Data Analysis with Microsoft Power BI

Brian Larson

New York   Chicago   San Francisco
Athens   London   Madrid
Mexico City   Milan   New Delhi
Singapore   Sydney   Toronto

Cataloging-in-Publication Data is on file with the Library of Congress

McGraw-Hill Education books are available at special quantity discounts to use as premiums and sales promotions, or for use in corporate training programs. To contact a representative, please visit the Contact Us pages at www.mhprofessional.com.

Data Analysis with Microsoft Power BI

1 2 3 4 5 6 7 8 9   LCR   23 22 21 20 19

ISBN   978-1-260-45861-9
MHID   1-260-45861-X

Sponsoring Editor	Technical Editor	Production Supervisor
Lisa McClain	Dan Corley	James Kussow
Editorial Supervisor	**Copy Editor**	**Composition**
Janet Walden	Bart Reed	Cenveo® Publisher Services
Project Editor	**Proofreader**	**Illustration**
Rachel Fogelberg	Paul Tyler	Cenveo Publisher Services
Acquisitions Coordinator	**Indexer**	**Art Director, Cover**
Emily Walters	Ted Laux	Jeff Weeks

Information has been obtained by McGraw-Hill Education from sources believed to be reliable. However, because of the possibility of human or mechanical error by our sources, McGraw-Hill Education, or others, McGraw-Hill Education does not guarantee the accuracy, adequacy, or completeness of any information and is not responsible for any errors or omissions or the results obtained from the use of such information.

This book is dedicated to my father-in-law, Len Martin. I had the great fortune to have in-laws who were also good friends. Len taught me many lessons on home improvement and was always ready to share his experience running a small business. A combat pilot in WWII, Air Force Reservist, and recreational pilot, he "slipped the surly bonds of earth" one last time on July 9, 2019.

About the Author

Brian Larson has focused his writing and consulting career around Microsoft reporting and analytics tools. That association began for Brian as a consulting member of the original Microsoft SQL Server Reporting Services development team. In that role, he contributed to the original code base of Reporting Services. Brian is currently a partner and chief creative officer for Superior Consulting Services in Minneapolis, Minnesota.

Brian has presented at national conferences and events, including the PASS Community Summit and the Microsoft Business Intelligence Conference, and has provided training and mentoring across the country. In addition to this book, Brian is the author of *Microsoft SQL Server 2016 Reporting Services, Fifth Edition* and *Delivering Business Intelligence with Microsoft SQL Server 2016, Fourth Edition*, and he is co-author of *Visualizing Data with Microsoft Power View,* all from McGraw-Hill Education.

Brian is a Phi Beta Kappa graduate of Luther College in Decorah, Iowa, with degrees in physics and computer science. He has 34 years of experience in the computer industry and 30 years of experience as a consultant creating custom database solutions. Brian is a Microsoft Certified Solutions Expert (MCSE) in Data Management and Analytics.

Brian and his wife, Pam, have been married for 34 years. Pam will tell you that their first date took place at the campus computer center. If that doesn't qualify someone to write a technology book, then Brian doesn't know what does. Brian and Pam have two children, Jessica and Corey.

About the Technical Editor

Dan Corley is a business intelligence architect with a strong passion for and expertise in the Microsoft data platform and business analytics technologies. He has worked in business intelligence for 20 years, architecting, managing, and developing business intelligence solutions in a variety of industries. Dan lives with his wife and eight children in Lakeville, Minnesota.

Contents at a Glance

Contents

Part II   Interacting with Power BI

Part V   Sharing Content

Acknowledgments

A project of this size is not completed alone. I need to thank many people for their assistance, professionalism, dedication, and support.

First, as always, a thank-you to Wendy Rinaldi, my original contact person at McGraw-Hill Education, who allowed me to lean on her as part editor, part coach, part literary agent, and part psychoanalyst. Her professionalism, humor, understanding, and faith have helped see me through many editions of many titles.

A huge thank-you to the rest of the McGraw-Hill Professional staff, who saw the project through to the end, kept prodding me as deadlines passed, and made sure there really was a book when all was said and done.

I am also indebted to Lisa Schmid and Paul Purington, my co-owners at Superior Consulting Services (SCS). They agreed to allow me to take on this project on company time and have agreed to create and support the ancillary materials on the SCS website (www.teamscs.com) that will keep this a relevant guide to a highly dynamic product.

An incredibly large thank-you to my wife, Pam, who, as always, serves as my best editor, alpha tester, and guardian of quality. Her incredible attention to detail has made this a much better learning tool.

Last, but certainly not least, to you, the reader, who plunked down your hard-earned cash for this purchase. I hope you view this as a helpful and informative means of jumpstarting your knowledge of the incredible set of tools that make up Microsoft Power BI.

All the best,
Brian Larson
blarson@teamscs.com

Part I

Understanding Business Intelligence and Power BI

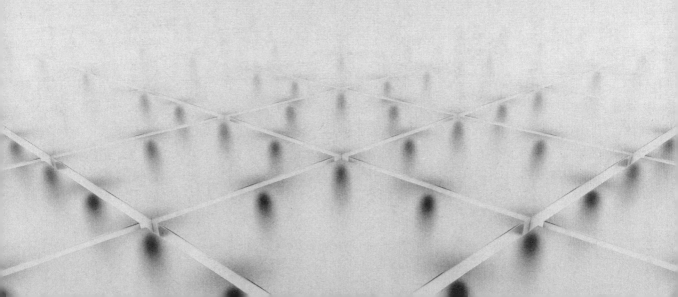

Chapter 1

How to Use This Book

In This Chapter

- The Tool Chest Called Power BI
- The Right Tool(s) for the Job
- Where to Find What You Need

"How to use this book?" you may think to yourself. "I already know how to use a book." In this chapter, I am not going to tell you to start on page one, reading from the upper left to the lower right, and then turn to page two. Instead, what I want to say right up front is that all parts of this book may not apply to all readers. This chapter's purpose is to provide a guide to planning your most efficient use of this book.

Microsoft Power BI is made up of many parts. You may not need to make use of all those parts to get what you need from Power BI. This chapter defines several ways in which Power BI can be used. All are valid ways to utilize Power BI, and all produce results valuable to our organizations. The way you interact with Power BI will depend on your role in your organization, what insights you are looking to gain through Power BI, and what other individuals are assisting and supporting you in that task.

The final section of this chapter tells you where to go for additional information that supports the content of this book. The code for all the examples and exercises in this book is available online. Because Power BI is constantly growing and evolving, updates to the content of this book are also available on my company's website.

The Tool Chest Called Power BI

Microsoft Power BI is not a single tool. It is important to understand this fact as you plan your approach to this book. Instead, Power BI is a set of tools. These tools began their lives as separate entities existing in a couple different environments. After several iterations and machinations, Microsoft brought these tools together into a single environment—the tool chest we call Power BI.

In most cases, when parts and pieces are assembled to try and make a whole new entity, we end up with a sort of Frankenstein's monster (a monster tapdancing to "Puttin' on the Ritz" for those of you who remember the movie *Young Frankenstein*). Power BI is one of those rare cases where the parts fit together extremely well. The process of creating a business intelligence (BI) infrastructure flows well from one tool to the next, and back again, as needed.

At the same time, you do not need to touch all the tools in the tool chest to get value from Power BI. It is possible to pick up the BI process midstream, selecting some tools while leaving others in their compartments. This is especially true if there are others within your organization fulfilling some of the various roles in the BI process.

The BI Process

Before we look specifically at the tools in the Power BI tool chest, we need to take a quick look at the basic BI process. How do we take data that is created and managed by our line-of-business systems—our enterprise resource planning (ERP) systems, our accounting systems, our human resource systems, and so on—and put it into an environment where we can use it to draw insights into our entire organization? There are five main steps to that process, as shown in Figure 1-1.

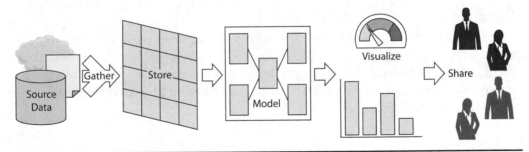

Figure 1-1   *The business intelligence (BI) process*

Gather

For ease and speed of analysis, data is gathered from various sources and placed in a single location. As data is gathered, it is also transformed. This transformation results in data that is cleansed of errors and inconsistencies. The transformation also aligns the data with the rest of the data store, allowing it to function as a consistent whole.

Store

The transformed data is stored in a specific location. This data store is often referred to as a data warehouse or data mart. The difference between these two is really a matter of scope. A data warehouse attempts to bring together data from across the entire organization, whereas a data mart brings together data that is limited to a particular subject area within the organization—sales or production, for example.

Data in the data warehouse or data mart is stored in a specialized format specifically designed to allow for quick retrieval during reporting and analysis. It is also structured so thousands or millions of individual transactions can be efficiently added together (aggregated) to determine, for example, the number of products produced in a given month or the total sales in a given year. This type of data store is said to be optimized for online analytical processing (OLAP).

Model

A data model is built on top of the data store to serve two purposes. First, it presents the data to the business user in a manner they are familiar with—no weird table and field names to decipher, and no complex language required to query the data.

Second, it provides a single location to store business calculations. Those internal formulas used to determine things like cost of goods sold, mean time between failure, and days beyond terms can be placed in a single location. When those calculations are needed within a report or on a dashboard, they are pulled from the data model, not re-created over and over again.

Visualize

Once the data is available in a model, it is ready for analysis and discovery. This is done by creating charts, tables, and gauges on reports and in dashboards. Some data visualizations will be created for one-time use as the data model is explored to answer a very specific question. Other visualizations will be created to be shared with many users and referred to again and again.

Share

For those visualizations that are meant to be shared, we need a mechanism for delivery throughout the organization. A common location is created where users can go to find the reports they need. This location has the proper security to ensure users can see only that data for which they have authorization.

Power BI Parts and Pieces

Now that we have reviewed the BI process, let's examine each of the tools in the Power BI tool chest. We will identify the current name for each tool and a bit more of the specifics of what it does. We will also briefly look at each tool's history.

The Query Editor

The Query Editor is the Power BI tool that makes it possible to do our data gathering and transformation. Data can be extracted from a wide variety of locations. Along the way, the data can be manipulated from its native form into a format that is more conducive for analysis.

The Query Editor can extract data from a wide range of sources—from text and Excel files to databases to Internet sites such as Facebook. Once the data is extracted, it can be manipulated through such processes as the following:

- Splitting data into multiple columns
- Pivoting and unpivoting
- Replacing values
- Modifying data types
- Merging data from multiple data extractions into a single table.

The Query Editor was originally known as Power Query.

The xVelocity In-memory Analytical Engine

xVelocity In-memory Analytical Engine is the long, official name of the technology that facilitates the storage (and retrieval) of data within Power BI. This technology was originally developed for use with the Power Pivot tool within Microsoft Excel. It is still often referred to by its shorter and catchier codename during its original development: the VertiPaq engine.

The VertiPaq engine enables fast retrieval of aggregated data by storing the data in memory, rather than on the drive, when the data is made available for querying. A highly efficient data compression algorithm is used so very large amounts of data can be crammed into memory. To further facilitate processing speed and data compression, the VertiPaq engine functions as a columnar store. This simply means that data is organized more around columns of values in a table rather than around rows of values in a table like most traditional databases.

The Tabular Model

Tables of data, relationships between those tables, and hierarchies within the tables are defined in Power BI using a Tabular data model. Business calculations are created in a Tabular model using measures. Measures can be very simple, such as calculating the sum of a set of values, or very complex, such as determining the cost of goods sold or year-over-year percent growth. Measures are defined using the Data Analysis Expressions language more commonly referred to as DAX.

Like the VertiPaq engine, the Tabular model was originally developed as part of Power Pivot in Microsoft Excel.

Power View

Data visualization within Power BI is done through a tool originally known as Power View. Power View was initially part of Microsoft SharePoint, and then Microsoft Excel, before ending up in Power BI. Power View was designed to allow users to create highly interactive, presentation-ready reports and dashboards in just a few clicks.

The Power BI Service, the Power BI Report Server, and Power BI Mobile

Power BI content is shared by publishing to the Power BI service or saving to the Power BI Report Server. The Power BI Service is a cloud-based portal otherwise known as PowerBI.com. While the Power BI Service can be used free of charge, most organization-level content sharing will require Power BI Pro or Power BI Premium licensing.

Those organizations that do not want to publish their content using a cloud service can install an instance of Power BI Report Server on premises. The Power BI Report Server is a version of the SQL Server Reporting Services (SSRS) server that can manage and render both SSRS and Power BI reports. The Power BI Report Server is licensed through Power BI Premium or through a SQL Server Enterprise Edition license as part of a Microsoft Enterprise Agreement/Software Assurance (EA/SA).

Both the Power BI service and the Power BI Report Server can be accessed through a modern browser. In addition, Microsoft has created native apps for iOS, Android, and Windows 10 mobile devices under the name Power BI Mobile. The Power BI Mobile app can connect to both the Power BI Service and a local instance of the Power BI Report Server to enable users to interact with Power BI reports on a tablet or smartphone.

The Right Tool(s) for the Job

As mentioned earlier in this chapter, Power BI can be used in a number of different ways. Therefore, you may not need to learn all the Power BI tools to use Power BI in the way that best suits your circumstances. This section examines the four main ways you can make use of Power BI as part of a business intelligence solution as well as notes which chapters you should work through to learn how to use Power BI in these four distinct ways.

Consuming Power BI Reports

Some of you looking to work with Power BI will be consumers only, meaning that others will create Power BI reports for you to use. What you need to know is how to find those reports and how to interact with them to obtain the answers you need.

Power BI consumers should complete Chapters 2 through 5 of this book.

Power BI as a Data Visualization Tool

In some organizations, others will bring together the data from the data sources and create one or more data models for you. In these situations, you simply need to connect to an existing data model and begin creating charts, tables, gauges, and so on. Power BI functions only as the data visualization tool.

There are two ways Power BI can be used solely as a visualization tool. The first is in business intelligence environments where a Microsoft SQL Server Analysis Services server is hosting one or more tabular data models. The second is in an environment where one or more Power BI data models have been published to the Power BI Service for your use.

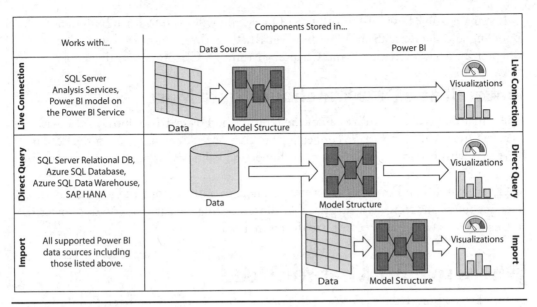

Figure 1-2   *Power BI connection types*

In both of these cases, a feature called "Live Connection" is used to interact with the existing data model (see Figure 1-2). No data is stored in your Power BI file. The data is queried from the data model each time it is needed to render a visualization, thus the name Live Connection.

If you are using Power BI solely as a data visualization tool, you need to complete Chapter 2 through Chapter 8 and Chapters 15 and 16 of this book.

Power BI as a Modeling Tool

In some situations, we do not want to store data within Power BI, but we do want to use Power BI for building our data model. This is true in situations where our analysis must be done in real time. We cannot add in any delay that would come from gathering the data and storing it in Power BI. For real-time analysis, we use a feature called "Direct Query" (refer to Figure 1-2).

Similar to Live Connection, Direct Query executes queries against the source data every time it is needed to render visualizations. Unlike Live Connection, Direct Query works with SQL Server relational databases and some other related data storage platforms. Because these relational data sources do not include the ability to define a data model, with Direct Query we define the data model within Power BI.

If you are using Power BI with Direct Query, you will need to learn both data modeling and data visualization with Power BI. Therefore, you need to complete Chapter 2 through Chapter 8 and Chapter 11 through Chapter 16 of this book.

Power BI as a Data Warehouse/Data Mart

The remaining scenario utilizes all of the tools in the Power BI toolbox. In this case, we use the Query Editor to create connections to the source data and import the data to be stored within Power BI. This type of connection is known as an "Import" connection (refer to Figure 1-2).

Given that all the Power BI tools are used here to gather, store, model, and visualize data, it should not come as a surprise that those wanting to learn how to use Power BI in this manner will need to complete the entire book.

Where to Find What You Need

In order to complete the exercises in this book, you will need to gather a few things. This section lets you know where to find those items. In addition, Power BI is updated frequently—usually once a month—so you will need other resources to stay up to date on what's new. Fortunately for you, dear reader, there is a location that provides information on all the new Power BI features while using the same sample data and teaching style used in this book.

Obtaining Power BI Desktop Software

To work through the exercises in this book, and indeed to create your own Power BI content, you will need to obtain the Power BI Desktop software. This is the authoring environment for all things Power BI. Power BI Desktop is available as a free download from Microsoft. The easiest way to locate the download page is to go to

www.powerbi.com

using any modern browser. At the top of the main page of the PowerBI.com site, you will see a menu. Select Products | Power BI Desktop. This will take you to the Power BI Desktop page.

On the Power BI Desktop page, click the Advanced Download Options link to go to the Microsoft Power BI Desktop page of the Microsoft Download Center. Click the Download button. If you are using a 32-bit version of Windows, check the box for the PBIDesktop.msi file, or if you are using a 64-bit version of Windows, check the box for the PBIDesktop_x64.msi file. Then click Next. Finally, open the file once the download is complete in order to execute the install program.

Sample Code and Supporting Materials

In addition to the Power BI Desktop software, you will need sample data and other supporting materials to complete the exercises in this book. You can download this material from the book's web page on the McGraw-Hill website at www.mhprofessional.com.

Once on the McGraw-Hill website, enter the book's title or ISBN in the search box. When you reach the page for this book, select the Downloads & Resources tab and then click the Source Code link. Follow the instructions in the ZIP file to install or prepare each item as needed.

Information on Power BI New Features and Enhancements

As updates to the Power BI environment are released by Microsoft, coverage of those updates will be available at www.teamscs.com/powerbi.

As new features and enhancements come out, I'll create examples and explanations of those features at this location. I will use the same sample datasets found throughout this book, so you will be familiar with the data and what it represents. The new features and enhancements will be placed into the Power BI context and framework presented in this book. The combination of this book and the supplemental web information will keep *Data Analysis with Microsoft Power BI* a dynamic learning device in the same way that Power BI is a dynamic tool for data analysis.

How to Succeed at Self-Service Analytics

Before we dive into the Power BI environment, Chapter 2 of this book will cover some of the basics of business intelligence and business intelligence projects. It provides tips on how to succeed at creating a functional self-service business intelligence environment.

Chapter 2

Successful Self-Service Analytics

In This Chapter

- What Is Business Intelligence?
- Is Your Organization Ready for BI?

- Implementation: Best Practices

When an organization implements Power BI, it is seeking to create an environment where business users can perform their own self-service analytics to create business intelligence. Knowing how to use Power BI is important to the success of these types of business intelligence projects. However, I am assuming you already knew that, because you bought this book. Beyond knowing the tool (or tools, given that you learned in Chapter 1 that Power BI is actually a set of tools), several other factors are also important to BI project success, such as the following:

- A common understanding of business intelligence and a definition of the building blocks that make up BI—namely, key performance indicators
- Verification that your organization is ready for a BI project
- Knowledge of the self-service BI project best practices

This chapter will lay the foundation in these vital areas.

What Is Business Intelligence?

Power BI contains the initialism "BI" right in its name, so there is little doubt that it is all about creating business intelligence. But just what is BI?

DEFINITION
Business intelligence is the delivery of accurate, useful information to the appropriate decision makers within the necessary time frame to support effective decision making.

The goal of a business intelligence project is better decisions. By better, I mean decisions based on factual data. This could be long-term strategic planning. It could be shorter-term tactical choices. It could be up-to-the-minute operational scheduling. Perhaps your organization's BI infrastructure will be used for all the above.

Defining KPIs

Based on this definition of business intelligence, one of the first requirements is to define what information is going to be useful to your decision makers. This is done by defining the key performance indicators (KPIs) for your organization. A KPI reflects some vital aspect of the operation of the organization. It shows your organization's health within a particular area.

Use the criteria in the following sections to ensure your KPIs appropriately reflect the overall health of your organization.

Actionability, Not Curiosity

As various values are proposed to serve as KPIs for your organization, it is important to ensure they are not just included to satisfy a decision maker's curiosity. The decision maker should be able to define specific actions the organization will take in response to variances in the KPI value. If values outside of a specified normal range do not trigger a response of some kind, then this is not a true KPI for your organization.

Organization-Wide

A wide range of KPIs should be selected to cover all aspects of the organization. The goal is to create a holistic picture. Financial KPIs are important. However, to have a complete view of the health of the organization, all areas of the organization must be represented. KPIs should be identified for sales, order fulfillment, production, customer retention, and so on.

Forward Looking

Design your KPIs to be as forward looking as possible. This provides more time to react when a number is out of the normal range. Last month's sales numbers may provide a key indicator of the organization's health, but it is too late in the process to provide time for any corrective intervention when that number dips. Instead, a KPI earlier in the sales pipeline may provide a better number to react to when making decisions.

Easily Understood

KPIs should be easily understood by those who use them. When a KPI is the result of a complex formula, it can be difficult to understand exactly what that numeric is saying about the business. Defining what constitutes a normal range for that KPI can be problematic. When that KPI strays from the defined normal range, it may be hard to know what changes must be made to bring it back to where it should be. Whenever possible, use simplicity when defining KPIs in order to lead to easier interpretation and clearer reactions.

When a more complex KPI is the only one that will suffice, be sure to include documentation and training so decision makers understand the KPI now and in the future.

Is Your Organization Ready for BI?

Once you have an understanding of business intelligence and what makes a good KPI, you can determine if your organization is ready to undertake a business intelligence project. This section details several indications that your organization will be successful implementing and utilizing a business intelligence infrastructure.

Desire

Take a realistic look at who is pushing for a business intelligence infrastructure project. If the only push for this type of project is coming from the technical staff, then your organization is not yet ready for BI. You need buy-in from the potential consumers of that BI infrastructure; otherwise, no matter how wonderfully it is created, it will go unused.

Is the impetus for a BI project coming only from middle management with no real desire coming from the C-level executives? If so, there is some preparatory work left to do. The corner office dwellers need to be shown the realistic expectations of return on investment (ROI) and competitive advantage to be realized from a well-functioning BI infrastructure. They need to be turned from skeptics to champions of the project before you begin. Without support from the top, a BI infrastructure project will be starved for both monetary and time resources.

Do the current keepers of the organization's data feel threatened by a BI implementation? Those who know the organization's data best may feel their value depends on their being the sole possessor of that inside information. Getting these information gatekeepers to cooperate in sharing inside information and explaining those calculations is essential. These key individuals must be shown how, with a functioning BI infrastructure, they will be able to move beyond shepherding data to shepherding the organization by concentrating on making the key business decisions they were hired to make.

Realistic Expectations

Does your organization have realistic expectations for a BI project? First, there must be an understanding that a full-featured BI infrastructure is not built using castoff equipment in a few weeks by the IT department in their spare time. The BI infrastructure will require investments in both computing power and personnel time to achieve satisfying results within a reasonable timeframe.

Second, there must a realization that a BI implementation project requires significant amounts of time, not only from the technical resources, but also from the business side of the organization. A BI solution cannot be created by the IT department in a vacuum. It requires the committed participation of the business stakeholders to clarify needs and define KPIs.

Ongoing Care and Feeding

Once the BI infrastructure is in place, is there an understanding that it will require resources to provide continuing support? These resources will need to monitor the infrastructure's operation to detect and correct any problems that might arise.

They will also need to make enhancements to the BI infrastructure as the organization grows and changes. In some cases, much of this ongoing support can be provided by external consulting resources. However, there should be at least one resource internal to the organization with a significant amount of their job description focused on overseeing BI operations.

Well-Defined KPIs

Will your organization be able to identify good KPIs? It can be difficult for different areas within an organization to agree on definitive formulas for given metrics. This is especially true if the organization is rather large, is spread out geographically, or tends toward a more autonomous management structure. In these cases, there must be someone in upper management who can be the final arbiter of conflicting formulas and interpretations. That person or group of people must shepherd the KPI definition process during implementation and also serve as an enforcer when departments try to drift away from agreed-upon standards later on.

Actionable KPIs

As mentioned previously, KPIs are only valuable when they lead to action within the organization. Therefore, it is important that decision makers can agree upon the normal range for each KPI. Further, they must be able to articulate the action to be taken when a KPI strays outside of that range. Without these actions, a BI infrastructure produces little ROI and no competitive advantage.

Reliable Sources of Data

Once the KPIs have been defined, the organization must identify the sources for the information to be used when performing these calculations. Is there a reliable electronic source for each component of each KPI calculation? In some cases, that source may come from outside of the organization. Once the sources are identified, it must be determined if there is a secure path to access that information and bring it into the BI infrastructure.

In cases where a reliable electronic source for a particular piece of information cannot be determined, an alternative must be developed. For each of these situations, is it possible to devise an accurate, timely, and repeatable process to capture the required information? This could mean manual data entry by internal personnel or by external vendors and business partners. It could also mean creating an electronic process where none currently exists.

Implementation: Best Practices

Once you have determined your organization is ready for BI and you have defined your KPIs according to the criteria provided earlier in this chapter, it is time to get down to the business of implementation. The following are best practices when implementing a BI infrastructure. Refer back to Figure 1-1 if you need to refresh your memory on the BI process.

Take an Iterative Implementation Approach

An iterative approach works best when implementing a BI infrastructure. BI projects that require six months or more to build and strive to deliver the BI infrastructure as a completed whole are extremely likely to fail. Incrementally delivering operational portions of the BI infrastructure over shorter periods of time helps ensure the project stays on target while generating excitement and providing a quicker path to return on investment.

Utilize a Data Warehouse/Data Mart

Users should not create their self-service content directly from the transactional, line-of-business data stores. Instead, a data warehouse or a series of data marts should be created to house a copy of the transactional data. This ensures a business user cannot bring the line-of-business systems to a screeching halt through a poorly performing query.

The copy of the transactional data can also be restructured from a format optimized for transactional processing to a format optimized for analytical processing. This helps to ensure the efficient operation of the self-service analytics environment. Additionally, data from multiple line-of-business systems can be brought together to allow for analysis across the entire enterprise.

Cleanse and Validate During Data Gathering

Data should be cleansed and validated as much as possible as it is gathered into the data warehouse or data marts. This includes the following tasks:

- Validating against lists of known entities like streets, cities, states, ZIP codes, gender, and so on.
- Making sure both sides of relationships exist. For example, if sales are attributed to a certain salesperson, make sure that salesperson exists in the salesperson table in the warehouse.
- Checking data types and lengths of data.

Any data that fails the validation process should be handled in a graceful manner. It should be logged in an appropriate manner and perhaps even saved to another location for manual cleansing and reloading. Notifications should be sent to the appropriate people to let them know a data validation issue occurred.

Audits should be run to ensure the data loaded completely and accurately. This may include counting certain entities or totaling certain quantities in the source systems and in the data warehouse after the data load to verify they match. Notifications of mismatches should be sent to the appropriate people to ensure remedial action is taken.

The source of each piece of information should be tracked through the extract, transform, and load (ETL) process. This may entail tagging it with an identifier indicating which source file or source record it came from. It may also include indicating the date and time it was loaded.

Create User-Friendly Data Models

Databases are complex beasts. It takes a technical aptitude and years of practice to efficiently navigate and retrieve data in these systems. Expecting the majority of business users to master the ins and outs of SELECT statements with INNER JOINs and GROUP BYs is going to lead to frustrated users and inaccurate data.

Instead, a data model with a business user–friendly metadata layer needs to be put in place. The data model presents the data to the business users with names, structures, and hierarchies with which they are familiar. The key to good data model design is to remember that this layer exists mainly to make things easier for the business users who will explore the data. Full English names with spaces should be used for all objects exposed to the business users. Further, the data model already knows how to make the proper connections within the data and which connections would lead to nonsense results.

Additionally, the data model can house definitions for the agreed-upon KPI calculations. Rather than re-creating these calculations over and over in multiple reports and visualizations, you can use a single definition in multiple locations. Finally, complex analysis like year-over-year growth or prorated percent of goal can be predefined for easy utilization.

Publish Latency

The data-gathering process and the loading of the data model both require time and are done on a periodic schedule. The time it takes for data to move from the source systems into the data model, via this schedule, is known as the latency of the BI environment. Be sure to design the BI infrastructure so it meets the latency requirements of the business users. Is it okay if data is loaded nightly, or do users need to see data no more than one hour after it is loaded into a transactional system?

Once the latency standards have been established, be sure users are aware of them. You may also want to implement a mechanism where users can quickly determine the time of the last data load.

Provide Training and Support

Many self-service analytics tools like to tout themselves as also being self-explanatory. Power BI is easy to use. However, I firmly believe every tool requires some type of training to get users acclimated to the tool and the way the tool wants them to approach the data. That is the reason this book includes coverage of the use of Power BI visualizations (Chapter 4). If nothing else, the training provides a structured way to give the users permission to dive in and manipulate the data for themselves.

If possible, the training should not be an off-the-shelf course with sample data. Users will get far more benefit from working with their own data. The training should guide the users to their first insights into their own operations and areas of responsibility.

After the initial training is complete, additional opportunities should be created to support the business users. This might include encouraging participation in a forum or local user group geared toward business users of the tool or perhaps even starting a user group within the organization. The users should be provided some forum to ask questions, share successes, and continue to grow their understanding of the tool.

Use the Right Tool for the Job

In a number of cases, I have seen organizations enter a self-service analytics project believing the self-service tool will fulfill all reporting needs. In almost all situations, this is not going to be the case. Power BI is a very powerful tool, but it cannot do everything—nor should it be expected to do so. There will still be a need for some set of reports to be developed and maintained by the IT department. There will be a need for reports that are printed or in other formats that are not readily produced by Power BI. Trying to create content of a certain type or in a certain format with a tool that is less than optimal for that purpose leads to frustrated users.

The best approach is one that looks at all the reporting and analysis needs of the organization and then chooses the appropriate tool and the appropriate author for each one. Some needs will be met by visualizations created in a more formal reporting environment, like SQL Server Reporting Services, by the IT department. Other needs may be met by visualizations created in Power BI by the IT department because of their widespread use and need for stricter management. Still other needs will be met by end users creating self-service content in Power BI. It may be the case that a visualization initially created by a business user becomes so widely used that it needs to transition from self-service content to IT-maintained content.

Establish Standards and Limits

Using the right tool for the job often means the organization will have more than one product in its visualization tool chest. However, that does not mean that every business user should be allowed to select whatever visualization tool they like. A set of standard tools should be established for the various visualization needs of the organization, and then business users should be required to work within that set of standards. This allows the organization to maximize its expertise and efficiency with this set of tools.

Business users are likely to come from other organizations with biases toward visualization tools used in those environments. Periodically, the organization's visualization tool choices should be evaluated to ensure they are still modern and well supported. Either of these influences—a user wanting to bring in a tool from another organization or a re-evaluation of the toolset—may create a desire to change toolsets. This needs to happen occasionally to get the optimal results from the visualization environment but should be done only after careful consideration. Once they are established, changing standard visualization tools is time consuming and disruptive.

Successfully Using Power BI

Implementing a BI infrastructure is not a trivial undertaking. But with the right knowledge, preparation, and attention to best practices, a well-implemented BI infrastructure provides a large return on investment and a tremendous competitive advantage for your organization.

Now that we have set some guidelines for the success of your BI project, it is time to begin looking at Power BI itself. However, before we explore the creation of visualizations in Power BI, you need to have a solid understanding of the way Power BI functions. Chapter 3 will take a more detailed look at the architecture of a BI infrastructure built around Power BI. Chapter 4 and Chapter 5 will then examine the ways we can interact with Power BI content.

Part II

Interacting with Power BI

Chapter 3

Power BI Architecture

In This Chapter

- The Power BI Architecture
- Power BI Desktop Optimizations
- Power BI Updates
- Microsoft On-Premises Data Gateway

In Chapter 1, we discussed the fact that Power BI is not a single tool but a set of tools. In that chapter, we also touched briefly on the software and services where these Power BI tools reside. In this chapter, we will take a close look at each of the various applications and websites that make up the Power BI architecture.

The Power BI Architecture

As noted previously, the capabilities that are now brought together under the name Power BI have shown up in a number of different places as parts of different tools and with different names. Microsoft rearranged the various pieces as it worked to find the right platform for business users to create self-service business intelligence. Here we examine where each of these tools has found a home within the Power BI architecture.

Power BI Desktop

Many of the Power BI parts and pieces have come together in a Microsoft Windows application called Power BI Desktop. This is the authoring environment for all things Power BI. Power BI Desktop allows a user to create their own business intelligence environment by gathering data from a variety of sources and loading it directly into a data model. Visualizations may then be created from that data model in the same workspace. The Power BI Desktop startup screen is shown in Figure 3-1.

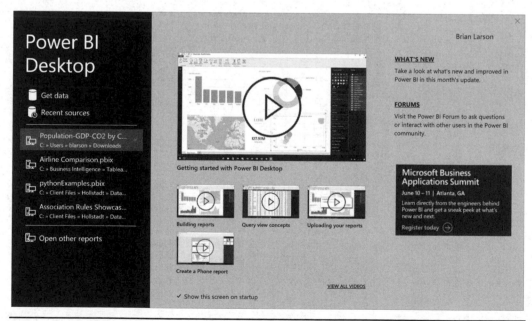

Figure 3-1   *The Power BI Desktop startup screen*

The tool that started life as Power Query now creates queries in Power BI Desktop. However, these queries do more than just select the data from the data sources. The queries in Power BI Desktop transform the data so it is ready to be loaded directly into a data model.

The xVelocity In-memory Analytical Engine (VertiPaq engine) stores and retrieves data within Power BI Desktop. The tool that began as Power Pivot now manages data models in Power BI Desktop. Last but not least, the tool once known as Power View now creates visualizations as part of Power BI Desktop. The visualization tool has grown and matured. Many new visualizations have been added, along with the ability to create and add your own.

Power BI Desktop brings all of these tools together in one BI creation tool. Within Power BI Desktop, the user can gather, store, model, and visualize data. Power BI Desktop does it all—almost. What Power BI Desktop doesn't do is share content with others.

NOTE
See the section titled "Power BI Desktop Optimizations" for information on the two distinct versions of the Power BI Desktop application.

The Power BI Service

One way to share the content created in Power BI Desktop is to publish it to the Power BI Service, otherwise known as PowerBI.com. Once the content is on PowerBI .com, it can be explored online in several different ways. Users can interact with existing visualizations or use a browser-based, Power BI Desktop–like interface to manipulate the model and create new visualizations. Users can also query the data using a natural language interface called Q & A. Content from the Power BI Service can also be shared with others and embedded in your own custom applications.

Each user obtains their own login to access the Power BI Service. This access is free within certain limitations. Check the PowerBI.com site for information on the current limitations on free access. Even if you need more capacity than the free access allows, the subscription access is currently just US$9.99 per month. Again, consult the PowerBI.com website to determine the current subscription cost and terms.

An example of the Power BI Service personal home page is shown in Figure 3-2.

NOTE
You may notice when you enter "powerbi.com" in your browser address bar that you are actually forwarded to "powerbi.microsoft.com" with the appropriate language added on the end. For simplicity, I will refer to this site as PowerBI.com in this book.

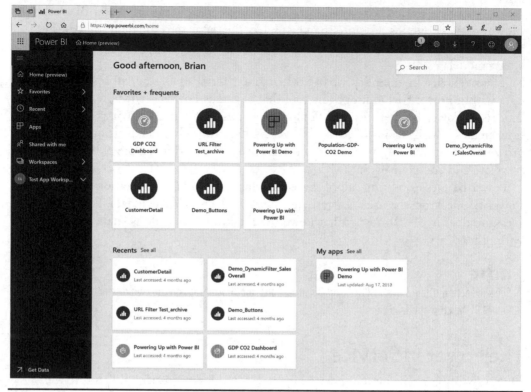

Figure 3-2   *The Power BI Service personal home page*

The Power BI Report Server

In addition to publishing to PowerBI.com, you have another option when you wish to share your Power BI content with others. While PowerBI.com provides a home for your content in the cloud, there is another tool that will host Power BI content on your own servers. That tool is the Power BI Report Server. An example of the Power BI Report Server home page is shown in Figure 3-3.

The Power BI Report Server is a customized version of the SQL Server Reporting Services (SSRS) server that can manage and render both SSRS content and Power BI reports. Users access reports on the Power BI Report Server using a version of the Reporting Services web portal. This browser-based application provides the interface for organizing, securing, and executing reports. Figure 3-3 shows an example of the Reporting Services web portal user interface. The groups of KPIs, mobile reports, and paginated reports are examples of SSRS content hosted on the Power BI Report Server.

All of the various types of content on the Power BI Report Server can be organized into folders. Categorizing reports in folders makes it easy for users to find the report

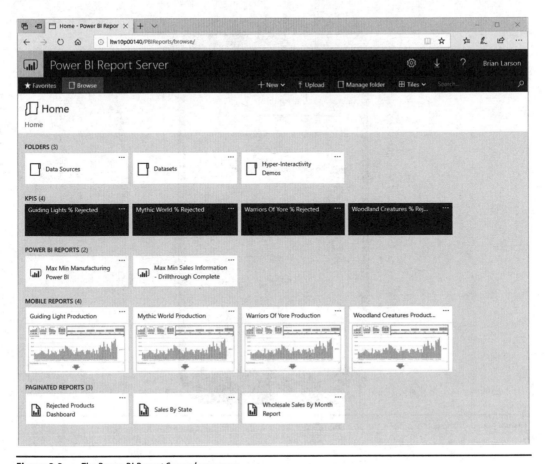

Figure 3-3   *The Power BI Report Server home page*

they are looking for. Folders also make it easier to manage the security access rights of a group of items all at the same time.

The Power BI Report Server is licensed through Power BI Premium or through a SQL Server Enterprise Edition license as part of a Microsoft Enterprise Agreement/Software Assurance (EA/SA).

The Power BI Mobile App

Content placed on PowerBI.com or on the Power BI Report Server can be viewed and interacted with using any modern browser. Those looking for a richer experience on a mobile device can download the Power BI native mobile app for their particular phone operating environment. The mobile app allows you to interact with the data in addition to simply viewing the content.

An example of a Power BI Mobile screen on a smartphone is shown in Figure 3-4.

Figure 3-4   *The Power BI Mobile app on a smartphone*

Power BI Desktop Optimizations

There are two distinct Power BI Desktop optimizations. One is optimized for publishing content to PowerBI.com. We will refer to this as the "Power BI Service" optimization of Power BI Desktop. The other is optimized for saving content to the Power BI Report Server. We will refer to this as the "Report Server" optimization of Power BI Desktop. It is important to use the correct optimization when creating your content, based on how you will be sharing that content. When building content to be shared using PowerBI.com, use the Power BI Service optimization. When building content to share using an on-premises Power BI Report Server, use the Report Server optimization.

NOTE
The Report Server optimization of Power BI Desktop is also able to publish content to PowerBI.com. The Power BI Service optimization of Power BI Desktop is not able to save content to a Power BI Report Server.

There are two ways to tell the difference between the optimizations of Power BI Desktop. The first is through the application icon, and the second is through the content of the File | Save As menu.

The Power BI Desktop application icon is a column chart within a rounded-corner rectangle. In the Power BI Service optimization of Power BI Desktop, the rectangle and column chart are black on a yellow background. In this version, there is no submenu under the File | Save As menu.

In the Report Server optimization of Power BI Desktop, the rectangle and column chart are yellow on a black background. In this version, there is a submenu under the File | Save As menu that includes an option for saving to a Power BI Report Server.

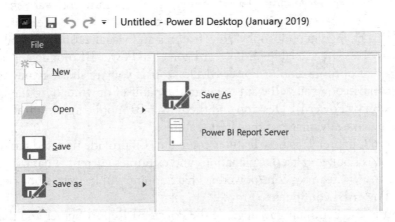

The best way to obtain a copy of the Power BI Server optimization of Power BI Desktop is from PowerBI.com. Follow the procedure described in the "Obtaining Power BI Desktop Software" section of Chapter 1. If you followed those instructions to get Power BI Desktop, that means you installed the Power BI Service optimization of

Power BI Desktop to complete the exercises in this book. In reality, either the Power BI Service optimization or the Report Server optimization of Power BI Desktop can be used to complete the data gathering, modeling, and visualization exercises in this book, as long as it is the July 2019 version or later.

The best way to obtain the Report Server optimization of Power BI Desktop for deploying to the Power BI Report Server is from Power BI Report Server. (Was that too obvious?) More specifically, from your installation of Power BI Report Server. More on why that is important can be found in the next section. Use the Download menu (the down-arrow icon) in Power BI Report Server to initiate the download of the corresponding version of the Report Server–optimized Power BI Desktop software.

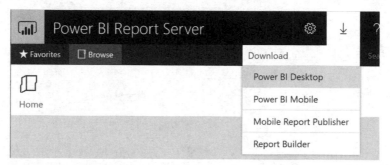

Power BI Updates

As Microsoft has embraced cloud-based computing, it has moved toward shorter and shorter delivery cycles. Power BI is one of the environments that has benefited the most from this change in philosophy. New features and visualizations, as well as any necessary bug fixes, are available on PowerBI.com, the Power BI mobile app, and the Power BI Server optimization of Power BI Desktop. If you are sharing your content through PowerBI.com, you will want to get in the habit of downloading the latest and greatest version of Power BI Desktop and the Power BI mobile app monthly to stay current and to take advantage of the latest features.

As noted in Chapter 1, as new features come out, I'll provide updated content to supplement this book and keep explanations and examples current. That content will be available at www.teamscs.com/powerbi. That content will keep this book alive and growing as Power BI continues to grow.

Microsoft is also continuing to upgrade the Power BI Report Server and the Report Server optimization of Power BI Desktop. However, this is happening about once a quarter. Your organization will need to decide how often to upgrade your installation of Power BI Report Server to the latest version. Each time that upgrade occurs, Power BI report authors will need to use the Download menu in Power BI Report Server to obtain and install the new version of Power BI Desktop.

When you're sharing data through Power BI Report Server, it is important to keep the versions of Power BI Report Server and Power BI Desktop in sync. If you obtain a newer version of Power BI Desktop elsewhere, you may use features in your reports that Power BI Report Server is not able to render. If you don't upgrade Power BI Desktop to match a Power BI Report Server upgrade, you will be missing out on new features!

Microsoft On-premises Data Gateway

In Chapter 1, we discussed the various ways Power BI can be utilized. We can use Power BI as a data visualization tool against a data model that exists elsewhere. We saw that this type of Power BI connection is called Live Connection. Alternatively, we can create our own data warehouse/data mart by storing the data within Power BI. This type of Power BI connection was called Import. Using either of these methods, you can see that, as we deploy content to PowerBI.com, we are going to have problems when our data sources exist on premises.

If we use Live Connection, how can a Power BI visualization existing in the cloud access a data model on our network? If we use Import, the data goes up to the cloud when we publish our content. However, we will eventually want to refresh that data in the cloud from our on-premises sources. How do we allow data to move securely from on-premises sources to Power BI content in the cloud, as shown in Figure 3-5?

This secure data movement is achieved using the Microsoft On-premises Data Gateway shown in Figure 3-6. While not technically part of Power BI, the On-premises

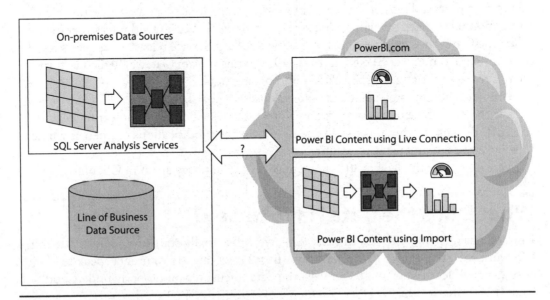

Figure 3-5   *Data access from the cloud to on-premises sources*

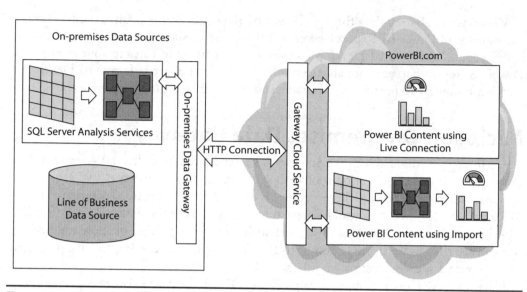

Figure 3-6   *The On-premises Data Gateway*

Data Gateway is an important piece of the Power BI architecture when sharing content via the cloud. Using the On-premises Data Gateway, we can successfully use Live Connection from the cloud as well as update imported data in the cloud.

The On-premises Data Gateway runs on a server within your network. It is constantly making Hypertext Transfer Protocol (HTTP) connections to PowerBI.com. This connection takes place through a feature of the Microsoft Azure cloud infrastructure called the Gateway Cloud Service. The Gateway Cloud Service relays any requests for data coming from Power BI content to the On-premises Data Gateway, which in turn queries the appropriate data source and returns the results.

As noted, the On-premises Data Gateway uses standard, outbound HTTP requests. This is the same type of communication a browser uses when communicating with the Internet. Because of this, there is no need to make any modifications or open any holes in your organization's network security.

We will look at the Microsoft On-premises Data Gateway again in Chapter 15.

What Does the Data Have to Say?

Enough background material. In Chapter 4, we will actually start using Power BI. You will work with real Power BI visualizations to see how they let your data speak to you. Also, you will learn how to interact with the data to ensure you properly understand what it is trying to say.

Chapter 4

Using Power BI Visualizations

In This Chapter

- Power BI Desktop
- Interacting with a Power BI Report
- Changing the Data with Slicers and Filters
- Navigating Power BI Reports

Part of what puts the power in Power BI is the fact that data visualizations are not static representations of your data. Instead, Power BI reports are highly interactive. We are able to navigate through the data to gain deeper meaning.

In this chapter, you will walk through these interactive features. You will learn how to use those features to truly analyze the data. This will enable you to follow the data where it leads you in the pursuit of insight.

Power BI Desktop

In most situations, when you are viewing and interacting with an existing Power BI report, you will do so through a browser. The report will be published and made available to you through PowerBI.com in the cloud or saved to a Power BI Report Server instance within your organization's infrastructure. In either case, you would access that report using a browser.

For the training exercises in this chapter, we are going to use a slightly different approach in order to keep things simple. In this chapter, we will open a Power BI report file (.pbix file extension) on your computer using the Power BI Desktop application. As explained earlier, Power BI Desktop is the authoring tool for Power BI content. However, because Power BI Desktop is a "what you see is what you get" (WYSIWYG) authoring tool, it can also be used to view and interact with the report.

By using Power BI Desktop for these exercises, we avoid the necessity of setting up a PowerBI.com location for publishing the report or having an existing Power BI Report Server available to which the report can be saved. With a couple of minor differences, which I will point out as we go along, you will get the exact same experience interacting with the report in Power BI Desktop as you would in either of the browser-based environments.

Obtaining What You Need

As you will have gathered from the preceding paragraphs, you need to install a copy of Power BI Desktop in order to complete the exercises in this chapter (and indeed, much of the rest of the book). You will also need to download the supporting materials for this book from the McGraw-Hill website to obtain the completed Power BI report we will be working with. The instructions for obtaining both of these items are found in the "Where to Find What You Need" section in Chapter 1 of this book.

Please follow the instructions found in Chapter 1 to download and install the Power BI Desktop software. If you already have Power BI Desktop installed, use the About button on the Help tab of the ribbon to verify that it is the July 2019 version or later. If you have an earlier version of Power BI Desktop, you will need to upgrade to the July 2019 or later version in order to successfully complete all the exercises in this book. If you need to upgrade, simply download and install the latest version using the instructions from Chapter 1. This will upgrade any existing Power BI Desktop version on your computer.

Also, please follow the instructions found in Chapter 1 to download the ZIP file containing the supporting materials (source code) for this book. Once you have downloaded the ZIP file, double-click the file to navigate its content. Locate the file called "Population-GDP-CO2 by Country.pbix," copy this file, and save it to a location in your file system (outside of the ZIP file). Be sure to remember the location where you saved this file.

Opening the Report/Preparing the Environment

With Power BI Desktop installed and the "Population-GDP-CO2 by Country.pbix" file in a convenient location, we are ready to begin. Follow these steps to open the report in Power BI Desktop and prepare the Power BI Desktop environment for our data exploration. In this chapter, we will be using Power BI Desktop only as a means of displaying the report so we can interact with it. We won't be needing any of the report authoring tools, so we will go ahead and hide those for now.

Opening the Population-GDP-CO2 by Country Report in Power BI Desktop

1. Locate the "Population-GDP-CO2 by Country.pbix" file in the file system location where you placed it.

2. Double-click the "Population-GDP-CO2 by Country.pbix" file. This will open the file in Power BI Desktop.

3. If this is the first time you have run Power BI Desktop, you will see the Welcome to Power BI dialog box, as shown in Figure 4-1. Unfortunately, this information is the "price" of the free software. Enter the required information and click Done.

4. Locate the Fields pane on the right side of the Power BI Desktop window. Click the arrow to the right of the "Fields" heading to hide the Fields pane.

Welcome to Power BI Desktop

Where can we send you the latest tips and tricks for Power BI?

First Name *

Last Name *

Email Address *

Enter your phone number *

Country/region *   ▾

Company name *

Company size... *   ▾

Job Title*   ▾

Microsoft may use your contact information to provide updates and special offers about Business
Intelligence and other Microsoft products and services. You can unsubscribe at any time. To learn more
you can read the privacy statement.

Done

Already have a Power BI account? Sign in

Figure 4-1   *The Welcome to Power BI dialog box*

5. Locate the Visualizations pane on the right side of the Power BI Desktop
    window. Click the arrow to the right of the "Visualizations" heading to hide the
    Visualizations pane.

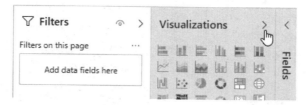

6. Locate the Filters pane on the right side of the Power BI Desktop window. Click the arrow to the right of the "Filters" heading to hide the Filters pane.

7. Locate the blue circle containing the question mark in the upper-right corner of the Power BI Desktop window. Click the arrow just to the left of the blue circle. This will hide the ribbon.

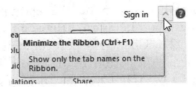

NOTE
If you have trouble minimizing either the Fields pane, the Visualizations pane, Filters pane, or the ribbon, try minimizing the entire Power BI Desktop window and then maximize the window again. Now retry the steps from this section that were unsuccessful.

Your Power BI Desktop window should now appear, as shown in Figure 4-2.

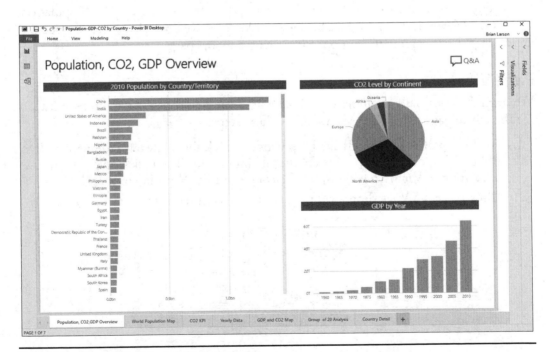

Figure 4-2 *Power BI Desktop, ready for report viewing*

Interacting with a Power BI Report

We will begin by looking at ways to interact with the items of the Power BI report itself. Most Power BI reports have multiple items on each report page. We will see how to make it easier to focus on a single report item. In addition, we will see how report items interact with each other when we consider the report page as a whole. At the end of this section, we will see how report items can help us interpret what we are seeing.

The "Population-GDP-CO2 by Country" report contains multiple pages. Each page is represented by a tab across the bottom of the report. The report should have defaulted to the "Population, CO2, GDP Overview" page. You can click the various tabs to page through the report if you like. We will spend more time exploring each report page in detail as we progress through this chapter.

The "Population, CO2, GDP Overview" page of the report contains several items. A title appears in the upper-left corner, and a "Q&A" button appears in the upper-right corner (more on that button later). Finally, three charts make up the bulk of the page content.

Working with a Single Report Item

Our report, shown in Figure 4-2, opened showing the entire content of the "Population, CO2, GDP Overview" report page by default. However, we don't always have to see the entire page. Let's explore the options for viewing a report page.

Page View

We begin by essentially zooming in to a portion of the report page or zooming out to see the entire page using Page View. Follow these steps:

1. At the top of the Power BI Desktop window, click the View tab. (Remember, the ribbon is hidden, so all you see are the ribbon tabs until you click one of them.) Clicking the View tab will display the content of the View tab of the ribbon.

2. Click the Page View dropdown item. You will see three Page View options.

3. Click Actual Size. Depending on your screen resolution and Power BI Desktop window size, you may now see only a portion of the report visible in the Power BI Desktop window and the content will be larger. You are now seeing the report content at its actual size. The content actually visible will vary depending on your screen resolution and the size of the Power BI Desktop window. This is one way to focus attention on one area of a Power BI report and make the content of that area easier to read. When a portion of the Power BI report is not visible, scrollbars allow you to move left and right, up and down to view the entire report.

4. Click the View tab and then the Page View dropdown item again. This time select Fit to Width. With this view option, you will see all of the report page content side to side but, depending on your screen resolution and window size, you may not see all of the report page content top to bottom.

5. Click the View tab and then the Page View dropdown item. Now select Fit to Page to return to our original view.

NOTE
Each page in a Power BI report can have its own default Page View setting. Be sure to always be aware of whether you are seeing the entire report page or only a portion of the page.

Focus Mode

Focus Mode provides another way to concentrate our attention on one particular item on the report page. To explore this mode, follow these steps:

1. Hover your mouse pointer over the "CO2 Level by Continent" pie chart. Notice that a new header bar appears above the chart with several icons. One of the icons shows a smaller rectangle inside a larger rectangle with an arrow going from the smaller to the larger. This is the Focus Mode icon.

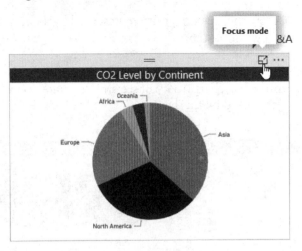

2. While being careful to keep your mouse pointer over the rectangle that defines the entire pie chart item, click the Focus Mode icon. Focus Mode gives the entire focus to one report item, making it easier to read and to interact with.

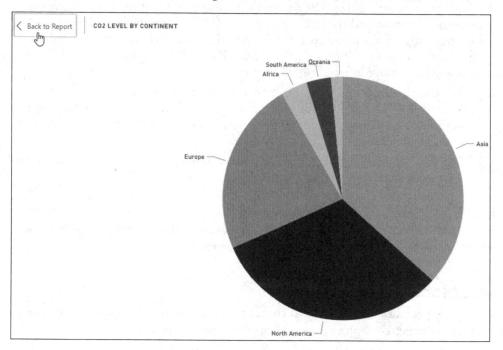

3. To return to the full report page, click "Back to Report" in the upper-left corner of the Focus Mode view.

Tooltips

Tooltips enable us to know the exact quantity represented by a chart item. To practice using these tooltips, follow these steps:

1. Hover your mouse pointer over the bar representing India in the 2010 Population by Country/Territory bar chart. You will see a tooltip showing the exact population amount being represented by this bar.

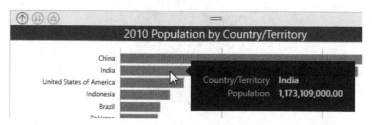

2. Now hover your mouse over the wedge representing Africa in the CO2 Level by Continent pie chart. Not only does the tooltip show the exact CO2 level being represented, but it also shows what percentage this is relative to the entire pie.

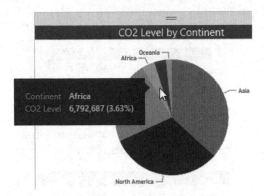

3. Click the World Population Map tab to switch to this page of the report. On this report page, population is represented by darker and lighter shading on a map rather than by bars on a bar chart.

4. Hover your mouse pointer over China on the map. You will see a tooltip showing the exact population amount represented by the shading.

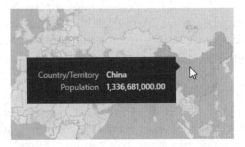

Changing Sort Order in a Table or a Matrix

We can change the order with which items are sorted within the report items. There are a couple different ways to change sort order depending on the type of data visualization with which you are working. We'll start by working with a table of values, as shown in the Country Data for 2010 table on the World Population Map page of our report.

The Country Data for 2010 table is sorted by Population in descending order (largest to smallest). This is indicated by the downward-pointing triangle underneath the Population column heading. Only table and matrix visualizations (visualizations with rows and columns of numeric values) have this sort indicator as part of a column header. (You'll learn more about matrix visualizations later in this chapter.)

Country Data for 2010		
Country/Territory	Population ▾	CO2 Le
China	1,336.68M	8,2
India	1,173.11M	2,0

1. Click the Population column heading in the Country Data for 2010 table. The sort order changes to ascending order by population (smallest to largest). The triangle underneath the Population column heading is now pointing upward.

Country Data for 2010		
Country/Territory	Population ▴	CO2 L
West Bank		
Montserrat	0.01M	
Saint Pierre and Miquelon	0.01M	

2. Click the GDP column heading in the Country Data for 2010 table. The sort order changes to descending order by GDP. The triangle has moved underneath the GDP column heading and it is pointing downward. Numeric columns default to descending order when you click the column heading for the first time. The assumption is the bigger quantities are more interesting than the smaller quantities.
3. Click the GDP column heading again to change the sort order to ascending order by GDP.
4. Click the Country/Territory column heading in the Country Data for 2010 table. The sort order changes to ascending order by Country/Territory. The triangle has moved underneath the Country/Territory column heading and it is pointing upward. Alphabetic columns default to ascending (alphabetic) order when you click the column heading for the first time. The assumption is ascending alphabetic order is most likely the desired result.

Change the Sort Order in Any Visualization

Whereas clicking the column heading to change sort order only works for a table or a matrix, there is another mechanism for changing sort order that works for all data visualizations. We will use this second method to return the Country Data for 2010 table to its original sort order, then we will try it out on a bar chart. Follow these steps:

1. In the upper-right corner of the Country Data for 2010 table, to the right of the Focus Mode icon, is the More Options icon represented by three dots (ellipsis). (If you don't see the More Options icon, you may need to hover your mouse pointer over the Country Data for 2010 table.) Click the More Options icon to view the More Options dropdown list.

2. Hover your mouse pointer over the Sort by option in the dropdown list. You will see a secondary dropdown list of the columns in the table. Note the yellow bar next to the Country/Territory item in the secondary dropdown list. This indicates the list is currently sorted by Country/Territory. The yellow bar next to the Sort ascending entry in the first dropdown list indicates the sort order is currently ascending. Click the Population item in the secondary dropdown list.

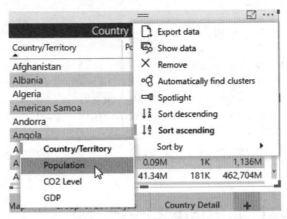

3. The table changes to sort by population, but the sort order remains ascending. The method does not default the sort of a numeric column to descending. We need to do that ourselves. Click the More Options icon. The More Options dropdown list appears.

4. Click Sort descending in the More Options dropdown list. The Country Data for 2010 table is once again sorted by population in descending order.

5. Click the Population, CO2, GDP Overview tab to return to the Population, CO2, GDP Overview page of the report.

6. Hover your mouse pointer over the 2010 Population by Country/Territory bar chart and click the More Options icon.

7. In the More Options dropdown list, hover your mouse pointer over Sort by. The Sort by dropdown list appears.

8. Click Country/Territory in the Sort by dropdown list.

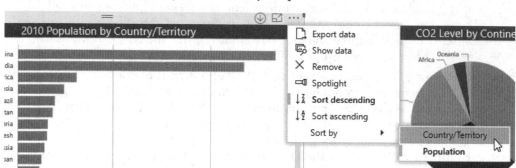

9. The chart is now sorted by Country/Territory, but in descending order. Click the More Options icon.

10. In the More Options dropdown list, select Sort ascending. We may like seeing the country/territory names in alphabetic order, but this sort order is not very helpful when trying to analyze population. Changing a visualization to sort by a particular quantity rather that alphabetically (or even chronologically) can be one way to aid your interpretation of the data.

11. Use the More Options menu to return the 2010 Population by Country/Territory bar chart to being sorted by population in descending order.

Interacting with Multiple Report Items

One of the most powerful features of Power BI is the fact that multiple data visualizations on a single report page will interact with one another. With that in mind, let's move from working with a single visualization to working with the entire report page.

Selecting a Chart Element

We can select an element within a chart—a single column in a column chart or a single wedge in a pie chart. Doing so focuses our attention on the selected item by dimming the other elements in that chart. Beyond that, the presentation of the data in the other visualizations on the page will also change. Follow these steps to try out this interaction:

1. In the GDP by Year column chart on the Population, CO2, GDP Overview page of the report, click the column for the year 2005. The 2005 column remains the same, but the other columns in the chart are dimmed. Note the wedges in the CO2 Level by Continent chart now contain a dual-color pattern. Part of each wedge is its original color while the rest of each wedge is now dimmed.

2. Hover over the wedge for Asia in the CO2 Level by Continent chart. There are now three lines in the resulting tooltip. The continent and the CO2 level represented by the full wedge are shown along with a new entry called "Highlighted." This is the value represented by the non-dimmed portion of the wedge. Because the year 2005 is selected in the other chart, this highlighted area represents the portion of the total Asia CO2 level from 2005.

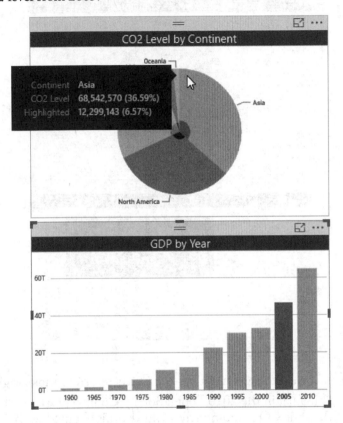

3. Click different year bars in the GDP by Year chart to compare the highlighted CO2 levels in the CO2 Level by Continent pie chart.

4. Click the Asia wedge in the CO2 Level by Continent pie chart. Notice that each of the columns in the GDP by Year column chart have both a dimmed and a highlighted portion. The highlighted portion represents the portion of that year's GDP coming from Asian countries.

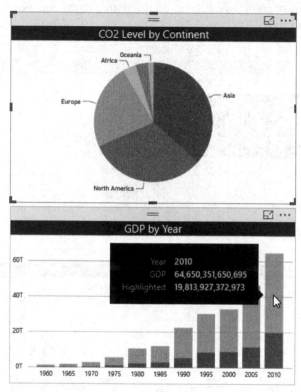

5. Click the Asia wedge again and all of the charts return to their original state.

6. Click the China bar in the 2010 Population by Country/Territory bar chart. The portion of the Asia CO2 coming from China is highlighted in the pie chart. The portion of the GDP coming from China is highlighted in the GDP by Year column chart, but only in the 2010 column. As the title indicates, the Population bar chart includes a filter that limits its data to the year 2010 (more on that later in this chapter). When we click a bar in this chart, we create highlighted regions in the other charts based not only on the country represented by that bar, but also by only 2010 data. This is done so that when we are looking at highlighted areas across multiple visualizations, we are comparing "apples to apples" as much as possible. In this case, we are comparing data for China in 2010 in all three charts.

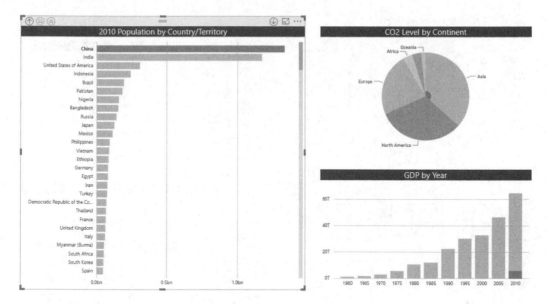

7. Hold down CTRL and click the United States of America bar in the 2010 Population by Country\Territory bar chart. This allows us to multi-select two items at the same time. The highlighted portion of the Asia wedge in the pie chart represents China's portion of the CO_2 level, and the highlighted portion of the North America wedge represents the United States' portion of the CO_2 level. The highlighted portion of the 2010 column in the GDP by Year chart represents the combined China and United States GDP for 2010.

Selecting a Map Region or Table Row

We have seen how things work with chart visualizations. Now let's try maps and tables.

1. Click the World Population Map tab to navigate to this page of the report.
2. Click China on the world map. This will limit the data in the Population Trend area chart and in the Country Data for 2010 table. Because the map is limited to 2010 data, when a country is selected, only that country's 2010 data is visible in the other items on the page.
3. Click China on the world map again and the page returns back to its original state. This is always the case; if you click a bar, column, wedge, country, or whatever, and then click that same item a second time, everything returns back to its original state.
4. Click Indonesia in the Country Data for 2010 table. Now, only the Indonesian data for 2010 is shown in the other items on the page. Because only Indonesia is highlighted on the map, the map auto-zooms in on Indonesia.

World Population in 2010

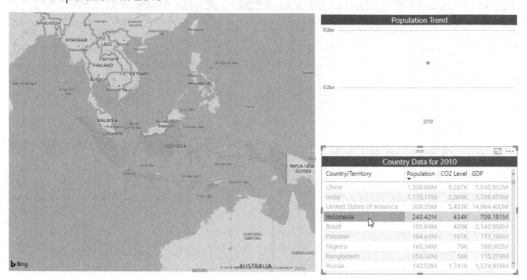

5. Click Indonesia in the Country Data for 2010 table again to return things to their original state.

Changing the Data with Slicers and Filters

Up to this point, we have manipulated the data that was provided to us on each page of the report. Next, we are going to look at ways to change the data displayed on a report page. To do this, we will look at slicers and filters.

Slicers and filters differ in form rather than in function. Both slicers and filters allow us to limit the data we are seeing in the visualizations on a report page. The big difference is how easy each of these is to get at and, therefore, how frequently each is meant to be changed.

Slicers

Slicers provide a way to change the data on a report page. Slicers are easily found, because they are laid out as part of the report page itself. Slicers come in multiple forms: buttons, dropdowns, lists, and even sliders, to name just a few.

A Dropdown Slicer

We begin by looking at a dropdown slicer:

1. Click the CO2 KPI tab to move to that page of the report.

2. The dropdown slicer for changing the year of the data being shown on this page is in the upper-right corner of the page itself. Click the down arrow to the right of "2010" to expand the dropdown list.

3. Scroll down in the list until the 2010 option with the filled-in selection box is visible.

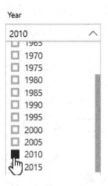

4. Click 2000 in the list. The report page changes to show data for the year 2000.

5. Click the up arrow to collapse the dropdown list. The dropdown slicer clearly indicates the year 2000 is selected.

6. Click the down arrow to expand the dropdown list.

7. Hold down CTRL and click 2005. Now data for both 2000 and 2005 is shown together on the report page. Note the slicer now says "Multiple selections" at the top of the dropdown list. You can select as many items as you like using CTRL.

8. Release CTRL and click 2010. As soon as an item is clicked without CTRL, only that single item is selected.

9. Click 2010 again. Clicking the only selected item causes it to become unselected. This shows you one of the unique things about slicers in Power BI. When nothing is selected in a slicer, Power BI acts like all the items in the slicer are selected. Note the slicer now says "All" at the top of the dropdown list. We are seeing data on the report page for all years added together.

10. Use CTRL and select several years in the dropdown list.

11. Hover your mouse pointer over the Year heading above the dropdown list. An icon will appear to the right of the heading. This icon is meant to evoke the big pink eraser some of us may have had back in grade school—although you may need to squint a little to see the resemblance. This is the Clear selections icon. There is a down arrow to the right of the Clear selections icon. That down arrow is used for report authoring, so we will ignore it for now.

12. Click the Clear selections icon. The Clear selections icon provides a quick way to clear out all the selected items in a slicer.

Interacting with Related Slicers

A report page can contain multiple slicers in different formats. In some cases, the data shown in the slicers will be interrelated. This can be useful, but can also lead to some odd interactions. Follow these steps to interact with related slicers:

1. Click the Yearly Data tab to move to that page of the report.
2. The rectangles showing six of the seven continents across the top of the page are slicer buttons. (We don't have any data from Antarctica, so that continent is not in the list.) There is another slicer showing a scrolling list of countries/territories down the right side of the page. This is a list slicer. Click the button for the Africa continent.

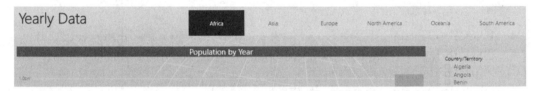

3. The reverse coloring clearly shows Africa is selected. Only data for African countries is included in the column chart. In fact, the Continent slicer is also filtering the values shown in the Country/Territory slicer. Only African countries/territories are shown in the list slicer. Click Angola in the Country/Territory slicer.

4. Now only data for Angola is displayed in the column chart. However, something odd has happened to the Continent slicer. It only has one big button for Africa. All of the other continents have disappeared. Just as the Country/Territory slicer is limiting what data is shown on the column chart, it is also limiting what data is shown in the Continent slicer. Only the continent associated with the selected value, Angola, is displayed. In order to select a different continent, we first have to clear the Country/Territory slicer. Click Angola again to deselect this item.
5. All of the continent options are back. Click South America.

Synchronized Slicers

Almost as graceful as synchronized swimming, synchronized slicers can save you time when working with multipage reports. Follow these steps to interact with synchronized slicers:

1. Click the GDP and CO2 Map tab to move to that page of the report.
2. Note that South America is selected in the Continent slicer and only data for South American countries is displayed. Click Africa in the Continent slicer.
3. Click the Yearly Data tab to move back to that page of the report. Now only data for African countries is displayed here.
4. Hold down CTRL and click Europe in the Continent slicer.
5. Click the GDP and CO2 Map tab.

As you can see, the Continent slicer is linked between these two pages. Any change made to the Continent slicer on one page also takes effect on the other page. When synchronized slicers are in place, you can make data selections on one page of the report and then view data from one or more other pages using the same selection criteria without having to reselect it.

A Range Slicer

In some cases, we may want to select a contiguous range of values. Holding down CTRL and clicking numerous values in that range could be tedious. The range slicer provides a convenient alternative.

The GDP and CO2 Map page of the report is designed to allow us to view data for a selected range of years. The Between Slider slicer makes this easy, as shown next:

1. Click the left end of the slider range and drag to the left until 1980 appears in the left (start of range) box.

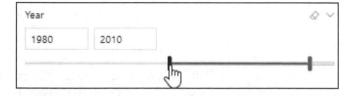

2. Click the right end of the slider range and drag it to the left until 2005 appears in the right (end of range) box. Note data for 1980 through 2005 now appears in the GDP and CO2 column chart and is reflected on the map.

3. Click in the left slicer box so you see an edit cursor.
4. Delete 1980.
5. Type **1965** and press ENTER.

6. Click in the right slicer box so you see an edit cursor.
7. Delete 2005.
8. Type **1990** and press ENTER. Now data from 1965 through 1990 is shown in the GDP and CO2 column chart and is reflected on the map.
9. Click the left end of the slider range and drag it until it is on top of the right end of the slider range. Now only a single value, 1990, is selected.

10. Double-click anywhere on the horizontal bar to the right of the slider range to see both the start and end points of the slider range.

11. Now click the right end of the slider range and drag it to the right until 2005 appears in the right box.

Filters

Filters work like slicers, but are somewhat hidden away. Whereas slicers are part of the report's user interface, filters are placed to the side on the Filters pane. Filters provide a less interactive but more flexible and powerful mechanism for modifying what is included in the report.

Power BI uses three different types of filters:

- Filters on this visual
- Filters on this page
- Filters on all pages

Filters on this visual affect the data shown in a single visualization on the report page. Filters on this page affect the data in all the visualizations on the report page. Filters on all pages affect the data in all the visualizations on all of the report pages.

Filters are located on the Filters pane. The Filters pane is often hidden on the right side of the screen. In order to view any filters or make changes to a filter, we need to show the Filters pane.

NOTE
The following instructions assume the updated Filters pane interface is being used. If you are seeing the filter definitions on the bottom of the Visualizations pane, go to File | Options and Settings | Options. In the Options dialog box, go to the Current File | Report Settings page and check the "Enable the updated filter pane, and show filters in the visual header for this report" option.

The Filters Pane

Let's use the Filters pane to modify one of the filters in our report. Earlier in this chapter we noted that the 2010 Population by Country/Territory bar chart on the Population, CO2, GDP Overview page of the report only displays population data for 2010. There is a filter on that visual that causes this behavior.

1. Click the Population, CO2, GDP Overview tab.
2. Click the arrow above the word "Filters" to show the Filters pane. Note there are no "Filters on this page" and no "Filters on all pages." No visualization is currently selected, so the "Filters on this visual" area is not visible.

3. Click somewhere in the 2010 Population by Country/Territory bar chart to select this visualization. The "Filters on this visual" area is now visible in the Filters pane. Most of the visual level filters show "(All)," indicating they are not restricting the data being shown. Only the Year filter says "Year is 2010," indicating only data for 2010 is being displayed in this visualization.

4. Hover over the Year area in the Filters pane and click the arrow to the right of the Year heading to expand the Year filter.

5. Scroll down in the year values until you can see 2000.

6. Check the box next to 2000, so both 2000 and 2010 are checked. You do not need to use CTRL to select multiple values for a filter. Despite what the heading is telling us, the 2010 Population by Country/Territory bar chart is now showing data for both 2000 and 2010.

7. Click the China bar in the 2010 Population by Country/Territory bar chart. In the GDP by Year column chart are highlighted regions for the years 2000 and 2010. As we saw previously, any filtering in effect for a given visualization becomes part of the interaction with other visualizations.

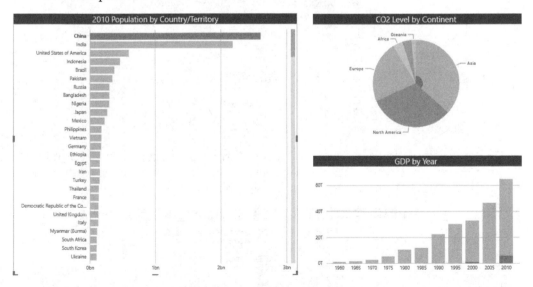

8. Let's put the filter back the way it was before we cause any confusion. Uncheck the 2000 entry in the Year visual level filter.

Excluded and Included

There are times when we are analyzing data when we may want to remove outlier values from a visualization in order to make it easier to evaluate the remaining values. The 2010 Population by Country/Territory bar chart is an example of this. The China and India population values are an order of magnitude larger than all the other population values. Because these bars are so much longer than the others, it is difficult to compare the relative lengths of the bars for the rest of the countries. The Excluded filter enables us to remove outliers.

At other times, we may want to create our own custom grouping of the data. We can then focus our analysis on the members of this custom grouping. The Included filter enables us to focus analysis on a select subset of the data. Let's explore using the Excluded and Included filters.

1. Click the China bar in the 2010 Population by Country/Territory bar chart so it is no longer highlighted.
2. Right-click the China bar in the 2010 Population by Country/Territory bar chart.
3. Select Exclude from the popup menu that appears. The China bar disappears from the chart.

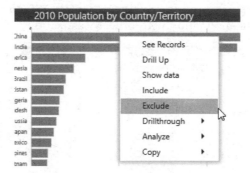

4. Right-click the India bar and select Exclude from the popup menu. The India bar disappears from the chart. It is now much easier to compare the relative populations of the next-largest countries in the chart.

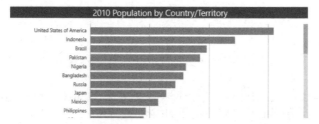

5. Scroll down until you see the entry for Nepal.
6. Click Nepal. Note you can click the "Nepal" label to select it or you can click the bar next to it.

7. Hold down CTRL and click the labels for the following countries:

   ● Peru

   ● Malaysia

   ● Uzbekistan

   ● Venezuela

   ● Saudi Arabia

8. Right-click the data bar for one of the six selected items and select Include from the popup menu. Note that you must right-click the data bar, not the label for this part of the operation. Now only these six countries/territories are included in the chart.

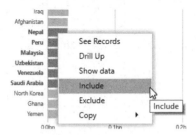

9. Look at the "Filters on this visual" area of the Filters pane. A new entry called Excluded has been created for the two countries/territories excluded from the chart. Also, a new entry called Included has been created for the six countries/ territories included in the chart. Click the down arrow to the right of the Included heading to see the items in the Included filter.

10. Click the "X" to the right of the Included filter entry for Peru (Country/Territory). This will remove Peru from the Included filter and consequently remove it from the chart. When an Included filter is present, only the items in the Included filter are present in the chart.

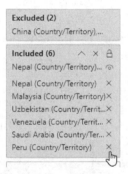

11. Click the "X" to the right of the Included filter heading to remove the entire Included filter. The chart now contains all of the countries/territories except for those in the Excluded filter.

12. Click the down arrow to the right of the Excluded heading to see the items in the Excluded filter.

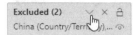

13. Click the "X" to the right of the Excluded filter entry for China (Country/Territory).

14. Click the "X" to the right of the Excluded filter heading to remove the entire Excluded filter.

Play Axis

One visualization within Power BI, the scatter chart, includes a feature that acts like a dynamic visual level filter. This feature is called the play axis. The play axis enables us to put the data in motion and animate it over a specified time period.

First, a bit about the scatter chart. The scatter chart allow us to analyze three variables at the same time—one on the horizontal axis, one on the vertical axis, and one controlling the size of each circle created on the chart. In the scatter chart on the Group of 20 Analysis page of our report, GDP is shown on the horizontal axis. The further to the right a country's circle travels, the bigger its GDP for that year. Population is shown on the vertical axis. The further up a country's circle travels, the bigger its population in that year.

Finally, CO2 level is shown by the size of the circle. The larger the circle, the bigger the CO2 level. The play axis runs from the year 1960 to 2010. So, we can see how all three of these variables interact over that 50-year period for the Group of 20 member nations.

1. Click the Group of 20 Analysis tab.
2. Click the play button to the left of the play (time) axis. The chart will animate the circles for each of the 20 nations.

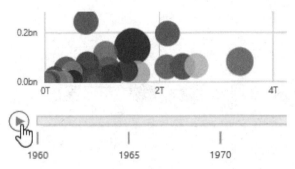

3. We can assist our analysis by highlighting certain countries. Click the light orange circle representing China. The path and size of the circle representing China are illustrated for each of the time stops along the play axis.

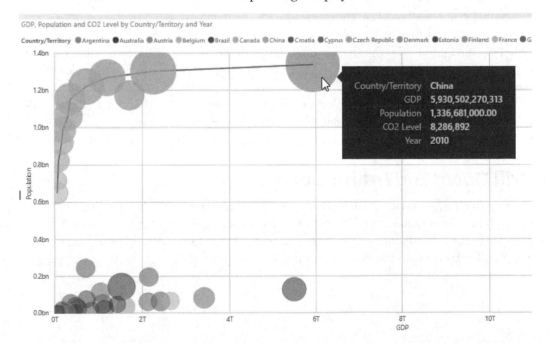

4. Hold down CTRL and click the gray circle representing the United States.
5. Click the play button again to observe the behavior of the highlighted data points.
6. Drag the cursor bar on the play axis from 2010 back to 2000.

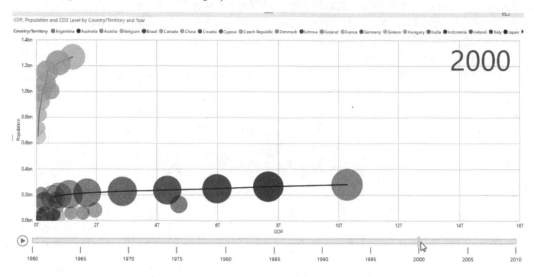

Navigating Power BI Reports

Up to this point, we have been interacting with the data contained in the report—selecting data and data elements as well as slicing and filtering. Now, we are going to switch to navigations. Navigating through levels of data using drill down and navigating through different pages of the report using drillthrough. After that we will look at buttons and bookmarks.

We will end the chapter by exploring ways to go after the underlying data directly. We will use an innovative method of querying our data using natural language statements. Finally, we will view and export the underlying data used to create our visualizations.

Drill Down and Drillthrough

Data analysis often takes us from looking at high-level summary data to digging through low-level detail data. We want to have a mechanism for finding a summary number that has some interest to us, and then drilling into the detail behind that number. Drill down and its corresponding drill up operation enable us to navigate up and down through levels of detail to find the answers we are looking for. Drillthrough takes us from a report page showing summary information to another report page showing the detail behind a particular number.

Drill Down in a Matrix

Several different types of Power BI visualizations support drill down. We begin by using drill down in a matrix.

NOTE
Drill down operations are available in a matrix only if the report author set up several levels of detail when the matrix was created. The presence or absence of the drill down context menu options and icons will let you know whether drill down is available in any given matrix. Drill down is not available in a table.

1. Click the CO2 KPI tab.
2. Select 2000 in the Year dropdown slicer.
3. In the CO2 Actual vs Goal matrix, we see that only Oceania is yellow at 116.69% of its CO2 reduction goal. Let's drill down to see what the values are for each Oceanian country. Right-click Oceania in the Continent column and select Drill Down from the context menu.

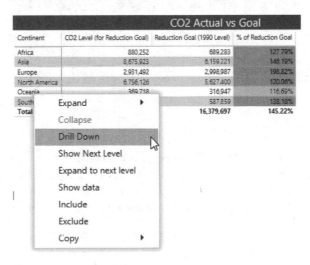

4. This drills into the Oceania continent, showing each of the countries that make up that continent along with the total for the continent as a whole. Right-click any of the countries and select Drill Up from the context menu.

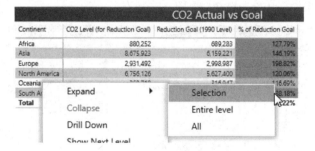

5. There are a number of alternative ways we can perform this drill down operation. Right-click Oceania again, but this time select Expand | Selection from the context menu.

Continent	CO2 Level (for Reduction Goal)	Reduction Goal (1990 Level)	% of Reduction Goal
Africa	880,252	689,283	127.79%
Asia	8,675,923	6,159,221	146.19%
Europe	2,931,492	2,998,987	198.82%
North America	6,756,126	5,627,400	120.06%
Oceania		316,947	116.69%
South A			8.18%
Total			22%

Expand ▸ | Selection
Collapse | Entire level
Drill Down | All
Show Next Level

6. Using this method, we continue to see all of the entries at the continent level along with the detail for the countries of Oceania. Rather than right-clicking to drill up this time, we will use the Drill Up icon in the upper-left corner of this visualization. This is the up arrow inside the circle. Click the Drill Up icon.

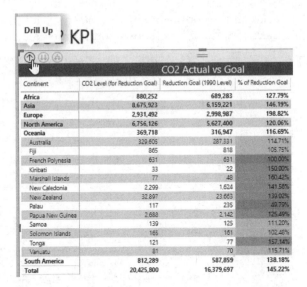

7. Right-click Oceania again and select Expand | Entire level from the context menu.

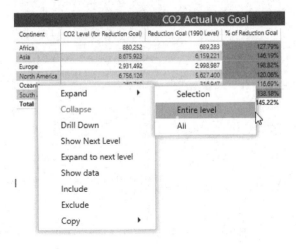

8. This method expands all the continent entries (the entire level) to show the countries within each continent. Scroll down to find the Oceanian countries.

Continent	CO2 Level (for Reduction Goal)	Reduction Goal (1990 Level)	% of Reduction Goal
Panama	5,790	2,769	209.10%
Saint Kitts and Nevis	103	66	156.06%
Saint Lucia	330	165	200.00%
Saint Vincent and the Grenadines	158	81	195.06%
Trinidad and Tobago	24,514	16,960	144.54%
United States of America	5,713,560	4,768,138	119.83%
Oceania	**369,718**	**316,947**	**116.69%**
Australia	329,605	287,331	114.71%
Fiji	865	818	105.75%
French Polynesia	631	631	100.00%
Kiribati	33	22	150.00%
Marshall Islands	77	48	160.42%
New Caledonia	2,299	1,624	141.56%
New Zealand	32,897	23,663	139.02%
Palau	117	235	49.79%
Papua New Guinea	2,688	2,142	125.49%
Samoa	139	125	111.20%
Solomon Islands	165	161	102.48%
Tonga	121	77	157.14%
Vanuatu	81	70	115.71%
South America	**812,289**	**587,859**	**138.18%**
Argentina	141,077	112,614	125.27%
Bolivia	10,224	5,504	185.76%
Brazil	327,984	208,887	157.02%
Chile	58,694	34,143	171.91%
Colombia	57,924	57,337	101.02%
Ecuador	20,942	16,835	124.40%
Guyana	1,610	1,140	141.23%
Paraguay	3,689	2,263	163.01%
Peru	30,297	21,170	143.11%
Suriname	2,127	1,811	117.45%
Uruguay	5,306	3,993	132.88%
Venezuela	152,415	122,162	124.76%
Total	**20,425,800**	**16,379,697**	**145.22%**

9. Click the Drill Up icon.
10. Right-click Oceania again and select Expand | All from the context menu.

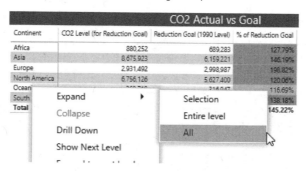

11. This method expands all items and drills down all levels. In this case, the capital city is included as a third level beneath continent and country. Again, scroll down to find the Oceanian countries and their capital cities.

CO2 Actual vs Goal			
Continent	CO2 Level (for Reduction Goal)	Reduction Goal (1990 Level)	% of Reduct.
~~Washington, D.C., United States of America~~			
Oceania	**369,718**	**316,947**	
Australia	**329,605**	**287,331**	
Canberra, Australia	329,605	287,331	
Fiji	**865**	**818**	
Suva, Fiji	865	818	
French Polynesia	**631**	**631**	
Papeete, French Polynesia	631	631	
Kiribati	**33**	**22**	
South Tarawa, Kiribati	33	22	
Marshall Islands	**77**	**48**	
Majuro, Marshall Islands	77	48	
New Caledonia	**2,299**	**1,624**	
Nouméa, New Caledonia	2,299	1,624	
New Zealand	**32,897**	**23,663**	
Wellington, New Zealand	32,897	23,663	
Palau	**117**	**235**	
Ngerulmud, Palau	117	235	
Papua New Guinea	**2,688**	**2,142**	
Port Moresby, Papua New Guinea	2,688	2,142	
Samoa	**139**	**125**	
Apia, Samoa	139	125	
Solomon Islands	**165**	**161**	
Honiara, Solomon Islands	165	161	
Tonga	**121**	**77**	
Nuku'alofa, Tonga	121	77	
Vanuatu	**81**	**70**	
Port Vila, Vanuatu	81	70	
South America	**812,289**	**587,859**	
Argentina	**141,077**	**112,614**	
Buenos Aires, Argentina	141,077	112,614	
Bolivia	**10,224**	**5,504**	
Sucre, Bolivia	10,224	5,504	
Total	**20,425,800**	**16,379,697**	

12. Click the Drill Up icon to remove the capital city level from the matrix.

13. Click the Drill Up icon again to remove the country level from the matrix so only the continents are visible.

14. Right-click Oceania and select Show Next Level from the context menu.

CO2 Actual vs Goal			
Continent	CO2 Level (for Reduction Goal)	Reduction Goal (1990 Level)	% of Reduction Goal
Africa	880,252	689,283	127.79%
Asia	8,675,923	6,159,221	146.19%
Europe	2,931,492	2,998,987	198.82%
North America	6,756,126	5,627,400	120.06%
Oceania	369,718	316,947	116.69%
Sou~~~~		587,859	138.18%
Tot~~~~		16,379,697	145.22%

Context menu:
- Expand ▸
- Collapse
- Drill Down
- **Show Next Level**
- Expand to next level
- Show data
- Include
- Exclude
- Copy ▸

15. This method shows all of the countries and no longer shows any of the continent information. Scroll down to find New Zealand in the list of countries.

CO2 Actual vs Goal			
Country/Territory	CO2 Level (for Reduction Goal)	Reduction Goal (1990 Level)	% of Reduction Goal
New Zealand	32,897	23,663	139.02%
Nicaragua	3,762	2,549	147.59%
Niger	796	832	95.67%
Nigeria	79,182	45,375	174.51%
North Korea	76,699	244,835	31.33%
Norway	38,808	31,364	123.73%
Oman	21,896	11,386	192.31%
Pakistan	106,449	68,566	155.25%
Palau	117	235	49.79%
Panama	5,790	2,769	209.10%
Papua New Guinea	2,688	2,142	125.49%
Paraguay	3,689	2,263	163.01%
Peru	30,297	21,170	143.11%
Philippines	73,307	41,763	175.53%
Poland	301,691	366,773	82.26%
Portugal	62,966	42,196	149.22%
Qatar	34,730	11,775	294.95%
Romania	89,985	158,862	56.64%
Rwanda	685	682	100.59%
Saint Kitts and Nevis	103	66	156.06%
Saint Lucia	330	165	200.00%
Saint Vincent and the Grenadines	158	81	195.06%
Samoa	139	125	111.20%
São Tomé and Principe	48	48	100.00%
Saudi Arabia	296,935	217,948	136.24%
Senegal	3,938	3,183	123.72%
Seychelles	565	114	495.61%
Sierra Leone	425	389	109.25%
Singapore	49,006	46,941	104.40%
Solomon Islands	165	161	102.48%
Somalia	517	18	2872.22%
South Africa	368,611	333,514	110.52%
South Korea	447,561	246,943	181.24%
Total	20,425,800	16,379,697	145.22%

16. Click the Drill Up icon.

17. Right-click Oceania and select "Expand to next level" from the context menu.

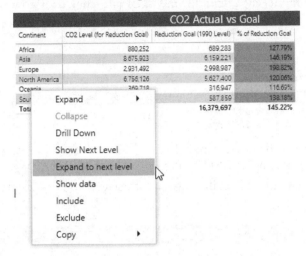

18. This method functions exactly the same as the Expand | Entire Level option. Click the Drill Up icon.

19. There are also icons that allow us to drill down. Click the circle containing the two parallel arrows. This is the "Go to the next level in the hierarchy" icon. (I will call this the double-arrow icon for short.)

20. This icon functions exactly the same as selecting Show Next Level from the context menu. Click the Drill Up icon.

21. Click the circle containing the arrow with one tail branching into two heads. This is the "Expand all down one level in the hierarchy" icon. (I will call this the forked-arrow icon.)

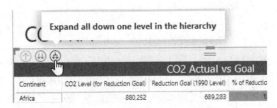

22. This icon functions exactly the same as the Expand | Entire Level option (and "Expand to next level" option). Click the Drill Up icon.

23. Finally, if that wasn't enough, there is an icon to turn on one-click drill down. This is the circle containing the down arrow on the right side of this item. Click the icon to turn on one-click drill down. When one-click drill down is on, its icon will have a gray background with a white down arrow.

24. Click Oceania in the Continent column. A simple click now executes a drill down equivalent to selecting Drill Down from the context menu.
25. Click New Zealand. This drills down another level to New Zealand's capital city.

Continent	CO2 Level (for Reduction Goal)	Reduction Goal (1990 Level)	% of Reduction Goal
Oceania	32,897	23,663	139.02%
New Zealand	32,897	23,663	139.02%
Wellington, New Zealand	32,897	23,663	139.02%
Total	32,897	23,663	139.02%

CO2 Actual vs Goal

26. Click the Drill Up icon twice.
27. Click the one-click drill down icon to turn off this feature. The icon returns to a white background with a gray down arrow.

Drill Down in a Chart

Drill down in a chart works in a manner similar to drill down in a matrix, but with slightly fewer options, as demonstrated next:

NOTE
Drill down operations are available in a chart only if the report author set up several levels of detail when the chart was created. The presence or absence of the drill down context menu options and icons will let you know whether drill down is available in any given chart.

1. Select the Population, CO2, GDP Overview tab.
2. It turns out the 2010 Population by Country/Territory bar chart is initially set to a lower level of drill down detail when the report opened. We will drill up and then examine the drill down options available to us. Click the Drill Up icon.

3. Right-click the bar for Africa and select Drill Down from the context menu.

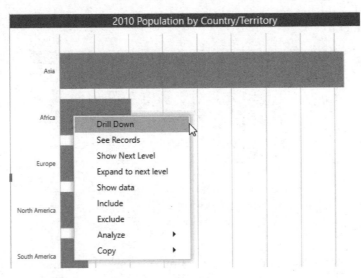

4. The chart shows the data for the African countries. Scroll down to find Somalia.

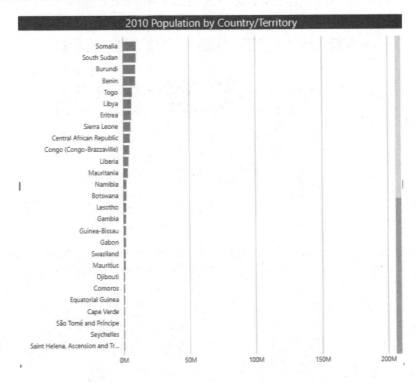

5. Click the Drill Up icon.

6. Right-click the bar for Africa again and select Show Next Level from the context menu.

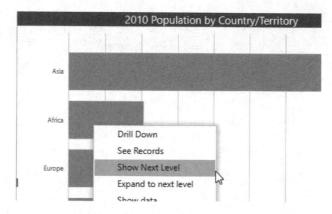

7. The chart shows the data for all the countries from all continents. This is the format the chart was in initially. Click the Drill Up icon.

8. Right-click the bar for Africa again and select "Expand to next level" from the context menu.

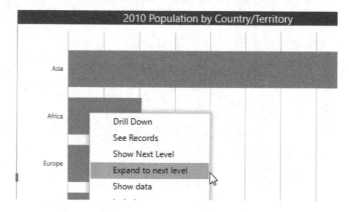

9. The chart shows the data for all the countries for all continents, but it has combined the continent name with the country name. Scroll down to find the entry for "Europe Ukraine."

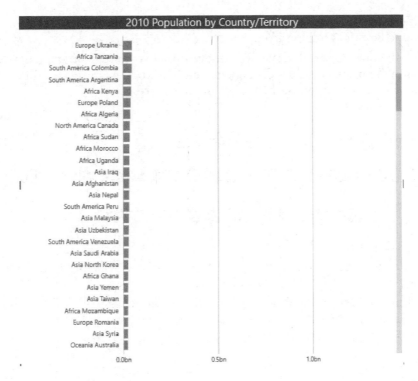

10. Click the Drill Up icon.
11. Click the double-arrow icon above this chart.

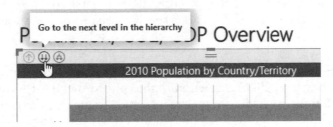

12. This icon functions the same as selecting Show Next Level from the context menu. Click the Drill Up icon.
13. Click the forked-arrow icon above this chart.

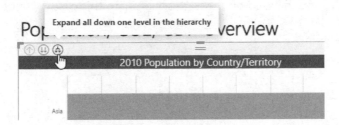

14. This icon functions the same as selecting "Expand to next level" from the context menu. Click the Drill Up icon.

15. Click the one-click drill down icon above this chart to turn on one-click drill down. When the one-click drill down feature is on, the one-click drill down icon will have a gray background with a white down arrow.

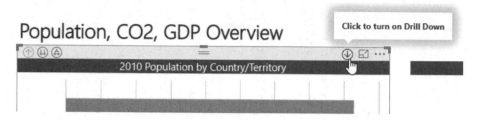

16. Click the bar for Africa.

17. Clicking a bar in the chart now functions the same as selecting Drill Down from the context menu. Click the Drill Up icon.

18. Click the one-click drill down icon to turn off one-click drill down. The icon returns to a white background with a gray down arrow.

19. Click the double-arrow icon to return the chart to the state in which we found it.

Drillthrough

We used drill down to get to a new level of data within a visualization. Now let's see how we can use drillthrough to get to an entire page of detail. In this case, let's suppose that, as we look at data for a country in one specific visualization, we want to see more detail about the country in general.

1. In the 2010 Population by Country/Territory bar chart, right-click the bar for Mexico. You will see there is an entry in the context menu for Drillthrough. Because we right-clicked a chart element linked to a particular country, the presence of the Drillthrough option indicates the report contains one or more pages that are set up for drillthrough.

2. Hover your mouse pointer over the Drillthrough entry. You see a submenu with an entry called Country Detail. This corresponds to the Country Detail page of the report. One entry will appear in this submenu for each report page that is set up for drillthrough based on the item selected (in this case, a country).

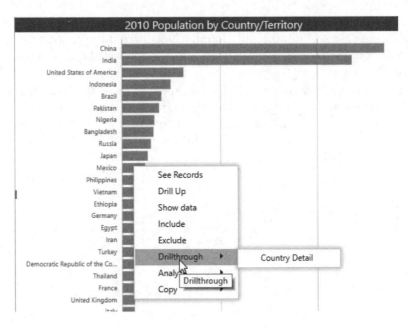

3. Click Country Detail in the submenu.
4. You navigate to the Country Detail page of the report (the Country Detail tab). Detail information for Mexico is shown.
5. There is a circle with a left arrow in the upper-left corner of the report page. This is a Back button. It will return us to whatever report page we were on when we made the selection from the Drill Down menu. Hover your mouse pointer over the Back button.

NOTE
The tooltip with this button instructs you to press CTRL and click the button. Interacting with buttons is one of the few things that functions differently when in Power BI Desktop versus interacting with a Power BI report through a browser. When clicking buttons in Power BI Desktop, we need to hold down CTRL. We can click a button without holding down CTRL when using a browser.

6. Hold down CTRL and click the Back button.

7. We return to the Population, CO2, GDP Overview page. Right-click the bar for Nigeria and select Drillthrough | Country Detail from the context menu. We are taken back to the Country Detail page, but information about Nigeria is being displayed.

8. Click the arrow above the word "Visualizations" to show the Visualizations pane. At the bottom of this pane is the Drillthrough area. (Scroll down within the pane, if necessary.) Notice the Drillthrough area contains a special filter that states "Country/Territory is Nigeria." This drillthrough filter is what enables us to see detail for the selected country.

9. Hold down CTRL and click the Back button.

10. Right-click the bar for Vietnam and select Drillthrough | Country Detail from the context menu.

11. The Country Detail page now contains information about Vietnam and the drillthrough filter has been changed to "Country/Territory is Vietnam." Hold down CTRL and click the Back button.

12. Click the Drill Up icon for the 2010 Population by Country/Territory bar chart.

13. Right-click the bar for Asia. Notice there is no Drillthrough option in the context menu. That is due to the fact that we are no longer at the country level in the chart. The drillthrough filter for the Country Detail page only reacts at the country level.

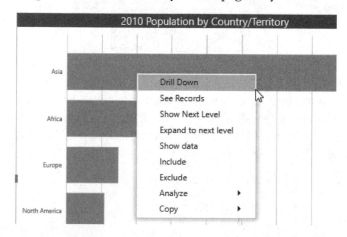

14. Click the double-arrow icon to return the bar chart to the country level.
15. Click the World Population Map tab.
16. Right-click Russia on the map.

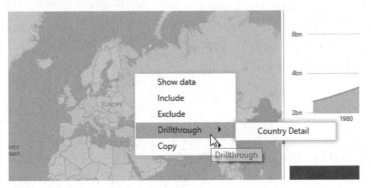

17. Because we are selecting a particular country, the Drillthrough option is available. Select Drilldown | Country Detail from the context menu.
18. Press CTRL and click the Back button.
19. In the Country Data for 2010 table, right-click Pakistan.

Country Data for 2010			
Country/Territory	Population	CO2 Level	GDP
China	1,336.68M	8,287K	5,930,502
India	1,173.11M	2,009K	1,708,459
United States of America	309.35M	5,433K	14,964,400
Indonesia	243.42M	434K	709,191
Brazil	195.84M	420K	2,143,068
Pakistan	184.41M	161K	177,166
Nigeria	.34M	79K	369,062
Bangla	.12M	56K	115,279
Russia	.53M	1,741K	1,524,916

Show data
Include
Exclude
Drillthrough ▸ Country Detail
Copy ▸ Country Detail

20. Again, because we are at a country level in the table, the Drillthrough option is available. Select Drillthrough | Country Detail from the context menu.
21. Press CTRL and click the Back button.
22. Click the CO2 KPI tab.

23. Right-click Oceania in the CO2 Actual vs Goal matrix. There is no Drillthrough option because we are not at a country level.
24. Select Drill Down from the context menu.
25. Right-click Australia in the CO2 Actual vs Goal matrix.
26. Now we are at the country level. Select Drillthrough | Country Detail.
27. Press CTRL and click the Back button.
28. Hide the Filters and Visualization panes.

Buttons

Buttons are used by the report author to create a richer user interface for our reports. Buttons can be used to navigate us to different pages within a report. They can also be used to change what we are seeing on a report page. Finally, they can be used to provide direct access to other features within Power BI.

Using a Button to Change Report Pages

We have already seen a button in action. The Back button allowed us to return from the Country Detail drillthrough page to whichever report page we were on when we activated drillthrough. Buttons can even be used to create a table of contents for a multipage report. I think you get the idea, so we won't be clicking any more buttons just to switch report pages.

Using a Button to Change Report Layout

What we haven't looked at yet is a button changing the report layout. Let's give that a try:

1. Click the Yearly Data tab.
2. There are three rectangles below the Population by Year column chart. These are buttons. Hover over the CO2 button.

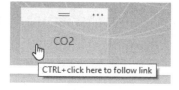

3. Again, notice the instruction to use CTRL when clicking this button. Press CTRL and click the CO2 button.

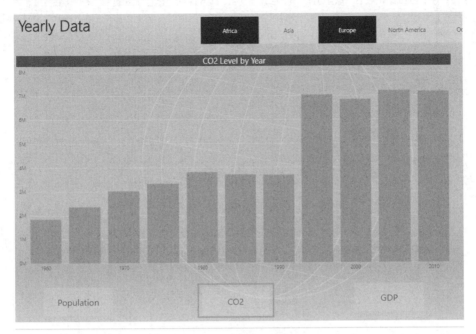

4. The Population by Year column chart is replaced by the CO2 Level by Year column chart. Press CTRL and click the GDP button.

5. Again, the chart changes, this time to GDP by Year. Press CTRL and click the Population button to change the page back to the way we found it.

Bookmarks

Bookmarks provide a way to save the setting of slicers, the drill down level within visualizations, and any selections in visualizations. This can be useful when we want to be able to return to a report page in a given state. Our report has some bookmarks saved for items on the GDP and CO2 Map page of the report. Let's see how these can be put to use.

Telling a Data Story

One way we often use bookmarks is to tell a story. By saving a series of states of a report page to a set of bookmarks, we step through states quickly to make a point with the data. This works much better than to have to manually change a number of slicers or drill downs to reach a certain point in the data when we have an audience.

1. Click View in the menu bar to see the View ribbon.
2. Check the box next to Bookmarks Pane.

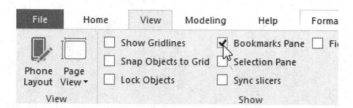

3. The Bookmarks pane appears. You may need to drag the Bookmarks pane wider so you can see the entire name of the bookmarks.

4. Click the "GDP & CO2 Map-Europe 1960-2010" entry. The entry will expand to show it is actually a grouping of several bookmarks. We can see they are for years 1960 to 2010.
5. Click the "GDP & CO2 Map-Europe 1960" entry. This will start us at the first bookmark in the grouping.
6. Click the View button.

7. Several things happen when you view the set of bookmarks. You are taken to the GDP and CO2 Map page of the report. Europe is selected in the continent slicer and 1960 is selected in the year slicer. The bottom of the report area shows a bookmark navigation control. Click the right arrow in the bookmark navigation control to move to the next bookmark.

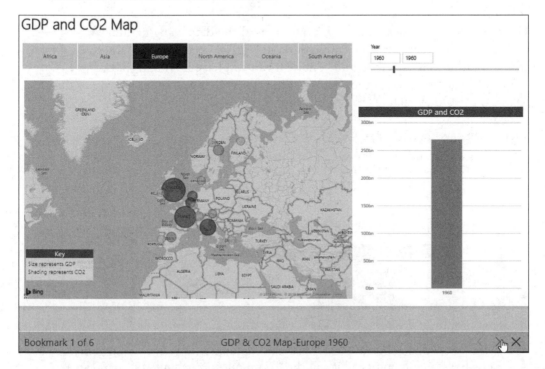

8. Continue to click the right arrow to walk through the bookmarks for the years up to 2010.
9. Click the "X" in the bookmark navigation control to exit the bookmark viewer.
10. Click the "GDP & CO2 Map-Asia 1960-2010" grouping entry to expand it.
11. Click the "GDP & CO2 Map-Asia 1960" bookmark.
12. Click the View button.
13. Use the bookmark navigator to move through the bookmarks in this grouping.
14. Close the bookmark navigator when you are done.

15. Use the "X" in the upper-right corner of the Bookmarks pane to close that pane.

Additional Data Interactions

Power BI provides a few ways for us to get at the underlying data. We aren't seeing the actual raw data behind the report. Instead, we are seeing representations of that data in various ways.

Q&A

The Q&A tool provides a way to ask questions of the data using natural language—sort of a Siri or Alexa for your Power BI data. "Sort of" because you have to type the question rather than speak it, and because it can still have its rough spots.

We will make use of another button in the report that was set up to give us direct access to the Q&A feature. To do so, follow these steps:

1. Click the Population, CO2, GDP Overview tab.
2. Press CTRL and click the Q&A button in the upper-right corner.

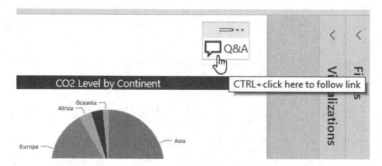

3. The Q&A dialog box appears. Several sample questions have been generated as possible starting points. Click in the "Ask a question about your data" area.

4. Type **total GDP by continent for 2010** and press ENTER.

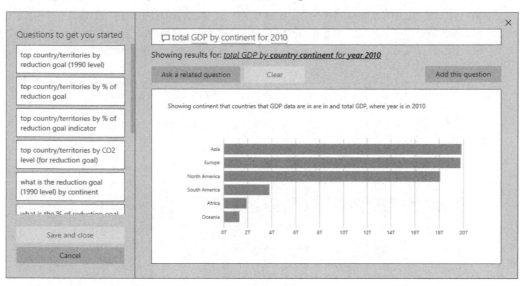

5. The Q&A feature creates a bar chart on the fly to answer our question. Click the "Ask a related question" button.

6. Type **total GDP by continent for 1990** and press ENTER.

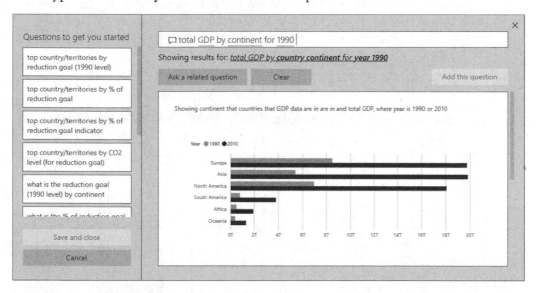

7. The Q&A feature created a second bar chart comparing the GDP for each continent in 1990 and 2010. Click the "X" in the upper-right corner to close the Q&A dialog box.

Show Data

The Show Data feature allows us to look at the data used to create a particular visualization. We see the data at the same level of granularity it is currently being shown at in the visualization. Follow these steps to use the Show Data feature:

1. Hover your mouse pointer over the 2010 Population by Country/Territory bar chart.
2. Click the Drill Up icon.
3. Click the More Options (…) icon in the upper-right corner of the 2010 Population by Country/Territory bar chart.
4. Select Show data from the popup menu.

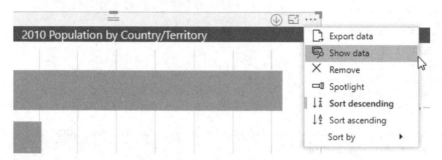

5. The visualization along with the underlying data is displayed. Note that we see the population totals at the continent level because that's the current drill down level of the visualization. Click the icon to show the visualization and data side by side rather than one atop the other.

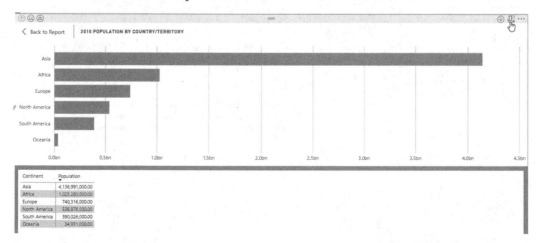

6. Click the double-arrow icon.
7. The visualization and the data are now shown at the Country level.
8. Click Back to Report.

Export Data

The Export Data feature works the same as the Show Data feature in that it exports the data used to create a particular visualization at the granularity level being shown in the visualization. The data is exported as comma-separated values, otherwise known as a CSV file. The CSV format is used because it can be easily opened in Excel. Follow these steps to use the Export Data feature:

1. Hover your mouse pointer over the 2010 Population by Country/Territory bar chart.
2. Click the More Options (…) icon.
3. Select Export Data from the popup menu.
4. The Save As dialog box appears. Select the folder where you would like to store the export file.
5. By default, the file is given the same name as the title of the visualization with ".csv" on the end. Click Save.
6. If you have Excel installed on your computer, navigate to the folder where you just saved the file and double-click the new CSV file.
7. The file will open in Excel. After viewing the data, close Excel.

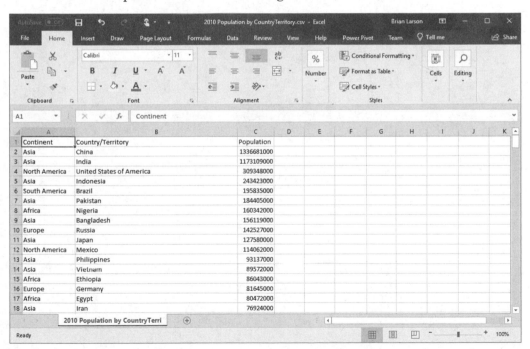

A Cloudy Forecast

You now have a good idea of the ways you can interact with and explore a Power BI report. In Chapter 5, we look at ways to manage Power BI reports in PowerBI.com. We will be headed from working in a local Windows application to life in the cloud.

Chapter 5

Using the Power BI Service (PowerBI.com)

In This Chapter

- PowerBI.com
- Workspaces
- Additional Areas and Items Within PowerBI.com

In the previous chapter, you learned how to interact with visualizations in a Power BI report. In this chapter, you learn how to interact with the environment most often used to share those reports across an organization—the Power BI Service, or more commonly known as PowerBI.com.

PowerBI.com

PowerBI.com is an online space within Microsoft's Azure cloud space created specifically for sharing Power BI content with others. You can create a sign-on for PowerBI.com and start using it for your Power BI content for free. However, you will quickly run into limitations when you try to share content. It is best to assume, when using PowerBI.com to publish content across an organization, that a Power BI Pro license is going to be necessary for each user who is going to be on either the sharing end or the receiving end of shared content.

The Organization of PowerBI.com

PowerBI.com organizes content into three areas: Workspaces, Apps, and Shared with Me. Each of these areas receives and manages content a bit differently. Content that lands in one of these areas cannot be moved to or intermingled with content from other areas.

Workspaces

The Workspaces area is made up of a number of named workspaces and a special workspace called My Workspace. The named workspaces are collaboration spaces that can be shared by a number of users. In this way, all of the members of that workspace can see all of the content stored there. These workspaces can be created in PowerBI.com or they may result from groups created within the Azure Active Directory space. For example, as of the writing of this chapter, groups created within the Microsoft Teams application will show up as workspaces in PowerBI.com.

The My Workspace area, as the name implies, manages content that only the signed-in user can see by default. Content in My Workspace can be packaged in a number of ways and made available to others. However, this requires additional steps.

When a report author publishes a report from Power BI Desktop, it is saved in a workspace. When a user installs a Power BI content pack, that content is also placed in a workspace. Content packs are a mechanism for packaging together dashboards, reports, and datasets and making that package available for others to install. Once installed, content pack content is simply mixed in with any other dashboards, reports, and datasets that happen to be in that workspace. We will look at publishing to PowerBI.com and creating content packs in Chapter 15.

Apps

Using apps is one of the preferred methods for sharing content in PowerBI.com. Like content packs, a Power BI app packages together dashboards, reports, and datasets for sharing with others. Unlike content packs, installed apps end up in their own area within PowerBI.com. This is the Apps page.

Each app has its own name and icon. The dashboards, reports, and datasets from each app remain separate. The app content is accessed by clicking the icon for that app.

Shared with Me

Individual dashboards and reports can also be shared from one user to another without packaging them into a content pack or an app. You will learn about sharing content in the Share section under Reports later in this chapter. Content that is shared in this manner ends up on the "Shared with me" page in PowerBI.com.

Connecting to PowerBI.com

To connect to PowerBI.com, open any modern browser and enter

```
powerbi.com
```

in the address bar. If you have a PowerBI.com (or Office 365 or Azure Active Directory) sign-in, click "Sign in" in the toolbar on the upper-right corner of the page. If you do not yet have a sign-in, click "Sign up free" and follow the steps to sign up.

When you click "Sign in," you will be taken to the Azure sign-in page. If the correct credentials are displayed on the sign-in page, click those credentials. If the correct credentials are not displayed, click "Use another account" and enter your sign-in. The sign-in process may be able to use your current Windows authentication to sign you in to PowerBI.com at this point in the process. If this is successful, you will be taken right into your PowerBI.com environment. If this is not successful, enter your password to complete the authentication.

Home

In most cases, once you are signed in to PowerBI.com, you will be taken to the Home page. This page contains the dashboards, reports, and apps you have accessed most frequently and most recently, along with any items you have marked as favorites. The bottom of the page also shows some recommended content and links to how-to videos and sites.

The "Set as featured" item on the Dashboard toolbar enables you to set a particular dashboard as the featured dashboard. This is noted in the Dashboard Toolbar section later in this chapter. If a dashboard has been set as featured, you will not be taken to the Home page upon signing in. Instead, your featured dashboard will be used as your landing page.

Signing Out

To sign out of PowerBI.com when you are done with your session, click the Profile icon in the upper-right corner. Select "Sign out" from the menu. Leave your browser window open until the sign-out process has completed.

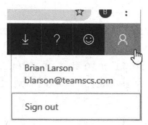

The Navigation Pane

The left side of the PowerBI.com pages contains the Navigation pane shown in Figure 5-1. The Navigation pane enables you to move between the PowerBI.com areas. You can hide or show the Navigation pane by clicking the button with the three horizontal lines located in the upper-left corner of the pane.

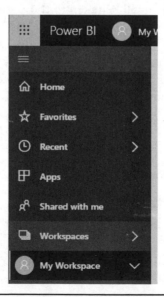

Figure 5-1   *The Navigation pane*

Workspaces

The lower portion of the Navigation pane shown in Figure 5-1 contains two references to workspaces. The "Workspaces" item, which is second from the bottom, will display a list of all workspaces available when it is clicked. This is shown in Figure 5-2. "My Workspace" is always shown at the top of the list. You use the Workspaces item on the Navigation pane to switch from working with one workspace to working with another.

The item at the bottom of the Navigation pane shows the workspace you are currently working in. In Figure 5-2, "My Workspace" is the current workspace. Clicking the down arrow to the right of the workspace name will expand this item to show its content right within the Navigation pane, as shown in Figure 5-3. You can click a content item in the Navigation pane to display that item in the main work area.

If you hover over an item, you will see the item's full name in a tool tip as well as an ellipsis button (…). Clicking the ellipsis button will display a context menu of more operations for each item. You will learn about each of these items as we cover them individually in the following sections of the chapter.

When we select a workspace, the content of that workspace appears in the main area of the page. The content is divided up into the various content types (dashboards, reports, and so on) with a selection menu across the top, as shown later in this chapter

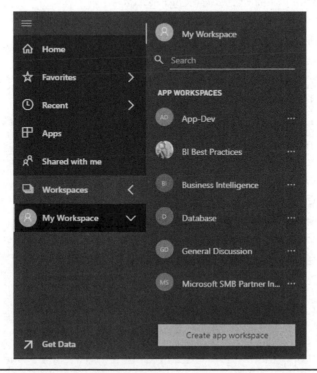

Figure 5-2   *The Navigation pane showing all workspaces*

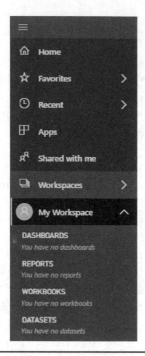

Figure 5-3 *The Navigation pane with the current workspace content*

in Figure 5-4. We can switch from viewing a list of dashboards to viewing a list of reports, and so on, using this selection menu.

Reports

We begin exploring the content in workspaces by looking at reports. The reports are the basic content created for user consumption in Power BI Desktop. They are the reason we need datasets, and their visualizations form the basis for the dashboards.

Publishing Reports to PowerBI.com

Let's try publishing two reports from this book to your My Workspace area on PowerBI.com. (This activity assumes you have a sign-in for PowerBI.com.) We will publish the "Population-GDP-CO2 by Country.pbix" report we worked with in Chapter 4 along with the "Max Min Sales Information.pbix" file that will be used later in this book. Both of these files are available in the supporting materials for this book (see Chapter 1 for more information).

Follow these steps:

1. Locate the "Population-GDP-CO2 by Country.pbix" file in your file system and double-click the file to open it in Power BI Desktop.

2. Click Publish on the Home tab of the ribbon.

3. If you have not signed in to PowerBI.com through Power BI Desktop, you will be prompted for your sign-in and password.

4. Once signed in, you will see a list of your workspaces in PowerBI.com. Ensure that "My workspace" is highlighted and click Select.

5. The publish process takes some time depending on the size of the Power BI file being sent to PowerBI.com. Once the publish process is successful, click the X in the upper-right corner to close the Publishing dialog box.

6. Close Power BI Desktop.

7. Locate the "Max Min Sales Information.pbix" file in your file system and double-click the file to open it in Power BI Desktop.

8. Click Publish on the Home tab of the ribbon.

9. Ensure that "My workspace" is highlighted and click Select.

10. Once the publish process is successful, click the X in the upper-right corner to close the Publishing dialog box.

11. Close Power BI Desktop.

You can now return to PowerBI.com, go to the Reports tab on My Workspace, and use these two reports to explore the report features described in the remainder of the "Reports" section.

The Report List

Figure 5-4 shows a list of reports in My Workspace. You can use the "Search content" area at the top to search for a report within a long list of reports. The search will look for any contiguous occurrence of the string you enter within the report name.

NOTE
The Usage Metrics feature is only available if you have a Power BI Pro or higher subscription. If you are using the free version of Power BI, you will not see the Usage Metrics button.

The various parts of the list entry for each report are labeled in the figure. This includes a number of function buttons. The function buttons are listed here with a brief description. Additional details about some of the functions are provided in sections later in this chapter.

● **Favorite**   Adds the report to the Favorites page.

● **Usage Metrics**   Displays a report showing the number of times this report has been accessed and how it ranks by number of views with other reports within the organization.

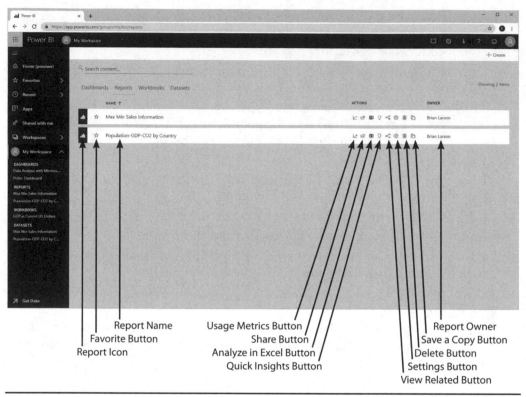

Figure 5-4   *The report list*

- **Share**   Shares the report with one or more other users.

- **Analyze in Excel**   Allows the data from the report to be analyzed in Microsoft Excel.

- **Quick Insights**   Causes Power BI to analyze the data used by this report, looking for correlations and other insights.

- **View Related**   Shows all the dashboards dependent on this report as well as the datasets on which this report depends.

- **Settings**   Enables the user to change the properties of this report.

- **Delete**   Removes the report from this workspace.

- **Save a Copy**   Saves a copy of this report in another workspace.

Clicking the report name within the report list will open the report.

File Menu

Once you are viewing a report, a File menu is available above the report display area. The File menu is shown in Figure 5-5. The File menu options are listed here with a brief description. Additional details about the pertinent functions are provided in sections later in this chapter.

- **Save as**   Saves the report under a new name in the same workspace on PowerBI.com.

- **Print**   Prints the single page of the report currently being viewed. The report page is printed in its current state.

- **Embed**   Enables this report to be securely embedded in a website.

- **Embed in SharePoint Online**   Enables this report to be securely embedded in a page in SharePoint Online.

- **Publish to web**   Enables this report to be made public so anyone who knows the appropriate URL address can access the report.

NOTE
Use the "Publish to web" option with great care! This option makes your report public on the Internet with no security restrictions. Anyone who knows the URL for the report—or can figure out that URL—has access to the data in the report!

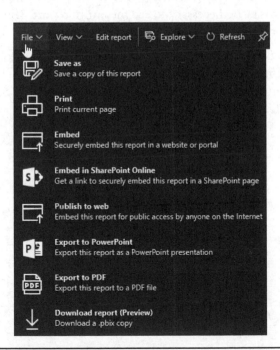

Figure 5-5   *The File menu for a report*

- **Export to PowerPoint** All pages of the report are exported to a PowerPoint file. The report is either exported in its current state or using the default values.

- **Export to PDF** All pages of the report are exported to a PDF file. The report is either exported in its current state or using the default values.

- **Download report** The report is downloaded in a .pbix file. This is usually done in order to edit the report locally using Power BI Desktop.

NOTE
The Embed and Publish features are not available with all Power BI subscriptions. You may not see these options on your File menu.

View Menu

When you are viewing a report, a View menu is available above the report display area. The View menu is shown in Figure 5-6. The View menu options are listed here with a brief description. Additional details about the pertinent functions are provided in sections later in this chapter.

- **Fit to page** Scales the report so the entire page is visible. This functions the same as the option of the same name in Power BI Desktop discussed in Chapter 4.

- **Fit to width** Scales the report so the entire width of the report page is visible. Vertical scrolling may be necessary to see the entire report. This functions the same as the option of the same name in Power BI Desktop discussed in Chapter 4.

- **Actual size** Shows the report without any scaling. Horizontal and vertical scrolling may be necessary to see the entire report. This functions the same as the option of the same name in Power BI Desktop discussed in Chapter 4.

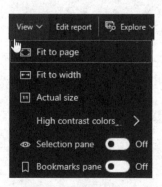

Figure 5-6 *The View menu for a report*

- **High contrast colors**   Enables the user to select from several color palette options with high contrast colors. These color palette options can make the report easier to read on certain monitors, in certain lighting situations, or in certain video projections situations.

- **Selection pane**   Displays the Selection pane. The Selection pane here functions the same as the Selection pane in Power BI Desktop. The Selection pane is discussed in Chapter 8.

- **Bookmarks pane**   Displays the Bookmarks pane. The Bookmarks pane here functions the same as the Bookmarks pane in Power BI Desktop. The Bookmarks pane was discussed in Chapter 4. It has additional features in PowerBI.com that are discussed in the Personal Bookmarks section of this chapter.

Explore Menu

When you select a visualization within a report, an Explore menu is available above the report display area. The Explore menu is shown in Figure 5-7. The Explore menu options are listed here with a brief description. The options in this menu control the drill down navigation and show data options for the selected visualization. This functionality was described in Chapter 4.

- **Show data**   Turning this on changes the selected visualization to show data mode where the visualization and the underlying data—at the same level of aggregation—are displayed. Turning this off returns the visualization to standard display mode.

- **Show Next Level**   Drills down to the next lower level across all items in the visualization. The higher level of aggregation is no longer shown.

Figure 5-7   *The Explore menu for a report when a visualization is selected*

- **Expand to next level**   Drills down to the next lower level across all items in the visualization while continuing to show the label from the higher level of aggregation.

- **Drill Up**   Drills up to the next higher level of aggregation.

- **Drill Down**   Turning this on enables one-click drill down. When this feature is turned on, you can drill down within an item on the visualization by clicking that item.

- **Drillthrough**   Turning this on enables one-click drillthrough. When this feature is turned on, you can display the drillthrough context menu for an item on the visualization by clicking that item.

- **See Records**   Turning this on enables the one-click See Records feature. When this feature is turned on, you can see the underlying records for an item on the visualization by clicking that item.

NOTE
One-click drill down, one-click drillthrough, and one-click see records are mutually exclusive. These three options function as radio buttons. Turning on one of these functions will automatically turn off either of the other two that had been turned on previously. It is also possible to have all three turned off.

Report Toolbar

When you are viewing a report, several toolbar-style buttons appear across the top of the report display area. Some of these items may appear in a popup menu under the ellipsis button (…) at the end of the toolbar, if your browser window is not wide enough. These items are shown in Figure 5-8. The Report toolbar items are listed here with a brief description. Additional details about the pertinent functions are provided in sections later in this chapter.

- **Edit report**   Opens the report in the browser-based version of the editor. Once in edit mode, a new button, "Reading view," takes its place. You can leave the edit view by clicking on "Reading view."

- **Refresh**   Updates the visualizations in the report from the current data in the dataset on PowerBI.com.

Figure 5-8   *The Report toolbar*

- **Pin Live Page**   Pins a thumbnail of the current report page to a dashboard.

- **Reset to default**   Resets the slicer selections and filter settings to the state they were in when the report was uploaded to PowerBI.com.

- **Comments**   Displays the Comments dialog box used to add comments to this report.

- **Bookmarks**   Enables the creation of personal bookmarks and provides an alternative method for displaying the Bookmarks pane.

- **Usage metrics**   Displays a report showing the number of times this report has been accessed and how it ranks by number of views with other reports within the organization.

- **View Related**   Shows all the dashboards dependent on this report as well as the datasets on which this report depends.

- **Favorite**   Adds the report to the Favorites page.

- **Subscribe**   Creates a subscription to the report. The subscription provides email delivery of the report on a regular basis.

- **Share**   Shares the report with one or more other users.

- **Generate QR Code**   Creates a QR code that can be copied and used elsewhere to provide quick access to the report. Anyone who uses the QR code must have been given rights to view the report through other means.

- **Analyze in Excel**   Allows the data from the report to be analyzed in Microsoft Excel.

Pin Visual/Pin Live Page to a Dashboard

Power BI enables you to take visualizations from one or more reports and combine them into a single dashboard view of some aspect of your organization—or even of your organization as a whole. In addition to providing a quick view of key visualizations, the dashboard can also act as a menu providing one-click access to each of the reports that the dashboard visualizations are drawn from.

The easiest way to create a dashboard is to view a report and find the first visualization (chart, gauge, table, and so on) that you want to put on your dashboard. Select that visualization and then click the pushpin icon, as shown in Figure 5-9. Power BI will display the "Pin to dashboard" dialog box.

In the "Pin to dashboard" dialog box, you can add the visual to an existing dashboard by clicking "Existing dashboard" and then selecting the dashboard name from the drop-down list. You can create a new dashboard with this visual by clicking "New dashboard"

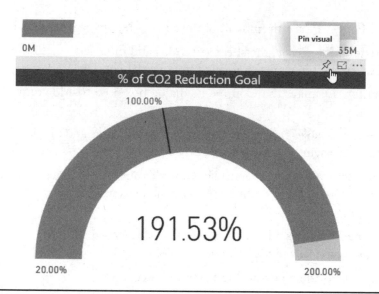

Figure 5-9   *Adding an item to a dashboard using the "Pin visual" button*

and typing the name of the new dashboard. This is shown in Figure 5-10. Finally, click Pin to complete the dashboard pinning operation.

In addition to pinning single visualizations to a dashboard, you can also pin an entire report page to a dashboard. Open the report containing the page to pin and then navigate to that page. Click the Pin Live Page button in the toolbar. You will again see the "Pin to dashboard" dialog box, shown in Figure 5-10. Select an existing dashboard or define a new dashboard as before and click "Pin live" to complete the process.

You will learn more about managing and interacting with dashboards in the "Dashboards" section of this chapter.

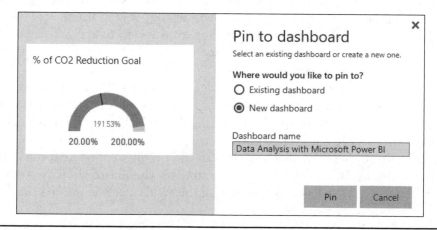

Figure 5-10   *The "Pin to dashboard" dialog box*

Share

When you select Share from the report list or from the report toolbar, the "Share report" dialog box will be displayed. The dialog box has two pages. The Share page is shown in Figure 5-11. On the Share page, you can enter email addresses for one or more people to whom you would like to grant access to this report. You can choose to send them email notification and, optionally, provide a custom message in that email. You can also choose whether recipients can reshare the report and whether they are allowed to create their own content using the datasets used in this report.

   If you have changed any slicers or filters from the report default settings when you choose to share the report, you will see a fourth checkbox. This allows you to share the report with the current slicers and filters in their current state. This is known as a shared report view. Leaving this box unchecked will share the report with the slicers and filters in their default state.

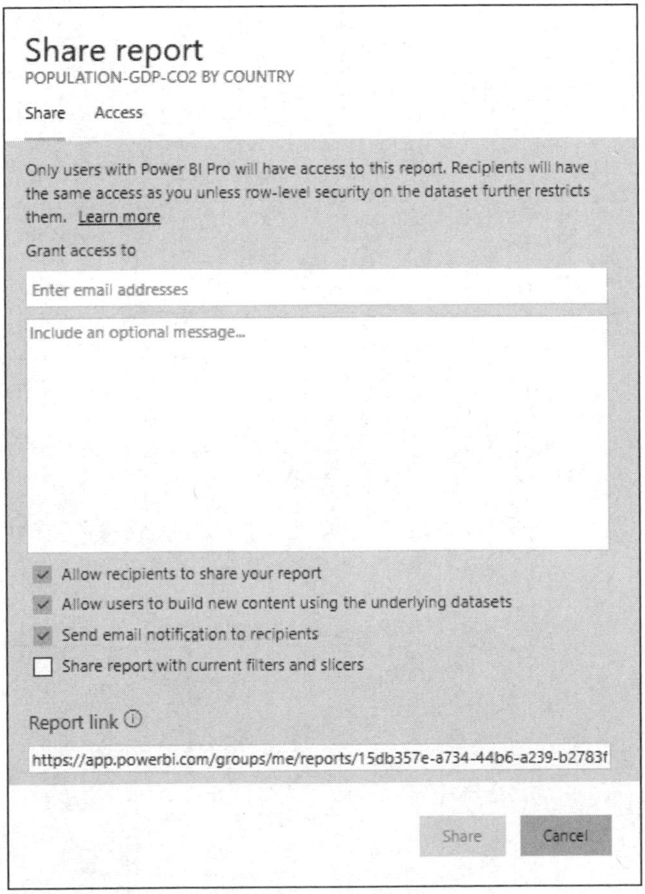

Figure 5-11   *The Share page of the Share report dialog box*

The Report link at the bottom of the dialog box can be used by people within your organization to access this report. In this case, being within your organization is defined as the members of your security structure (tenant) within Azure Active Directory. The link can be copied to an email or used elsewhere to provide access to the report.

The second page of the Share report dialog box is the Access page. The Access page is shown in Figure 5-12. The Access page shows you who currently has access to the report. Any non-owners can have one of two levels of access:

- **Read**   Users with read access can simply view the report.
- **Read and reshare**   Users with read and reshare access can view the report and can also share the report with others.

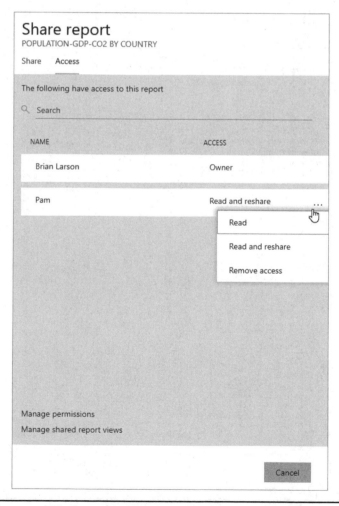

Figure 5-12   *The Access page of the Share report dialog box*

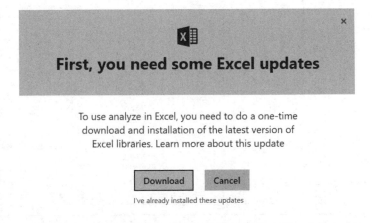

URL	DATE SHARED	DAYS UNTIL EXPIRED	
https://app.powerbi.com/groups/me/reports/15db357e-a734-44b6-a239-b2783f8e7299?bookmarkGuid=25dfcbdb-f766-4d75-ad17-2f...	Apr 7, 2019	89	🗑
https://app.powerbi.com/groups/me/reports/15db357e-a734-44b6-a239-b2783f8e7299?bookmarkGuid=930dae44-ade4-4b3b-b360-...	Apr 7, 2019	89	🗑

Figure 5-13   *The "Manage shared report views" page*

The More options (…) button next to a non-owner name allows you to change that user's access rights or remove their access. The "Manage permissions" link at the bottom of the page allows you to change access rights for or remove access from multiple users in one operation. The "Manage shared report views" link at the bottom of the page shows you a list of the URLs for each report view you have shared. This is shown in Figure 5-13.

The Delete button can be used to remove one of these shared report views. Removing a shared report view does not remove a user's access rights to the report. However, the user will no longer be able to use that URL to access the report with that particular set of slicer and filter settings preselected.

Analyze in Excel

The Analyze in Excel feature enables you to use a Pivot Table in Microsoft Excel to query a Power BI data model. The first time you select this option, you may see the dialog box shown in Figure 5-14. If you see this dialog box, click Download to install the appropriate Excel libraries to support this operation. Clicking Download will begin

First, you need some Excel updates

To use analyze in Excel, you need to do a one-time download and installation of the latest version of Excel libraries. Learn more about this update

Download   Cancel

I've already installed these updates

Figure 5-14   *The Excel Updates dialog box*

the download of an install (.msi) file. Once the download is complete, open the install file to begin the install. Follow the prompts of the install program to complete the install process. Once the install is completed, you can click the "Analyze in Excel" button.

Once the proper libraries are in place, PowerBI.com will download an Office Data Connection (.odc) file. Once the file is downloaded, open the file. This will launch Microsoft Excel. You may receive a security warning about the .odc file. Click Enable.

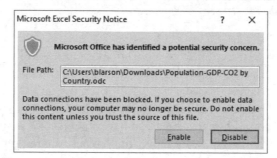

Excel will open a Pivot Table with a connection to the data model contained within the Power BI report. You can now begin exploring the data model in the Pivot Table, as shown in Figure 5-15.

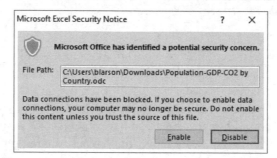

Figure 5-15 *Analyzing a Power BI data model in a Microsoft Excel Pivot Table*

Quick Insights

The Quick Insights option uses advanced analytics to find correlations and trends within the data model associated with this Power BI report. Once initiated, Power BI will run the data in the model through a number of analytics algorithms. When this is complete, you will see a message telling you that you can view the insights. Click "View insights."

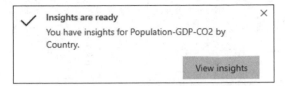

Power BI will take you to the Quick Insights page to show you the results of the analysis. This is shown in Figure 5-16. Scroll down the page to view the insights that were found. Some will be odd, or even incredibly obvious, but some just may provide a

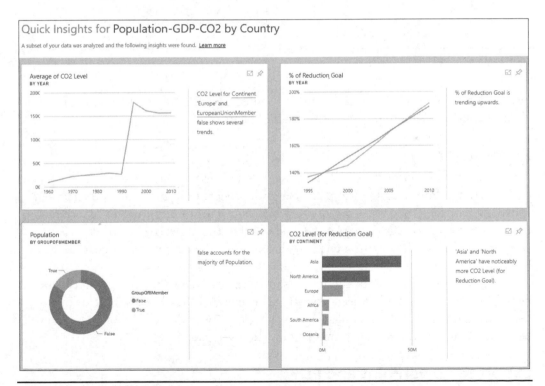

Figure 5-16   *The Quick Insights page*

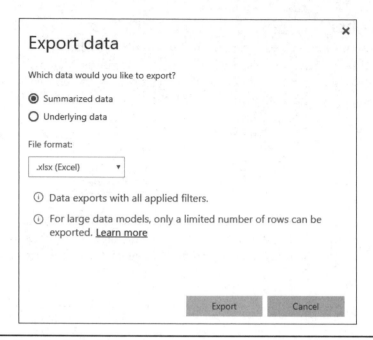

Figure 5-17   *The "Export data" dialog box*

new understanding of your data. If you find something particularly interesting, you can click the pushpin icon to pin the item to a dashboard.

Export Data

The export data functionality in PowerBI.com is a bit more sophisticated than what we encountered in Power BI Desktop. You begin the export process in the same manner. Hover over or select the visualization for which you want to perform the export data function and click the "More options" (…) button in the upper-right corner. Select "Export data" from the popup menu. The Export data dialog box will appear, as shown in Figure 5-17.

We now have the option to export the summarized data or the underlying (detail) data. We can also choose between exporting the data in an Excel (.xlsx) file or in a comma-separated values (.csv) file. Make your selections and click Export. The file will be downloaded for you to save or to open in Microsoft Excel.

Export to PowerPoint and PDF

In addition to exporting the data behind a single visualization, we now have the ability to export the entire report to either a PowerPoint file or a PDF file. To begin your export, select the appropriate option from the File menu. For both the PowerPoint and PDF file exports, the Export dialog box will appear, as shown in Figure 5-18.

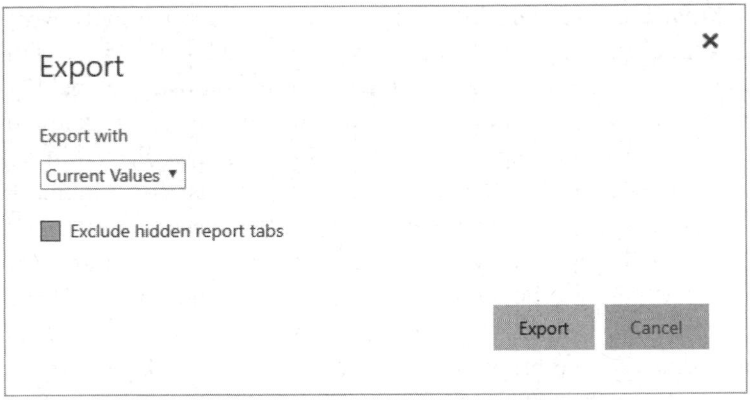

Export

Export with

Current Values ▾

☐ Exclude hidden report tabs

Export   Cancel

Figure 5-18 *The Export dialog box*

You can export the report using either the current settings for slicers and filters or the default values. If there are any hidden tabs in the current report, you can use the checkbox to determine whether those are included in the export file. Finally, click Export to launch the export process.

The generation of the export file will take some time. This process runs in the background, and you are free to do other operations within PowerBI.com while this is executing. A message box in the upper-right corner lets you know the export file is being generated.

Export to PDF in progress ×
Your report Population-GDP-CO2 by Country is being exported to a PDF file. This might take a few minutes.

Once the file is exported and ready for viewing, a new message box will appear.

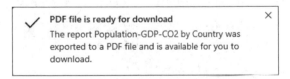

✓ **PDF file is ready for download** ×
The report Population-GDP-CO2 by Country was exported to a PDF file and is available for you to download.

Personal Bookmarks

In Chapter 4, you learned how bookmarks can be used to tell a story. In PowerBI.com, you can use personal bookmarks to mark your place in a report. This includes remembering what page of the report you were viewing and what the slicers and filters were set to at the time you created the personal bookmark.

Where bookmarks created within the report travel with that report every time it is shared, personal bookmarks are, as the name says, personal. Personal bookmarks are tied to your sign-in and are only available for your use. You use personal bookmarks to quickly move to report pages in the states in which you want to see them. If you frequently look at a particular report page with certain values selected in the slicers, you can create a bookmark reflecting that state. Then you can use the bookmark to return to that state without having to reselect the values from the slicers.

To create a personal bookmark, you need to get the report page into the state you want to capture. Navigate to the report page you want to bookmark. Set the slicers and filters to the desired values. Next, drill down to the appropriate levels in the visualizations and select an item within a visualization, if you like.

Once the page is just the way you will want to return to it in the future, click the Bookmarks item in the toolbar. The Bookmarks popup menu appears. Click "Add personal bookmark" to create a new personal bookmark. Type the name of the bookmark and click Save. If you would like to start on this page, in this state, whenever you open this report, check the "Make default view."

The personal bookmarks you have created for the current report will show up in the Bookmarks popup menu. You can use the ellipsis (…) button to the right of a bookmark name to manage this bookmark. Using the secondary popup menu, you can update the bookmark to remember the current state as the new bookmarked state. You can also set this bookmark as your default or, if it is already the default, you can clear the default designation. Finally, you can rename the bookmark or delete it.

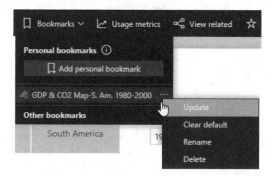

The "Other bookmarks" option on the Bookmarks popup menu will open the Bookmarks pane. This functions the same as if you selected to view the Bookmarks pane from the View menu. The Bookmarks pane provides access to the bookmarks saved with the report in the same manner you saw in Chapter 4. In addition, you can access your personal bookmarks from the Bookmarks pane.

Subscribe

The Subscribe toolbar button enables you to create subscriptions to the current report. A subscription will deliver a copy of the report page to you and others via email. The report page will appear as an image embedded in the body of the email. The report will appear in its default state with the slicers and filters set as they were when the report was published. The email will also include links to access the report on PowerBI.com and to manage the subscription.

To create a subscription, click the Subscribe button in the toolbar. The "Subscribe to emails" dialog box will appear. This is shown in Figure 5-19. Your email address is automatically included in the Subscribe textbox. You can remove your email address and/or add other email addresses to the subscription. You can also enter a subject and optional message. The subscription defaults to the report page you are viewing, but you can change that using the Report page drop-down list.

You can set the frequency with which the report is delivered. The "After data refresh (once daily)" setting will deliver the report once a day immediately after a scheduled refresh of the data in this report's data sets. The Daily setting will deliver the report every day. The Weekly setting allows you to choose the days of the week on which you want it to be delivered. You can select the time of day for the delivery along with a starting date and an ending date. Finally, you can select to give the recipients rights to the report using the "Also give access to this report" checkbox. Once you have completed filling in the subscription information, click "Save and close."

You can manage existing subscriptions for this report by clicking the Subscribe toolbar button. Use the Run Now button to force an immediate delivery of the subscription. Use the On/Off slider button to enable (On) or disable (Off) the subscription. Use the trashcan button to delete the subscription. If you enable the subscription, disable the subscription, or delete the subscription, you also have to click "Save and close" in order for your changes to take effect. Clicking the "Manage all subscriptions" link takes you to the Subscriptions page, where you can manage all the subscriptions for this workspace.

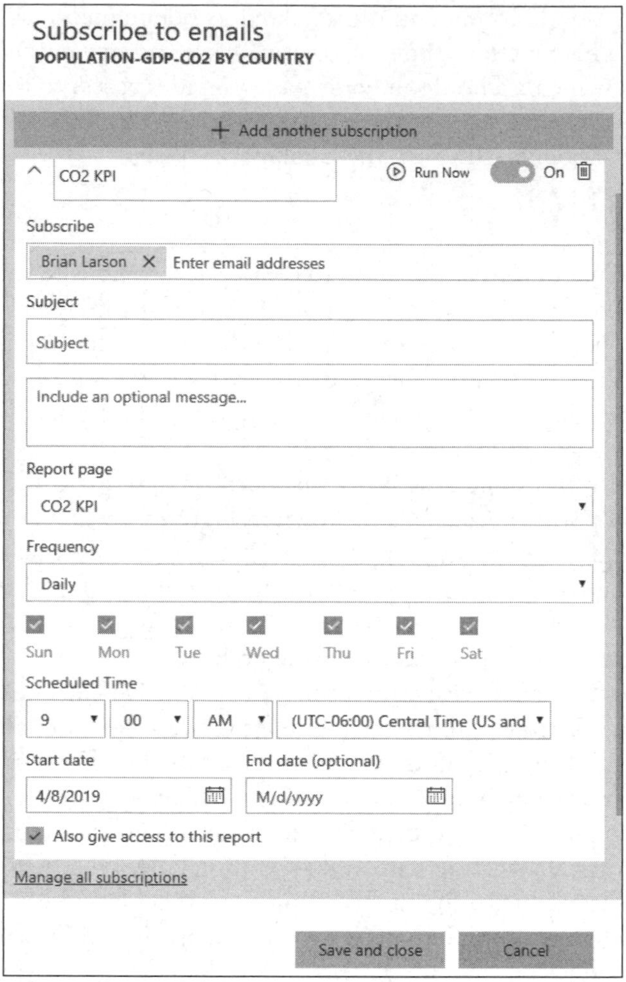

Figure 5-19 *The Subscribe to emails dialog box*

Report Settings

Clicking the Settings button for a report in the report list displays the Settings dialog box. This is shown in Figure 5-20. Using the Settings dialog box, you rename a report by editing the content of the "Report name" textbox and clicking Save.

You can also change the behavior of several aspects of the report. By default, each report will return to the state (slicer and filter selections) in which you last left it. If you instead want the report to open in its default state each time you return to it, you can turn on the "Don't allow end user to save filters on this report" switch.

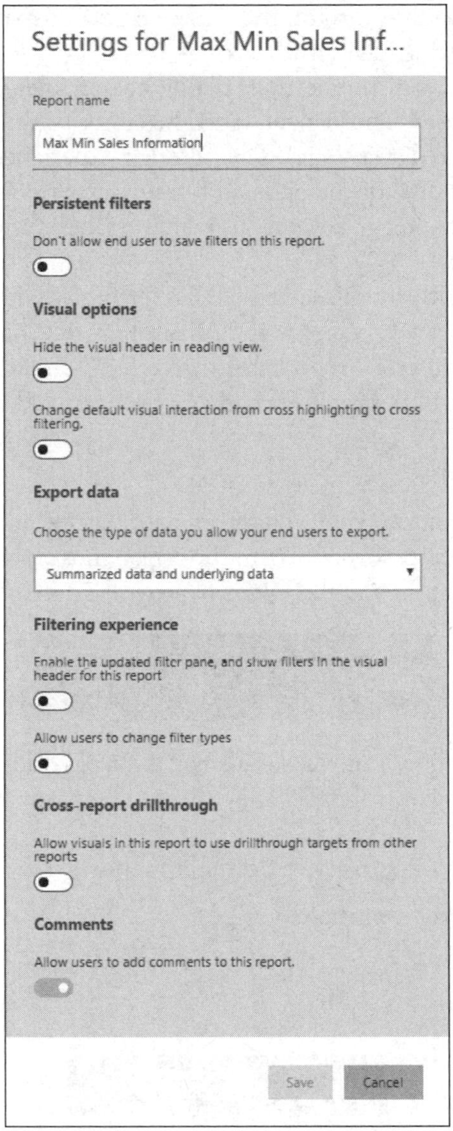

Figure 5-20   *The Settings dialog box for a report*

Visual headers are the popup toolbars that appear above each visualization when you hover over or select it. If you do not want the visual headers to appear when you are viewing this report, you can turn on the "Hide the visual header in reading view" switch.

As you learned in Chapter 4, by default when you select an item in one visualization, it highlights the pertinent areas in the other visualizations. This is known as *cross highlighting*. You can instead change this behavior from highlighting to simply filtering other visualizations. To do this, turn on the "Change default visual interaction from cross highlighting to cross filtering" switch.

The Export data section of the Settings dialog box enables you to determine what data is included when a user exports data. It can be either summarized data, summarized and underlying data, or no data (None). The Filtering experience section enables you to toggle between the traditional or the updated filtering experience. More on the updated filtering experience in Chapter 6. You can also choose whether to allow users to change the filter types.

The Cross-report drillthrough section of the Settings dialog box enables you to determine if this report can participate in drillthrough that navigates between two different reports. More on cross-report drillthrough in Chapter 6. Finally, in the Comments section, you can determine whether a user can add comments to this report.

Full Screen Mode

While viewing a report, you can enter full screen mode. Enter full screen mode by clicking the double-headed diagonal arrow button in the upper-most toolbar. In full screen mode, you will see the report content and the Filters pane with no menus or toolbars.

While in full screen mode, you will see a small control panel in the lower-right corner of the report. This control panel allows you to perform the following tasks:

- Go back to the report list to select a different report.
- Move between the pages of the report.
- Print the report.
- Exit full screen mode.

Dashboards

Dashboards enable you to provide a summary view of the overall state of your organization or of a particular aspect of your organization. Dashboards are created by picking key visualizations for one or more reports and assembling them in a single layout area. Dashboards can also serve as a sort of menu to the reports. Clicking on a visualization in a dashboard takes you to the report page that contains that visualization.

Creating a Dashboard

Let's create a dashboard that you can use to explore the concepts in the "Dashboards" section of this book. Follow these steps:

1. Open the "Max Min Sales Information" report from My Workspace in PowerBI.com.
2. Click the "Sales Units by Promotion" tab.
3. Hover over the donut chart until the pushpin and other icons appear in the upper-right corner.
4. Click the pushpin.
5. In the "Pin to dashboard" dialog box, select "New dashboard."
6. Type **Data Analysis with Microsoft Power BI** and click Pin.
7. Click the Sales Units Gauge tab.
8. Hover over the gauge until the pushpin appears.
9. Click the pushpin.
10. In the "Pin to dashboard" dialog box, ensure that the "Existing dashboard" radio button is selected and the "Data Analysis with Microsoft Power BI" dashboard is selected in the drop-down list.
11. Click Pin.
12. Click the Units/Dollars Comparison tab.
13. Pin the top column chart to the "Data Analysis with Microsoft Power BI" dashboard (steps 8 through 11).
14. Pin the bottom column chart to the "Data Analysis with Microsoft Power BI" dashboard (steps 8 through 11).
15. Open the "Population-GDP-CO2 by Country" report from My Workspace.
16. On the "Population, CO2, GDP Overview" page of the report, click the Pin a Live Page button in the toolbar.
17. In the "Pin to dashboard" dialog box, ensure that the "Existing dashboard" radio button is selected and the "Data Analysis with Microsoft Power BI" dashboard is selected in the drop-down list.
18. Click "Pin live."
19. Click the CO2 KPI tab.
20. Pin the CO2 Level gauge to the "Data Analysis with Microsoft Power BI" dashboard.
21. Pin the "% of CO2 Reduction Goal" gauge to the "Data Analysis with Microsoft Power BI" dashboard.
22. Go to the "Data Analysis with Microsoft Power BI" dashboard.
23. Hover over the Sales in Units donut chart. Use the sizing handle in the lower-right corner to change the chart to the desired size. Drag the chart to the desired location, as shown in Figure 5-21.
24. Size and arrange the remaining dashboard items to match Figure 5-21.

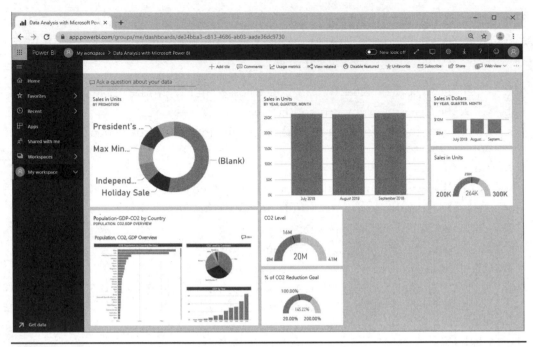

Figure 5-21   *The Data Analysis with Microsoft Power BI dashboard*

You can now use this dashboard to explore the dashboard features described in the remainder of the "Dashboards" section.

The Dashboard List

Figure 5-22 shows the dashboard list in My Workspace. You can use the "Search content" area at the top to search for a dashboard within a long list of dashboards. The search will look for any contiguous occurrence of the string you enter as part of the dashboard name.

The various parts of the list entry for each dashboard are labeled in the figure. This includes a number of function buttons. The function buttons are listed here with a brief description. Additional details about some of the functions are provided in sections later in this chapter.

- **Favorite**   Adds the dashboard to the Favorites page.
- **Usage Metrics**   Displays a report showing the number of times this dashboard has been accessed and how it ranks by number of views with other dashboards within the organization.

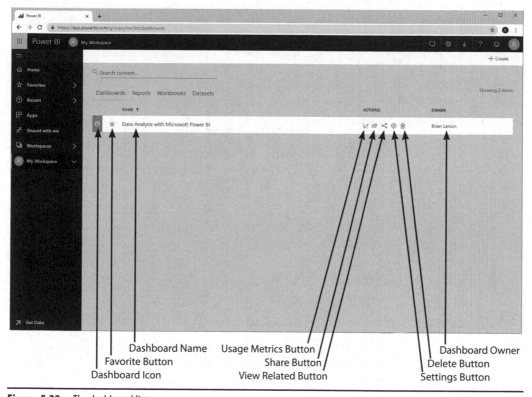

Figure 5-22   *The dashboard list*

- **Share**   Shares the dashboard with one or more other users. Dashboards are shared and access is managed in the same manner as reports. See the "Share" section under "Reports" in this chapter for more information.

- **View Related**   Shows all the reports and datasets on which this dashboard depends.

- **Settings**   Enables the user to change the properties of this dashboard.

- **Delete**   Removes the dashboard from this workspace.

Clicking on the dashboard name within the dashboard list will open the dashboard.

Dashboard Toolbar

When viewing a dashboard, you see several toolbar-style buttons across the top of the report display area. Some of these items may appear in a popup menu under the ellipsis button (…) at the end of the toolbar, if your browser window is not wide enough. These items are shown in Figure 5-23. The Dashboard toolbar items are listed here with a brief

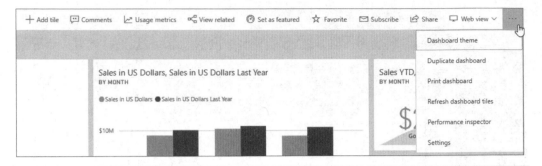

Figure 5-23   *The dashboard toolbar*

description of each. Additional details about the pertinent functions are provided in sections later in this chapter.

- **Add tile**   Creates a new tile on the dashboard displaying web content, an image, text, a video, or custom streaming data.

- **Comments**   Allows the user to add a comment about the dashboard.

- **Usage metrics**   Displays a report showing the number of times this dashboard has been accessed and how it ranks by number of views with other dashboards within the organization.

- **View related**   Shows all the reports and the datasets on which this dashboard depends.

- **Set as featured**   Sets this dashboard as the featured dashboard. The featured dashboard becomes the landing page.

- **Favorite**   Adds the dashboard to the Favorites page.

- **Subscribe**   Creates a subscription to the dashboard. The subscription provides email delivery of the dashboard on a regular basis. Dashboard subscriptions are created and managed in the same manner as report subscriptions. See the "Subscribe" section under "Reports" in this chapter for more information.

- **Share**   Shares the dashboard with one or more other users. Dashboards are shared and access is managed in the same manner as reports. See the "Share" section under "Reports" in this chapter for more information.

- **Web view**   Switches between the web view and the phone view of the dashboard. You can change which visualizations are included in the phone view of the dashboard as well as the size and arrangement of visualizations in phone view.

- **Dashboard theme**   Enables the user to set a color theme for the dashboard. Custom themes can be created using a JSON file and uploaded for use with this and other dashboards. A JSON file can be downloaded to use as a starting point when creating a custom theme.

- **Duplicate dashboard**   Creates a copy of this dashboard within this workspace.

- **Print dashboard**   Prints the dashboard.

- **Refresh dashboard tiles**   Refreshes the dashboard content from the underlying sources.

- **Performance inspector**   Analyzes the performance of the dashboard and the network.

- **Settings**   Enables the user to change the properties of this dashboard.

Add Tile

When you select Add tile from the Dashboard toolbar, the "Add tile" dialog box will be displayed. The dialog box has two pages. The first page, shown in Figure 5-24, allows you to select one of the following to be the source of the content for the tile:

- **Web content**   This option utilizes embedded HTML code.

- **Image**   The image must come from a location on the Internet that can be reached by a URL.

- **Text box**   Enter your own custom text. The text can be formatted and the font can be changed within the text string.

- **Video**   The video must come from a location on the Internet that can be reached by a URL.

- **Custom Streaming Data**   The data comes from a streaming dataset within your workspace. The streaming dataset can be created on the second page of the dialog box. The streaming datasets use an API, Azure Stream, or PubNub as a data source.

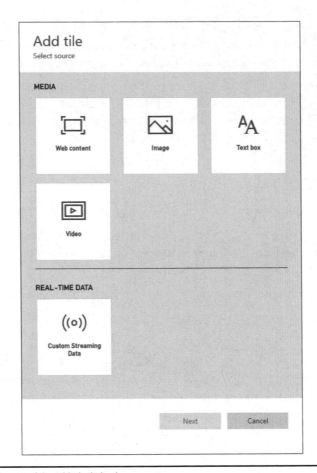

Figure 5-24 *The first page of the Add tile dialog box*

The second page of the dialog box allows you to provide the necessary information about the selected content type. In addition, the second page of the dialog box allows you to set a custom link for this dashboard tile. The custom link is the location the browser will be directed to when this dashboard tile is clicked. The custom link can be an external URL or an existing dashboard or report in the same workspace. You can choose to have the custom link open in the same browser tab or in a new browser tab.

Comments

Clicking the Comments button displays the Comments dialog box. This is shown in Figure 5-25. The Comments dialog box allows users who have access to this dashboard to share their thoughts on values seen on the dashboard.

Figure 5-25 *The Comments dialog box*

Dashboard Settings

Clicking the Settings button displays the Settings dialog box. This is shown in Figure 5-26. Using the Settings dialog box, you rename a dashboard by editing the content of the "Dashboard name" textbox and clicking Save.

You can also enable or disable several features for this dashboard:

- **Q&A**   Use the Q&A slider switch to enable or disable the Q&A feature for this dashboard.

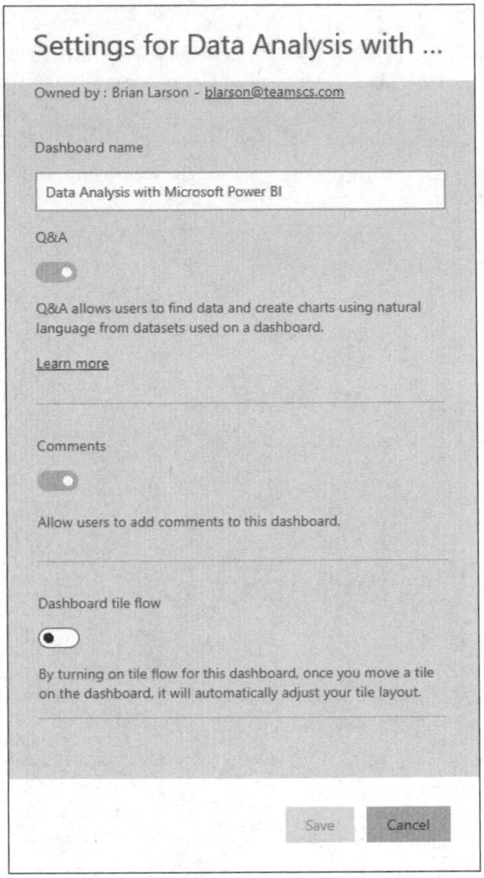

Settings for Data Analysis with ...

Owned by : Brian Larson – blarson@teamscs.com

Dashboard name

Data Analysis with Microsoft Power BI

Q&A

Q&A allows users to find data and create charts using natural language from datasets used on a dashboard.

Learn more

Comments

Allow users to add comments to this dashboard.

Dashboard tile flow

By turning on tile flow for this dashboard, once you move a tile on the dashboard, it will automatically adjust your tile layout.

Save   Cancel

Figure 5-26   *The Settings dialog box for a dashboard*

- **Comments**   Use the Comments slider switch to enable or disable comments on this dashboard.
- **Dashboard tile flow**   Use the "Dashboard tile flow" slider switch to enable or disable the automatic flow and arrangement of tiles within the dashboard layout.

Full Screen Mode

While viewing a dashboard, you can enter full screen mode. Enter full screen mode by clicking the double-headed diagonal arrow button in the uppermost toolbar. In full screen mode, you will see only the dashboard content with no menus or toolbars.

While in full screen mode, you will see a small control panel in the lower-right corner of the dashboard. This control panel allows you to perform the following tasks:

- Go back to the dashboard list to select a different report.
- Print the dashboard.
- Fit the dashboard to the screen.
- Fit the width of the dashboard to the screen.
- Exit full screen mode.

Workbooks

The workbooks area within a workspace is one location that can hold Excel spreadsheet content. Workbooks can be viewed with Excel Online right within your browser. In this way, you can upload Excel content that performs analysis on the same data or same subject matter as your workspace to support and supplement Power BI dashboards and reports.

Publishing Excel Content to Power BI

We can use two mechanisms to publish Excel content to Power BI. Both are accessed from the Publish page of the File tab in Microsoft Excel. The Upload option will send the entire workbook file (.xlsx) to Power BI. The workbook can then be explored right from PowerBI.com using Excel Online. In addition, workbook content can be added to a dashboard. The Export option will send data from a table or a data model to a Power BI dataset (more on that in the "Datasets" section of this chapter).

NOTE
To complete this exercise, ensure you are using Office 365 and that Office 365 is signed in with the same user you have been using to access PowerBI.com.

Let's create a workbook that you can use to explore the concepts in the "Workbooks" section of this book. Follow these steps:

1. Open the "GDP 2013 Analysis.xlsx" file (available in the supporting materials for this book) in Microsoft Excel.
2. Click File.

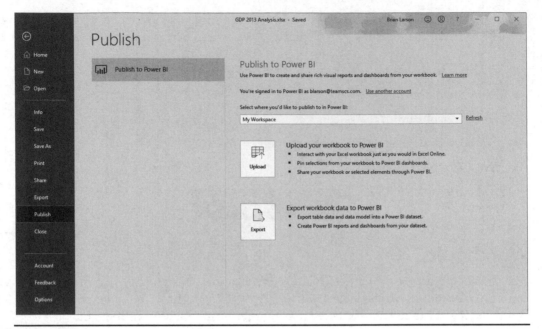

Figure 5-27   *The Publish page in Microsoft Excel*

3. Click Publish. The Publish page appears, as shown in Figure 5-27.
4. Sign in to PowerBI.com, if required.
5. Select My Workspace from the "where you'd like to publish" drop-down list.
6. Click Upload.
7. In PowerBI.com, select My Workspace and go to the list of workbooks, as shown in Figure 5-28.
8. Click the "GDP 2013 Analysis" item to view the workbook in Excel Online.
9. If a message about pinning a selection appears, click "Got it."
10. Click the "GDP in 2013" column chart to select it.
11. Click the Pin toolbar button in the upper-right corner, as shown in Figure 5-29.
12. In the familiar "Pin to dashboard" dialog box, ensure the "Existing dashboard" radio button is selected and "Data Analysis with Microsoft Power BI" is selected in the drop-down list. Click Pin.
13. Go to the "Data Analysis with Microsoft Power BI" dashboard. The chart from the workbook is now part of the dashboard.

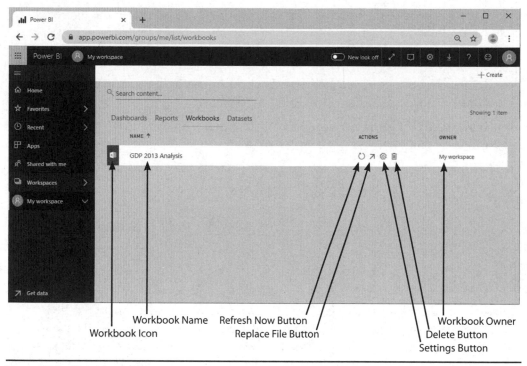

Figure 5-28   *The workspace list*

The Workbook List

Figure 5-28 shows the workbook list in My Workspace. You can use the "Search content" area at the top to search for a workbook within a long list of workbooks. The search will look for any contiguous occurrence of the string you enter as part of the workbook name.

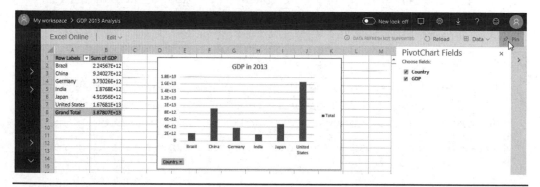

Figure 5-29   *Pin workbook content to a dashboard*

The various parts of the list entry for each workbook are labeled in the figure. This includes a number of function buttons. The function buttons are listed here with a brief description.

- **Refresh Now** If the workbook was loaded from an online source, this button will refresh the content of the workbook from that source.
- **Replace File** Opens a dialog box to enable you to upload the latest copy of the workbook file.
- **Settings** Enables the user to change the name of this workbook.
- **Delete** Removes the workbook from this workspace.

Clicking the workbook name within the workbook list will open the workbook in Excel Online.

Datasets

Datasets contain the imported data used to create reports and dashboards. When a Power BI report using imported data is published to PowerBI.com, the data is automatically placed in a dataset in the same workspace. In addition to serving as the source of the data for the report it was uploaded with (and any dashboards created from the report), a dataset can be used to create new reports right within the PowerBI.com browser-based interface.

The Dataset List

Figure 5-30 shows the dataset list in My Workspace. You can use the "Search content" area at the top to search for a dataset within a long list of datasets. The search will look for any contiguous occurrence of the string you enter as part of the dataset name.

The various parts of the list entry for each dataset are labeled in the figure. This includes a number of function buttons and a drop-down menu displayed by the "More options" button. The function buttons and menu items are listed here with a brief description of each.

- **Endorsements** Endorsements will appear in this area to indicate the dataset is being promoted for use by others or is certified by data professionals within the organizations. The endorsements are defined using the dataset settings menu.
- **Create Report** Opens the report editor in the browser window with this dataset as the selected data model.
- **Refresh Now** If the dataset was loaded from an online source or if its source is available through a data gateway, this button will refresh the content of the dataset from that source.

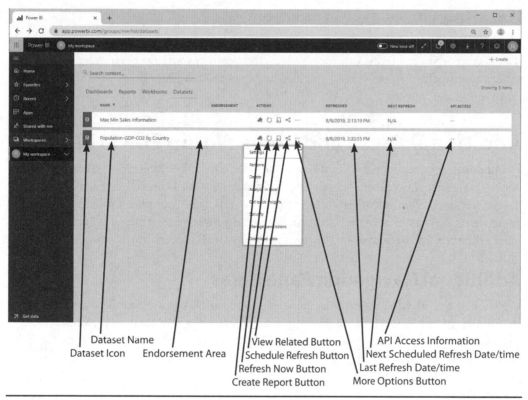

Figure 5-30 *The dataset list*

- **Schedule Refresh** If the dataset was loaded from an online source or if its source is available through a data gateway, this button allows you to create a regularly scheduled refresh of the dataset from that source.

- **View Related** Shows all of the dashboards and reports that depend on this dataset.

- **Settings** Enables the user to change the settings for this dataset.

- **Rename** Allows the user to rename this dataset.

- **Delete** Removes the dataset from this workspace.

- **Analyze in Excel** Allows the data from the dataset to be analyzed in Microsoft Excel.

- **Get quick insights** Causes Power BI to analyze the data in this dataset looking for correlations and other insights.

- **Security** Manages role-based security in this dataset.

- **Manage permissions** Manages who has rights to this dataset.

- **Download .pbix** Downloads the content of this dataset in a Power BI report (.pbix) file.

Dataflows

Some workspaces contain a fifth list for managing dataflows. A *dataflow* is a process that extracts data from one or more sources and performs any necessary clean up or other manipulation to get it ready for use in a data model. Data flows are discussed in more detail in Chapter 15.

Additional Areas and Items Within PowerBI.com

Dashboards, reports, workbooks, datasets, and dataflows are the items we manage and ultimately use to gain business insight when working with PowerBI.com. However, we haven't yet covered a few other areas within PowerBI.com that play a role in managing these items. In this section, we examine the remaining items within the Navigation pane and a few of the remaining buttons in the PowerBI.com user interface.

Additional Navigation Pane Items

We've seen that the Navigation pane enables us to quickly move among the workspaces that make up our PowerBI.com environment. There are a few areas in PowerBI.com that allow us to organize content across workspaces and outside of workspaces. Let's quickly touch on each of these.

Favorites

On the Dashboards List page and on the Reports List page, we have the ability to mark an item as a favorite. Items marked as favorites show up on the Favorites page. This enables each user to create their own custom list of most-used content.

   We reach the Favorites page by clicking Favorites in the Navigation pane. The Favorites page looks like the other list pages but contains a list of both dashboard and report content. From the Favorites page, you can perform the following tasks:

- Unfavorite an item.
- Launch an item.
- Share an item.

Recent

The Recent page shows a list of the recently accessed items. Items of every type are included here. The functionality that is normally available in the list for each type of item is also available from the Recent page.

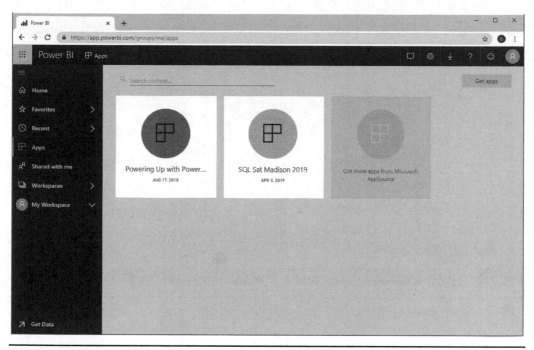

Figure 5-31   *The Apps page*

Apps

As noted earlier, using apps is one of the ways content can be made available to you.
Any apps you have installed are displayed on the Apps page, as shown in Figure 5-31.
Clicking an app you have installed will take you to the landing page (dashboard or
report) for that app.

To see the apps available for you to install, click the "Get apps" button. This brings
up the AppSource dialog box showing apps available within your organization and apps
available from other sources outside your organization (see Figure 5-32). To install an
app, click the "Get it now" link.

Shared with Me

Items that are shared with you appear on the "Shared with me" page, as shown in
Figure 5-33. The shared items can be seen in a single list, or they can be grouped by
the workspace they came from. Shared items can be reshared, if you were given rights
to do so.

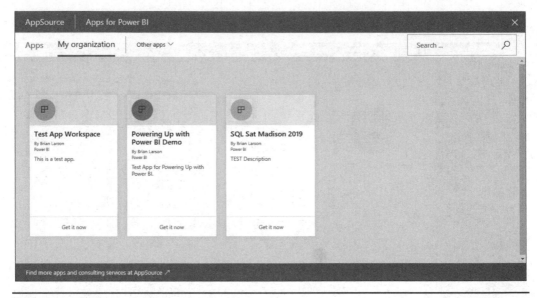

Figure 5-32 *The AppSource dialog box*

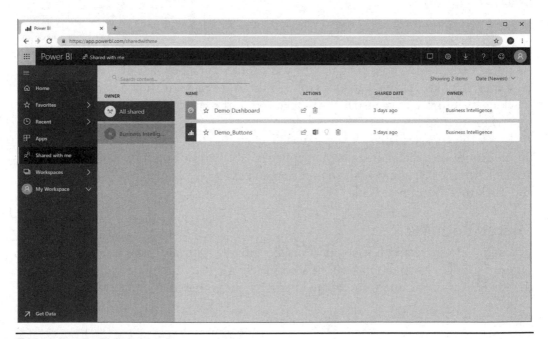

Figure 5-33 *The "Shared with me" page*

Additional Buttons

We should touch on a few additional buttons in the PowerBI.com user interface as we wrap up this chapter. The Get Data button is found in the lower-left corner. The Notifications and Settings buttons are in the toolbar at the upper right.

Get Data

The Get Data button takes you to the Get Data page, shown in Figure 5-34. While getting additional data is one of the functions available from this page, you can also get additional content. Clicking the Get button in either the "My organization" item or the "Services" item in the "Discover content" area allows you to find additional apps to install. The Get buttons in either the Files item or the Databases item in the "Create new content" area actually provide the ability to get data that the page name suggests. The "Organizational Content Packs" and "Service Content Packs" links at the bottom of the page provide the ability to install content packs. The remaining links at the bottom of the screen provide access to sample data and partner solutions for sale.

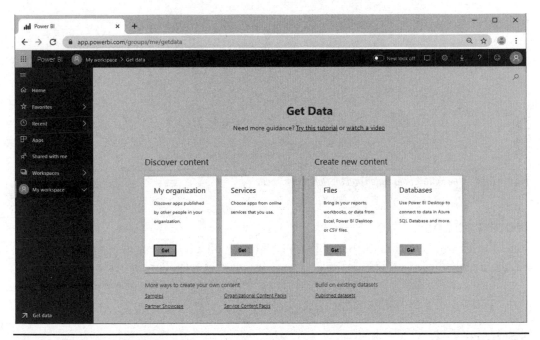

Figure 5-34   *The Get Data page*

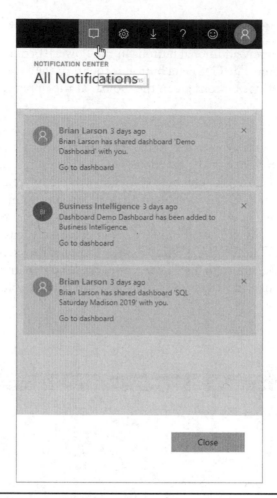

Figure 5-35 *The Notifications button and the Notifications pane*

Notifications

The Notifications button in the toolbar displays the Notifications pane, as shown in Figure 5-35. These notifications tell you of content that has been shared or changes to content you have previously installed. When you have unread notifications, an unread notification count will appear within the Notifications button.

Settings

The Settings button displays the Settings menu. The Settings menu enables you to manage certain aspects of your PowerBI.com environment. The Settings item on the Settings menu will display the Settings page. Both the Settings menu and the Settings page are shown in Figure 5-36.

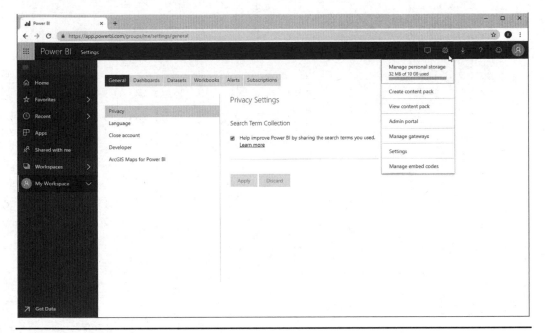

Figure 5-36   *The Settings page*

How It All Gets Made

Those of you who will be using Power BI content, but will not be creating your own custom Power BI content, can stop at this point. We have covered the use of Power BI reports and the workings of the PowerBI.com interface. If you want to go from user to creator, continue on to Chapter 6 to learn how to create your own content in Power BI Desktop.

Part III

Creating Visualizations

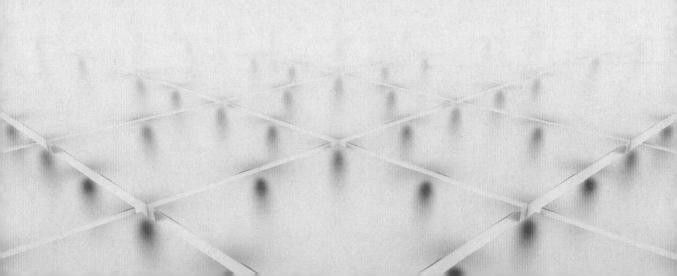

Chapter 6

Basic Data Visualizations

In This Chapter

- Learn By Doing
- Basic Visualizations
- Interactivity
- Geographic Visualizations
- Other Visual Elements

In Chapters 4 and 5, you learned how to interact with Power BI reports in Power BI Desktop and in the Power BI Service (PowerBI.com). In this chapter, you go from using Power BI content to creating Power BI content. Your transition from consumer to producer is about to begin.

In this chapter, you learn to create visualizations in the report layout area. The focus will be on assigning the proper data elements to the proper locations to obtain the appropriate results. In most cases, we will be content with the default look of the visualizations produced. Chapter 7 is where we dive into the formatting side of Power BI reports.

This chapter begins with a look at basic visualizations, both text-based and graphical. From there, we add interactivity to our report. Next, we work with the geographic visualizations. We end the chapter with a look at some of the other visualization elements that enable us to add information and interest to our reports.

Learn By Doing

While this book is not entirely a "step-by-step" learning book, I have employed interactive learning activities in recent chapters. After all, the whole point of this book is to enable you to work with Power BI to obtain your desired results. Therefore, it only seems right there should be some hands-on content.

This chapter will be heavily focused on interactive learning activities. There really isn't that much to tell about creating visualizations in Power BI. It is really something you need to see. In other words, the best way for you to see how report authoring works is to actually author reports.

In previous chapters, you could get a good deal of information reading them without completing the activities. In this chapter, almost all the learning is in the doing. Therefore, I encourage you to take the time to work through the steps to complete these reports. You will be rewarded with a solid understanding of the process of creating visualizations within Power BI.

Starting Point

After our one-chapter move to PowerBI.com, we shift back to the Power BI Desktop environment. As has been mentioned previously, this is the place, in most organizations, where the majority of Power BI report authoring will be done. Even if you do author reports in the PowerBI.com browser-based environment, the user interface is almost identical.

In order to create a report in Power BI, you need to have a data model to work from. You may create this data model yourself in Power BI Desktop. This will be covered in Chapters 9 through 14. Alternatively, you may be creating your Power BI reports from data models that have been created by others. These data models may reside on premises on a SQL Server Analysis Services server or they may reside in PowerBI.com.

For the activities in this chapter, we are going to simulate having a data model created and available to us by starting with a Power BI report file (.pbix) that already contains a data model. That file is called "Max Min Sales Information No Visualizations .pbix" and is located in the supporting materials you should have downloaded from the McGraw-Hill Education website. Copy this file and save it to a location in your file system (outside of the .zip file it came in). Remember the location where you saved this file. If you need help downloading the supporting materials for the book, refer to the instructions in Chapter 1.

Basic Visualizations

We begin by working through some of the basic visualizations. These visualizations will make up the meat of your reports. They provide the mechanisms for Power BI to represent data both in textual form and graphically.

Maximum Miniatures Manufacturing

For the reports in this chapter, we will use data from a fictional company called Maximum Miniatures, Incorporated. Maximum Miniatures, or Max Min for short, manufactures and sells small, hand-painted figurines. It has several product lines, including the Woodland Creatures collection of North American animals; the Mythic World collection, which includes dragons, trolls, and elves; the Warriors of Yore collection, containing various soldiers from Roman times up through World War II; and the Guiding Lights collection, featuring replica lighthouses from the United States. The miniatures are made from clay, pewter, or aluminum.

Max Min markets these miniatures through three different channels. It operates five of its own "Maximum Miniature World" stores dedicated to selling the Max Min product line. Max Min also operates an online store to sell its products via the Web. In addition, Max Min sells wholesale to other retailers.

The "Max Min Sales Information No Visualizations.pbix" file referenced previously contains a data model created by importing data on Max Min sales. This data covers calendar years 2013 to 2015. The data model in this file will serve as the basis for all the reports created in this chapter.

Our First Report Page

We start with a very basic report page that includes the following elements:

- Column chart
- Slicer

The goal is to display the total sales in U.S. dollars for each sales person for a selected year.

Opening the Max Min Sales Information No Visualizations File in Power BI Desktop

1. Locate the "Max Min Sales Information No Visualizations.pbix" file in the file system location where you placed it.
2. Double-click the "Max Min Sales Information No Visualizations.pbix" file. This will open the file in Power BI Desktop.
3. If the Visualizations pane or the Fields pane is hidden on the right side of the window, click the arrow to expand.

Creating the Column Chart

1. In the Fields area on the right, expand the Orders table shown in Figure 6-1. Note the calculator icons and the Greek letter sigma next to many of the fields in the Orders table. This signifies the model knows how to add up the values for these fields across multiple records in the table. For example, we can get the total "Sales in Dollars" for a customer or get the total "Sales in Units" for a particular month.
2. Click the check box next to "Sales in Dollars" in the Fields area. A column chart showing the total sales in dollars across all of the data in the model is displayed. You may need to make the Fields area wider or hover over the item to see the tooltip to determine which field to select.
3. On the View tab of the ribbon, click the Page View button and select Actual Size from the drop-down menu. Depending on your screen resolution, the bar chart may be bigger and easier to read.
4. In the Fields area, expand the Sales Person table.
5. Click the check box next to Sales Person.

Creating the Slicer

1. Click somewhere in the report layout area that is outside of the chart so the chart is no longer selected.
2. In the Fields area, expand the Date table.
3. Expand the Date Hierarchy entry.
4. Click the check box next to Year. A table of the data in the Year field is created.

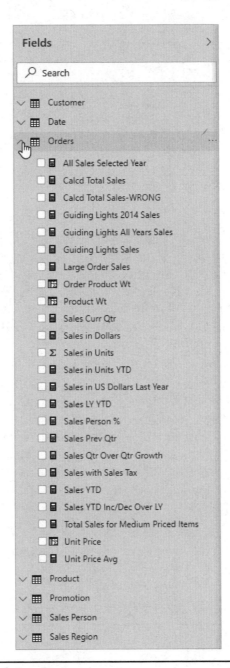

Figure 6-1   *The Fields area on the Report page*

Figure 6-2 *The Slicer button in the Visualizations area*

5. Drag this table so it is on the right side of the report layout area near the top.

6. In the Visualizations area, click the Slicer button, as shown in Figure 6-2. The Year table is now a slicer. As you learned in Chapter 4, a slicer filters the values on the report page by what is selected. Note that having no items selected in the slicer is the same as having all items selected in the slicer.

7. Use the sizing handles to remove the whitespace surrounding the year names in the slicer, as shown in Figure 6-3.

8. Size and arrange the two items on the report page, as shown in Figure 6-4.

9. Click the Calendar 2018 entry in the slicer. The chart shows sales for each sales person in calendar year 2018.

10. Click the Calendar 2017 entry in the slicer. The chart shows sales for 2017. Note that, by default, the chart is sorted by "Sales in Dollars" descending. When we use the slicer to switch the data from one year to another, the sort order changes according to who were the top sellers in that year.

Figure 6-3 *Sizing the slicer*

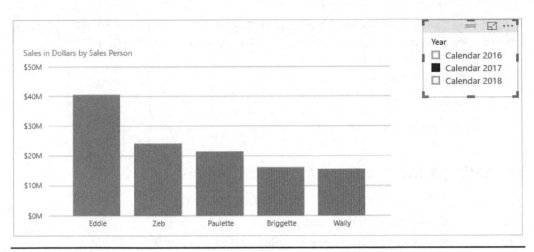

Figure 6-4   *A Power BI report with slicer*

Saving the Report

1. Click the File tab of the ribbon.
2. Select Save As from the drop-down menu. The Save As dialog box appears.
3. Navigate to the location where you would like to save the content created in this chapter and the next.
4. Remove "No Visualizations" from the filename.
5. Click Save.

Congratulations. You've built your first Power BI report page.

Text-based Visualizations

Next, we work with the text-based visualizations in Power BI. Text-based visualizations are as follows:

- The table
- The matrix
- The card
- The multi-row card

Text-based visualizations are often used to show data at a detail level. While working with the text-based visualizations, you will also learn to do the following:

- Rename report tabs.
- Set a visual level filter.
- Change the sort order.

Renaming a Tab and Creating a New Tab

1. Right-click the Page 1 tab and select Rename Page from the context menu.
2. Type **Sales by Sales Person** and press ENTER.
3. Click the yellow tab containing the plus sign to add a new report page.
4. Right-click the new page and select Rename Page from the context menu.
5. Type **Sales by State** and press ENTER.
6. On the View tab of the ribbon, click the Page View button and select Actual Size from the drop-down menu.

Creating the Table and Matrix Visualizations

1. In the Fields area, scroll down and expand Orders, if it is not already expanded.
2. Check the box for "Sales in Dollars." A column chart appears on the report page.
3. In the Fields area, expand Customer.
4. Check the box for State. A column is added to the chart for each state.
5. In the Visualizations area, select the Table visualization, as shown in Figure 6-5. The column chart becomes a table of values.

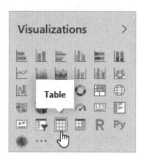

Figure 6-5 *Selecting the Table visualization*

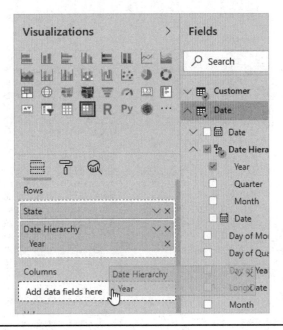

Figure 6-6 *Moving fields to the Columns area*

6. In the Fields area, expand Date, if it is not already expanded.

7. Expand the Date Hierarchy and check the box for Year. Year is added to the table.

8. In the Visualizations area, select the Matrix visualization. We do this to demonstrate the difference between the Table and the Matrix. The Matrix enables us to create groupings on both rows and columns.

9. In the area below Visualizations, click the Date Hierarchy/Year entry and drop it on Columns | Add data fields here, as shown in Figure 6-6. The years are pivoted to become columns in the matrix layout.

10. Click the State column heading so the data is sorted by state in ascending order.

11. Use the sizing handles to size the matrix appropriately. The visualization should appear as shown in Figure 6-7.

12. Click Save in the upper-left corner of the Power BI Desktop window.

Using the Card and Multi-row Card Visualizations

1. Click the yellow tab containing the plus sign to add a new report page.

2. Right-click the new page and select Rename Page from the context menu.

3. Type **Customer Info** and press ENTER.

State	Calendar 2016	Calendar 2017	Calendar 2018	Total
AK	$9,402,574.68	$9,411,419.20	$9,367,863.16	$28,181,857.04
AL	$125,509.60	$129,953.88	$133,462.80	$388,926.28
AR	$375,367.08	$352,402.88	$382,163.36	$1,109,933.32
AZ	$452,117.68	$482,518.12	$458,350.40	$1,392,986.20
CA	$1,494,093.04	$1,504,961.04	$1,492,673.48	$4,491,727.56
CO	$720,256.44	$708,663.60	$702,126.56	$2,131,046.60
CT	$5,151,180.04	$5,067,532.24	$5,100,552.84	$15,319,265.12
DE	$1,155,546.36	$1,145,798.68	$1,141,506.24	$3,442,851.28
FL	$599,476.08	$614,590.48	$594,893.96	$1,808,960.52
GA	$394,165.36	$376,568.80	$374,001.00	$1,144,735.16
HI	$696,683.20	$634,412.08	$647,713.72	$1,978,809.00
IA	$844,321.96	$834,043.52	$858,178.88	$2,536,544.36
ID	$408,404.72	$379,396.48	$394,124.60	$1,181,925.80
IL	$2,687,570.00	$2,630,308.60	$2,585,482.68	$7,903,361.28
IN	$874,105.04	$854,209.20	$851,639.80	$2,579,954.04
KS	$6,934,789.44	$6,818,224.40	$6,754,413.48	$20,507,427.32
KY	$4,683,191.32	$4,524,527.24	$4,713,125.60	$13,920,844.16
LA	$90,682.72	$96,584.44	$96,998.72	$284,265.88
MA	$113,304.24	$114,070.52	$113,156.24	$340,531.00
MD	$7,061,677.20	$6,959,244.12	$7,301,314.48	$21,322,235.80
ME	$8,209,307.72	$8,029,731.44	$7,762,738.52	$24,001,777.68
MI	$2,153,910.44	$2,134,164.12	$2,152,050.76	$6,440,125.32
MN	$2,131,571.48	$2,137,109.88	$2,166,029.44	$6,434,710.80
MO	$1,802,474.24	$1,814,270.04	$1,807,464.72	$5,424,209.00
MS	$2,166,754.44	$2,106,460.84	$2,170,998.12	$6,444,213.40
Total	$120,558,366.44	$117,875,913.72	$119,353,112.92	$357,787,393.08

Figure 6-7   *The Sales by State page*

4. On the View tab of the ribbon, click the Page View button and select Actual Size from the drop-down menu.
5. In the Fields area, check the Customer field in the Customer table.
6. In the Visualizations area, select the Card visualization. The Card visualization displays a single value. Therefore, it displays only the first customer.
7. In the Visualizations area, select the Multi-row Card visualization. The visualization changes to a scrolling list with one card layout for each customer. The card layout is pretty simple at the moment. It only includes the customer name.
8. In the Fields area, check the Address field. The address is added to each customer card.
9. Add the following fields to the visualization:
   - City
   - State
   - Zip Code
   - Married?

- Number of Cars Owned
- Number of Children at Home

Formatting and Sorting the Card Visualizations

1. Select the Format tab below the Visualizations area. This is the paint roller icon shown in Figure 6-8.
2. Expand the Data labels area.
3. Click the Color drop-down.
4. Select the gold color shown in Figure 6-9.
5. Expand the Card area in the Format tab.
6. From the Outline drop-down list, select Bottom only.
7. From the Outline color drop-down list, choose your favorite yellow color.
8. Use the Bar thickness control to set the thickness to 10.
9. Expand the Title area.
10. Toggle the Title switch to On.
11. In the Title Text area, type **Customer Information** and press ENTER.
12. Click the report layout area outside of the multi-row card visualization to unselect it.
13. In the Fields area, check the State field in the Customer table. A map of the states appears.
14. In the Visualizations area, select Slicer.
15. Click the top of the slicer and drag it beside the multi-row card.
16. Select a state in the slicer to view the customers in that state.
17. Click the ellipsis (…) button in the upper-right corner of the multi-row card visualization.

Figure 6-8   *The Format tab*

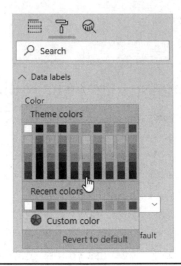

Figure 6-9   *Selecting a data label color*

18.   Select Sort By | City from the pop-up menu. The customer cards are sorted by city in descending order.

19.   Click the ellipsis button again.

20.   Select Sort ascending. The multi-row card visualization should appear similar to Figure 6-10.

21.   Click Save.

Customer Information		State
Gary D Elert *Customer*	8393 Baker Ave. *Address*	☐ AK
		☐ AL
Appleford *City*	CO *State*	☐ AR
		☐ AZ
80203 *Zip Code*	Y *Married?*	☐ CA
		☐ CO
0 *Number of Cars Owned*	2 *Number of Children at Home*	☐ CT
		☐ DE
Greg U Wellington *Customer*	3948 40th St. *Address*	☐ FL
		☐ GA
		☐ HI
Appleford *City*	CO *State*	☐ IA
		☐ ID
80203 *Zip Code*	N *Married?*	☐ II
2 *Number of Cars Owned*	2 *Number of Children at Home*	

Figure 6-10   *The Customer Info page*

Graphical Visualizations

We now return to the graphical visualizations available in Power BI. There are a number of stacked and clustered column and bar charts available in Power BI. They all function in a manner similar to the column chart we already created, so we won't do any more with those visualizations in this section.

In this section we will create the following visualizations:

- A pie chart
- A donut chart
- A treemap
- A gauge

While working with the graphical visualizations, you will also learn how to do following:

- Format labels.
- Begin a page from the ribbon.
- Begin a visualization from the ribbon.

Creating a Pie Chart, a Donut Chart, and a Treemap

1. Click the yellow tab containing the plus sign to add a new report page.
2. Right-click the new page and select Rename Page from the context menu.
3. Type **Sales Units by Promotion** and press ENTER.
4. Using the Page View drop-down list on the View tab of the ribbon, select Actual Size.
5. In the Fields area, check the Sales In Units field in the Orders table.
6. In the Fields area, select the Promotion field in the Promotion table.
7. In the Visualizations area, select Pie chart. A pie chart is created.
8. Select the Format tab under Visualizations.
9. Expand the Detail Labels area.
10. Use the Text Size control to set the text size to 12 pt.
11. Expand the Title area.
12. Use the Text Size control to set the text size to 18 pt.
13. Use the sizing handles to make the pie chart large enough so all of the labels are displayed in full.

14. Click the pie chart to give it focus and press CTRL-C to copy it.
15. Press CTRL-V to paste a copy of the pie chart onto the report page.
16. Move the copy of the pie chart so it is to the right of the original.
17. In the Visualizations area, select Donut chart.
18. Press CTRL-V again to paste another copy of the pie chart onto the report page.
19. Move this copy of the pie chart below the original.
20. In the Visualizations area, select Treemap.
21. Size the treemap visualization so it fits below the pie chart. The visualization should appear similar to Figure 6-11.

NOTE
Although all of these visualizations show the relative number of orders for each of the promotional categories, the current opinion is that the human brain is better at comparing relative sizes of rectangles than pie slices or donut sections.

22. Click Save.

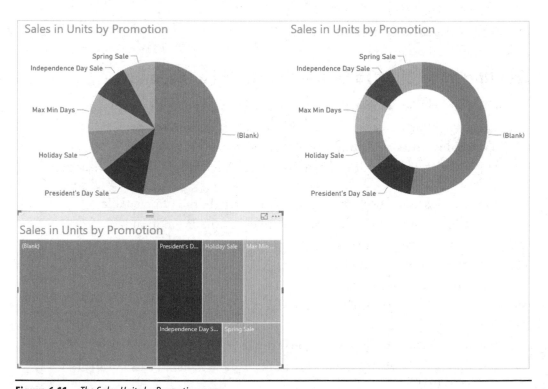

Figure 6-11 *The Sales Units by Promotion page*

Creating a Gauge

1. On the Home tab of the ribbon, click the drop-down arrow on the New Page button.
2. Select Blank Page from the drop-down menu to add a new report page.
3. Right-click the new page and select Rename Page from the context menu.
4. Type **Sales Units Gauge** and press ENTER.
5. From the Page View drop-down list on the View tab of the ribbon, select Actual Size.
6. On the Home tab of the ribbon, click New Visual. A placeholder for a new visual is created.
7. In the Fields area, check Sales in Units in the Orders table.
8. In the Visualizations area, select Gauge. A gauge showing the total sales in units across all time is created.
9. Use the sizing handles to make the gauge larger.
10. On the Home tab of the ribbon, click New Visual. A placeholder for a new visual is created.
11. In the Visualizations area, select Slicer. The placeholder becomes an empty slicer.
12. In the Fields area, check Month from the Date Hierarchy.
13. Drag the slicer up to the right of the gauge and size it appropriately.
14. Select January 2016 in the slicer.
15. Select the gauge and then select the Format tab under Visualizations.
16. Expand the Gauge axis area.
17. For Min, type **200000** and click in the Max entry area. The left end of the gauge scale is set to 200K.
18. For Max, type **300000** and click in the Target entry area. The right end of the gauge scale is set to 300K.
19. For Target, type **250000**. After a moment, a target line is created at 250K.

NOTE
In this example, we are hardcoding the values for Min, Max, and Target. It is also possible to use fields from the model to make Min, Max, and Target more dynamic. This is done using the "Minimum value," "Maximum value," and "Target value" drop areas on the Fields tab rather than these entry areas on the Format tab.

20. Expand Data labels.
21. From the Display units drop-down list, select Thousands.
22. For Text Size, type **17**.
23. Expand Callout Value.

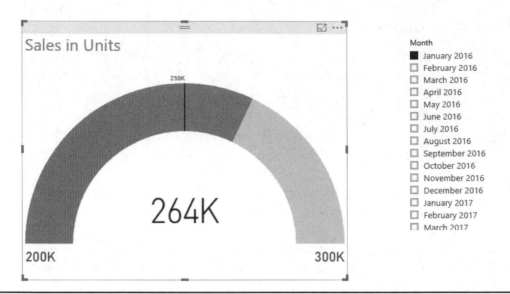

Figure 6-12 *The Sales Units Gauge page*

24. From the Display units drop-down list, select Thousands.
25. Scroll up and expand Data colors.
26. From the Target drop-down, select the darkest red color.
27. Scroll down and expand Title.
28. For Text Size, type **19**. The report page should appear as shown in Figure 6-12.
29. Select different months from the slicer and note the sales performance against the goal.
30. Click Save.

Interactivity

Now that we have worked with many of the basic visualizations in Power BI, let's add in more interactivity. You saw these interactive features in operation in Chapter 4. Here you will see how to put them in place.

Slicers

We begin our look at interactivity by taking a closer look at slicers. Slicers can take many forms. We created a few slicers as simple lists in previous reports in this chapter. In this section, we will branch out and create slicers using a number of different formats.

Creating Sales in Units and Sales in Dollars Charts

1. Click the yellow tab containing the plus sign to add a new report page.
2. Right-click the new page and select Rename Page from the context menu.
3. Type **Units/Dollars Comparison** and press ENTER.
4. In the Fields area, check the "Sales in Units" field in the Orders table.
5. In the Fields area, check the Month field in the Date Hierarchy of the Date table. Note that Month along with the other levels of the hierarchy are added to the chart axis. This is one way to create the drill down functionality.
6. Select the Format tab under Visualizations.
7. Expand Title.
8. Enter **15** for Text Size.
9. Scroll up and expand General.
10. Enter **800** for Width.
11. Click the Sales in Units by Year column chart again to give it focus. It should remain selected.
12. Press CTRL-C.
13. Press CTRL-V. A copy of the chart is pasted on top of the existing chart.
14. Drag the new chart below the existing chart.
15. Select the Fields tab in the area below Visualizations.
16. We are going to add "Sales in Dollars" to the new chart. From the Fields area, click on "Sales in Dollars" from the Orders table to drag and drop it on top of "Sales in Units," as shown in Figure 6-13.

Figure 6-13   *Adding a field to an existing chart*

17. Under Value where we just dropped the "Sales in Dollars" field, click the "X" next to "Sales in Units" to remove it from the chart.

18. Hold down CTRL and select the Sales in Units by Year chart. Both charts should now be selected. We want to make sure the two charts are exactly aligned for comparison.

19. On the Visual Tools | Format tab of the ribbon, click Align.

20. Select Align Left from the drop-down list.

Creating Slicers of Various Types

1. On the Home tab of the ribbon, click New Visual.

2. In the Visualizations area, select Slicer.

3. In the Fields area, check Product Type in the Product table.

4. Select the Format tab under Visualizations.

5. Expand General.

6. In the Orientation drop-down list, select Horizontal.

7. Expand Items.

8. In the Background drop-down list, select a light gray color.

9. Use the sizing handles to size the Product Type slicer appropriately.

10. On the Home tab of the ribbon, click New Visual.

11. In the Visualizations area, select Slicer.

12. In the Fields area, check Product Subtype in the Product table.

13. Click the down arrow in the upper-right corner of the Product Subtype slicer, as shown in Figure 6-14.

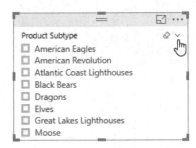

Figure 6-14 *Changing the slicer type*

14. Select Dropdown from the list. The slicer will change from a list of values to a drop-down list.

15. Size and position the Product Subtype slicer appropriately.

16. On the Home tab of the ribbon, click New Visual.

17. In the Visualizations area, select Slicer.

18. In the Fields area, check Date from the Date Hierarchy in the Date table. A slider with both begin and end points is created for the Date slicer.

19. Click the down arrow in the upper-right corner of the Date slicer.

20. Select After from the list. The slider now has only a begin point.

21. Size and position the Date slicer appropriately. Your completed report page should appear similar to Figure 6-15. Go ahead and try out the drill down and slicers on your new report page.

 NOTE
Once you select a Product Subtype, you only see its corresponding Product Type in the slicer. You must clear the selection from the Product Subtype slicer to see all of the Product Types again.

22. Click Save.

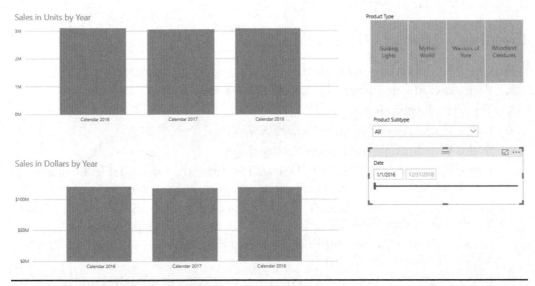

Figure 6-15   *The Units/Dollars Comparison page*

Filters

Filters work in a manner similar to slicers. Both provide a way for us to limit what is being displayed in the report. Whereas slicers are part of the layout of the report and are meant to be changed frequently, filters are a bit more hidden in their own Filters pane. The user viewing the report can change filter values, but it is expected this will happen with less frequency than slicer interaction.

We can add filters at several different levels:

- **Filters on this Visual**   Visual level filters change the data displayed by the visual that is selected at the time they are set. Visual level filters do not affect any other visualizations on the page. The Visual level filters option is only available when a visual is selected on the report page.

- **Filters on this Page**   Page level filters change the data displayed by all visuals on the page where they are set.

- **Filters on all Pages**   These filters change the data displayed by all visuals on all pages of the report.

In this section, we also create a scatter chart. Scatter charts provide a means of analyzing three measures at the same time. They also provide a mechanism to animate the way values change over time.

Creating a Scatter Chart

1. Click the yellow tab containing the plus sign to add a new report page.
2. Right-click the new page and select Rename Page from the context menu.
3. Type **Sales Analysis** and press ENTER.
4. In the Home tab of the ribbon, select New Visual.
5. In the Visualizations area, select Scatter chart.
6. In the Fields area, click "Sales in Units YTD" from the Orders table. Drag and drop it on X Axis | Add data fields here, as shown in Figure 6-16.
7. In the Fields area, click Sales YTD from the Orders table. Drag and drop it on Y Axis | Add data fields here.
8. In the Fields area, click Unit Price Avg from the Orders table. Drag and drop it on Size | Add data fields here.
9. In the Fields area, click Product Type from the Product table. Drag and drop it on Details | Add data fields here.

Figure 6-16   *Adding a field to the scatter chart visualization*

10. In the Fields area, click Month from the Date Hierarchy in the Date table. Drag and drop it on Play Axis | Add data fields here.
11. Select the Format tab.
12. Click the slider next to Color by category.

Setting a Visual Level Filter

1. Expand the Fields pane.
2. Click Store Type from the Store table. Drag and drop it on the "Add data fields here" area under "Filters on this visual."
3. In the newly created Store Type filter, check Wholesale, as shown in Figure 6-17.
4. Click Date from the Date Hierarchy in the Date table. Drag and drop it in the "Filters on this visual."
5. In the newly created Date filter, use the drop-down list to change from "Basic filtering" to "Advanced filtering."
6. In the "Show items when the value:" drop-down list, select "is on or after."
7. Below this drop-down list, use the date picker to select or type **1/1/2017**.
8. Be sure the And option is selected. In the drop-down list below the And option, select "is on or before."
9. Below this drop-down list, use the date picker to select or type **12/31/2017**.
10. Click Apply Filter.
11. Click the right arrow at the top of the Filters pane to minimize that pane.
12. Use the sizing handles to make the scatter chart as large as the report page.
13. Click the Format tab below the Visualizations area.

Figure 6-17   *Setting a Visual level filter*

14. Expand Title.
15. Replace the title with **Sales Analysis for 2017**.
16. Change the Text size to 20.
17. Click the play button in the lower-left corner of the scatter chart. Watch the visualizations change as the play axis moves from January 2017 to December 2017. The scatter chart should appear as shown in Figure 6-18.
18. Click Save.

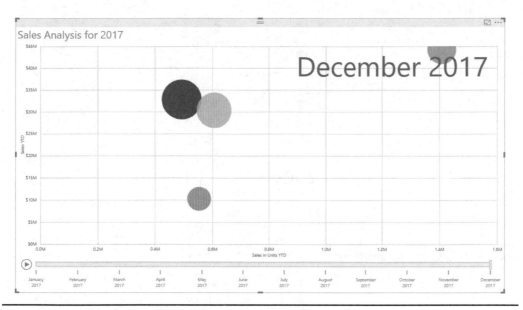

Figure 6-18 *The Sales Analysis page*

Drillthrough

The drillthrough feature of Power BI allows us to create a special type of page using a special type of filter. Using drillthrough, we can provide the report user with additional detail about a specific item. This enables the user to dig into the data to answer questions raised by the higher-level data.

To facilitate drillthrough, we must do two things. First, we create a page whose content provides the detail information. Second, we define a drillthrough filter that will allow the report user to navigate to our detail page with a specific item selected.

Let's see how it works.

Creating the Product Type Detail Page

1. Click the yellow tab containing the plus sign to add a new report page.
2. Right-click the new page and select Rename Page from the context menu.
3. Type **Sales Person Detail** and press ENTER.
4. In the Fields pane, click Sales Person from the Sales Person table. Drag and drop it on the "Add drillthrough fields here" area, as shown in Figure 6-19.
5. In the Drillthrough filters area, check Briggette, as shown in Figure 6-20. This will be our default selection used when we build this report page. When users actually drill through to this page, the sales person they select will be present in the drillthrough filter. Note that a Back button was automatically added for us.

Figure 6-19   *Creating a drillthrough filter*

Figure 6-20   *Setting a drillthrough filter default value*

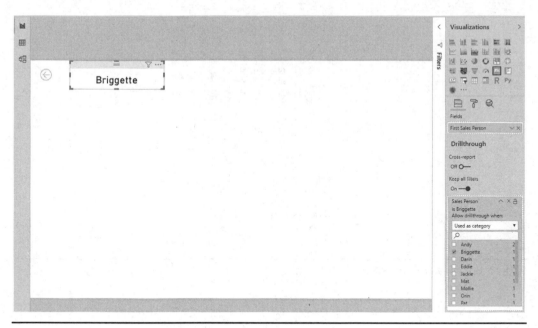

Figure 6-21   *The sales person heading using the Card Visualization*

6. In the Fields pane, check Sales Person in the Sales Person table to create a new visualization.

7. In the Visualizations area, select Card.

8. Select the Format tab.

9. Use the slider switch next to "Category label" to turn off the category label.

10. This card will be the heading showing which sales person is currently selected. Size it appropriately and position it at the top of the page, as shown in Figure 6-21.

11. In the Home tab of the ribbon, click New Visual.

12. In the Visualizations area, select "Line and stacked column chart."

13. In the Fields pane, check "Sales in Dollars" in the Orders table.

14. Select the Fields tab.

15. In the Fields pane, click "Sales in Units" in the Orders table. Drag and drop it on Line values | Add data fields here, as shown in Figure 6-22.

16. In the Fields pane, check Date Hierarchy/Month. We now have a chart showing sales in dollars shown as columns with the scale on the left and sales in units with the scale on the right. This chart has drilldown enabled.

Figure 6-22 *Adding a line to a line and stacked column chart*

17. Size and position the chart appropriately, as shown in Figure 6-23.
18. In the Home tab of the ribbon, click New Visual.
19. In the Visualizations area, select Treemap.

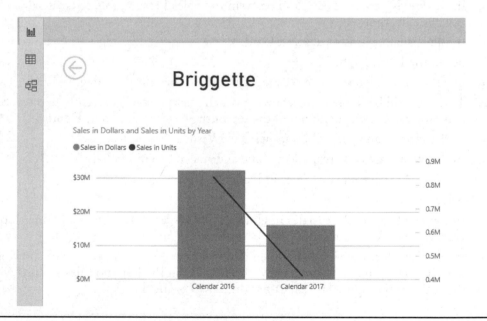

Figure 6-23 *The Sales Person Detail report page with one chart*

20. In the Fields pane, check "Sales in Units" in the Orders table.
21. In the Fields page, check Product Type in the Product table.
22. Size and position the chart appropriately, referencing the completed report page shown in Figure 6-24.
23. In the Home tab of the ribbon, click New Visual.
24. In the Visualizations area, select Treemap.
25. In the Fields pane, check "Sales in Units" in the Orders table.
26. In the Fields page, check Promotion in the Promotion table.
27. Size and position the chart appropriately, referencing Figure 6-24.
28. In the Home tab of the ribbon, click New Visual.
29. In the Visualizations area, select Treemap.
30. In the Fields pane, check "Sales in Units" in the Orders table.
31. In the Fields pane, check Sales Region in the Customer table.
32. Size and position the chart appropriately. The report page should appear similar to Figure 6-24.
33. Click Save.

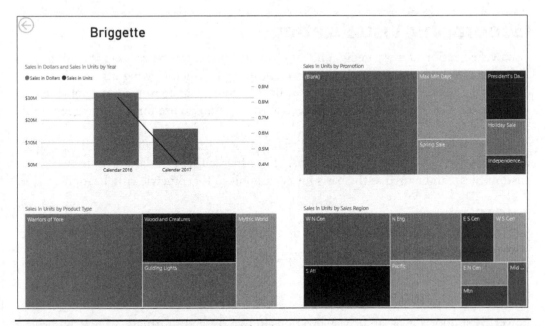

Figure 6-24 *The Sales Person Detail report page with four charts*

Testing the Report

1. Select the "Sales by Sales Person" report page. You many need to scroll left in the list of tabs at the bottom of the report to see the tab for this report page.
2. Right-click the column for Eddie and select Drillthrough | Sales Person Detail from the context menu. You are taken to the Sales Person Detail report page.

NOTE
Eddie is now selected in the Sales Person drillthrough filter. Also, the "Keep all filters" slider switch is on, which means in this case the year selected in the slicer on the Sales by Sales Person report page is still active and filtering values on this report page.

3. Hover over the "Line and stacked column chart" and click the forked arrow in the upper-left corner of the chart to drill down to the quarter level. We now see all of the quarters for the year selected by the Year slicer on the Sales by Sales Person report page.
4. Press CTRL and click the Back button in the upper-left corner of the report page. You return to the Sales by Sales Person report page.

Geographic Visualizations

Data visualization across a geographic or geometric space can be very enlightening. Relationships between data points not readily apparent when viewing information organized alphabetically by country name or state name can be immediately obvious when data is presented on a map. These days, there is no excuse for avoiding geographic presentations.

Power BI includes support for two different types of map visualizations. Bing maps can be used for geographic visualizations. Shape files, either standard or your own custom files, can be used as the basis for geographic and geometric visualizations.

NOTE
GIS-based visualizations can be created using a third-party custom visualization. See Chapter 7 for more information on custom visualizations.

Bing Map Visualizations

Power BI supports geographic visualizations in two different formats. Values can be represented by shaded areas with the color or intensity of the shading representing the relative amounts. Power BI calls this visualization a "Filled map."

Alternatively, values can be represented on a map by a "bubble." The size of the bubble represents the relative amounts. Power BI simply calls this visualization a "Map." (I suspect this was the first geographic visualization in Power BI, so it got the short name and all other geographic visualizations after that had to have a differentiator in the name.)

When using the Bing map visualizations, you have two methods available to specify the location associated with a value. If your data is geocoded and latitude and longitude are available in your dataset, you can use those fields. If you are not working with geocoded data, you can let Bing do the geocoding for you. Simply use a country name, state name, or city name to specify location. If you are using city names to specify location, create a field containing both the city and state or city and country separated by a comma. This will give Bing a much better chance of selecting the right geographic location to associate with that place name.

You do not need any additional licensing to use the Bing map visualizations in Power BI. This is included as part of Power BI, even if you are using the free license. However, you need access to the Internet from the computer running Power BI Desktop in order for the Bing maps to function in your report-authoring environment.

Creating a Map

1. Click the yellow tab containing the plus sign to add a new report page.
2. Right-click the new page and select Rename Page from the context menu.
3. Type **Sales by State Map 1** and press ENTER.
4. In the Home tab of the ribbon, click New Visual.
5. In the Visualizations area, select Map.
6. In the Fields pane, check State in the Customer table. The State field is used to specify Location in the visualization.
7. In the Fields pane, check "Sales in Dollars" in the Orders table. The size of the bubbles is determined by the "Sales in Dollars."
8. Size the map visualization to cover the entire report page.
9. Expand the Filters pane.
10. In the Fields pane, click Date Hierarchy | Year. Drag and drop it in the Filters pane on Filters on this page | Add data fields here.
11. In the newly created Year filter, check Calendar 2018. Your report page and Filters pane should appear similar to Figure 6-25.
12. Click Save.

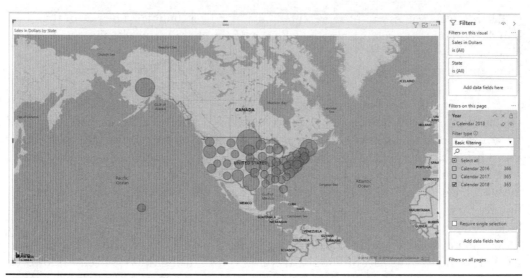

Figure 6-25   *The Sales by State Map 1 page*

Creating a Filled Map

1. In the Home tab of the ribbon, click the drop-down area on the New Page button.
2. Select Duplicate Page from the drop-down list.
3. Right-click the tab for this new page and select Rename Page from the context menu.
4. Change the report page name to **Sales by State Map 2** and press ENTER.
5. Select the existing Map visualization in the report page layout area.
6. In the visualizations area, select "Filled map" to change this from a Map visualization to a Filled map visualization.
7. Select the Format tab.
8. Expand the "Data colors" area.
9. Hover over the "Default color" header and click the ellipsis (…) button that appears. Select "Conditional formatting" from the context menu. The "Default color – Data colors" dialog box appears.
10. Click the "Based on field" drop-down list.
11. Expand the Orders table entry.
12. Select "Sales in Dollars."
13. Use the color picker for the Minimum value to select the lightest green. See Figure 6-26.
14. Use the color picker for the Maximum value to select the darkest green.

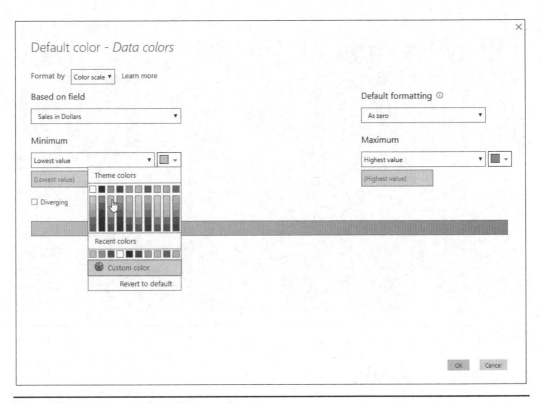

Figure 6-26   *Selecting a color for the Minimum value*

15. Click OK. The Filled map should appear as shown in Figure 6-27.
16. Click Save.

Shape Map Visualizations

At the time of this writing, maps based on shape files is a preview feature in Power BI, which means it is available for you to try but is not yet considered a production feature. I am assuming the maps based on shape files feature makes the cut and eventually becomes a production feature, so I will cover it here. In the following exercise, we will check to see if the "Shape map" is available in your Visualizations area. If it is not, we will follow steps to turn on this preview feature.

Power BI includes shape files for several countries by default. You see the list in Step 14 in this exercise. There are also a number of projections or different views of each country's shape file available. You see the list of projections for the "USA: states" map in Steps 16 through 18. You can also create your own custom shape file using JSON. We will complete that task in Chapter 7.

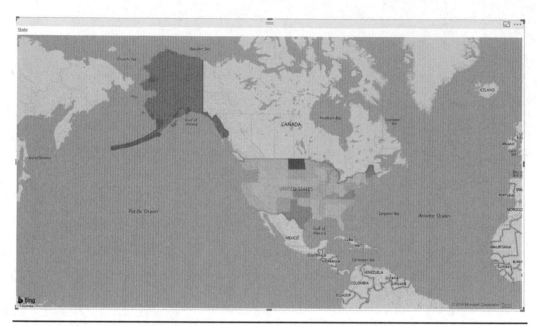

Figure 6-27 *The Sales by State Map 2 page*

Creating a Shape Map

1. As part of this report page, we will use the "Globe Background.jpg" image file. Locate this file in the supporting materials download and copy it to a location in your file system.

2. Right-click the "Sales by State Map 2" tab and select Duplicate Page from the context menu.

3. Right-click the tab for this new page and select Rename Page from the context menu.

4. Change the report page name to **Sales by State Map 3** and press ENTER.

5. Look at the Visualizations area to see if the "Shape map" visualization is available (see Figure 6-28). If it is present in your Visualizations area, jump to step 10.

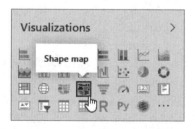

Figure 6-28 *Shape map in the Visualizations area*

6. Select File | Options and settings | Options. The Options dialog box will appear.

7. Select the Preview features page of the dialog box.

8. Check "Shape map visual," as shown in Figure 6-29.

9. Click OK. This may require you to exit and restart Power BI Desktop.

10. Click the Filled map on the report page so it is selected.

11. In the Visualizations area, select Shape map. The Filled map becomes a Shape map.

12. Select the Format tab.

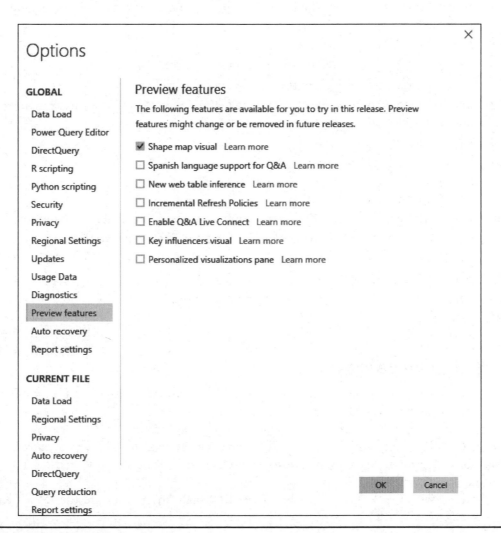

Figure 6-29   *Activating the Shape map visual*

13. Expand the Shape area.
14. Click the drop-down arrow for the Map drop-down list. Note the shape files for the various countries that are available by default.
15. Click the drop-down arrow to collapse the Map drop-down list.
16. Select Equirectangular from the Projection drop-down list. Note the different perspective shown by this version of the "USA: states" map.
17. Select Mercator from the Projection drop-down list. Note the different perspective shown by this version of the "USA: states" map.
18. Select "Albers USA" from the Projection drop-down list to return to the default projection.
19. Expand the "Data colors" area.
20. Select the lightest green from the Minimum color picker.
21. Select the darkest green from the Maximum color picker.
22. Click the report page layout area outside of the Shape map so the Shape map is no longer selected.
23. Click the Format tab.
24. Expand the "Page background" area.
25. Select the lightest blue from the Color drop-down color picker. The report page is now light blue.
26. Click "Add image" in the Page background area. The Open dialog box appears.
27. Locate and select the "Globe Background.jpg" file in your file system.
28. Click Open.
29. Select Fit from the Image Fit drop-down list.
30. The Shape map and Format area should appear similar to Figure 6-30.
31. Click Save.

GIS Map Visualizations

Many organizations have been visualizing geographic information using the Geographic Information Systems (GIS) standard. It is possible to create GIS-based maps in Power BI using a third-party visualization tool called ArcGIS Maps for Power BI. You may even see an ArcGIS Maps for Power BI icon in your Visualizations area. However, clicking this icon will simply take you to an informational dialog box until you license this custom visualization.

Working with the ArcGIS Maps for Power BI visualization is beyond the scope of this book.

Figure 6-30   *The Sales by State Map 3 page*

Other Visual Elements

In addition to the items found in the Visualizations area, Power BI provides a few more visual reporting elements on the Home tab of the ribbon:

- Text box
- Image
- Shapes
- Buttons

Text boxes, images, and shapes can be used to add clarity and interest to your reports. Buttons can be used to enhance interactivity.

We take a quick look at text boxes, images, and shapes in the following section. We work with buttons in Chapter 7.

Text Boxes, Images, and Shapes

Text boxes, images, and shapes are used to put the finishing touches on your reports. They can provide logos, headers, and footers on your report pages. You can even use these items to annotate your visualizations.

Remember, your visualizations should tell the story. However, when you want to add a little window dressing, the tools are there for you to do it. Just don't clutter your report pages with so much fluff that it gets in the way of interpreting the data.

Adding a Text Box, an Image, and a Shape to a Report

1. As part of this report page, we will use the "Sales Person Icon.jpg" image file. Locate this file in the supporting materials download and copy it to a location in your file system.
2. Select the Sales Person Detail tab.
3. On the Home tab of the ribbon, click Text box. A text box and a text formatting bar will appear.
4. Using the text formatting bar, change the font to Arial.
5. Change the font size to 28.
6. Turn on bold formatting.
7. Set the text justification to Right.
8. Type **Sales Person**.
9. Drag the text box to a position at the top of the report page with its right side even with the right side of the Sales in Units by Promotion treemap.
10. Size the text box appropriately. The result is shown in Figure 6-31.
11. On the Home tab of the ribbon, click Image. The Open dialog box appears.
12. Locate and select the "Sales Person Icon.jpg" file in your file system.
13. Click Open. The image appears on the report page.
14. Drag the resulting image to the left of the text box.

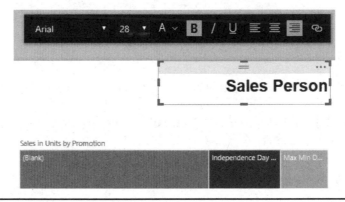

Figure 6-31   *Adding a text box*

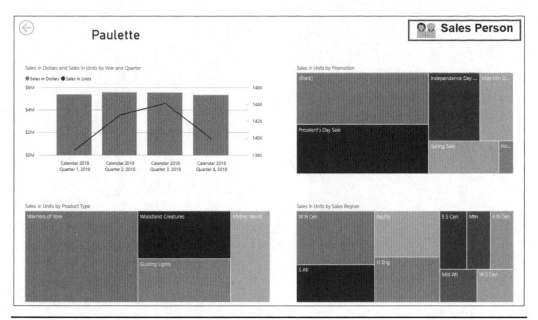

Figure 6-32 *The Sales Person Detail page with additional heading*

15. Size the image so it fits nicely next to the text box.
16. On the Home tab of the ribbon, click the Shapes drop-down.
17. Select Rectangle from the drop-down list. A rectangle appears on the report page.
18. The Visualizations pane is replaced by the Format Shape pane. Use the slider switch next to Fill to turn off the shape fill.
19. Expand the Line area.
20. Use the Line color drop-down color picker to select the darkest blue.
21. Size and position the rectangle so it surrounds the text box and the image. The completed Sales Person Detail report page appears as shown in Figure 6-32.
22. Click Save.

Fancy Formatting

In this chapter, we concentrated on putting visualizations on report pages. Although we did some work on the Format tab of the Visualizations pane, that was not our focus. In Chapter 7, we spend more time with visualization formatting. We will also work with the Analytics tab of the Visualization pane. In addition, we examine some of the ways we can create and utilize custom visualizations.

Chapter 7

Visualization Formatting

In This Chapter

- The Visualization Format Tab
- Advanced Formatting Dialog Boxes
- The Visualization Analytics Tab
- Themes

In the previous chapters, you learned to create visualizations using Power BI. As part of that process, we used the Format tab in the Visualizations pane to control the way a report item looks and acts. In this chapter, we take a more complete look at the options available on the Format tab. We also look at the third tab available in some situations on the Visualizations pane, the Analytics tab.

This chapter does not provide step-by-step examples of each and every formatting property available in Power BI. That would make for a very long and tedious chapter. Instead, much of this chapter functions as a reference to the formatting options available.

The Visualization Format Tab

The Format tab, with the paint roller icon, enables us to change the look and the behavior of our Power BI reports. When a report item is selected within a Power BI report, we can use the Format tab to change the formatting properties of that item. When no item is selected, we see the formatting properties of the report page in the Format tab.

Formatting properties are grouped by functional area. Clicking the title of a functional area will expand it to show us the properties available in that area. The functional areas for the report page are shown in Figure 7-1.

Figure 7-1   *The Format tab of the Visualizations pane*

Report Page

The following functional areas apply to the report page.

Page Information

Property	Description
Name	The name of the report page. This is the text that appears in the tab at the bottom of the report.
Tooltip	Activates the Tooltip filter in place of the Drillthrough filter for this report page. This enables the page to be used as a tooltip page.
Q&A	When this property is on, the Q&A feature may use this report page as the answer to a question.
Q&A Alternate Names	A list of names that might also identify this page as the answer to a Q&A or Cortana question

Page Size

Property	Description
Type	The type of page size being specified. The 16:9 and 4:3 options are most often used for pages designed to be displayed on a screen. The Letter option is optimal for pages that will be printed. The Tooltip option is used for pages designed to be used as tooltips. The Custom option allows you to specify your own width and height.
Width	The width of a custom page size
Height	The height of a custom page size

Page Background

Property	Description
Color	The background color of the page
Transparency	The transparency of the page color
Image	An image file to load in the background
Image Fit	The method used to fit the image to the page size

Page Alignment

Property	Description
Vertical Alignment	Position of the report page if the page does not fill the area between the ribbon and the report page tabs

Wallpaper

Property	Description
Color	The color of the borders around and behind the page
Transparency	The transparency of the wallpaper color
Image	An image file to load as the wallpaper
Image Fit	The method used to fit the image to the wallpaper area

Filter Pane

Property	Description
Background Color	The background color of the Filters pane
Transparency	The transparency of the background color of the Filters pane
Font + Icon Color	The color of the text and icons in the Filters pane
Header Text Size	The font size of the headers in the Filters pane
Font Family	The font family of the text in the Filters pane
Left Border	When this property is on, the Filters pane has a left border.
Left Border Color	The color of the left border
Width	The width of the Filters pane

Filter Cards

Property	Description
Type	When Type is set to Available, the properties affect filter cards containing conditions created but not yet affecting the report data. When Type is set to Applied, the properties affect filter cards containing conditions affecting the report data.
Background Color	The background color of the filter cards
Transparency	The transparency of the background color of the filter cards
Border	When this property is on, the filter cards have a border around them.
Border Color	The color of the filter card border
Font + Icon Color	The color of the text and icons in the filter cards
Text Size, Font Family	The font used in the filter cards
Input Box Color	The color of the text boxes in the filter cards

All Items

The following functional areas apply to all report items. The properties within the functional areas may vary slightly for some report items. Those differences are noted within the descriptions of those properties. For example, the General properties area for a clustered column chart is shown in Figure 7-2.

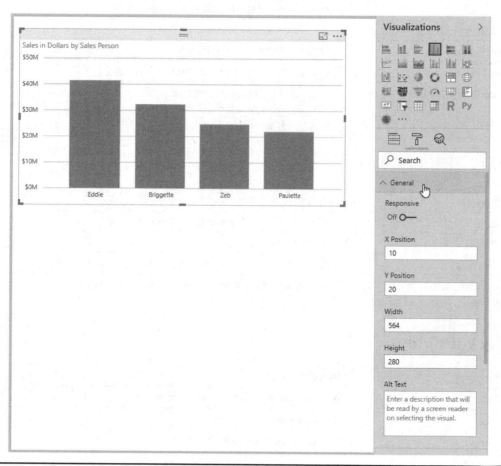

Figure 7-2   *The General properties area of a clustered column chart*

General

Property	Description
Responsive	When this property is on, the item responds to changes in the size of the browser window when the report is viewed. The item's layout will adapt to continue to provide the user with optimal data viewing. The Responsive property is available for all bar charts and all column charts as well as the line chart, area chart, stacked area chart, ribbon chart, waterfall chart, and scatter chart.
X Position, Y Position	Properties controlling the position of the item
Width, Height	Properties controlling the size of the item
Alt Text	Text said aloud by a screen reader when this item is selected
High Density Sampling	When on, the High Density Sampling property will improve the appearance of certain charts displaying a large volume of data. This property is only available for line chart, area chart, scatter chart, and map.

Title

Property	Description
Title	When this property is on, an item title is displayed.
Title Text	The content of the title
Word Wrap	When this property is on, the title text is word-wrapped rather than cut off.
Font Color, Background Color, Alignment, Text Size, Font Family	The font color, background color, alignment, and font of the title

Background

Property	Description
Background	When this property is on, the item has a background color.
Color	The background color
Transparency	The transparency of the background color

Lock Aspect

Property	Description
Lock Aspect	When this property is on, the aspect ratio of the item is maintained when you resize the item using the corner sizing handles. This option does not change the behavior of the sizing handles in the middle of each side of the item.

Border

Property	Description
Border	When this property is on, the item has a border around it.
Color	The border color
Radius	The extent to which the corners of the border are rounded

Tooltip

The Tooltip functional area is available for all report items except multi-row card, KPI, slicer, text box, image, shape, and button.

Property	Description
Tooltip	When this property is on, a tooltip is displayed if the user hovers the mouse over an item element.
Type	When Type is set to default, the default tooltip appears showing the values for the item element being hovered over. When Type is set to Report Page, a report page with its Tooltip property turned on is displayed when an item element is hovered over.
Page	The report page used as the tooltip
Label Color	The font color used for labels on the default tooltip
Value Color	The font color used for values on the default tooltip
Text Size, Font Family	The font used by the default tooltip
Background Color	The background color used by the default tooltip
Transparency	The transparency of the background color used by the default tooltip

Visual Header

This property works in conjunction with the "Use the modern visual header with updated styling options" setting on the Report Settings tab of the Options dialog box. You reach the Options dialog box by selecting File | Options and Settings | Options. (You can find more about the Options dialog box in Chapter 8.) When the "Use the modern visual header with updated styling options" setting is not checked, the only formatting option available in the Visual Header area is the toggle to turn the visual header on or off when the report is published. When the "Use the modern visual header with updated styling options" setting is checked, all of the properties are available for formatting the modern visual header on the item.

Property	Description
Visual Header	When this property is on, a visual header is displayed for this item when the report is published and viewed online. When it's off, no visual header is available for this item when the report is published and viewed online. The visual header is always displayed in the authoring environment.
Background Color	The background color behind each icon in the visual header
Border	The color of the border around each icon in the visual header
Transparency	The transparency of the background color behind each icon in the visual header
Icon Color	The color of each icon in the visual header
Visual Information Icon	When this property is on, the Visual Information icon is visible in the visual header.
Visual Warning Icon	When this property is on, the Visual Warning icon is visible in the visual header.
Visual Error Icon	When this property is on, the Visual Error icon is visible in the visual header.
Drill On Dropdown	When this property is on, the "Drill on" drop-down is visible in the visual header.
Drill Up Icon	When this property is on, the Drill Up icon is visible in the visual header.
Drill Down Icon	When this property is on, the Drill Down icon is visible in the visual header.
Show Next Level Icon	When this property is on, the Show Next Level icon is visible in the visual header.
Expand Next Level Icon	When this property is on, the Expand Next Level icon is visible in the visual header.
Pin Icon	When this property is on, the Pin icon is visible in the visual header.
Focus Mode Icon	When this property is on, the Focus Mode icon is visible in the visual header.
See Data Layout Icon	When this property is on, the See Data Layout icon is visible in the visual header.
More Options Icon	When this property is on, the More Options icon is visible in the visual header.
Filter Icon	When this property is on, the Filter icon is shown in the visual header.
Visible Header Tooltip Icon	When this property is on, the Visible Header Tooltip icon is shown.

Charts

The following functional areas apply to all bar charts and all column charts as well as the line chart, area chart, stacked area chart, ribbon chart, waterfall chart, and scatter chart.

Legend

The following functional area is visible when there is information to display in a legend.

Property	Description
Legend	When this property is on, a legend is displayed.
Position	The position of the legend
Title	When this property is on, the legend includes a title.
Legend Name	The legend title
Color, Font Family, Text Size	The color and font of the legend text, including the title
Style	The style of graphic shown next to each legend label to link it with a line on the chart. Style may be set to "Markers only," "Line and markers," or "Line only." This property is only available for the line chart, area chart, stacked area chart, line and stacked column chart, and line and clustered column chart.
Match Line Color	This property is available when style is set to "Markers only." When this property is on, the legend matches the line color.
Circle Default Icon	This property is available when style is set to "Markers only." When this property is on, the legend uses circle markers in front of each legend label instead of a line segment.

Y Axis

The following functional area is available for all charts listed at the beginning of the Charts section except for ribbon chart.

Property	Description
Y Axis	When this property is on, the Y axis is displayed.
Position	The position of this axis relative to the chart area
Scale Type	The type of scale used for this axis. This property is only available in the Y axis grouping on column charts as well as the line chart, area chart, stacked area chart, and scatter chart.

(Continued)

Property	Description
Start, End	The range of values to include on the axis. These properties are only available in the Y axis grouping on column charts as well as the line chart, area chart, stacked area chart, waterfall chart, and scatter chart.
Color, Text Size, Font Family	The color and font of the axis text
Minimum Category Width	The minimum width (vertical) allotted for each category label. This property is only available in the Y axis grouping on bar charts.
Maximum Size	The maximum size (horizontal) allotted for each category label as a percent of the chart width. This property is only available in the Y axis grouping on bar charts.
Inner Padding	The space between each bar as a percent of the bar width. This property is only available in the Y axis grouping on bar charts.
Display Units, Value Decimal Places	The units (none, thousands, millions, and so on) and decimal places used to display the axis values. These properties are only available in the Y axis grouping on the column charts as well as the line chart, area chart, stacked area chart, waterfall chart, and scatter chart.
Title	When this property is on, the axis includes a title.
Style, Title Color, Axis Title, Title Text Size, Font Family	The style, color, content, and font of the axis title
Gridlines	When this property is on, gridlines are displayed on the chart. This property is only available in the Y axis grouping on the column charts as well as the line chart, area chart, stacked area chart, waterfall chart, and scatter chart.
Color, Stroke Width, Line Style	The color, width, and style (solid, dotted, dashed) of the grid lines. These properties are only available in the Y axis grouping on the column charts as well as the line chart, area chart, stacked area chart, waterfall chart, and scatter chart. (These properties are only visible when the Gridlines property is on.)
Show Secondary	When this property is on, a secondary Y axis scale is shown. This property is only available in the Y axis grouping on the line and stacked column chart and the line and clustered column chart. When the Show Secondary property is on, many of the above properties are displayed again for the secondary Y axis.
Align Zeros	This is only available when the secondary Y axis scale is shown. When this property is on, the 0 lines on the primary and secondary scales remain aligned. This property is only available in the Y axis grouping on the line and stacked column chart and the line and clustered column chart.
Show Blank Values	When this property is on, blank values are visualized as zeros in order to prevent breaks in the scatter chart tracks. This property is only available in the Y axis grouping on the scatter chart.

X Axis

Property	Description
X Axis	When this property is on, the X axis is displayed.
Scale Type	The type of scale used for this axis. This property is only available in the X axis grouping on bar charts as well as the scatter chart.
Start, End	The range of values to include on the axis. These properties are only available in the X axis grouping on bar charts as well as the scatter chart.
Type	The type of X axis. Type may be set to Continuous or Categorical. This property is only available in the X axis grouping on line charts, area charts, and stacked area charts.
Color, Text Size, Font Family	The color and font of the axis text
Minimum Category Width	The minimum width (vertical) allotted for each category label. This property is only available in the X axis grouping on column charts as well as the line chart, area chart, stacked area chart, ribbon chart, and waterfall chart.
Maximum Size	The maximum size (horizontal) allotted for each category label as a percent of the chart width. This property is only available in the X axis grouping on column charts as well as the line chart, area chart, stacked area chart, ribbon chart, and waterfall chart.
Inner Padding	The space between each bar as a percent of the bar width. This property is only available in the X axis grouping on column charts as well as the waterfall chart.
Display Units, Value Decimal Places	The units (none, thousands, millions, and so on) and decimal places used to display the axis values. These properties are only available in the X axis grouping on the stacked bar chart, clustered bar chart, and scatter chart.
Concatenate Labels	When this property is on, axis labels are concatenated when using the "Expand all down one level in the hierarchy" function. When it's off, groupings are created in the axis labels. This property is only available in the X axis grouping on column charts as well as the line chart, area chart, stacked area chart, and ribbon chart.
Title	When this property is on, the axis includes a title.
Style, Title Color, Axis Title, Title Text Size, Font Family	The style, color, content, and font of the axis title
Gridlines	When this property is on, gridlines are displayed on the chart. This property is only available in the X axis grouping on the bar charts as well as scatter chart.
Color, Stroke Width, Line Style	The color, width, and style (solid, dotted, dashed) of the gridlines. These properties are only available in the X axis grouping on the bar chats as well as the scatter chart.
Show Blank Values	When this property is on, blank values are visualized as zeros in order to prevent breaks in the scatter chart tracks. This property is only available in the X axis grouping on the scatter chart.

Data Colors

The following functional area is available for all charts listed at the beginning of the Charts section except for the waterfall chart.

Property	Description
(Color Picker for each legend value)	The color to be used when displaying values for that legend value

Data Labels

The following functional area is available for all charts listed at the beginning of the Charts section except for the scatter chart.

Property	Description
Data Labels	When this property is on, data labels are displayed.
Color	The color of the data labels
Display Units, Value Decimal Places	The units (none, thousands, millions, and so on) and decimal places used to display the data labels. The Display Units property is not available on 100% stacked column chart and 100% stacked bar chart.
Orientation	The orientation of the data labels (horizontal or vertical). This property is available on all column charts as well as the ribbon chart and waterfall chart.
Position	The position of the data labels relative to the data bar.
Overflow Text	When this property is on, data labels are displayed even if the data bar is not large enough to contain them. This works best with non-stacked bars. This property is available on all bar charts as well as the stacked column chart, clustered column chart, 100% stacked column chart, and ribbon chart.
Text Size, Font Family	The font of the data labels
Show Background	When on, this property shows a box behind each data label.
Background Color, Transparency	The color and transparency of the box behind each data label
Customize Series	When this property is on, the formatting and visibility of the data labels for each line series on the chart can be set individually. The following properties are only available when this property is on. This property is available on all charts except the waterfall chart.
Series Selection Dropdown	The line series to modify
Show	When this property is on, data labels for the selected line series are shown.
Color	The color of the data labels for the selected line series
Display Units, Value Decimal Places	The units (none, thousands, millions, and so on) and decimal places used to display the data labels for the selected line series
Position	The position of the data labels relative to the data bar for the selected line series

Property	Description
Text Size, Font Family	The font of the data labels for the selected line series
Show Background	When on, this property shows a box behind each data label for the selected line series.
Background Color, Transparency	The color and transparency of the box behind each data label for the selected line series

Plot Area

Property	Description
Transparency	The transparency of the plot area
Image	An image file to load as the background of the plot area
Image Fit	The method used to fit the image to the plot area

Additional Chart Functional Groups

The following functional groups are available on one or more charts, as described.

Shapes

This functional group is available on the line chart, area chart, stacked area chart, line and stacked column chart, and the line and clustered column chart. The Size, Marker shape, and Customize series properties are the only properties in this section available on a scatter chart.

Property	Description
Shade Area	When this property is on, the area below the line is shaded. This property is only available on the line and stacked column chart and the line and clustered column chart.
Stroke Width	The width of each line on the chart
Join Type	The shape of the joints (miter, round, bevel) at each data point on the lines
Line Style	The style of the lines (dashed, solid, dotted)
Show Marker	When this property is on, markers are shown at each data point.
Marker Shape, Marker Size, Marker Color	The shape, size, and color used for the markers
Stepped	When this property is on, lines are drawn in a stepped manner.
Customize Series	When this property is on, the formatting and visibility of the data labels for each line series on the chart can be set individually. This property is only available on the line chart, area chart, stacked area chart, and scatter chart. When the Customize Series property is on, the above properties are displayed again for the series being customized.
Series Selection Dropdown	The line series to customize

Ribbons

This functional group is available on the ribbon chart.

Property	Description
Spacing	Determines the amount of whitespace between ribbons
Match Series Color	When this property is on, the ribbons between the data bars match the data series colors.
Transparency	The transparency of the ribbons
Border	When this property is on, a border appears along the top and bottom of each ribbon.

Sentiment Colors

This functional group is available on the waterfall chart.

Property	Description
Increase	The color for increasing bars in the waterfall
Decrease	The color for decreasing bars in the waterfall
Other	The color for other bars in the waterfall
Total	The color for total bars in the waterfall

Breakdown

This functional group is available on the waterfall chart.

Property	Description
Max Breakdowns	The maximum number of breakdowns in the waterfall

Category Labels

This functional group is available on the scatter chart.

Property	Description
Category Labels	When this property is on, category labels are displayed on the scatter chart.
Color, Text Size, Font Family	The color and font of the category labels
Show Background	When on, this property shows a box behind each category label.
Background Color, Transparency	The color and transparency of the box behind each category label

Fill Point

This functional group is available on the scatter chart.

Property	Description
Fill Point	When this property is on, each point on the scatter chart is filled in. This is available only if there is no data series determining the size of each point.

Color Border

This functional group is available on the scatter chart.

Property	Description
Color Border	When this property is on, each point on the scatter chart has a border.

Table and Matrix

The following functional groups apply to tables and matrixes.

Style

Property	Description
Style	The style used to format the table or matrix

Grid

Property	Description
Vertical Grid	When this property is on, vertical grid lines separate each column.
Vertical Grid Color, Vertical Grid Thickness	The color and thickness of the vertical grid lines
Horizontal Grid	When this property is on, horizontal grid lines separate each row.
Horizontal Grid Color, Horizontal Grid Thickness	The color and thickness of the horizontal grid lines
Row Padding	The spacing between rows
Outline Color, Outline Weight	For tables, this is the color and thickness of the line separating the headings from the data area and separating the data area from the totals. For matrixes, this is the color and thickness of the line separating the row and column values from the values area.
Text Size	The size of the text in the table or matrix
Image Height	The height of an image shown in the table or matrix

Column Headers

Property	Description
Font Color	The font color of the column header text
Background Color	The background color of the column headers
Outline	How the column headers are outlined
Auto-size Column Width	When this property is on, column widths are adjusted to the size of the data displayed.
Font Family, Text Size, Alignment	The font and alignment of the column header text
Title Alignment	The alignment of the title text. This property is only available in matrixes.
URL Icon	When this property is on, an icon is shown in place of a URL. This property is only available in matrixes.
Word Wrap	When this property is on, the column header text is word-wrapped rather than truncated.

Row Headers

This functional group is only available in matrixes.

Property	Description
Font Color	The font color of the row header text
Background Color	The background color of the row headers
Outline	How the row headers are outlined
Stepped Layout	When this property is on, the row data layout is stepped.
Stepped Layout Indentation	The amount of indentation used for the stepped layout
URL Icon	When this property is on, an icon is shown in place of a URL.
Word Wrap	When this property is on, the row header text is word-wrapped rather than truncated.
Font Family, Text Size, Alignment	The font and alignment of the row header text
+/- Icon	When this property is on, an icon is displayed to facilitate drill down or drill up. The icon will only be visible in situations where the row data supports drill down.
Icon Color, Icon Size	The size and color of the Drill Down icon

Values

Property	Description
Font Color	The font color of the values area
Background Color	The background color of the values

Property	Description
Alternate Font Color	The font color of the values when alternating color formatting is used
Alternate Background Color	The background color of the values when alternating color formatting is used
Banded Row Style	When this property is on, alternating color formatting is used in the row headers area in addition to the values area. This property is only available in matrixes.
Show On Rows	When this property is on, multiple values are shown as multiple rows rather than multiple columns. This property is only available in matrixes.
Outline	How the values area is outlined
URL Icon	When this property is on, an icon is shown in place of a URL.
Word Wrap	When this property is on, the value text is word-wrapped rather than truncated.
Font Family, Text Size	The font of the value text

Subtotals

This functional group is only available in matrixes.

Property	Description
Row Subtotals	When this property is on, row subtotals are included.
Row Subtotal Label	The label placed on each subtotal row
Column Subtotals	When this property is on, column subtotals are included.
Column Subtotal Label	The label placed above each subtotal column
Font Color	The font color of the subtotals
Font Family	The font family of the subtotals
Background Color	The background color of the subtotals
Text Size	The text size of the subtotals
Apply To Labels	When this property is on, these font and color settings are applied to the subtotal row and subtotal column headings.
Row Subtotal Position	The position of the row subtotals relative to the values being totaled
Per Row Level	When this property is on, additional sliders appear to allow for subtotals to be turned on or off at each row grouping level.
Per Column Level	When this property is on, additional sliders and text boxes appear to allow for subtotals to be turned on or off at each column grouping level and for subtotal labels to be entered.

Grand Total

This functional group is only available in matrixes.

Property	Description
Font Color	The font color of the grand total
Font Family	The font family of the grand total
Background Color	The background color of the grand total
Apply To Labels	When this property is on, these font and color settings are applied to the grand total row and grand total column headings.
Text Size	The text size of the grand total

Totals

This functional group is only available in tables.

Property	Description
Total	When this property is on, column totals are included.
Total Label	The label placed on the total row
Font Color	The font color of the totals
Background Color	The background color of the totals
Outline	How the totals area is outlined
Font Family	The font family of the totals
Text Size	The text size of the totals

Field Formatting

Property	Description
Field Dropdown	The field to format
Display Units, Value Decimal Places	The units (none, thousands, millions, and so on) and decimal places used to display the field values. This property is only available in matrixes.
Font Color	The font color of the selected field
Background Color	The background color of the selected field
Alignment	The alignment of the selected field
Apply To Header	When this property is on, these font and color settings apply to the header for the selected field.
Apply To Values	When this property is on, these font and color settings apply to the values area for the selected field.

Property	Description
Apply To Subtotals	When this property is on, these font and color settings apply to the subtotals area for the selected field. This property is only available in matrixes.
Apply To Total	When this property is on, these font and color settings apply to the totals area for the selected field.

Conditional Formatting

Property	Description
Field Dropdown	The field to format
Background Color	When this property is on, the Conditional Formatting Advanced Controls dialog box can be used to define conditional background color formatting for the selected field. See the "Conditional Formatting Advanced Controls Dialog Box" section of this chapter for more detail.
Font Color	When this property is on, the Conditional Formatting Advanced Controls dialog box can be used to define conditional font color formatting for the selected field. See the "Conditional Formatting Advanced Controls Dialog Box" section of this chapter for more detail.
Data Bars	When this property is on, the Data Bars Advanced Controls dialog box can be used to define data bar formatting for the selected field. See the "Data Bars Advanced Controls Dialog Box" section of this chapter for more detail.
Icons	When this property is on, icons are displayed to show the conditional status.

Card and Multi-row Card

The following functional groups apply to cards and multi-row cards.

Data Label/Data Labels

This is the Data Label functional group in card and the Data Labels functional group in multi-row card. For simplicity, data labels will be referred to in the plural in the following explanations.

Property	Description
Color	The color of the data labels
Display Units, Value Decimal Places	The units (none, thousands, millions, and so on) and decimal places used to display the data labels. This property is only available in card.
Text Size, Font Family	The font of the data labels
Source Spacing	When this property is on, extra spaces in the data label are displayed rather than being automatically trimmed. This property is only available in card.

Category Label/Category Labels

This is the Category Label functional group in card and the Category Labels functional group in multi-row card. For simplicity, category labels will be referred to in the plural in the explanations below.

Property	Description
Category Labels	When this property is on, category labels are displayed.
Color, Text Size, Font Family	The color and font of the category labels

Word Wrap

This functional group is only available in card.

Property	Description
Word wrap	When this property is on, text on the card is word-wrapped rather than truncated.

Card

This functional group is only available in multi-row card.

Property	Description
Outline	How each card is outlined
Show Bar	When this property is on, a bar is shown to the left of each card.
Bar Color	The color of the bar to the left of each card
Bar Thickness	The thickness of the bar to the left of each card
Padding	The whitespace between each car
Background	The background color of each card

Pie Chart, Donut Chart, Treemap, and Maps

The following functional groups apply to pie chart, donut chart, treemap, map, filled map, and shape map.

Legend

This property only appears when there is information to display in a legend.

Property	Description
Legend	When this property is on, a legend is displayed.
Position	The position of the legend

Property	Description
Title	When this property is on, the legend includes a title.
Legend Name	The legend title
Color, Font Family, Text Size	The color and font of the legend text including the title

Data Colors

Property	Description
(Color Picker for each legend value)	The color to be used when displaying values for that legend value

Detail Labels/Data Labels

This functional group is available as Detail Labels in pie chart and donut chart. It is available as Data Labels in treemap.

Property	Description
Detail Labels	When this property is on, detail or data labels are displayed.
Label Style	Select the style of the label. This property is only available in pie chart and donut chart.
Color	The color of the labels
Display Units, Value Decimal Places	The units (none, thousands, millions, and so on) and decimal places used to display the labels
Text Size, Font Family	The font of the labels
Label Position	The position of the labels. This property is only available in pie chart and donut chart.

Category Labels

This functional group is only available in treemap and map.

Property	Description
Category Labels	When this property is on, category labels are displayed.
Color, Text Size, Font Family	The color and font of the category labels
Show Background	When on, this property shows a box behind each category label. This property is only available in map.
Background Color, Transparency	The color and transparency of the box behind each category label. This property is only available in map.

Shapes

This functional group is only available in donut chart.

Property	Description
Inner Radius	The radius of the inner "donut hole" as a percent of the radius of the outer circle

Bubbles

This functional group is only available in map.

Property	Description
Bubble Size	The size of the circles on the map

Map Controls

This functional group is only available in map and filled map.

Property	Description
Auto Zoom	When this property is on, the map will auto zoom to show regions of the map with values.
Zoom Buttons	When this property is on, the map displays plus and minus buttons to facilitate zooming in and out. When not on, zooming must be done using the mouse wheel or a pinch movement on a touch screen.

Map Styles

This functional group is only available in map and filled map.

Property	Description
Theme	The appearance of the Bing map

Shape

This functional group is only available in shape map.

Property	Description
Map	The preloaded map to use
View Map Keys	This link displays the Map Keys dialog box showing the key values associated with each shape on the map.
Map	A custom shape file to load into the map
Projection	The map projection to display

Default Color

This functional group is only available in shape map.

Property	Description
Show	When this property is on, the default color is shown in shapes with no data value.
Color	The default color shown in shapes with no data value
Border Color	The color of the shape borders
Border Thickness	The thickness of the shape borders

Zoom

This functional group is only available in shape map.

Property	Description
Auto Zoom	When this property is on, the map will auto zoom to show regions of the map with values.
Selection Zoom	When this property is on, the map zooms in on a selected region.
Manual Zoom	When this property is on, zooming may be done using the mouse wheel or a pinch movement on a touch screen.

Funnel

The following functional groups apply to funnel.

Category Labels

Property	Description
Category Labels	When this property is on, category labels are displayed.
Color, Text Size, Font Family	The color and font of the category labels

Data Colors

Property	Description
Default Color	The default color for the data
Show All	When this property is on, a color picker is shown for each data grouping.
(Color Picker for each data grouping)	The color to be used when displaying values for that data grouping

Data Labels

Property	Description
Data Labels	When this property is on, data labels are displayed.
Label Style	The style of the data labels
Color	The color of the data labels
Display Units, Value Decimal Places	The units (none, thousands, millions, and so on) and decimal places used to display the data labels
% Decimal Places	The decimal places used to display percentages in the data labels
Position	The position of the data labels
Text Size, Font Family	The font of the data labels

Conversion Rate Labels

Property	Description
Conversion Rate Labels	When this property is on, conversion rate labels are displayed.
Color, Text Size, Font Family	The color and font of the conversion rate labels

Gauge

The following functional groups apply to gauge.

Gauge Axis

Property	Description
Min	The minimum value at the start of the gauge axis
Max	The maximum value at the end of the gauge axis
Target	The target value to display on the gauge axis

Data Colors

Property	Description
Fill	The fill color of the gauge
Target	The color of the target line

Data Labels

Property	Description
Data Labels	When this property is on, data labels are displayed.
Color	The color of the data labels
Display Units, Value Decimal Places	The units (none, thousands, millions, and so on) and decimal places used to display the data labels
Text Size, Font Family	The font of the data labels

Target

Property	Description
Target	When this property is on, a target label is displayed.
Color	The color of the target label
Display Units, Value Decimal Places	The units (none, thousands, millions, and so on) and decimal places used to display the target label
Text Size, Font Family	The font of the target label

Callout Value

Property	Description
Callout Value	When this property is on, the value on the gauge is also displayed as text.
Color	The color of the callout value
Display Units, Value Decimal Places	The units (none, thousands, millions, and so on) and decimal places used to display the callout value

KPI

The following functional groups apply to KPI.

Indicator

Property	Description
Display Units, Value Decimal Places	The units (none, thousands, millions, and so on) and decimal places used to display the indicator value
Text Size	The font size of the indicator value

Trend Axis

Property	Description
Trend Axis	When this property is on, a trend graph is displayed.

Goals

Property	Description
Goal	When this property is on, a goal value is displayed.
Distance	When this property is on, the distance of the value from the goal is displayed.

Color Coding

Property	Description
Direction	Specifies which direction is good (high is good or low is good)
Good Color	The color for a good value
Neutral Color	The color for a neutral value
Bad Color	The color for a bad value

Slicer

The following functional groups apply to slicers.

Selection Controls

Property	Description
Single Select	When this property is on, the slicer only allows a single value to be selected.
Multi-select With CTRL	When this property is on, multiple values can only be selected by holding down CTRL while selecting.
Show "Select all" Option	When this property is on, a "Select all" option is included in the slicer.

Slicer Header

Property	Description
Slicer Header	When this property is on, the slicer includes a header.
Font Color	The font color of the slicer header text
Background	The background color of the slicer header
Outline	Selects how the slicer header is outlined
Text Size, Font Family	The font of the slicer header text
Show Summary	When this property is on, a summary of the selected item or items is shown.

Items

Property	Description
Font Color	The font color of the slicer item text
Background	The background color of the slicer items
Outline	Selects how the slicer items are outlined
Text Size, Font Family	The font of the slicer item text

Button, Shape, and Image

The following functional groups apply to buttons, shapes, and images.

Button Text

This function group is only available in buttons.

Property	Description
Button Text	When this property is on, text may be added to the button.
Button State Dropdown	The button state you are selecting properties for (default state, on hover, or on press)
Button Text	The text on the button
Font Color	The font color of the button text
Padding	The padding around the button text
Vertical Alignment	The vertical alignment of the text within the button
Horizontal Alignment	The horizontal alignment of the text within the button
Text Size, Font Family	The font of the button text

Icon

This functional group is only available in buttons.

Property	Description
Icon	When this property is on, the button includes an icon.
Button State Dropdown	The button state you are selecting properties for (default state, on hover, or on press)
Shape	The icon to be displayed in this button
Padding	The padding between the icon and the sides of the button
Vertical Alignment	The vertical alignment of the icon within the button
Horizontal Alignment	The horizontal alignment of the icon within the button
Line Color	The color of the icon
Transparency	The transparency of the icon
Weight	The line width of the icon

Outline

This functional group is only available in buttons.

Property	Description
Outline	When this property is on, the button has an outline.
Button State Dropdown	Select which button state you are selecting properties for (default state, on hover, or on click).
Outline Color	The color of the outline
Transparency	The transparency of the outline
Outline Weight	The line width of the outline
Round Edges	The degree to which the corners are rounded

Line

This functional group is only available in shapes.

Property	Description
Line Color	The color of the line
Transparency	The transparency of the line
Weight	The thickness of the line
Rounded Edges	The degree to which the corners are rounded

Fill

This functional group is only available in shapes and buttons.

Property	Description
Fill	When this property is on, the button or shape has a fill color.
Button State Dropdown	Select which button state you are selecting properties for (default state, on hover, or on click). This property is only available in buttons.
Fill Color	The fill color
Transparency	The transparency of the fill color

Rotation

This functional group is only available in shapes.

Property	Description
Rotation	The rotation of the shape

Scaling

This functional group is only available in images.

Property	Description
Scaling	Select the method used to display the image file within the height and width of the image item.

Action

Property	Description
Action	When this property is on, an action is taken when this report item is clicked.
Type	The type of action taken
Bookmark	When the bookmark action type is selected, this property selects the bookmark to activate.
Web URL	When the Web URL action type is selected, this property specifies the URL to navigate to.
Tooltip	The tooltip text to display when the mouse pointer hovers over this report item

Advanced Formatting Dialog Boxes

In addition to the controls in the functional groups of the Visualizations pane's Format tab, two dialog boxes also control visualization formatting: the Conditional Formatting Advanced Controls dialog box and the Data Bars Advanced Controls dialog box. These dialog boxes are opened through links within the functional groups, as noted previously in the chapter.

Conditional Formatting Advanced Controls Dialog Box

Conditional formatting is used to change the formatting, often the color, of a value or visualization element in response to the condition of the data. In some cases, conditional formatting is used to assist the viewer with an indication of how to interpret the data.

This is the case when we color the font or the background of numeric values in a table or chart. In other cases, conditional formatting is used to provide the only visualization of a value. We saw this in Chapter 6 when we used the Advanced Controls dialog box to define the shading on the filled map (see Figures 6-26 and 6-27).

Conditional formatting can be defined three different ways with the Advanced Controls dialog box. We can create a color scale where the color of the objects pass through a color gradient that is proportional to their values. We can also create color rules where objects receive their color based on a set of specific rules. Finally, we can use field values that contain color definitions to directly specify colors. The type of conditional formatting in use is determined by the "Format by" drop-down list in the upper-left corner of the Conditional Formatting Advanced Controls dialog box.

Color Scale

When we use the Color Scale setting in the Advanced Controls dialog box, we create a color gradient to be applied to a set of values. We specify the definition for the low end, the high end, and, optionally, the middle of the gradient. We can use relative formatting, where the gradient start, end, and, optionally, midpoint are defined by the lowest value included in the group, the highest value included in the group, and, optionally, the center value in the group, respectively. When the Diverging box is checked, we can configure the Center value. When the Diverging box is not checked, only the Minimum and Maximum values can be specified.

Figure 7-3 shows the Font Color Conditional Formatting Advanced Controls dialog box configured to use red for the lowest Sales in Dollars value, yellow for the middle Sales in Dollars value, and green for the highest Sales in Dollars value. The values are relative because "Lowest value," "Middle value," and "Highest value" are selected from the drop-downs. Whatever the lowest value for Sales in Dollars happens to be in the set of values displayed will be colored red. Whatever the highest value for Sales in Dollars happens to be in the set of values displayed will be colored green. Similarly, the middle value will be yellow and the gradients will be determined relative to those points.

We can also use specific numbers to determine the end points and the midpoint of our color gradient scale. This is shown in Figure 7-4. In this example, we are using a count of an item (in this case, customers) rather than a measure to determine our color scale. When a non-measure is used to determine the scale, we have the option of determining how the field is aggregated in the color scale calculation. This is done using the Summarization drop-down.

In Figure 7-4, the drop-downs under Minimum and Maximum have been changed to "Number" and specific values have been entered below each. With this configuration, any state with a count of 500 customers or fewer will appear as the specified red color. Any state with a count of 8,000 or more customers will appear as the specified green color. The gradient will be determined from red to green between 500 and 8,000. (In this example, Diverging is not checked, so no midpoint value is specified.)

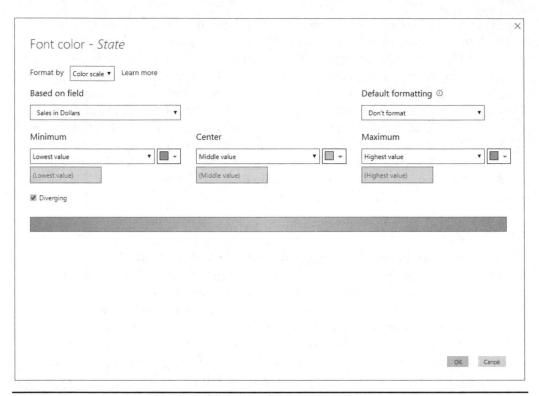

Figure 7-3   *Conditional Formatting Advanced Controls dialog box using a relative color scale*

One additional drop-down to note in Figure 7-4 is the "Default formatting" drop-down. This specifies how blank values should be handled. We have three options:

- Format as if it was a zero value
- Format it with a specific color (selected right next to the "Default formatting" drop-down)
- Do not format

In Figure 7-4, states with no customers are formatted with their own specific color.

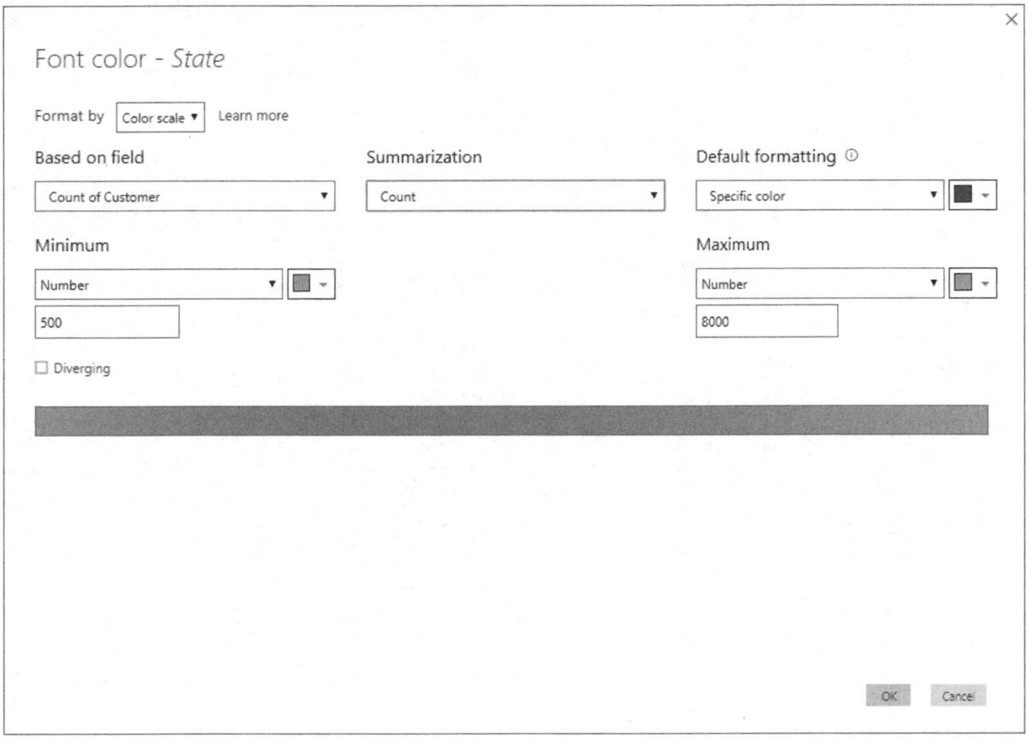

Figure 7-4   *Conditional Formatting Advanced Controls dialog box using a specific color scale*

Rules

The gradient created using the Color Scale setting is great for situations where there are varying degrees of good and bad. In Figure 7-4, we are telling those viewing the report that having only 500 customers in a state is bad, having somewhere between 500 and 8,000 customers is better, and having 8,000 customers is best. In some cases, however, our interpretation of performance against a goal might be more hard and fast—either there are 750 or more customers in a state or there are not. For these situations, we use the Rules setting of the Advanced Controls dialog box. This is shown in Figure 7-5.

With the Rules setting, we define specific conditions for each color. If a value meets the conditions of the first rule in the list, it is assigned that color. If not, the evaluation moves on to the next rule. Rules can be based on percentages or numbers. In Figure 7-5, three rules are defined. Blank values are a dark purple. Any count of customers that is under 750 is red. Any count of customers that is 750 or over is green.

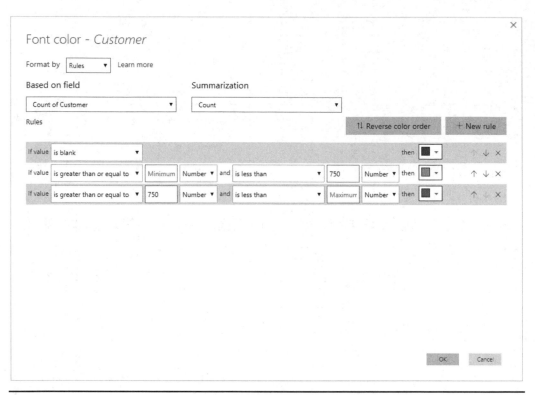

Figure 7-5 *Conditional Formatting Advanced Controls dialog box using rules*

NOTE
If you want to specify the minimum number or the maximum number as shown in Figure 7-5, delete the content of the text box and press TAB.

Field Value

In some cases, the data itself may contain information on the color to use when displaying a given value. This could be a specific color that identifies an object to the report viewer. It could be a specific color that a product comes in that was selected by the consumer for that particular sale. It could be an interpretation color (bad, okay, excellent) that is calculated outside of the data model.

Figure 7-6 shows the Advanced Controls dialog box configured to use a field value. In this case, the background color of the Product Type column will have a color based on the content of the Product Type Color field. This value will be taken from the first row in the data grouping. The content of the Product Type Color field must be a valid color name or a hexadecimal color specification with a leading # character.

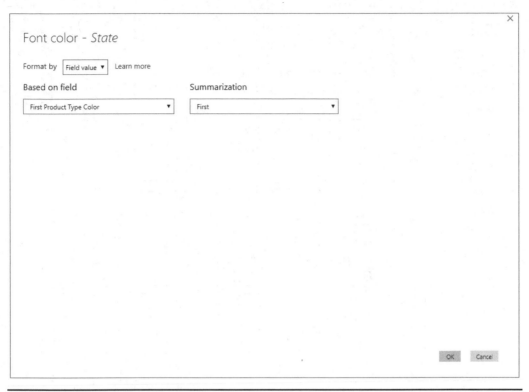

Figure 7-6   *Conditional Formatting Advanced Controls dialog box using a field value*

Data Bars Advanced Controls Dialog Box

In addition to changing the foreground and background colors, conditional formatting also enables us to add data bars to numeric values. This is done using the Data Bars Advanced Controls dialog box, as shown in Figure 7-7. In the example, data bars are added to the Sales in Dollars column with the shortest bar based on the minimum value and the longest bar based on the maximum value.

Alternatively, we could have chosen specific numeric values for the Minimum and Maximum fields. When a specific minimum is chosen, any value at or below the minimum will not have a data bar. When a specific maximum is chosen, any value at or above the maximum will not have a data bar spanning the entire column width.

In addition to the minimum and maximum values, the Data Bars Advanced Controls dialog box allows us to specify the color of the positive bar and the negative bar.

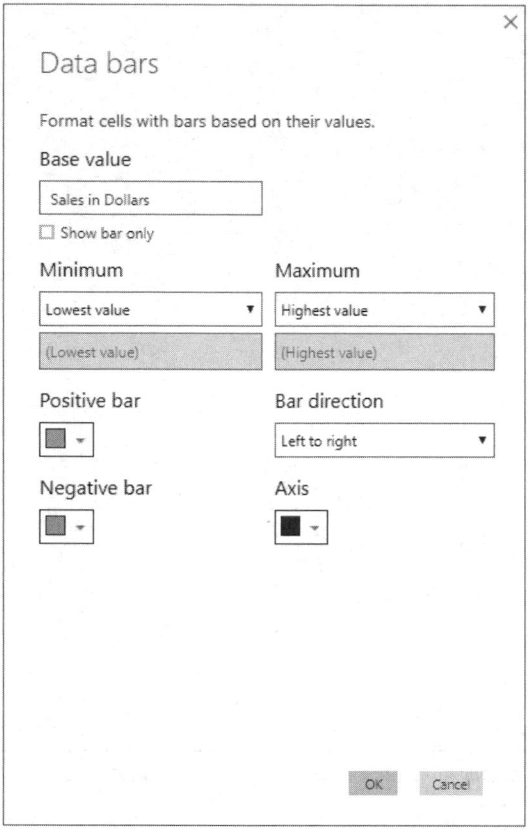

Figure 7-7 *Data Bars Advanced Controls dialog box*

If there are both positive and negative values in the set, the axis line will be shown in the specified color. Finally, we can determine if the data bars go from left to right or from right to left.

The data bars created by the settings in Figure 7-7 are shown in Figure 7-8.

Product Type	Sales in Dollars
Guiding Lights	$30,816,660.00
Mythic World	$100,489,797.52
Warriors of Yore	$134,901,539.08
Woodland Creatures	$91,579,396.48
Total	**$357,787,393.08**

Figure 7-8 *A table column with data bars*

The Visualization Analytics Tab

The Analytics tab, with the chart in a magnifying glass icon, enables us to add analytics lines to our charts. This is shown in Figure 7-9. When certain report items are selected within a Power BI report, we can use the Analytics tab to enable and format these lines. If a report item that does not support analytics lines is selected, the Analytics icon disappears.

Figure 7-10 shows a chart with analytics lines. A Constant Line shows the sales goal of $25 million. An Average Line shows the average sales among the sales people listed.

Figure 7-9   *The Visualizations pane's Analytics tab*

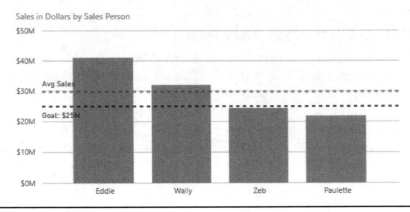

Figure 7-10 *A chart with analytics lines*

Types of Analytics Lines

Power BI provides the following types of analytics lines:

Line Type	Description
Constant Line	A line at a specified axis value. This is often used as a goal line on a chart.
X-Axis Constant Line	This functions the same as a Constant Line but appears on the X axis of a scatter chart. The scatter chart is the only chart with two value axes.
Y-Axis Constant Line	This functions the same as a Constant Line but appears on the Y axis of a scatter chart. The scatter chart is the only chart with two value axes.
Min Line	A line indicating the minimum value on the chart
Max Line	A line indicating the maximum value on the chart
Average Line	A line indicating the average value on the chart
Median Line	A line indicating the median value on the chart
Percentile Line	A line indicating the specified percentile on the chart
Symmetry Shading	A line defining the symmetry of a scatter chart. The area above the symmetry line is shaded one color and the area below the symmetry line is shaded another color.
Ratio Line	The line defining the ratio of all Y axis values over all X axis values on a scatter chart

Controls for Editing Analytics Lines

Power BI provides the following controls for creating and managing analytics lines:

Property	Description
Line Names	If you have added more than one analytics line, the top area allows you to select the line whose properties you want to modify. Double-click a line name to edit that name. Click the "x" next to a line name to remove that line from the chart.
+Add	Click here to create a new line.
Value	The value to use for a Constant Line. This property is only available for Constant Line, X-Axis Constant Line, and Y-Axis Constant Line.
Measure	The measure from the chart to use when calculating the value for the line. This property is only available for Min Line, Max Line, Average Line, Median Line, and Percentile Line.
Percentile	The percentile used for a Percentile Line. This property is only available for Percentile Line.
Upper Shading	The color of the shading above the symmetry line. This property is only available for Symmetry Shading.
Lower Shading	The color of the shading below the symmetry line. This property is only available for Symmetry Shading.
Color	The color of the line. This property is not available for Symmetry Shading.
Transparency	The transparency of the line or shading
Line Style	The style of the line (dashed, solid, dotted). This property is not available for Symmetry Shading.
Position	The position of the line relative to the items on the chart (In Front or Behind). This property is not available for Symmetry Shading or Ratio Line.
Data Label	When this property is on, a data label appears with the line. This property is not available for Symmetry Shading or Ratio Line.
Color (Data Label)	The color of the data label. This property is not available for Symmetry Shading or Ratio Line.
Text	The content of the data label. This can be the value, the name of the line, or the name of the line and the value. This property is not available for Symmetry Shading or Ratio Line.
Horizontal Position	The horizontal position of the label (Left or Right). This property is not available for Symmetry Shading or Ratio Line.
Vertical Position	The vertical position of the label relative to the line (Above or Under). This property is not available for Symmetry Shading or Ratio Line.
Display Units, Decimal Places	The units (none, thousands, millions, and so on) and decimal places used to display the label values. These properties are not available for Symmetry Shading or Ratio Line.

Themes

Themes can be used to create a set of desired colors and fonts to use across multiple Power BI reports. A theme can be created to make your Power BI reports consistent with your organization's branding. They can also be used to create a set of colors that work well together for a specific purpose. For example, you can use a theme to make sure your visualizations can be interpreted properly by someone with red-green color blindness.

Themes are selected using the Switch Theme drop-down on the Home tab of the ribbon. Several themes are preloaded in Power BI Desktop, as shown in Figure 7-11.

Additional themes are available from the Power BI Community Themes Gallery. Select "Theme gallery" from the Switch Theme drop-down to open a browser and view the Themes Gallery. If you find a theme you like, download its .JSON file and use "Import theme" from the Switch Theme drop-down to load it.

Figure 7-11 *Selecting a theme*

You can also create a .JSON file for your own custom theme. This can then be imported into Power BI Desktop using "Import theme" from the Switch Theme drop-down. Use "How to create a theme" from the Switch Theme drop-down for more information on creating your own custom themes.

New Ways to Interact and Visualize

In Chapter 8, you'll learn how to work with advanced interactivity in Power BI. You'll also see some of the ways to take visualization beyond what is available by default in Power BI Desktop. Finally, you'll publish reports to PowerBI.com.

Chapter 8

Advanced Interactivity and Custom Visualizations

In This Chapter

- Controlling Interactivity
- Creating Interactivity
- Customizing Visualizations

Power BI allows us to create reports with rich interactivity and informative data visualizations with just a few clicks. Crisp, clean layouts and interactive slicing happen with very little input required on our part. The rich data exploration experience is baked right in.

However, there are times when we or our report users want more. Fortunately, Power BI provides additional features for controlling and creating interactivity. Power BI also provides several mechanisms for adding custom visualizations to our reports. In this chapter, we work through a number of exercises to learn how these features enable us to take our reporting to the next level.

Controlling Interactivity

Clicking on almost any given element in a visualization or a cell in a table or matrix causes portions of the other visualizations on the report page to be highlighted or dimmed. Making a selection in a slicer filters the data on the current report page. These behaviors happen automatically. However, that doesn't mean these are the only actions that can occur. In this section, we work through a couple ways we modify Power BI's default interactivity.

Controlling Interactions

We begin by changing the default interaction between visualizations. To do this, we need to return to the Options dialog box. In Chapter 6, we used the Preview Features page of the Options dialog box to ensure you had access to the Shape Map visualization. Here, we look at the Report Settings page of the Options dialog box.

Looking at the Default Interaction Behavior

1. Locate the "Max Min Sales Information.pbix" file in the file system location where you saved it in Chapter 6. (This file is also available in the download of the supporting materials for this book, if you did not create it in Chapter 6.)
2. Double-click the "Max Min Sales Information.pbix" file. This will open the file in Power BI Desktop.
3. Select the Sales by Sales Person tab.
4. In the Year slicer, select Calendar Year 2016.
5. In the Sales in Dollars by Sales Person column chart, right-click the column for Paulette and select Drillthrough | Sales Person Detail from the context menu.
6. In the Sales in Units by Product Type treemap in the lower-left corner of the report page, click the Warriors of Yore rectangle. Now, the bars and rectangles in the other visualizations each contain a highlighted and a dimmed section.

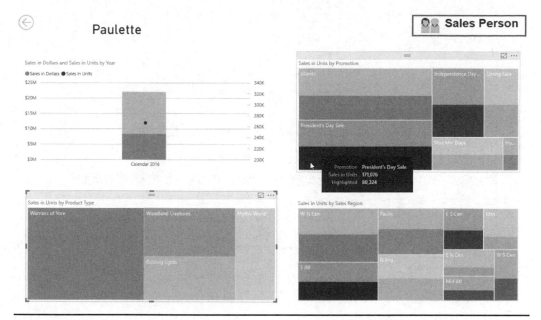

Figure 8-1   *Standard visualization interactivity*

7. In the Sales in Units by Promotion treemap, hover over the President's Day Sale rectangle. We see that a total of 171,076 units have been sold as part of the President's Day Sale promotion, and 80,324 of those units were from the Warriors of Yore product type. This is shown in Figure 8-1.

8. In the Sales in Units by Product Type treemap, click the Warriors of Yore rectangle again so it is not selected.

Testing the New Interactivity

1. Select File | Options and settings | Options. The Options dialog box will appear.

2. Select the "Report settings" page in the CURRENT FILE section of the dialog box.

3. Check "Change default visual interaction from cross highlighting to cross filtering," as shown in Figure 8-2.

4. Click OK.

5. In the Sales in Units by Product Type treemap, click the Warriors of Yore rectangle. Now, the other visualizations are cross-filtered so only the numbers for the Warriors of Yore data is shown.

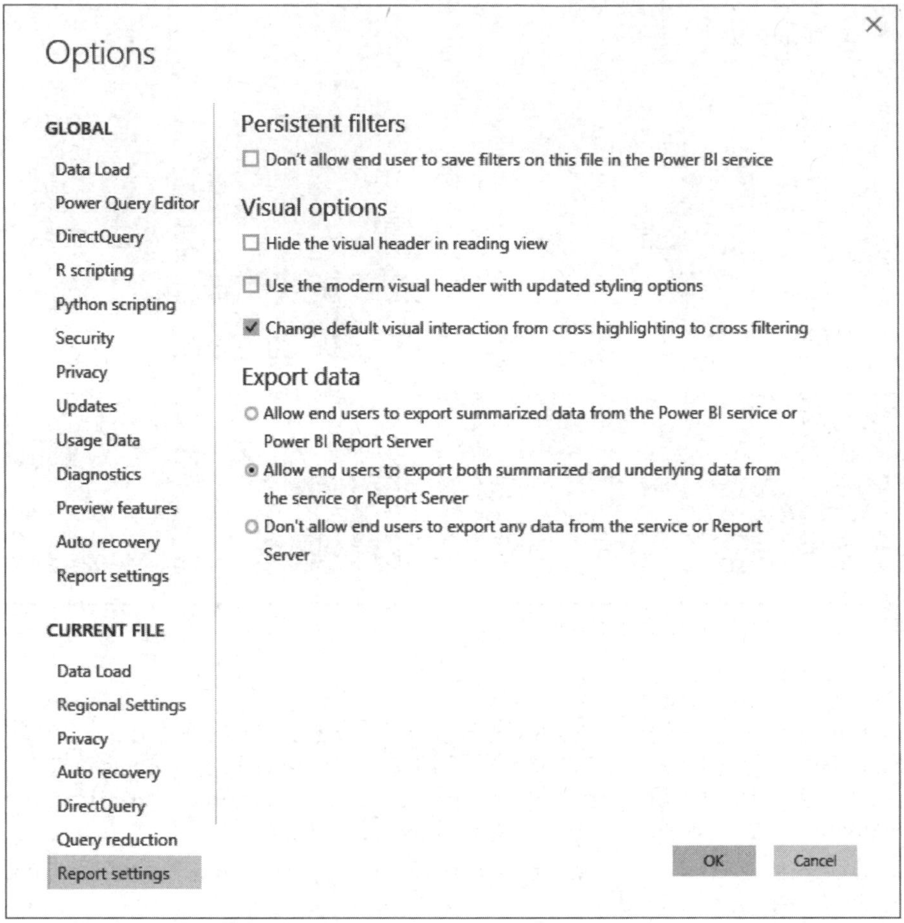

Figure 8-2 *The "Report settings" page of the Options dialog box*

6. In the Sales in Units by Promotion treemap, hover over the President's Day Sale rectangle. We see that only the 80,324 units for the Warriors of Yore product type are shown, as seen in Figure 8-3.
7. Click Save.

You can decide if you want to keep the cross-filtering behavior or return to the Options dialog box and turn it off. This option change only affects the current report file. You need to make the same change in each file where you want to enable the cross-filtering behavior.

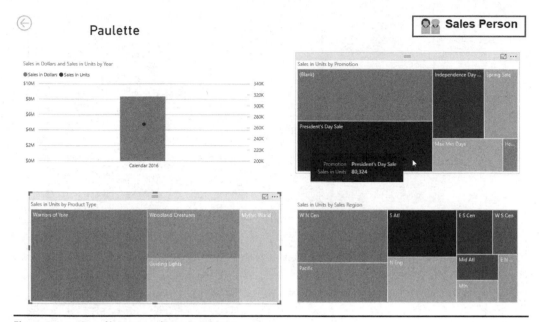

Figure 8-3 *Cross-filtering visualization interactivity*

Synchronizing Slicers

When we created slicers on our report pages in Chapter 6, they filtered the data on a single page. However, in Chapter 4, you saw that slicers can be synchronized to filter data across two or more report pages. In this exercise, you learn how that is accomplished.

Synchronizing Slicers – Slicer Not Visible on Second Report Page

1. In the "Max Min Sales Information.pbix" report, select the Units/Dollars Comparison tab.
2. On the View tab of the ribbon, check the box to view the "Sync slicers" pane.
3. Click the Product Type slicer to select it, as shown in Figure 8-4.

   The "Sync slicers" pane shows the selected slicer is only visible on the Units/Dollars Comparison report page (the single check mark in the column with the eye at the top). This slicer is not synchronized to slice data on any other report pages.

4. Check the box in the Sync column (the column with the two arrows in a circle) for the Units/Dollars Comparison report page.
5. Check the box in the Sync column for the Sales by State Map 1 report page.

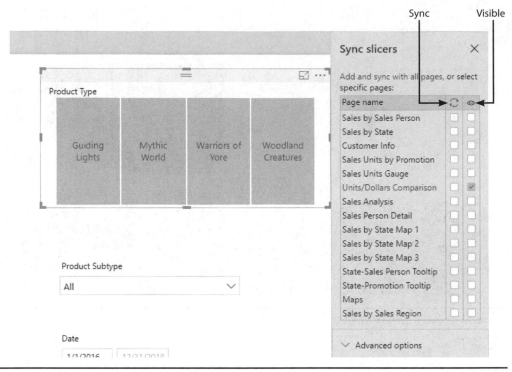

Figure 8-4 *The "Sync slicers" pane with no synchronization*

6. Select Guiding Lights in the Product Type slicer. The Product Type slicer and the "Sync slicers" pane appear, as shown in Figure 8-5.

7. Select the Sales by State Map 1 tab. Figure 8-6 shows the map data without the effect of the slicer on the left and the map data with the slicer in effect on the right.

Using this approach, you can create slicers on a main report page (or perhaps a dedicated slicer report page) and then have those slicers filter data on multiple pages throughout the report without requiring layout space for the slicers on the subsequent pages. In this situation, the report user must have a clear understanding that data is being filtered even though the slicer is not visible.

Synchronizing Slicers – Slicer Is Visible on Second Report Page

Now, let's turn on visibility so the slicer is synchronized and visible on both pages.

1. Select the Units/Dollars Comparison tab.

2. Select the Product Type slicer.

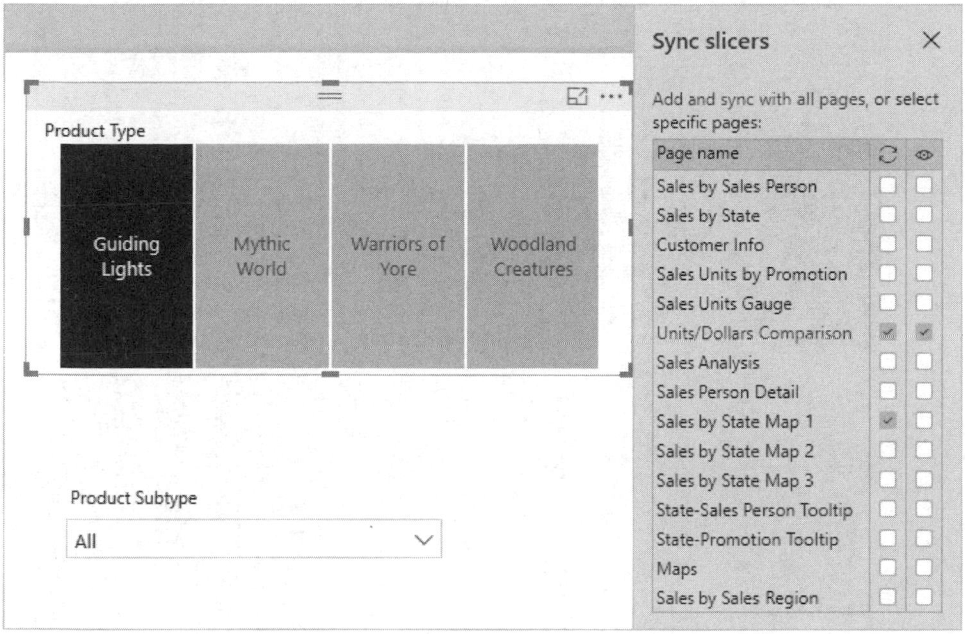

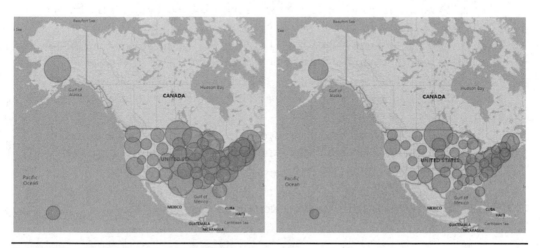

Figure 8-5   *A synchronized slicer with no visibility on the second page*

Figure 8-6   *Nonsliced data on the left and sliced data on the right.*

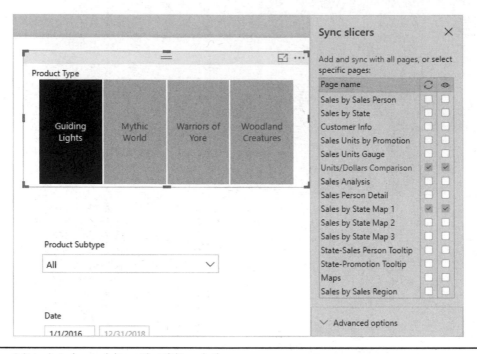

Figure 8-7 *A synchronized slicer with visibility on both pages*

3. In the "Sync slicers" pane, check the box in the Visible column for the Sales by State Map 1 page, as shown in Figure 8-7.
4. Select the Sales by State Map 1 tab. The Product Type slicer is now visible on this page. It is positioned on top of the map visualization.
5. Click the map visualization to select it. The map now comes to the top and hides the slicer. This allows the user to view and interact with any data elements that may have been covered by the slicer.
6. Click the report page background above or below the map visualization. This will unselect the map visualization. The Product Type slicer is visible once more.
7. In the Product Type slicer, select Warriors of Yore.
8. Select the Units/Dollars Comparison tab. The slicer on this report page also has Warriors of Yore selected. The two slicers are in sync.

Synchronizing Slicers Using Copy and Paste

You can also synchronize slicers by copying a slicer on one report page and pasting it on to another page.

1. Select the Product Type slicer.
2. Press CTRL-C to copy the slicer.

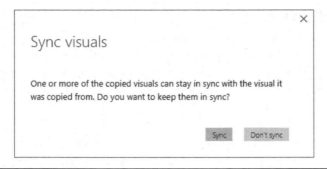

Figure 8-8   *The "Sync visuals" dialog box*

3. Select the Sales by State Map 2 tab.

4. Press CTRL-v to paste the slicer on this page.

5. You will see the "Sync visuals" dialog box, as shown in Figure 8-8.

6. Click Sync to synchronize the newly pasted slicer with the slicer it was copied from. Note that all three slicers are marked as synchronized in the "Sync slicers" pane, as shown in Figure 8-9.

7. Click Mythic World in the Product Type slicer.

8. Select the Sales by State Map 1 tab. Note the Product Type slicer has Mythic World selected.

9. Click the Units/Dollars Comparison tab. Mythic World is also selected here.

Figure 8-9   *The pasted copy of the slicer is synchronized.*

Synchronization Groups

In some cases, we may want to synchronize slicers using the same data field on some report pages, but not on all of them. We achieve this functionality using synchronization groups. In this example, we synchronize the Product Type slicers on the two map pages and allow the Product Type slicer on the Units/Dollars Comparison page to function independently.

1. On the Units/Dollars Comparison report page, select the Product Type slicer.
2. Expand the "Advanced options" area at the bottom of the "Sync slicers" pane.
3. In the group name area, enter **Product Type Non-Map**. Note that this slicer is no longer synchronized to the other Product Type slicers on the other pages, as shown in Figure 8-10.

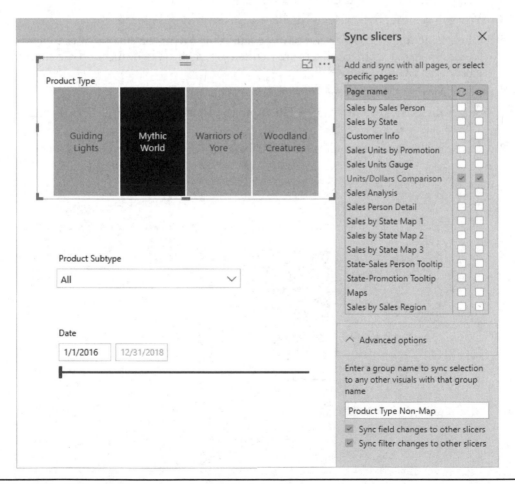

Figure 8-10 *Naming a synchronization group using Advanced options*

4. Select Guiding Lights in the Product Type slicer.
5. Select the Sales by State Map 1 tab. Note that Mythic World is still selected in the Product Type slicer on this page.
6. Select the Product Type slicer. The "Sync slicers" pane shows this slicer is still synchronized with the Product Type slicer on the Sale by State Map 2 report page with a group name of "Product Type."
7. Close the "Sync slicers" pane.
8. Click Save.

Creating Interactivity

In the previous section, you learned how to control existing interactivity in a Power BI report. In this section, you learn how to create additional interactivity. The most powerful way to create interactivity is through the combination of the Bookmarks pane, the Selection pane, and buttons. Before we work with that potent combination, however, you learn how to create a custom tooltip.

Custom Tooltips

Power BI creates a tooltip for every visualization element showing the number or numbers being represented. This tooltip is a great way to make the actual numbers easily available to the user without having to turn on data labels on every chart and graph. There may be times, however, that we would like this tooltip to convey different information to the user when they hover over an item.

Fortunately, Power BI provides a mechanism for doing just that. We can create custom tooltips. This is a two-step process very similar to the steps used to create a drillthrough page. First, we create a specially formatted report page displaying the desired tooltip content. Second, we associate this page with a specific filtering data item.

Let's give it a try. Here we create a tooltip that shows the sales in dollars for each sales person when you hover over a state.

Formatting a Tooltip Report Page

1. Click the yellow tab containing the plus sign to add a new report page.
2. Right-click the new page and select Rename Page from the context menu.
3. Type **State-Sales Person Tooltip** and press ENTER.
4. In the Visualizations pane, select the Format tab.
5. Expand the "Page information" section.

6. Change the Tooltip slider switch to On in order to identify this page as a tooltip page.
7. Expand the "Page size" section.
8. In the Type dropdown list, select Tooltip. The Format tab will appear, as shown in Figure 8-11.
9. In the Visualizations pane, select the Fields tab.
10. In the Fields pane, select State from the Customer table and drop it on Tooltip | "Drag tooltip fields here." See Figure 8-12.

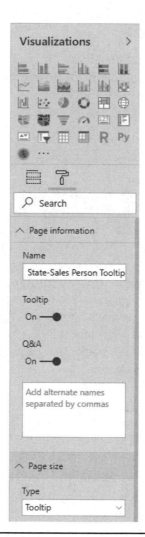

Figure 8-11 *Formatting for a tooltip report page*

Figure 8-12 *Setting the tooltip filter*

Creating Tooltip Page Content

1. In the View tab of the ribbon, select "Actual Size" from the Page View dropdown. The report page becomes the appropriate size for a tooltip.
2. In the Fields pane, click the check box next to "Sales in Dollars" in the Orders table.
3. Click the check box next to "Sales Person" in the Sales Person table.
4. In the Visualizations area, select treemap.
5. Use the sizing handles of the treemap to expand this visualization so it covers the entire report page.
6. In the Visualizations pane, select the Format tab.

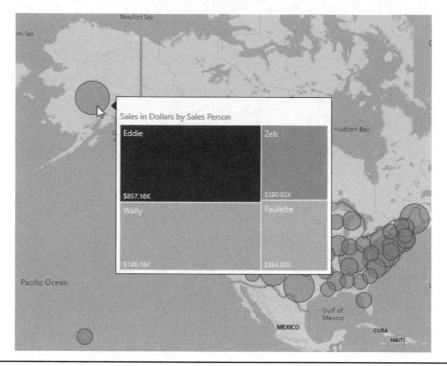

Figure 8-13   *A custom tooltip*

7. Change the "Data labels" slider switch to On.
8. Select the Sales by State Map 1 tab.
9. Hover over any of the state bubbles on the map. The new custom tooltip is displayed automatically because you are hovering over a visualization for a particular state and the tooltip filter is set to State. See Figure 8-13.

Tooltips with the Same Filter

1. Click the yellow tab containing the plus sign to add a new report page.
2. Right-click the new page and select Rename Page from the context menu.
3. Type **State-Promotion Tooltip** and press ENTER.
4. In the Visualizations pane, select the Format tab.
5. Expand the "Page information" section.
6. Change the Tooltip slider switch to On in order to identify this page as a tooltip page.

7. Expand the "Page size" section.

8. In the Type dropdown list, select Tooltip.

9. In the Visualizations pane, select the Fields tab.

10. In the Fields pane, select State from the Customer table and drop it on Tooltip | "Drag tooltip fields here."

11. In the View tab of the ribbon, select "Actual Size" from the Page View dropdown. The report page becomes the appropriate size for a tooltip.

12. In the Fields pane, click the check box next to "Sales in Dollars" in the Orders table.

13. Click the check box next to Promotion in the Promotion table.

14. In the Visualizations area, select Donut chart.

15. Use the sizing handles of the donut chart to expand this visualization so it covers the entire report page.

16. In the Visualizations pane, select the Format tab.

17. Select the Sales by State Map 1 tab.

18. Hover over any of the state bubbles on the map. The custom tooltip with the promotion donut chart is displayed. If there is more than one tooltip filtering on the same field, Power BI selects the most recent custom tooltip created. However, we can override that behavior.

19. Click the map visualization so it is selected.

20. In the Visualizations pane, select the Format tab.

21. Expand the Tooltip area.

22. In the Page dropdown list, select "State-Sales Person Tooltip." This is the name of the first tooltip we created.

23. Hover over any of the state bubbles on the map. Now, the custom tooltip with the sales person treemap is displayed.

24. Select the Sales by State Map 2 tab.

25. Click the filled map visualization so it is selected.

26. In the Visualizations pane, select the Format tab.

27. Expand the Tooltip area.

28. In the Page dropdown list, select "State-Promotion Tooltip." This is the name of the second tooltip we created.

29. Hover over any of the shaded states on the map. Now, the custom tooltip with the promotion donut chart is displayed.

30. Click Save.

Bookmarks

Bookmarks enable you to save the current state of a report page and give it a name. You (or your report user) can then use that bookmark to easily return to that state at a later time. This can be used to quickly view data for a popular combination over time without having to constantly reselect those slicer elements. Bookmarks can also be used to create a set of "points of interest" you want to show as you are presenting using live data.

In this exercise, we will create a series of bookmarks that allow us to quickly show various selections of data on the Units/Dollars Comparison and Sales By State Map 1 report pages.

Creating Bookmarks

1. Select the Units/Dollars Comparison tab.
2. In the Product Type slicer, select Guiding Lights.
3. In the Product Subtype slicer, select World Lighthouses.
4. In the "Sales in Units by Year" chart, drill down in Calendar Year 2018.
5. Drill down again in Quarter 3, 2018.
6. In the "Sales in Dollars by Year" chart, drill down in Calendar Year 2018.
7. Drill down again in Quarter 3, 2018. This is the state of the report page we would like to save for our first bookmark.
8. In the View tab of the ribbon, check the box for Bookmarks Pane.
9. At the top of the Bookmarks pane, click Add. A new bookmark called "Bookmark 1" is created.
10. Click the "More options" (…) button next to "Bookmark 1." The "More options" context menu appears, as shown in Figure 8-14.

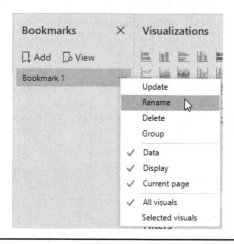

Figure 8-14   *The "More options" context menu*

Using the "More options" context menu, you can:

- Update an existing bookmark to save the current state of the report page.
- Rename a bookmark.
- Delete a bookmark.
- Group bookmarks.
- Determine what the bookmark includes in the saved state:
  - **Data**   The current slicer selections and drilldown levels
  - **Display**   Which items are visible and hidden (more on this in the next section)
  - **Current page**   Whether the user is brought back to this page
- Determine which items are affected by the bookmark:
  - **All visuals**   All items on the page
  - **Selected visuals**   Only those visuals that were selected when the bookmark was created/updated

11. Select Rename from the context menu.
12. Type **Wld LH Q3 18** and press ENTER.
13. Clear the Product Subtype slicer using the "Clear selections" button (the eraser icon).
14. In the Product Type slicer, select Warriors of Yore.
15. In the Product Subtype slicer, select Roman Legion.
16. In the Sales in Units chart, drill up to the year level and then drill down to the quarter level in Calendar 2017.
17. In the Sales in Dollars chart, drill up to the year level and then drill down to the quarter level in Calendar 2017.
18. In the Bookmarks pane, click Add.
19. Double-click "Bookmark 2" to rename it.
20. Type **Rmn Lgn 2017** and press ENTER. Your report page should appear as shown in Figure 8-15.
21. Select the Sales by State Map 1 tab.
22. In the Product Type slicer, select Warriors of Yore.
23. In the Bookmarks pane, click Add.
24. Double-click "Bookmark 3" to rename it.
25. Type **Warriors Map** and press ENTER.
26. Click each of the three bookmarks. You will return to the report page and state of that page when the bookmark was created.

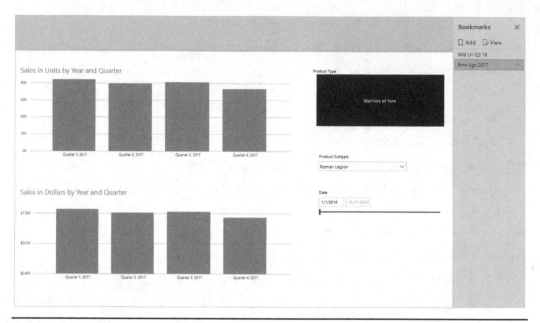

Figure 8-15   *The Bookmarks pane with two bookmarks*

Grouping Bookmarks and Presenting

1. In the Bookmarks pane, click "Wld LH Q3 18."
2. Hold down CTRL and select "Rmn Lgn 2017."
3. Hold down CTRL and select "Warriors Map." All three bookmarks are now selected.
4. Right-click "Warriors Map" and select Group from the context menu, as shown in Figure 8-16.
5. Double-click "Group 1" to rename it.
6. Type **Presentation A** and press ENTER.
7. Click View at the top of the Bookmarks pane. We are now in bookmark view mode. Note the bookmark bar at the bottom of the report page area.
8. Click the arrows at the right end of the bookmark bar to move between the three bookmarks in this group. You have a readymade presentation using live data.
9. Click the "X" at the right end of the bookmark bar to exit bookmark view mode.
10. Click Save.

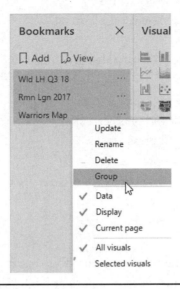

Figure 8-16   *Creating a bookmark group*

Selection Pane

The Selection pane serves three functions:

- Determine the layer order of items on the report page. In other words, determine which visualization, button, and so on is on top of the other if they overlap.

- Determine the tab order of items on the report when using TAB to move from one selected item to another.

- Determine whether each item is visible or hidden.

We are going to use the last capability (visibility) along with bookmarks to create a dynamic report page layout.

Creating a Report Page with Overlapping Visualizations

1. Select the Sales by State Map 1 tab.
2. Click the map to select it.
3. Press CTRL-C to copy the map.
4. Click the yellow tab containing the plus sign to add a new report page.
5. Right-click the new page and select Rename Page from the context menu.
6. Type **Maps** and press ENTER.
7. Click in the report area and press CTRL-V to paste the map onto the new report page.

8. In the Visualizations pane, select the Format tab.
9. Expand the Title area.
10. Change the Title text to **Map of Sales in Dollars** and press ENTER.
11. Expand the General area.
12. For X Position, type **0** and press ENTER.
13. For Y Position, type **100** and press ENTER.
14. For Width, type **1280** and press ENTER.
15. For Height, type **620** and press ENTER.
16. Select the Sales by State Map 2 tab.
17. Click the filled map to select it.
18. Press CTRL-C to copy the filled map.
19. Select the Maps tab.
20. Press CTRL-V to paste the filled map onto this report page.
21. In the Visualizations pane, select the Format tab.
22. Expand the Title area.
23. Change the Title text to **Filled Map of Sales in Dollars** and press ENTER.
24. Expand the General area.
25. For X Position, type **0** and press ENTER.
26. For Y Position, type **100** and press ENTER.
27. For Width, type **1280** and press ENTER.
28. For Height, type **620** and press ENTER.
29. Select the Sales by State Map 3 tab.
30. Click the shape map to select it.
31. Press CTRL-C to copy the shape map.
32. Select the Maps tab.
33. Press CTRL-V to paste the shape map onto this report page.
34. In the Visualizations pane, select the Format tab.
35. Expand the Title area.
36. Change the Title text to **Shape Map of Sales in Dollars** and press ENTER.
37. Expand the General area.
38. For X Position, type **0** and press ENTER.
39. For Y Position, type **100** and press ENTER.
40. For Width, type **1280** and press ENTER.
41. For Height, type **620** and press ENTER.
42. Select the Sales by State Map 2 tab.
43. Click the Product Type slicer to select it.

44. Press CTRL-C to copy the slicer.

45. Select the Maps tab.

46. Press CTRL-V to paste the slicer onto this report page.

47. In the "Sync visuals" dialog box, click "Don't sync."

48. Move the slicer so it is up against the top of the report page.

Using Visibility and Bookmarks

1. If the Bookmarks pane is not visible, check the box for Bookmarks Pane in the View tab of the ribbon.

2. In the View tab of the ribbon, check the box for Selection Pane.

3. In the Selection pane, click the "Hide this visual" icon next to "Shape Map of Sales in Dollars." The shape map will no longer be visible.

4. In the Selection pane, click the "Hide this visual" icon next to "Filled Map of Sales in Dollars." The filled map will no longer be visible.

5. In the Bookmarks pane, click Add.

6. Double-click the new bookmark to rename it.

7. Type **Map Visible** and press ENTER.

8. Click the "More options" (…) icon next to the Map Visible bookmark.

9. In the context menu, uncheck Data. In this configuration, the bookmark will remember the visibility setting of each item on the current page but will not remember the slicer setting. Your report should appear similar to Figure 8-17.

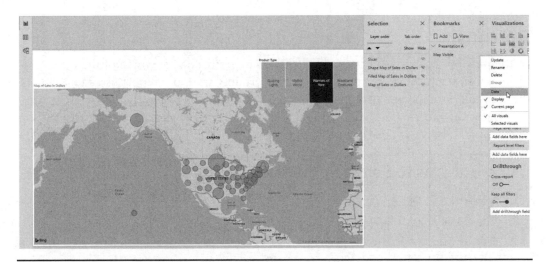

Figure 8-17   *Using bookmarks and visibility to layer visualizations*

10. In the Selection pane, click the "Hide this visual" icon next to "Map of Sales in Dollars." The map will no longer be visible.

11. In the Selection pane, click the "Hide this visual" icon next to "Filled Map of Sales in Dollars" to toggle it from hidden to visible. The filled map is now visible.

12. In the Bookmarks pane, click Add.

13. Double-click the new bookmark to rename it.

14. Type **Filled Map Visible** and press ENTER.

15. Click the "More options" (…) icon next to the Filled Map Visible bookmark.

16. In the context menu, uncheck Data.

17. In the Selection pane, click the "Hide this visual" icon next to "Filled Map of Sales in Dollars." The map will no longer be visible.

18. In the Selection pane, click the "Hide this visual" icon next to "Shape Map of Sales in Dollars" to toggle it from hidden to visible. The shape map is now visible.

19. In the Bookmarks pane, click Add.

20. Double-click the new bookmark to rename it.

21. Type **Shape Map Visible** and press ENTER.

22. Click the "More options" (…) icon next to the Shape Map Visible bookmark.

23. In the context menu, uncheck Data.

24. Click on each of three new bookmarks in the Bookmarks pane. Note how a different map becomes visible with each one.

25. Select a different product type in the Product Type slicer and then try the new bookmarks again. Note the bookmarks do not affect the slicer value.

26. Click Save.

Buttons

In the previous section, you created bookmarks to easily change which of the three maps is visible on the report page. You could certainly train the report users to open the Bookmarks pane and use these bookmarks to change between the maps. However, that is not the most natural or convenient user interface. Instead, we can link these bookmarks to buttons right on our report page.

Using Buttons to Select Bookmarks

1. Close the Selection pane.

2. Close the Bookmarks pane.

3. Ensure you are on the Maps tab (Maps report page). In the Home tab of the ribbon, click the Buttons dropdown.

4. Click Blank in the dropdown list, as shown in Figure 8-18.

Figure 8-18 *Adding a button to the report page*

5. In the Visualizations pane, change the Button Text slider switch to On.
6. Expand the Button Text area.
7. For Button Text, type **Bubble Map** and press ENTER.
8. Change the Fill slider switch to On.
9. Expand the Fill area.
10. In the dropdown list at the top of the Fill area, select "On hover."
11. Select a light green from the Fill color dropdown. The button will be light green when the user hovers the mouse over it.
12. In the dropdown list at the top of the Fill area, select "On press."
13. Select a darker green from the Fill color dropdown. The button will be darker green when it is being clicked.
14. Expand the General area.
15. Change X Position to **200**.
16. Change the Action slider switch to On.
17. Expand the Action area.
18. In the Type dropdown list, select bookmark.
19. In the Bookmark dropdown list, select "Map Visible."
20. In the Home tab of the ribbon, click the Buttons dropdown.
21. Click Blank in the dropdown list.
22. In the Visualizations pane, change the Button Text slider switch to On.
23. Expand the Button Text area.
24. For Button Text, type **Filled Map** and press ENTER.

25. Change the Fill slider switch to On.
26. Expand the Fill area.
27. In the dropdown list at the top of the Fill area, select "On hover."
28. Select a light green from the Fill color dropdown.
29. In the dropdown list at the top of the Fill area, select "On press."
30. Select a darker green from the Fill color dropdown.
31. Expand the General area.
32. Change X Position to **400**.
33. Change the Action slider switch to On.
34. Expand the Action area.
35. In the Type dropdown list, select bookmark.
36. In the Bookmark dropdown list, select "Filled Map Visible."
37. On the Home tab of the ribbon, click the Buttons dropdown.
38. Click Blank in the dropdown list.
39. In the Visualizations pane, change the Button Text slider switch to On.
40. Expand the Button Text area.
41. For Button Text, type **Shape Map** and press ENTER.
42. Change the Fill slider switch to On.
43. Expand the Fill area.
44. In the dropdown list at the top of the Fill area, select "On hover."
45. Select a light green from the Fill color dropdown.
46. In the dropdown list at the top of the Fill area, select "On press."
47. Select a darker green from the Fill color dropdown.
48. Expand the General area.
49. Change X Position to **600**.
50. Change the Action slider switch to On.
51. Expand the Action area.
52. In the Type dropdown list, select bookmark.
53. In the Bookmark dropdown list, select "Shape Map Visible." Your report page should appear similar to Figure 8-19.
54. Press CTRL and click the Bubble Map button. This activates the Map Visible bookmark, and the map visualization is displayed. (Remember, you need to press CTRL when you click a button in Power BI Desktop. Clicking the button without pressing CTRL will simply select the button. Users will not need to CTRL-click in the deployed environments.)

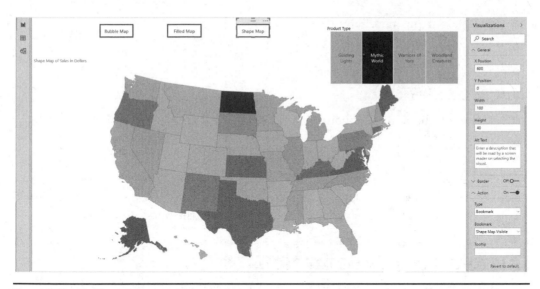

Figure 8-19   *The Maps report page with buttons*

55. Press CTRL and click the Filled Map button. This activates the Filled Map Visible bookmark, and the filled map visualization is displayed.

56. Click Save.

Button Actions and Icons

Buttons can perform several different types of actions when clicked, as follows:

- **Back**   Navigates to the previously active report page
- **Bookmark**   Activates a bookmark
- **Q&A**   Activates the Q&A natural language query feature
- **Web URL**   Opens the default browser and navigates to the specified web address

In addition to putting text on a blank button as you did in the previous exercise, you can also combine text with an icon. The following icon options are available:

- Left Arrow
- Right Arrow
- Reset (U-turn arrow)

- Back (left arrow in a circle)
- Information (lowercase I in a circle)
- Help (question mark in a circle)
- Q&A (cartoon balloon)
- Bookmark (bookmark ribbon)
- Blank (no icon)

For several of the button's property areas, you can set properties separately for the default state, the hover-over state, and the pressed state. This enables you to give feedback to the user when the mouse hovers over a button or when the button is clicked.

Customizing Visualizations

In addition to the visualizations included by default at the top of the Visualizations pane, Power BI offers several ways to add new visualizations to the environment. You can obtain visualizations others have created and made available in the Marketplace. You can also create your own custom visualizations using the R language or the Python language. You can also customize the appearance of the Shape Map visualization by providing your own custom shape files.

Custom Visualizations from the Marketplace

A number of companies have created custom visualizations that can be added into your Power BI environment. These custom visualizations can be downloaded from the Marketplace. Many of these custom visualizations are available free of charge; however, some may require a purchase or licensing fee.

To view the list of custom visualizations, click the "Import a custom visual" button (…) in the Visualizations area. Select "Import from marketplace," as shown in Figure 8-20. You will need a Microsoft Power BI login in order to access and download from the Marketplace. If you are not yet signed in to PowerBI.com, you will be prompted to do so.

Once you're signed in, the list of custom Power BI visualizations available in the Marketplace will be displayed in a dialog box. This is shown in Figure 8-21. To include a custom visualization in your report, click Add. To remove a custom visualization from your report, click the "Import a custom visual" button and select "Delete a custom visual" from the context menu. If you have downloaded a custom visualization definition in a file, you can import that custom visualization into your report using the "Import from file" option on the "Import a custom visual" context menu.

Figure 8-20 *The "Import a custom visual" button*

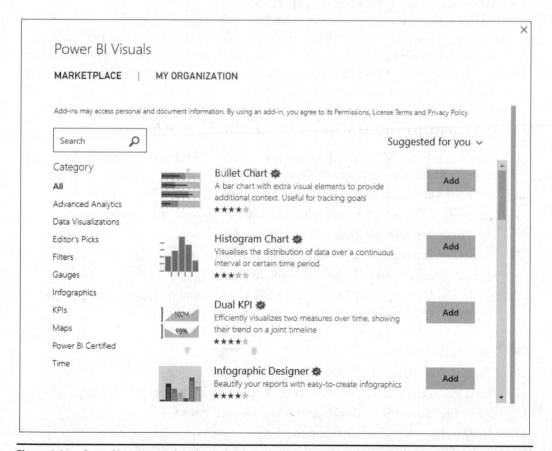

Figure 8-21 *Power BI custom visuals in the Marketplace*

Custom Visualizations from R and Python

The R statistical analytics and graphics language and the Python programming language can both be used to create custom visualizations in Power BI. The "R" and "Py" buttons in the Visualizations area along with the "R script" and "Python script" create containers for R script or Python script to produce a data set and generate visualizations. Creating custom visualizations with R or Python are beyond the scope of this book.

Creating a Custom Shape Map

In Chapter 6, you used the Shape Map visualization and saw the maps available by default for this visualization. One of the most exciting things about this visualization is it uses a standard known as TopoJSON. You can load a custom TopoJSON file into the Shape Map visualization for additional visualizations.

In the following exercise, we use the "Max Min Sales Regions.json" TopoJSON file to create a map of sales by territory. This file is available in the supporting materials for this book. My apologies in advance to those living in Alaska and Hawaii. For simplicity, I did not include those states in my crude Max Min Sales Regions map. No offense was meant to the residents of those beautiful U.S. states!

Using a Custom TopoJSON File with the Shape Map

1. Locate the "Max Min Sales Regions.json" file in the supporting materials download and copy it to a location in your file system.
2. Click the yellow tab containing the plus sign to add a new report page.
3. Right-click the new page and select Rename Page from the context menu.
4. Type **Sales by Sales Region** and press ENTER.
5. In the Fields pane, check "Sales in Dollars" in the Orders table.
6. In the Visualizations pane, select Shape map.
7. In the Fields pane, select "Sales Region" in the Customer table and drop it on Location | "Add data fields here."
8. In the Visualizations pane, select the Format tab.
9. Expand the Shape area.
10. Click "+ Add Map." The Open dialog box appears.
11. Navigate to the location where you saved the "Max Min Sales Regions.json" file.
12. Select the "Max Min Sales Regions.json" file and click Open.
13. Use the sizing handles to expand the shape map so it covers the entire report page.
14. Expand the Data colors area.
15. In the Minimum color dropdown, select the lightest green.

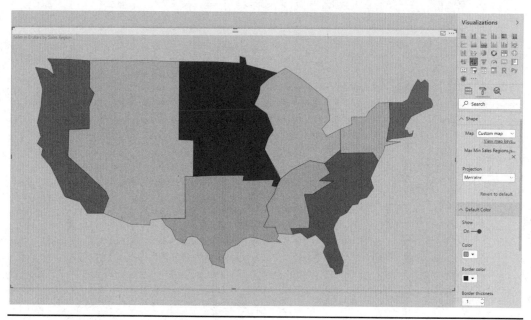

Figure 8-22   *The shape map with a custom map file*

16. In the Maximum color dropdown, select the darkest green.
17. Expand the Default Color area.
18. In the Border color dropdown, select black.
19. Change the Background slider switch to On.
20. Expand the Background area.
21. In the Color dropdown, select a light blue. The report page should appear similar to Figure 8-22.
22. Click Save.

Moving on to Modeling

This brings us to the end of Part III on creating visualizations. You have had a chance to use Power BI's features for visualizing data and creating interactivity surrounding those visualizations—at least all of Power BI's features at the time of the writing of this book. Remember, you can go to

www.teamscs.com/powerbi

for information on the latest features added to Power BI.

We now move from using an existing data model for creating visualizations to learning to create our own data models. It's time to become model citizens!

Part IV

Building Data Models

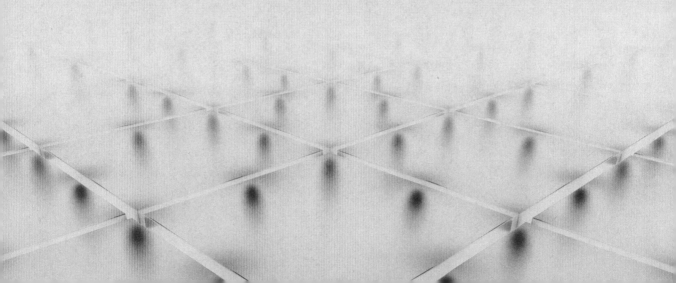

Chapter 9

Loading Data
with Power BI

In This Chapter

- Gathering Data
- Transforming Data During the Data Import
- Repeating and Changing the Data Import

- Relationships and Intermediate Tables
- Parameters

Up to this point, this book has concentrated on creating and interacting with visualizations from an existing data model. However, those of you interested in Part IV and Part V of this book will probably approach Power BI development from a different direction. You may spend a significant amount of your "Power BI time" gathering and modeling data in a PBIX file before you create your first visualization on a report page.

The approach in this book is based on the belief that it is much easier to grasp the more abstract concepts of data modeling if you already have familiarity with the more concrete concepts that a data model facilitates—namely, data visualization and exploration. So, now that you understand how tables and measures are used when creating visualizations and exploring data, let's circle back and see how the data models themselves are created.

Gathering Data

We begin the data model creation process by gathering data. This data may come from on premises line-of-business systems, from cloud-based software-as-a-service applications, or even from export files and manually maintained Excel spreadsheets. Wherever the source data resides, there is almost certainly a way for Power BI to get ahold of it and pull it into a data model.

The process of gathering data and building data models will be done using Power BI Desktop. Rather than opening existing PBIX files that already contain a data model, now we will open Power BI Desktop and start from scratch. Whether we start Power BI Desktop by clicking the icon or from the Start menu, the first thing we see is the Start dialog box. This is shown in Figure 9-1.

The right side of the dialog box includes links to Power BI–related forums, blog sites, and tutorials along with announcements of upcoming events. The center section gives you access to Power BI how-to videos. The lower section of the left side of the dialog box provides access to the most recently opened files as well as the Open dialog box to open any existing PBIX file.

Get Data

The remaining two buttons on the left side of the dialog box allow us to begin a new Power BI report by getting new data for a new data model. We use the "Recent sources" button to gather new data from a data source we have connected to in the past. The "Get data" button enables us to make a brand-new data connection.

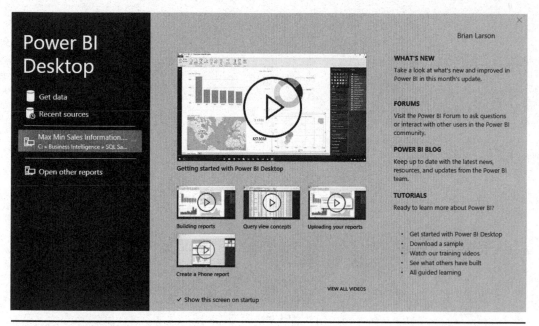

Figure 9-1   *The Power BI Desktop Start dialog box*

While the Start dialog box makes it easy to begin the data-gathering process, we are not required to come to this dialog box every time we want to add data to a model. There are also Get Data and Recent Sources buttons on the Home tab of the Power BI Desktop ribbon. Both the "Get data" button on the Start dialog box and the Get Data button on the ribbon take us to the same starting place—the Get Data dialog box, shown in Figure 9-2.

Data Sources

As you can see from Figure 9-2, Power BI can pull data from a wealth of sources. In fact, new data sources are being added each month. As you scroll down the list of supported sources, you will probably see a few marked as "(Beta)." These data sources are so new they haven't gone through the entire testing process yet. You are welcome to try them out and help Microsoft make sure they are ready for production use.

Because the list of supported data sources is ever changing, I won't try to explain every data source here. The truth is, if you don't know what a particular data source is for, you probably don't need it. Conversely, if you recognize the name of a given data source because you've heard it talked about around your organization, it is probably something you will need to use.

Figure 9-2 *The Get Data dialog box*

Power BI data sources fall into several categories. The lists in each category are not all-inclusive. The list of Power BI data sources is shown in Table 9-1.

Power BI Connection Types

In Chapter 1, you learned about the three different connection types in Power BI: Import, Live Connection, and Direct Query. They are shown in Figure 9-3. Let's review the characteristics of these connection types.

Import

When we use the Import method to access the data for a model, that data is loaded and stored within the Power BI PBIX file at the time the model is created. The original source for that data is not accessed again until we choose to update the data contained in the model. This allows Power BI to keep the model data in memory when it is being queried so we get great data exploration performance.

Data Source Category	Examples
Databases	Most popular database systems are covered. Examples include: ● SQL Server Relational Databases ● SQL Server Analysis Services Databases ● Oracle ● MySQL ● IBM DB2 ● Teradata
Files	Many different types of files can be used as data sources. Some examples include: ● Excel ● CSV ● XML ● JSON ● Text
Azure	If your data is stored on Microsoft Azure, the odds are good you will be able to load that data into a Power BI model. Some examples: ● Azure SQL Database ● Azure SQL Data Warehouse ● Azure Analysis Services ● Azure HDInsight (HDFS) ● Azure HDInsight Spark ● Azure Blob Storage ● Azure Data Lake Storage
Power BI	Data published to or gathered in PowerBI.com can be used to create other data sets: ● Power BI Datasets ● Power BI Dataflows
Online Services	Extract data from cloud-based services for your own analysis. Examples include: ● Microsoft Exchange Online ● Dynamics 365 (online) ● Dynamics NAV ● Facebook ● Salesforce Objects ● Salesforce Reports ● GitHub ● MailChimp ● QuickBooks Online
Standard Drivers	Power BI provides support for several data access standards. Some examples include: ● OData Feed ● ODBC

Table 9-1   *Types of Power BI Data Sources*

Data Source Category	Examples
File Systems	You can use a file system as a data source with information about the files it contains as the data. Here are some examples: ● Folder *(Windows File System)* ● Hadoop File System (HDFS)
Websites	Scrape web page content for information or analyze website usage statistics. Examples include: ● Web ● Google Analytics ● Webtrends
SharePoint	Load data from SharePoint both on premises and in the cloud. Here are some examples: ● SharePoint List ● SharePoint Folder ● SharePoint Online List
Other	Popular data sources that don't fit into any of the preceding categories: ● Microsoft Exchange ● Microsoft Exchange Online ● Active Directory ● R Script ● Python Script

Table 9-1   *Types of Power BI Data Sources (Continued)*

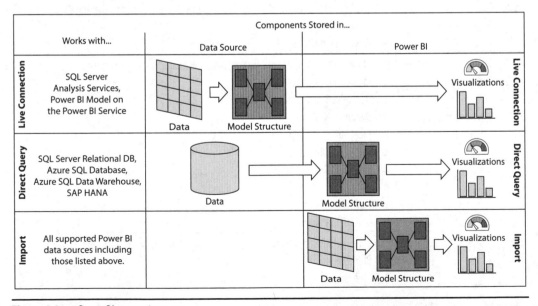

Figure 9-3   *Power BI connection types*

Once we have the data loaded into the Power BI model, additional structure can be added—things like relationships between tables and the ability to quickly aggregate quantities across a number of records. These additions, which make up the structure of the data model, are created in and stored as part of the Power BI model itself. We will see this in Chapters 11 through 14.

To summarize, when you use Import mode, the data and the model structure are both stored within the Power BI file. This is represented by the bottom row in Figure 9-3. The big advantage of Import mode is the speed gained from use of the in-memory model versus the query performance of whatever might be providing the underlying data. In the remainder of this chapter, we will also discover features that allow us to manipulate the data as it is imported into the Power BI file. The major disadvantage of Import mode is the data is refreshed from the data source on a periodic basis—at most eight times per day. That means the data can be out of date. Also, there is some model downtime required each time the data is being reloaded.

Live Connection

The Live Connection mode only works with Tabular and Multidimensional data models. These models may be stored in SQL Server Analysis Services, in Azure Analysis Services, or in a Power BI dataset. With Live Connection, we don't load any data into our Power BI model. Instead, Power BI queries the Tabular model whenever it needs data. Figure 9-4 shows an example using the Live Connection mode to connect to a SQL Server Analysis Services data source. The "Connect live" option selects the Live Connection mode.

When using Live Connection, we do not create any model structure within Power BI. Any definition as to how we aggregate values or what tables are related to each other, and so on, comes from the underlying Tabular or Multidimensional model. It is all prepared for us ahead of time by some nice model developer.

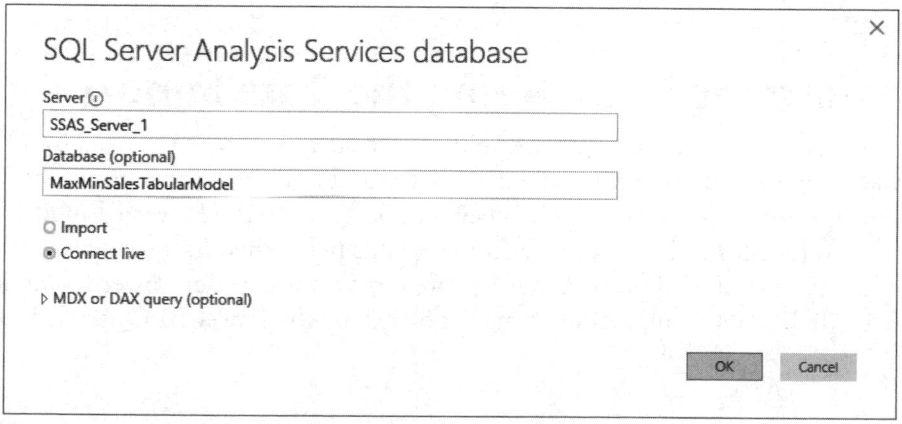

Figure 9-4   *Using Live Connection to get data from SQL Server Analysis Services*

10. Click OK. Only the selected columns remain.

11. We need to replace the ".." entries in the table with a null value. Click the 1960 column heading.

12. Hold down SHIFT and click the 2010 column heading to select all of the columns from 1960 to 2010.

13. On the Home tab of the ribbon, click Replace Values. The Replace Values dialog box appears.

14. Enter .. for Value To Find. We want to leave Replace With blank.

15. Click OK.

16. On the Transform tab of the ribbon, select Unpivot Columns.

17. Click the Attribute column to select that column by itself.

18. Right-click the Attribute column and select Rename from the context menu.

19. Type **Year** and press ENTER.

20. Right-click the Value column and select Rename from the context menu.

21. Type **CO2 Level** and press ENTER.

22. Click the data type indicator in the GDP column. The data type dropdown list appears.

23. Click Whole Number.

24. On the Home tab of the ribbon, click Close & Apply. The data is pulled from the Excel file, the transformations are applied, and the result is loaded into the data model.

25. Click Save.

Repeating and Changing the Data Import

As we configure transformations and see them applied in real time in the Query Editor, it seems like we are performing a one-time data manipulation to load data into our model. Fortunately, this is not the case. What we are really doing is generating a script of data manipulations that can be repeated and modified. We can repeat the data transformation process each time we need to bring updated data into the model. We can modify the transformation process if we discover an error or if the source data should change.

Refreshing Data in Power BI Desktop

We can manually update the data in our data model in Power BI Desktop anytime we need to. Once the data model is deployed to PowerBI.com, we can schedule this refresh to occur on a regular basis. More on that in Chapter 15.

Even though our source files haven't changed, let's do a manual refresh of the data in our model to see how it works.

Manually Refreshing Data in the Population-GDP-CO2 by Country from Scratch Model

In the Home tab of the ribbon, click Refresh. The Refresh dialog box appears, as shown in Figure 9-12.

That's all there is to it. This may take a minute or two to complete, depending on the size of your data model and the responsiveness of the data sources. Fortunately, the Refresh dialog box gives us feedback on the status of the refresh process and disappears once the refresh is complete.

Remember, when we refresh the data, Power BI Desktop is not only getting a fresh copy of the data from the source systems, but it is also reapplying all the transformations we created for each table. The data goes through the same cleansing process as before. The fresh data ends up in the data model in the same format we created during its original import.

It is also possible to refresh the data in a single table rather than reloading the whole model. Let's give this a try.

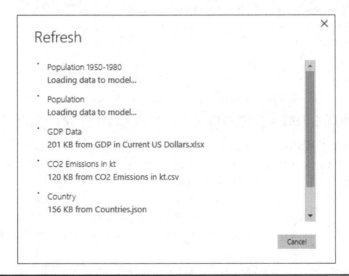

Figure 9-12   *Refreshing all data in a data model*

Manually Refreshing Data in a Single Table in the Data Model

1. In the Fields pane, right-click the Population table.
2. Select "Refresh data" from the context menu. The Refresh dialog box will appear briefly while the data in this table is reloaded.

Modifying Queries

To modify a query, we reopen the Query Editor. Once the Query Editor is open, we can move among the queries created for each of the tables in the data model. We can make modifications to one or more of these queries, as necessary, and then apply all of those changes at the same time. It is also possible to change the connection information used for queries.

Let's look at both of the steps to examine and change connection information and the steps to modify queries.

Editing Connection Information

1. On the Home tab of the ribbon, click the Edit Queries dropdown, as shown in Figure 9-13.
2. Select "Data source settings" from the dropdown list. The "Data source settings" dialog box appears.

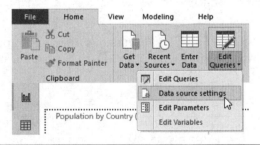

Figure 9-13 *Using the Edit Queries dropdown*

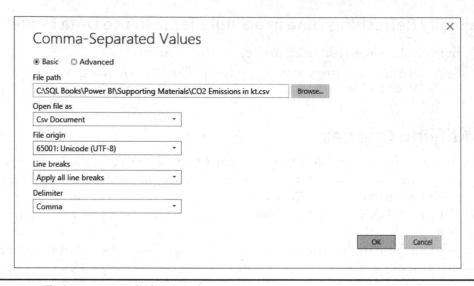

Figure 9-14 *The Comma-Separated Values dialog box*

3. Make sure the entry for "CO2 Emissions in kt.csv" is selected and click Change Source. The Comma-Separated Values dialog box appears, as shown in Figure 9-14. This dialog box enables you to change any of the parameters related to this comma-separated values file. The Advanced option button enables you to build the file path from multiple segments rather than entering it as one long string. More on this in the "Parameterizing Connections" exercise later in this chapter.

4. Click Cancel.

5. Click Edit Permissions. The Edit Permissions dialog box appears, as shown in Figure 9-15. More on permissions in the "Data Source Permissions" section of this chapter.

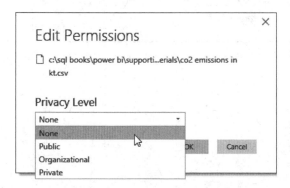

Figure 9-15 *The Edit Permissions dialog box*

6. Click Cancel.
7. Click Close.

Editing Queries

1. On the Home tab of the ribbon, click the Edit Queries dropdown.
2. Select "Edit Queries" from the dropdown list. The Query Editor appears.
3. The left side of the Query Editor shows all the tables in the model that use a query for their data load.
4. Click the Population table. The Query Editor appears just as it did when we completed the creation of its data transformation process. You can make changes to the transformations here as might be necessary.

NOTE
If the data has not been loaded from the source in the past day or two, you will receive a message asking if you want to refresh the data in the model. This is shown in Figure 9-16.

The Advanced Editor and the Power Query Formula Language

Previously in this chapter, you learned how easy it is to use the Query Editor to manipulate and cleanse the data as it is loaded into a Power BI data model. Chapter 10 provides a reference to the broad range of transformations available to us. The Query Editor is a good example of a well-designed user interface that makes a complex task simpler.

Queries [6]	◀	ⓘ This preview may be up to 6 days old.	Refresh	
▦ Population 1950-1980		✕ ✓ *fx*	= Table.Combine({#"Changed Type1", #"Population 1950-1980"})	
▦ **Population**		▦ ▾	A^B_C Country (or dependent territory) ▾	A^B_C Year ▾	1^2_3 Population ▾
▦ GDP Data		1	Afghanistan	1985	13120000
▦ CO2 Emissions in kt		2	Afghanistan	1990	13569000
▦ Year		3	Afghanistan	1995	19446000
▦ Country		4	Afghanistan	2000	22462000
		5	Afghanistan	2005	26335000
		6	Afghanistan	2010	29121000

Figure 9-16 *A data source query with old data*

However, as was mentioned earlier in this chapter, there is a text-based language lurking behind the scenes. The formal name of this language is the Query Formula Language. The informal name is "M," which comes from Mashup Query Language. That is, after all, what we are doing—creating data mashups.

When you are in the Query Editor, you can view the Query Formula Language by clicking Advanced Editor on the View tab of the ribbon. This displays the Advanced Editor dialog box, shown in Figure 9-17. There is one line in the text for each applied step in your query. The context is very straightforward. It isn't difficult to determine which text defines which step.

You can use the Advanced Editor to make a quick change to the data query process without having to work through the user interface. The Advanced Editor is most useful, however, when something has changed in a data source that breaks the query used to extract data from that data source. Using the Advanced Editor, you may be able to get the query back into a valid state rather than starting all over again.

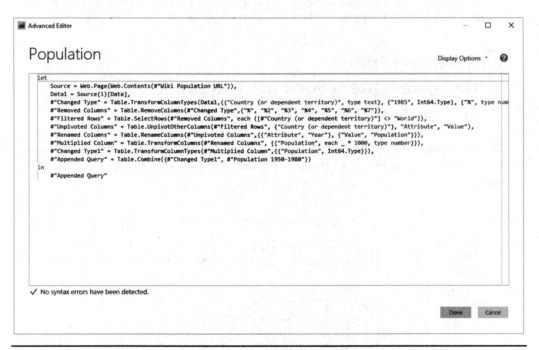

Figure 9-17 *The Advanced Editor with Query Formula Language*

Data Source Permissions

In the earlier exercises in this chapter, we saw how data can be combined into a single table. We did this by combining the 1950 to 1980 population data with the 1985 to 2010 population data into a single table. In this case, the data came from the same data source—the Wikipedia page. However, it is possible to combine data coming from two different data sources in a similar manner.

This can cause an issue if data of a sensitive nature is combined with data that does not need to be safeguarded. To prevent this, we can set the permission level of each data source. (Refer back to Figure 9-15.) Four permission levels are possible:

- None
- Public
- Organizational
- Private

When a permission level other than None is applied to a data source, Power BI can enforce rules governing combining data from this data source with data from other data sources. Those rules are as follows:

- Data from a Private data source may not be combined with data from any other data source.
- Data from an Organizational data source can only be combined with data from other Organizational data sources.
- Public data sources do not have any restrictions.

In addition to the Permissions settings on each data source, there is also an Options setting that determines whether the privacy level rules are enforced in the data model. To see this option, go to File | Options and settings | Options | Current File: Privacy. This is shown in Figure 9-18.

The privacy level rules are enforced by default. You can select the "Ignore the Privacy Levels and potentially improve performance" option to ignore the privacy level rules. This may improve data load speed, but in most cases the difference will be very slight.

Figure 9-18   *The Privacy Levels options*

Relationships and Intermediate Tables

In Chapter 11, we will begin defining the inner workings of our data models. One of the first things we will do is set relationships between the tables created as we gathered data. Looking at the tables in our Population-GDP-CO2 by Country model, there are two obvious relationships we need to have in place to do effective data exploration across multiple tables. We need relationships between the Country columns in the tables. We should be able to compare the population for a given country with the GDP or CO_2 emissions for that country. Likewise, we need relationships between the Year columns in the tables. We need to be able to compare the population in given years with the gross domestic product (GDP) or carbon dioxide (CO_2) emissions in those same years.

It is tempting to simply create connections between Country fields and the Year fields in the three tables. This would create a number of many-to-many relationships.

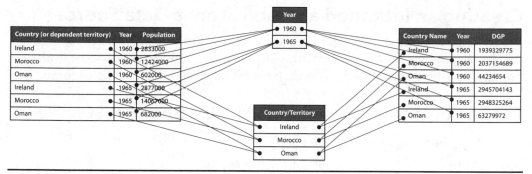

Figure 9-19 *Implementing many-to-many relationships with intermediate tables*

Many records in the Population table have the same value in the Country field as many records in the GDP Data table. Many records in the GDP Data table have the same value in the Year field as many records in the CO_2 Emissions in kt table, and so on.

Power BI will support this type of many-to-many relationship, but it makes for a somewhat confusing data exploration experience. The user would select a country from the Population table to filter the GDP Data table. The user would select a year from the CO_2 Emissions in kt table to filter the Population table, and so on.

A better way to link these tables is through intermediate tables. This Year intermediate table will have one record for each year. The Country intermediate table will have one record for each country. Once we have the intermediate tables built, we can create several one-to-many relationships, as shown in Figure 9-19.

To prevent confusion as users work with the data model, we will hide the Year and Country fields in the initial tables. Only the Year field in the Year intermediate table and the Country (or dependent territory) field in the Country table will be visible in the data model as users work with it to explore the data. When we select a year in the Year intermediate table, it will filter all the other tables for that year. When we select a country in the Country intermediate table, it will filter all the other tables for that country. This is shown in Figure 9-20.

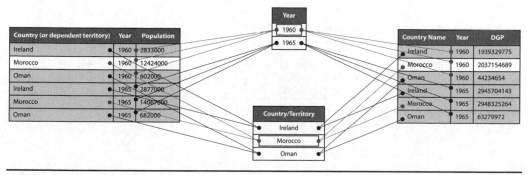

Figure 9-20 *Filtering through the intermediate tables*

Creating an Intermediate Table from a Data Source

We begin by creating the Country intermediate table. The "Countries.json" file contains the data needed for the Country intermediate table. We will need to do some work in our data transformation process to unpack the JSON structure into a usable format.

Loading the Countries Intermediate Table from the JSON File

1. Close the Query Editor, if it is open.
2. Click Get Data. The Get Data dialog box appears.
3. Select JSON and click Connect. The Open dialog box appears.
4. Navigate to the location where you saved the "Countries.json" file.
5. Select the "Countries.json" file and click Open. The Query Editor opens, showing a single column named "List" that says "Record" in each row. We need to unpack these JSON structures into table columns.
6. A new ribbon tab called "List Tools/Transform" is visible. On that new ribbon tab, click "To Table," as shown in Figure 9-21. The To Table dialog box appears.
7. Leave the defaults selected in the To Table dialog box and click OK. The column name changes to "Column1."
8. Click the icon to the right of the "Column1" heading, as shown in Figure 9-22.
9. In the pop-up dialog box, uncheck "Use original column name as prefix."
10. Click OK. The JSON items become columns.
11. On the right under Properties, replace the content of Name with **Country** and press ENTER.

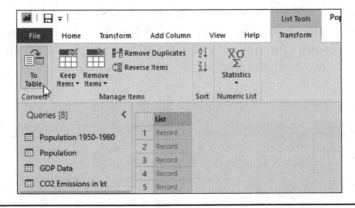

Figure 9-21 *Using the To Table button on the List Tools/Transform ribbon tab*

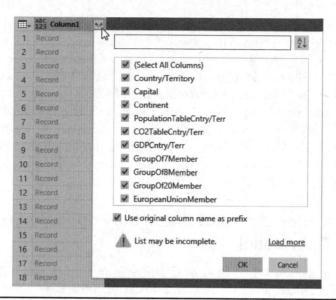

Figure 9-22 *Expanding the record into columns*

12. On the Home tab of the ribbon, click Close & Apply. The data is parsed from the JSON file and loaded into the data model.

13. Click Save.

Manually Creating Intermediate Tables

Up to this point, we have added data to our model by importing that data from external sources. This is by far the most common way to obtain data for data models that use the import method to gather data. (That is why it is called the import method.)

However, importing is not the only way to create a new table in our data model. We can also manually create tables. This can be done one of two ways. First, you can simply type in the values for each row in your manually created table. Obviously, this is only practical for small tables that do not change very often.

The second approach is to programmatically generate the rows in the table. This is done using the DAX expression language. We will dive deeply into DAX in Chapters 12 and 13. In this chapter, we will get a sneak peak at what DAX looks like and how we can use it to create a table.

We begin the exercises in this section by adding the second intermediate table to the "Population-GDP-CO2 by Country from Scratch" model. This is the Year table. This is the last bit of data we need to gather for this model.

We will then switch to a different data model that has already been started for you. You worked with the "Max Min Sales Information" model when we created data visualizations. Now you will see how some parts of that model were created. We will use a version of that model that has been started for us, but it has some features missing. This is in the "Max Min Sales Information Incomplete Model.pbix" file. This file is located in the supporting materials that you should have downloaded from the McGraw-Hill Education website. Copy this file and save it to a location in your file system (outside of the ZIP file it came in). Remember the location where you saved this file. If you need help downloading the supporting materials for the book, refer to the instructions in Chapter 1.

Manually Creating the Year Table in the Population-GDP-CO2 by Country Data Model

1. In your "Population-GDP-CO2 by Country from Scratch.pbix" file, click Enter Data on the Home tab of the ribbon. The Create Table dialog box appears.
2. In row 1 under Column1, double-click to edit.
3. Type **1950** and press ENTER.
4. In row 2 under Column1, double-click to edit.
5. Type **1955** and press ENTER.
6. In row 3 under Column1, double-click to edit.
7. Type **1960** and press ENTER.
8. Continue this process until you have rows for every five years from 1950 to 2015. If you end up with a blank row 15, right-click the blank row and select Delete from the context menu.
9. Double-click the Column1 heading to rename the column.
10. Type **Year** and press ENTER.
11. Replace "Table" with **Year** for Name at the bottom of the dialog box. The Create Table dialog box appears, as shown in Figure 9-23.
12. Click Load. The Year table is created in the data model.
13. Click the report background so nothing is selected.
14. In the Fields pane, expand the Year table and select the Year field.
15. Click Save.
16. Close Power BI Desktop.

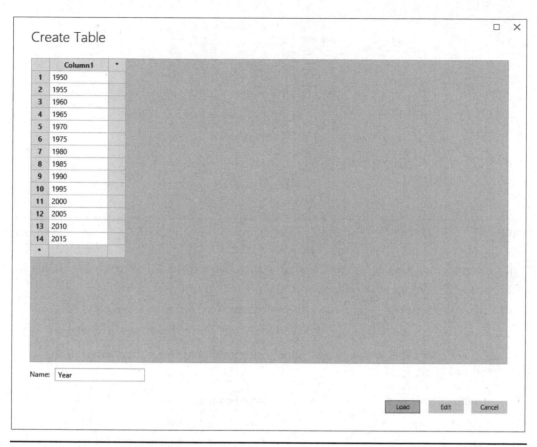

Figure 9-23   *The Create Table dialog box*

Creating a Calculated Table to Add a Date Table to the Max Min Sales Information Model

1. Locate the "Max Min Sales Information Incomplete Model.pbix" file in the file system location where you saved it.

2. Double-click the "Max Min Sales Information Incomplete Model.pbix" file. This will open the file in Power BI Desktop.

3. On the far left, click the Data tab, as shown in Figure 9-24.

4. On the Modeling tab of the ribbon, click New Table. The formula bar appears directly below the ribbon.

5. Enter the following in the formula bar:

```
Date = CALENDAR(DATE(2016, 1, 1), DATE(2018, 12, 31))
```

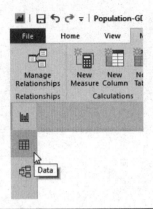

Figure 9-24 *Selecting the Data tab*

6. Press ENTER. This will generate a table with dates from 1/1/2016 to 12/31/2018.

7. In the Modeling tab of the ribbon, click New Column.

8. Enter the following expression in the formula bar and then press ENTER:

```
Long Date Name = FORMAT('Date'[Date], "dddd, MMMM dd, yyyy")
```

9. Repeat Steps 7–8 to create additional calculated columns, as indicated in the following table:

Column Name	Column Formula
YearSort	YearSort = YEAR('Date'[Date])
Year	Year = "Calendar " & YEAR([Date])
QtrSort	QtrSort = FORMAT('Date'[Date], "yyyyq")
Quarter	Quarter = "Quarter " & FORMAT('Date'[Date], "q, yyyy")
MnSort	MnSort = FORMAT('Date'[Date], "yyyymm")
Month	Month = FORMAT('Date'[Date], "MMMM yyyy")
MnOfYrSort	MnOfYrSort = MONTH('Date'[Date])
Month of Year	Month of Year = FORMAT('Date'[Date], "MMMM")

When this is completed, the Date table should appear as shown in Figure 9-25.

10. On the Modeling tab of the ribbon, click Mark as Date Table | Mark as Date Table. The "Mark as date table" dialog box appears.

11. In the Date column dropdown list, select Date. The "Mark as date table" dialog box should appear, as shown in Figure 9-26.

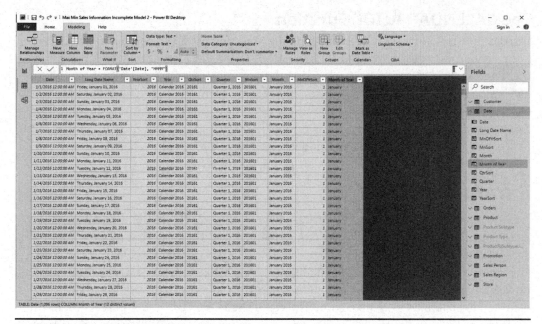

Figure 9-25 *The calculated Date table*

12. Click OK to exit the "Mark as date table" dialog box.
13. Click Save in the toolbar.
14. Close Power BI Desktop.

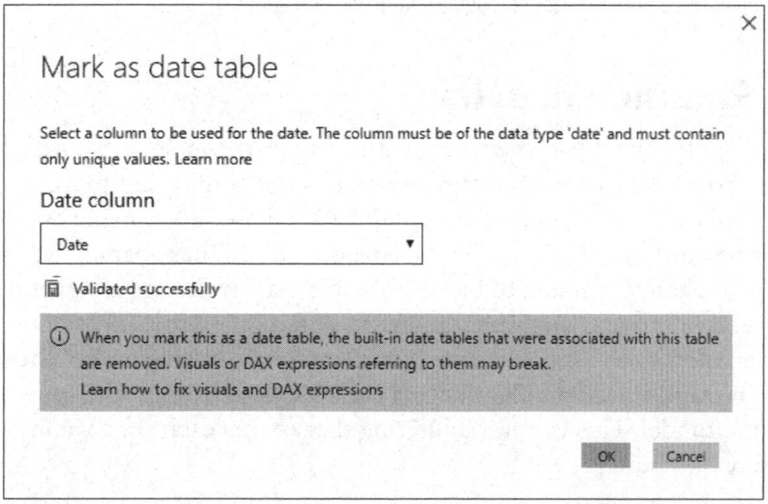

Figure 9-26 *The "Mark as date table" dialog box*

The CALENDARAUTO() Function

Instead of using the CALENDAR() function and specifying the begin and end dates for our calendar, we could have used the CALENDARAUTO() function, which explores the date values in the model to determine the minimum date value and the maximum date value in the model. It then creates date records from the first day of the year that contains the minimum date value to the last day of the year that contains the maximum date value. If your dates utilize a fiscal calendar, you can specify the month number of the first month of the fiscal year as an optional parameter for this function.

Parameters

Next we examine the ability to add parameters to a Power BI model. Parameters allow us to collect user input in a very structured manner and then use that input within the data model.

Parameters are not meant to facilitate interactivity like a slicer or a report filter. In Power BI, parameters function more like the entries in a configuration file. Power BI parameters enable us to change some aspects of the Power BI model in reaction to the environment where the model is operating. The values specified for the parameters are used when data is loaded into the model. Usually, the model is loaded infrequently—at most just once at the beginning of an interactive data session. Therefore, we are not going to use parameters as part of our routine when exploring the data.

 NOTE
As of this writing, Power BI parameters can be entered when working with the model in Power BI Desktop. They cannot be entered once the model is published to PowerBI.com.

Putting Parameters to Use

Power BI parameters have two main uses within our data model. First, we can use parameters as part of the connection information when connecting to a data source. For example, we can set up a parameter to hold a database server name or a file path. The connection configuration can then be changed to use these parameter values. In this way, we can change a model to move from using a development server to using a production server without going into the model and making modifications.

Parameters can also be used when we filter the rows in a table within the data model. Again, keep in mind this particular filtering comes into play only when the data is loaded into the model. This is not the filtering that occurs each time we interact with a visualization on a report.

Let's make this parameter concept a bit more concrete with an exercise.

Creating a Power BI Parameter

1. Locate the "Population-GDP-CO2 by Country from Scratch.pbix" file in the file system location where you saved it.

2. Double-click the "Population-GDP-CO2 by Country from Scratch.pbix" file. This will open the file in Power BI Desktop.

3. Click Edit Queries (the upper part of the button, not the dropdown) on the Home tab of the ribbon. The Query Editor appears.

4. Click the Manage Parameters dropdown on the Home tab of the ribbon in the Query Editor.

5. Select New Parameter from the dropdown list. The Parameters dialog box appears.

6. Replace Parameter1 with **Wiki Population URL** for Name.

7. For Description, type the following:

   ```
   The URL for the population tables in Wikipedia.
   ```

8. Select Text from the Type dropdown list.

9. For Current Value, type the following:

   ```
   http://en.wikipedia.org/wiki/List_of_countries_by_past_and_future_
   population
   ```

   The Parameters dialog box will appear, as shown in Figure 9-27.

NOTE
You can create a list of valid values for this parameter using the Suggested Values dropdown list. Selecting "List of values" enables you to manually enter the list of values. Selecting Query enables you to specify a column in a data model table to be used as the list of values. The table column must be converted to a list using the "Convert to List" option on the Transform tab of the Query Editor ribbon before it can be selected in the Parameters dialog box.

10. Click the New link to create a new parameter.

11. Replace Parameter1 with **Source Folder** for Name.

12. For Description, type the following:

    ```
    The path to the folder containing the files used to load this model.
    ```

13. Select Text from the Type dropdown list.

14. For Current Value, type the drive letter and path to the folder containing the CO2 Emissions in kt.csv, GDP in Current US Dollars.xlsx, and Countries.json files. Be sure to end the path with a backslash (\) character.

15. Click OK.

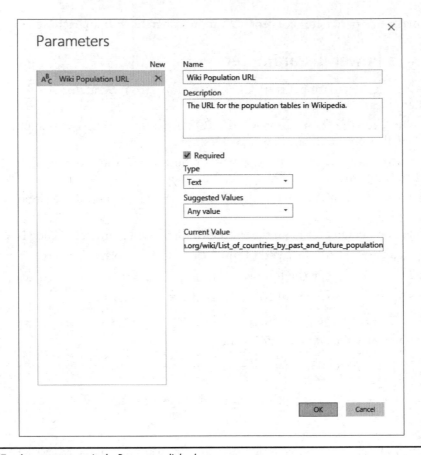

Figure 9-27   *A new parameter in the Parameters dialog box*

Parameterizing Connections

1. Click Data Source Settings in the Home tab of the Query Editor ribbon. The Data Source Settings dialog box appears.
2. Select the "CO2 Emissions in kt.csv" data source.
3. Click Change Source. The Comma-Separated Values dialog box appears.
4. Select the Advanced option.
5. In the top text box under "File path parts," delete the entire file path except for the filename and extension (CO2 Emissions in kt.csv).
6. Hover over the top text box under "File path parts" and click the ellipsis (…) button.
7. Select Move Down from the context menu. This text box is now the bottom text box under "File path parts."

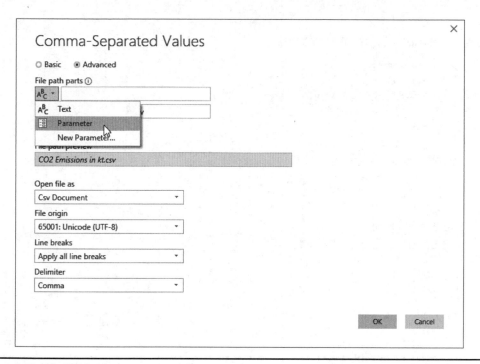

Figure 9-28   *The ABC dropdown*

8. Click the top ABC dropdown under "File path parts," as shown in Figure 9-28.

9. Select Parameter from the dropdown list.

10. The blank text box becomes a dropdown list with "Wiki Population URL" selected. From this dropdown list, select Source Folder. The dialog box will appear as shown in Figure 9-29.

11. Click OK.

12. Select the "gdp in current us dollars.xlsx" data source.

13. Click Change Source. The Excel dialog box appears.

14. Select the Advanced option.

15. In the top text box under "File path parts," delete the entire file path except for the filename and extension (GDP in Current US Dollars.xlsx).

16. Hover over the top text box under "File path parts" and click the ellipsis (…) button.

17. Select Move Down from the context menu. This text box is now the bottom text box under "File path parts."

18. Click the top ABC dropdown under "File path parts" and select Parameter.

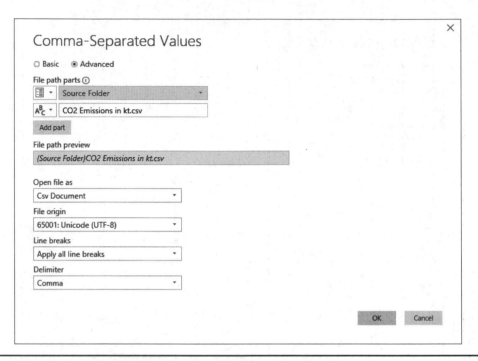

Figure 9-29   *The Comma-Separated Values dialog box with a parameterized file path*

19. The blank text box becomes a dropdown list with "Wiki Population URL" selected. From this dropdown list, select Source Folder.

20. Click OK.

21. Select the "countries.json" data source.

22. Click Change Source. The JSON dialog box appears.

23. Select the Advanced option.

24. In the top text box under "File path parts," delete the entire file path except for the filename and extension (Countries.json).

25. Hover over the top text box under "File path parts" and click the ellipsis (…) button.

26. Select Move Down from the context menu. This text box is now the bottom text box under "File path parts."

27. Click the top ABC dropdown under "File path parts" and select Parameter.

28. The blank text box becomes a dropdown list with "Wiki Population URL" selected. From this dropdown list, select "Source Folder."

29. Click OK.

30. Select the Web data source (the data source that has the globe icon and begins with "http://").

31. Click Change Source. The From Web dialog box appears.

32. Click the top ABC dropdown under URL and select Parameter. The Wiki Population URL parameter is selected by default.

33. Click OK.

34. Click Close.

35. In the Home tab of the Query Editor ribbon, click Close & Apply. The data is reloaded using the parameterized connections. Again, this may take a minute or so.

36. Click Save.

With our parameterized connections, if you need to move the source files to a different folder or if the Wikipedia URL should change, all you need to do is change the parameter value. You don't have to modify each affected data source. In our case, this is especially beneficial for the three data sources that share the same file path.

Transformers

In this chapter, we focused on the steps used to get data and transform it as it is loaded into the data model. We utilized some of the transformations available in the Query Editor, but really just scratched the surface. The following chapter provides a reference to all of those transformations.

Chapter 10

Power BI Transformation Reference

In This Chapter

- **Transformation Reference**

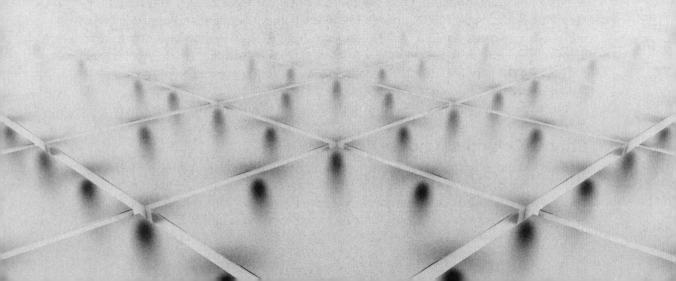

I n the previous chapter, you got a taste of the power and flexibility of the Query Editor. We touched on a few of the transformations available as we loaded data into our models. But there are a number of transformations we have not touched upon. It is time to fix that.

Transformation Reference

In this chapter, we look at all the transformations the Query Editor provides. These transformations are accessed using the Query Editor ribbon. They are spread across several ribbon tabs. In fact, some of the transformations appear on more than one tab of the ribbon. In addition, some of the transformations can be found in the context menu when you right-click a column heading.

Informational-Only Transformations

Certain transformations provide information to the person creating the query but don't add content to the query. These are noted as "informational only." When an informational-only transformation is used, the result is displayed to the user. Once the user has noted the information, the transformation should be deleted using the Applied Steps area to allow for the continuation of the query creation.

Transformations on the Query Editor Home Tab

We begin with the transformations available on the Home tab of the Query Editor. This tab functions as a "favorites" collection. It contains some of the most frequently used transformations.

Append Queries

Append Queries is a dropdown with two options: Append Queries and Append Queries as New. This transformation takes the content of two or more queries and combines them into a single query in the model. The selected query or queries are appended to an initial query to create a union of the queries involved. All queries involved must have an identical structure. If Append Queries is selected from the dropdown, the result takes the place of the current query. If Append Queries as New is selected from the dropdown, the result becomes a new query.

The append operation is defined with the Append dialog box shown in Figure 10-1.

Choose Columns | Choose Columns

Choose Columns is a dropdown with two options. The Choose Columns | Choose Columns option displays a dialog box where the set of columns to remain in the query is selected. Only columns checked on the Choose Columns dialog box, shown in Figure 10-2, stay in the query after this transformation is applied.

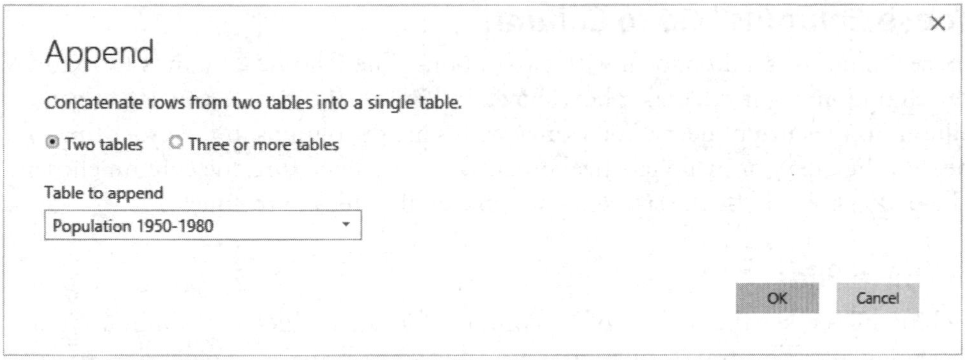

Figure 10-1   *The Append dialog box*

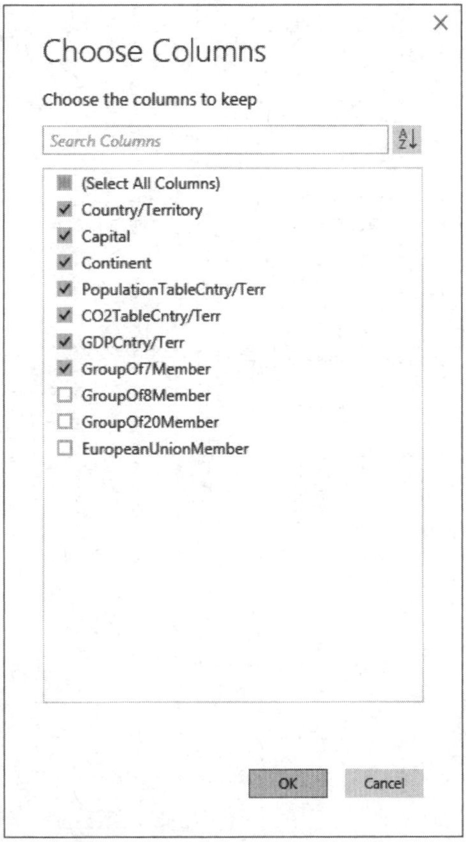

Figure 10-2   *The Choose Columns dialog box*

Choose Columns | Go to Column

Choose Columns is a dropdown with two options. The Choose Columns | Go to Column option displays a dialog box, shown in Figure 10-3, where you can select a column in the current query. You can view this list of columns in the order they appear in the query or in alphabetical order. Once you click OK, the column chosen in the dialog box will be the selected column (highlighted) in the query.

Combine Files

Combine Files takes the content of two or more files in a folder and combines them into a single file. This transformation is available when using the Folder data source. The files are combined at the binary level.

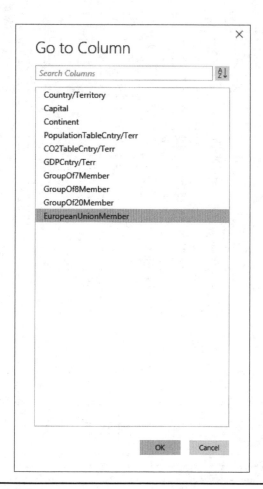

Figure 10-3   *The Go to Column dialog box*

Data Type

Data Type specifies the data type of the currently selected column or columns. Use the dropdown list to set the desired data type. Alternatively, click the data type indicator in a column heading to select the desired data type for that column.

Group By

Group By aggregates multiple rows into single rows using grouping criteria. Each column to be included in the result must either be part of the group by or be derived from an aggregation. The grouping criteria are created using the Group By dialog box, shown in Figure 10-4.

Keep Rows

Keep Rows is a dropdown that specifies rows to keep in the query. You can use any of the following to specify which rows to keep:

- Keep Top Rows
- Keep Bottom Rows

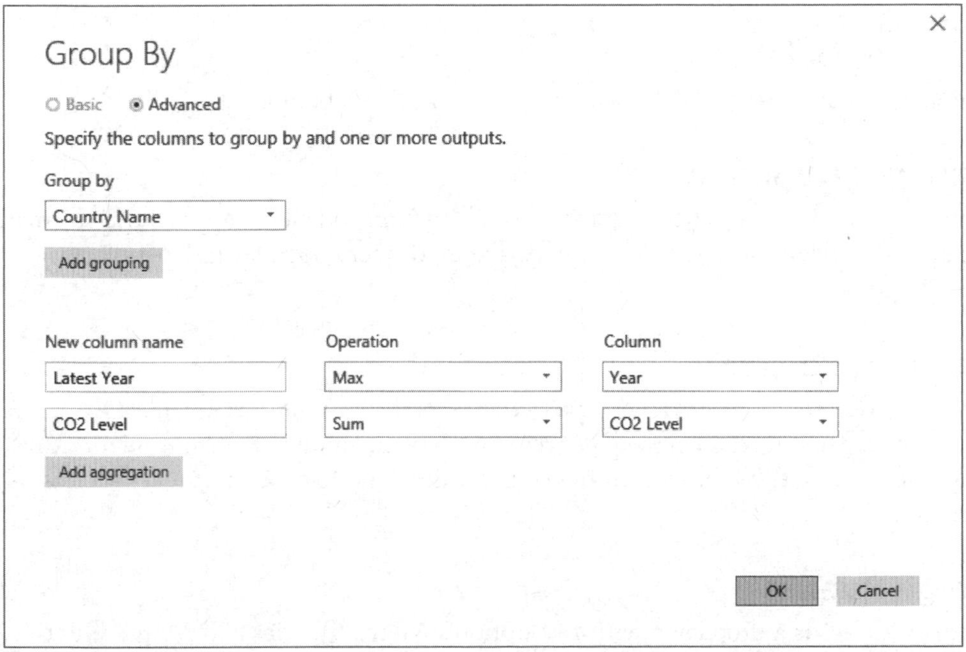

Figure 10-4 *The Group By dialog box*

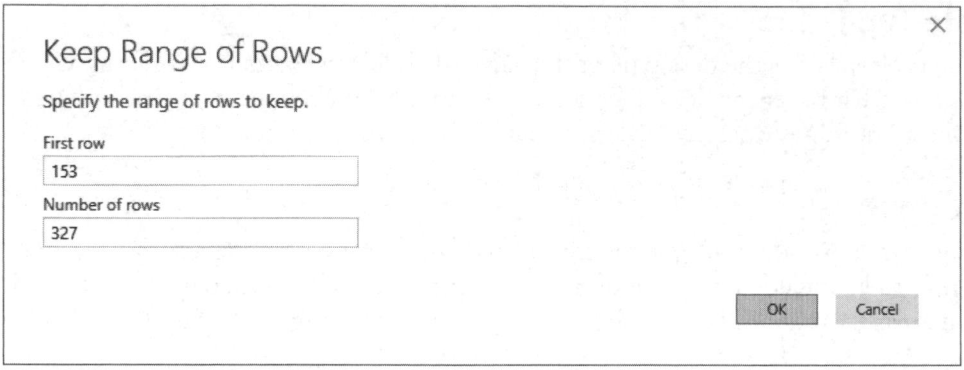

Figure 10-5   *The Keep Range of Rows dialog box*

- Keep Range of Rows
- Keep Duplicates
- Keep Errors

   The Keep Range of Rows dialog box, shown in Figure 10-5, is used when specifying a range of rows to keep.

Manage | Delete
Manage | Delete removes the selected query from the data model.

Manage | Duplicate
Manage | Duplicate copies the data source information and all the applied transformation steps in the current query to a new query. The new query operates independently of the current query.

Manage | Reference
Manage | Reference creates a new query that uses the current query as its starting data source. Therefore, the new query remains dependent on the current query. Any subsequent changes to the current query affect the data that the new query sees as its data source.

Merge Queries
Merge Queries is a dropdown with two options: Merge Queries and Merge Queries as New. This transformation takes the content of two queries and joins them using one of several join options. If Merge Queries is selected from the dropdown, the result

takes the place of the current query. If Merge Queries as New is selected from the dropdown, the result becomes a new query.

The join condition options are as follows:

- **Left Outer**   Includes all rows from the first query and only rows satisfying the join condition from the second query
- **Right Outer**   Includes all rows from the second query and only rows satisfying the join condition from the first query
- **Full Outer**   Includes all rows from both queries, merging those rows that satisfy the join condition
- **Inner**   Includes only rows from each query that satisfy the join condition
- **Left Anti**   Includes only rows from the first query that did not satisfy the join condition
- **Right Anti**   Includes only rows from the second query that did not satisfy the join condition

The join condition is defined in the Merge dialog box, shown in Figure 10-6. The join condition is created by selecting one or more columns in the first query and the same number of columns in the second query. The merge is done using fuzzy matching, when the "Use fuzzy matching to perform the merge" is checked. Use CTRL-click or SHIFT-click to select multiple columns.

Data source permissions may apply when using Merge Queries. These permissions are associated with privacy levels. See the "Data Source Permissions" section of Chapter 9 for more information.

Remove Columns

Remove Columns is a dropdown with two options: Remove Columns and Remove Other Columns. If Remove Columns is selected from the dropdown, the selected columns are deleted. If Remove Other Columns is selected from the dropdown, the non-selected columns are deleted.

Remove Rows

Remove Rows is a dropdown that specifies rows to remove from the data set. You can use any of the following to specify which rows to remove:

- Remove Top Rows
- Remove Bottom Rows

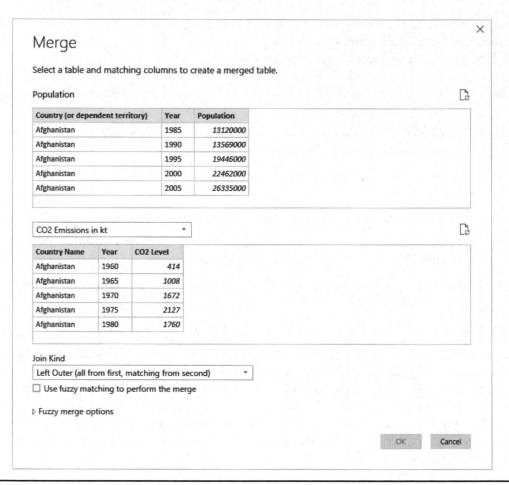

Figure 10-6 *The Merge dialog box*

- Remove Alternate Rows
- Remove Duplicates
- Remove Blank Rows
- Remove Errors

The Remove Alternate Rows dialog box, shown in Figure 10-7, is used when specifying an alternating pattern of rows to remove.

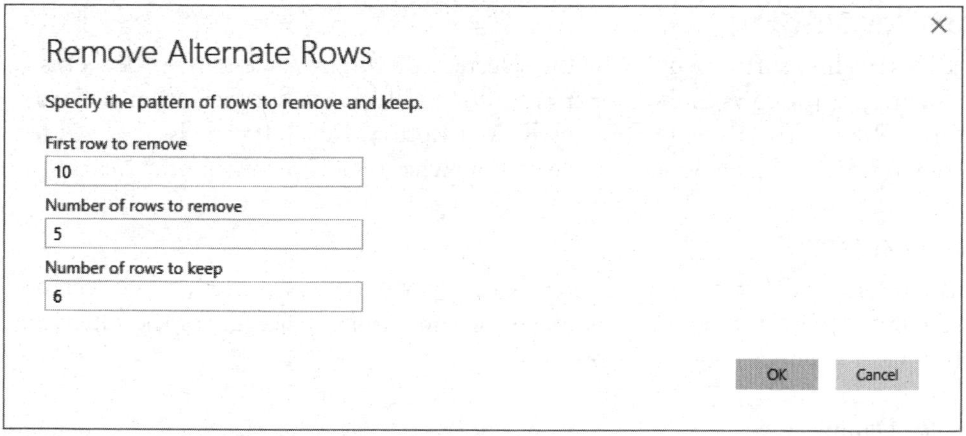

Figure 10-7   *The Remove Alternate Rows dialog box*

Replace Values

Replace Values substitutes a specified value for another specified value in the selected column. The values are entered in the Replace Values dialog box, shown in Figure 10-8.

Sort Ascending

Sort Ascending sorts the query by the selected column in ascending order. This can be used to put the rows in the proper order for a follow-on transformation such as Remove Rows | Top Rows or Remove Rows | Bottom Rows. It can also be used for your own reference purposes as you determine what data is present in the query.

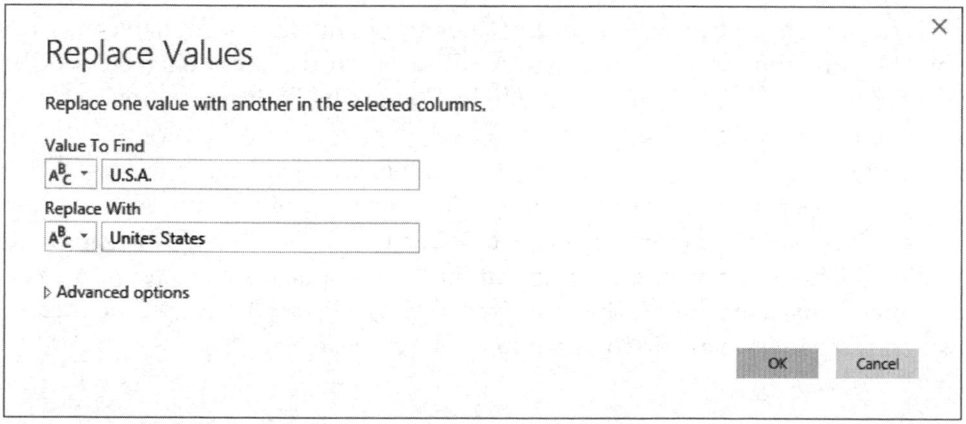

Figure 10-8   *The Replace Values dialog box*

Sort Descending

Sort Descending sorts the query by the selected column in descending order. This can be used to put the rows in the proper order for a follow-on transformation such as Remove Rows | Top Rows or Remove Rows | Bottom Rows. It can also be used for your own reference purposes as you determine what data is present in the query.

Split Column

Split Column is a dropdown that allows you to parse the text content of a selected column and split it into two or more new columns. You can use any of the following techniques to split the column content:

- By Delimiter
- By Number of Characters
- By Positions
- By Lowercase to Uppercase
- By Uppercase to Lowercase
- By Digit to Non-digit
- By Non-digit to Digit

Split Column by Delimiter uses occurrences of a delimiter character for the breakpoints. You can split at the first delimiter encountered from the right, the first delimiter encountered from the left, or at all occurrences of the delimiter. The Split Column by Delimiter dialog box, shown in Figure 10-9, is used when a delimiter is to be specified.

Split Column by Number of Characters uses a fixed number of N characters as the breakpoints. You can split at the first N characters, at the last N characters, or at every N characters in the column. Use Split Column by Positions to break at a specified position. Split Column by Lowercase to Uppercase splits every time there is a transition from a lowercase character to an uppercase character in the text. Split Column by Uppercase to Lowercase splits every time there is a transition from an uppercase character to a lowercase character in the text. Split Column by Digit to Non-digit splits every time there is a transition from a numeric character (0–9) to a non-numeric character. Split Column by Non-digit to Digit splits every time there is a transition from a non-numeric character to a numeric character.

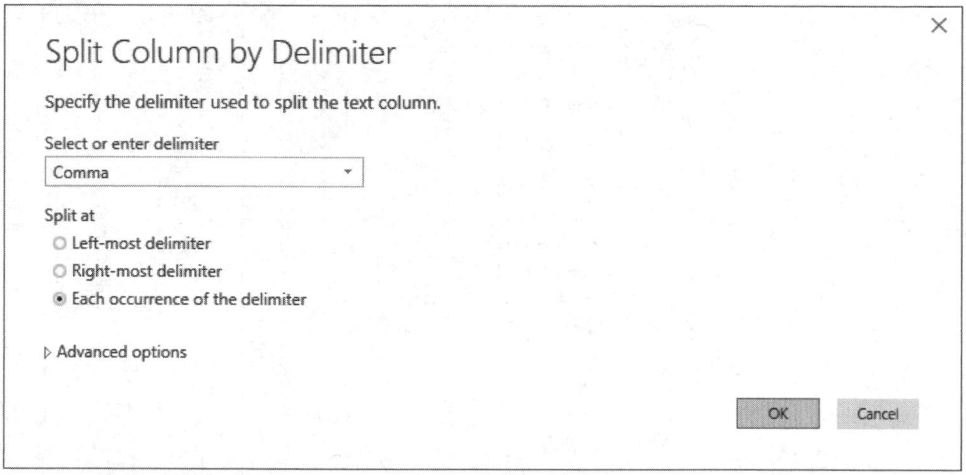

Split Column by Delimiter

Specify the delimiter used to split the text column.

Select or enter delimiter

Comma

Split at
○ Left-most delimiter
○ Right-most delimiter
● Each occurrence of the delimiter

▷ Advanced options

OK   Cancel

Figure 10-9   *The Split Column by Delimiter dialog box*

Use First Row As Headers

Use First Row As Headers takes the first row of data in the query and promotes these values to the names of the columns in the query. In doing so, the first row of data is removed from the query. Use First Row As Headers also has an option to perform the opposite operation, taking the names of the columns and adding them as the first row of data in the query result.

Transformations on the Query Editor Transform Tab

The Transform tab of the Query Editor contains transformations that manipulate the existing data. Some of these transformations affect the structure of the entire query. Others will change the data in a single column.

Aggregate

The Aggregate transformation will aggregate values found in a linked query and place the result in the related record in the current query. The Aggregate dialog box is used to select the columns from the related table and the type of aggregation used for each. This is shown in Figure 10-10.

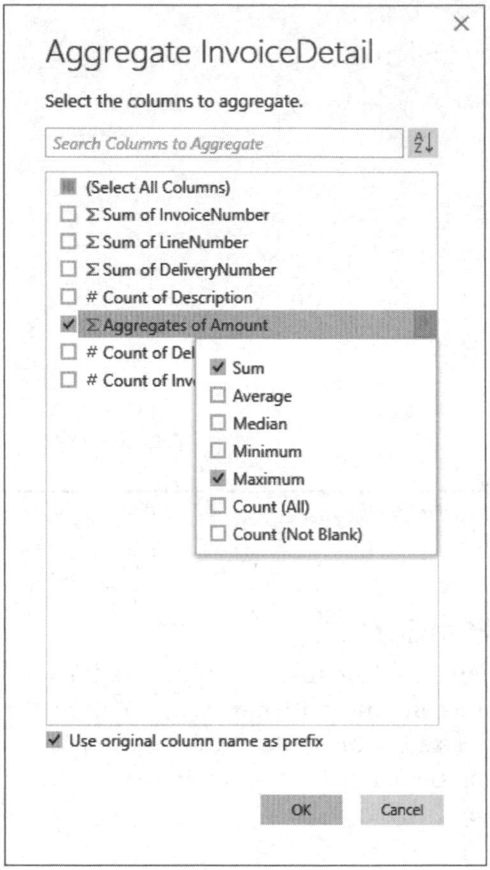

Figure 10-10 *The Aggregate dialog box*

Convert to List

Convert to List takes the selected column and converts it to a list of values, which can then be used as a list of valid values for a parameter. The list can be further cleansed and sorted using the List Tools/Transform tab of the Query Editor. This tab will only appear when you're working with a list.

Count Rows

Count Rows simply counts the number of rows satisfying the current query and displays the result. Count Rows is informational only. Once you have noted the number of rows, you can delete this transformation from the Applied Steps list.

Data Type

Data Type specifies the data type of the currently selected column or columns. Use the dropdown list to set the desired data type. Alternatively, click the data type indicator in a column heading to select the desired data type for that column.

Date

When the Date transformation is applied to a column containing values of any of the date-related data types, it changes the content of the column to a value calculated from the original date value in the column. When Date is applied to a column of type Text, it converts the text to a date. Alternatively, a date and a time value can be combined into a single value.

The following values can be calculated from a date-related data type:

Age	The amount of time between the current system date and time and the value in the row
Date Only	Removes any time portion of the value
Parse	Parses a text column to extract a date value
Year | Year	The year portion of the value
Year | Start of Year	The first day of the year containing the value
Year | End of Year	The last day of the year containing the value
Month | Month	The month portion of the value as a number
Month | Start of Month	The first day of the month containing the value
Month | End of Month	The last day of the month containing the value
Month | Days in Month	The number of days in the month containing the value
Month | Name of Month	The name of the month containing the value
Quarter | Quarter of Year	The quarter containing the value as a number
Quarter | Start of Quarter	The first day of the quarter containing the value
Quarter | End of Quarter	The last day of the quarter containing the value
Week | Week of Year	The number of the week containing the value within that year
Week | Week of Month	The number of the week containing the value within that month
Week | Start of Week	The first day of the week containing the value
Week | End of Week	The last day of the week containing the value
Day | Day	The day portion of the value as a number
Day | Day of Week	The number of the day specified by the value within that week
Day | Day of Year	The number of the day specified by the value within that year

(Continued)

Day | Start of Day	The earliest time within the day containing the value
Day | End of Day	The latest time within the day containing the value
Day | Name of Day	The name of the day containing the value
Combine Date and Time	Combines a selected date column and a selected time column into a single value
Earliest	The earliest value in the column (informational only)
Latest	The latest value in the column (informational only)

Detect Data Type

Detect Data Type examines the content of the selected column and determines the data type. It then changes the data type of the column to that data type. The Detect Data Type transformation will result in a Changed Type step added to the Applied Steps list.

Duration

Duration takes an age and translates it to various durations. Here are the possible durations:

- Days
- Hours
- Minutes
- Seconds
- Total Years
- Total Days
- Total Hours
- Total Minutes
- Total Seconds

Duration will also multiply an age by a value or divide an age by a value. Alternatively, Duration will perform statistical analysis on an age. The statistical analysis is informational only. Available statistics include the following:

- Sum
- Minimum

- Maximum
- Median
- Average

Expand

Expand parses a structured column and replaces the structured column with new columns in the query. The structured column will contain the following words in every row rather than displaying the actual content of the column:

- List
- Record
- Table
- Value

A structured column may be a reference to a related table or may contain structured content such as JSON data.

You can select which data items from the structure should become columns using the Expand JSON Data dialog box, as shown in Figure 10-11.

Extract

Extract creates new values based on information about or the partial content of a selected column. One of the following methods is used:

- **Length**   New value is the length of the value in each row.
- **First Characters**   New value is the first N characters of the value in each row.
- **Last Characters**   New value is the last N characters of the value in each row.
- **Range**   New value is N characters starting at character X.
- **Text Before Delimiter**   New value is the characters before a specified delimiter.
- **Text After Delimiter**   New value is the characters after a specified delimiter.
- **Text Between Delimiters**   New value is the characters between the delimiter specified as the start delimiter and the delimiter specified as the end delimiter.

An example of the Extract Text Range dialog box is shown in Figure 10-12.

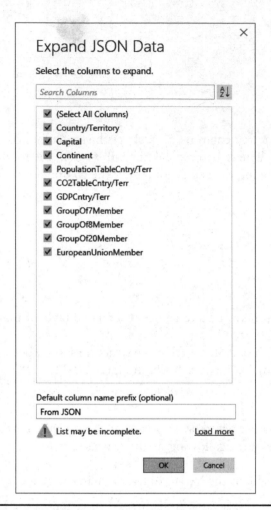

Figure 10-11 *The Expand JSON Data dialog box*

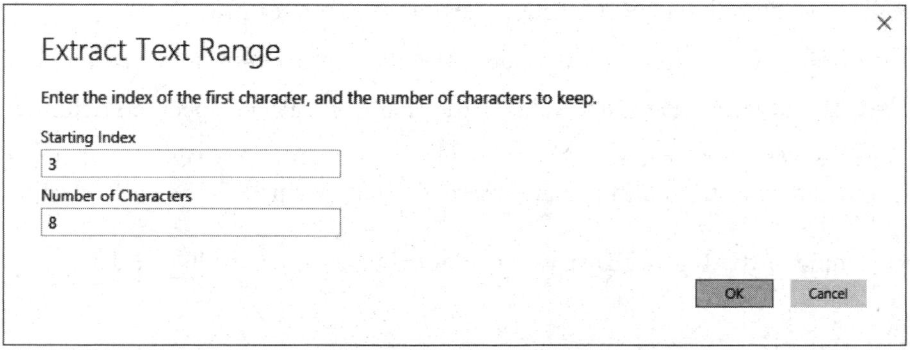

Extract Text Range

Enter the index of the first character, and the number of characters to keep.

Starting Index

3

Number of Characters

8

OK   Cancel

Figure 10-12 *The Extract Text Range dialog box*

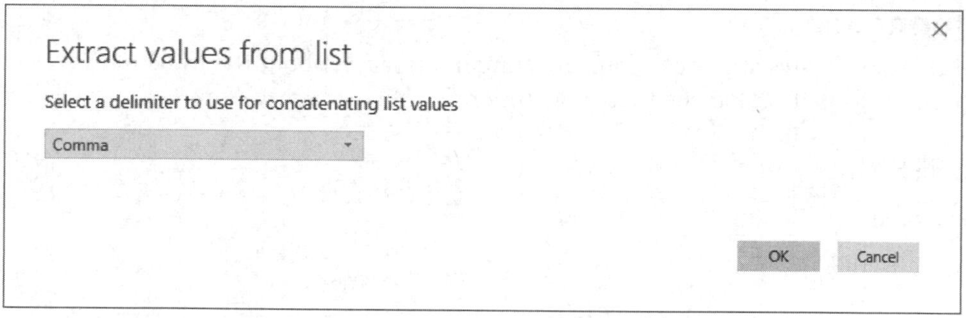

Figure 10-13 *The Extract values from list dialog box*

Extract Values

Extract Values takes values from a List column and converts them to a delimited string of values. The Split transformation can then be used to create multiple columns from the list values. The delimiter is specified on the "Extract values from list" dialog box, as shown in Figure 10-13.

Fill

Fill inserts the selected values into any empty cells either above or below the selected cell in the query.

Format

Format applies formatting to text in a given column. Here are the valid formats:

- Lowercase
- Uppercase
- Capitalize Each Word
- Trim (Remove leading and trailing whitespace)
- Clean (Remove non-printable characters)
- Add Prefix
- Add Suffix

Group By

Group By aggregates multiple rows into single rows using grouping criteria. Each column to be included in the result must either be part of the group by or must be derived from an aggregation. The grouping criteria are created using the Group By dialog box, shown earlier in Figure 10-4.

Information

Information creates a new column, reflecting information about the value in the selected column. Information has the following options:

- Is Even
- Is Odd
- Sign

When indicating the sign, 1 means positive, −1 means negative, and 0 means the value was 0.

Merge Columns

Merge Columns joins the content of two columns into a new column. The new column replaces the source columns in the query. A separator can be specified for insertion between the two values. The Merge Columns dialog box is used to define the new column, as shown in Figure 10-14.

Move

Move changes the position of the selected column. A column can be moved in the following ways:

- Left
- Right
- To Beginning
- To End

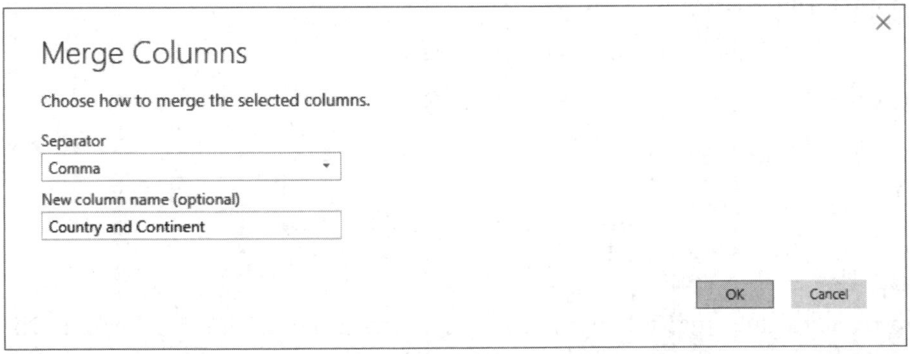

Figure 10-14 *The Merge Columns dialog box*

Parse

Parse interprets the selected column as either an XML or JSON structure. The contents are parsed and placed in an embedded table. Click the button to the right of the column header to expand the embedded record into columns.

Pivot Column

Pivot Column takes values in a selected column and converts them into multiple columns in the query. The column selected when Pivot Column is clicked becomes the column to pivot. The values in this column become column headings. The data in the selected Values Column becomes the values in the new columns created by the pivot operation. Using the Advanced options, you can specify an aggregate to use when determining the values in the new columns.

The Pivot Column dialog box is shown in Figure 10-15.

Rename

Rename enables the entry of a new name for a column. The name is edited right in the column heading area.

Replace Values

Replace Values substitutes a specified value for another specified value in the selected column. The values are entered in the Replace Values dialog box, shown earlier in Figure 10-8.

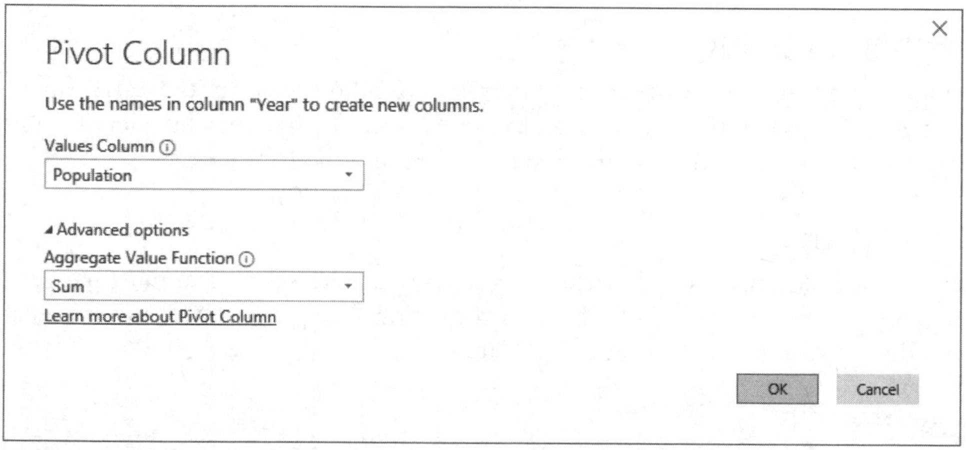

Figure 10-15 *The Pivot Column dialog box*

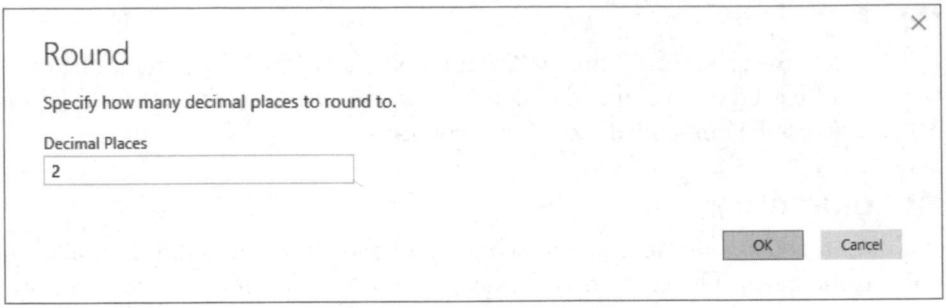

Figure 10-16 *The Round dialog box*

Reverse Rows

Reverse Rows reverses the order of the rows in the query. Reverse Rows, Sort Ascending, and Sort Descending all change the order of the rows in the query. However, whereas the sort transformations use the content of a column for reordering, Reverse Rows works off the physical order of the rows.

Rounding

Rounding removes some or all of the decimal portion of a value. Round Up moves the value up to the closest integer. Round Down moves the value down to the closest integer. Round ... performs rounding to the specified decimal place. The Round dialog box, shown in Figure 10-16, is used to specify the number of decimal places to round to.

Run Python Script

Run Python Script executes a script written in Python to transform the data. You must have a Python engine installed in order to use this transformation. The query data is made available to the Python script through a data set called "dataset."

Run R Script

Run R Script executes a script written in R to transform the data. You must have an R engine installed in order to use this transformation. The query data is made available to the R script through a data set called "dataset."

Scientific

Scientific applies one of the following scientific operations to the values in a numeric column, replacing each value with the result:

- Absolute Value
- Power
- Square Root
- Exponent
- Logarithm
- Factorial

Split Column

Split Column is a dropdown that allows you to parse the text content of a selected column and split it into two or more new columns. You can use any of the following techniques to split the column content:

- By Delimiter
- By Number of Characters
- By Positions
- By Lowercase to Uppercase
- By Uppercase to Lowercase
- By Digit to Non-digit
- By Non-digit to Digit

Split Column by Delimiter uses occurrences of a delimiter character for the breakpoints. You can split at the first delimiter encountered from the right, the first delimiter encountered from the left, or at all occurrences of the delimiter. The Split Column by Delimiter dialog box, shown earlier in Figure 10-9, is used when a delimiter is to be specified.

Split Column by Number of Characters uses a fixed number of N characters as the breakpoints. You can split at the first N characters, at the last N characters, or at every N characters in the column. Use Split Column by Positions to break at a specified position. Split Column by Lowercase to Uppercase splits every time there is a transition from a lowercase character to an uppercase character in the text. Split Column by Uppercase to Lowercase splits every time there is a transition from an uppercase character to a lowercase character in the text. Split Column by Digit to Non-digit splits every time there is a transition from a numeric character (0–9) to a non-numeric character. Split Column by Non-digit to Digit splits every time there is a transition from a non-numeric character to a numeric character.

Standard

Standard applies one of the following standard mathematical operations to the values in a numeric column, replacing each value with the result:

- Add
- Multiply
- Subtract
- Divide
- Integer-Divide
- Modulo
- Percentage
- Percent Of

Statistics

Statistics performs one of the following statistical analyses on the selected column:

- Sum
- Minimum
- Maximum
- Median
- Average
- Standard Deviation
- Count Values
- Count Distinct Values

The statistical analysis is informational only. Once you have noted the statistic that was requested, you can delete this transformation from the Applied Steps list.

Time

When Time is applied to a column containing time-related values, it changes the content of the column to a value calculated from the time value. When Time is applied to a column of type Text, it converts the text to a time value. Alternatively, a date and a time value can be combined into a single value.

The following values can be calculated from a time-related data type:

Time Only	Removes any date portion of the value
Local Time	Changes the values to local time
Parse	Parses a text column to extract a time value
Hour | Hour	The hour portion of the value as a number
Hour | Start of Hour	The first minute and second of the hour containing the value
Hour | End of Hour	The last minute and second of the hour containing the value
Minute	The minute portion of the value as a number
Second	The second portion of the value as a number
Earliest	The earliest value in the column (informational only)
Latest	The latest value in the column (informational only)

Transpose

Transpose changes the query to treat all rows as columns and all columns as rows. As such, one column will be created in the query after the transformation for every row that was present in the query before the transformation. Columns will be named "Column1" through "ColumnN."

Trigonometry

Trigonometry applies one of the following trigonometric operations to the values in a numeric column, replacing each value with the result:

- Sine
- Cosine
- Tangent
- Arcsine
- Arccosine
- Arctangent

Unpivot Columns

Unpivot Columns is a dropdown with three options: Unpivot Columns, Unpivot Other Columns, and Unpivot Only Selected Columns. This transformation takes values in a selected set of columns and converts them into a single column in the query. The column headings of the unpivoted columns become values in a new column called Attribute. The values in the unpivoted columns become values in a new column called Value.

If Unpivot Columns is selected from the dropdown, this transformation unpivots all selected columns. If Unpivot Other Columns is selected from the dropdown, the transformation unpivots all non-selected columns. If Unpivot Only Selected Columns is selected from the dropdown, the transformation unpivots all selected columns using an explicit list of columns to pivot.

If you look in the Advanced Editor, you will see the Unpivot Columns option actually creates an Unpivot Other Columns operation in the Query Formula Language. This results in an explicit list of the non-affected columns in the code. That means, if new columns are added to the source and this process is rerun to do a table refresh, the new columns will be included in the pivot operation. If this situation is not desirable, use the Unpivot Only Selected Columns option to create an explicit list of the columns included in the pivot operation.

Use First Row As Headers

Use First Row As Headers takes the first row of data in the query and promotes these values to the names of the columns in the query. In doing so, the first row of data is removed from the query. Use First Row As Headers also has an option to perform the opposite operation, taking the names of the columns and adding them as the first row of data in the query result.

Transformations on the Query Editor Add Column Tab

The Transformations on the Add Column tab of the Query Editor add to the data. These transformations create a new column in the query. The new column is based on data in one or more existing columns.

Column From Examples

Column From Examples is a dropdown with two options: From All Columns and From Selection. This transformation creates a new column based on a manually entered sample of what you want the data in the new column to look like. For example, you may have a Country column and a Continent column and want to create a new column with data in the form *country, continent*. You can enter "Abkhazia, Asia" in the first row of the example column. When you press ENTER, the Query Editor populates the data in the rest of the rows. This is shown in Figure 10-17. If the Query Editor does not get the new data correct based on the example in one row, you can add example data in more rows to provide the Query Editor with a more complete example.

If From All Columns is selected from the dropdown, all columns in the query are used to determine the appropriate expression for the new column. If From Selection is selected from the dropdown, only the selected columns are used to determine the appropriate expression for the new column.

Figure 10-17 *Creating a new column by example*

Conditional Column

Conditional Column defines a new column in the query based on one or more conditional expressions. This enables the value of the new column to be determined by the content of one or more existing columns in that row. The conditional expressions are defined using the Add Conditional Column dialog box, shown in Figure 10-18.

Custom Column

Custom Column creates a new column in the query based on a custom DAX formula. The custom formula is defined in the Custom Column dialog box, shown in Figure 10-19.

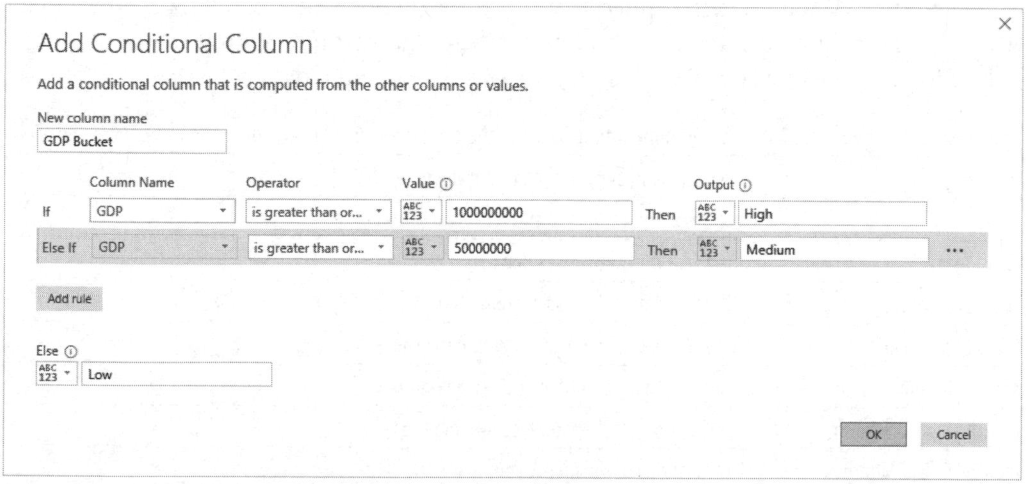

Figure 10-18 *The Add Conditional Column dialog box*

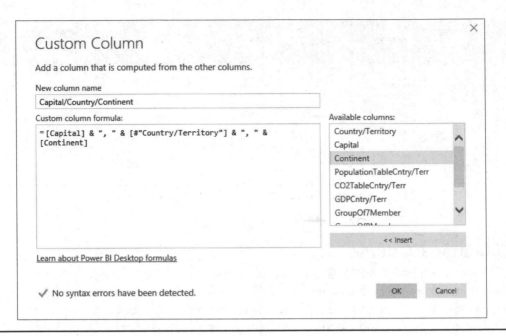

Figure 10-19 *The Custom Column dialog box*

Date

When Date is applied to a column containing values of any of the date-related data types, it creates a new column containing a value calculated from the original date value in the column. When Date is applied to a column of type Text, it converts the text to a date. Alternatively, a date and a time value can be combined into a single value.

The following values can be calculated from a date-related data type:

Age	The amount of time between the current system date and time and the value in the row
Date Only	Removes any time portion of the value
Parse	Parses a text column to extract a date value
Year | Year	The year portion of the value
Year | Start of Year	The first day of the year containing the value
Year | End of Year	The last day of the year containing the value
Month | Month	The month portion of the value as a number
Month | Start of Month	The first day of the month containing the value
Month | End of Month	The last day of the month containing the value
Month | Days in Month	The number of days in the month containing the value
Month | Name of Month	The name of the month containing the value
Quarter | Quarter of Year	The quarter containing the value as a number

Quarter | Start of Quarter	The first day of the quarter containing the value
Quarter | End of Quarter	The last day of the quarter containing the value
Week | Week of Year	The number of the week containing the value within that year
Week | Week of Month	The number of the week containing the value within that month
Week | Start of Week	The first day of the week containing the value
Week | End of Week	The last day of the week containing the value
Day | Day	The day portion of the value as a number
Day | Day of Week	The number of the day specified by the value within that week
Day | Day of Year	The number of the day specified by the value within that year
Day | Start of Day	The earliest time within the day containing the value
Day | End of Day	The latest time within the day containing the value
Day | Name of Day	The name of the day containing the value
Subtract Days	The number of days between two selected date columns
Combine Date and Time	Combines a selected date column and a selected time column into a single column
Earliest	The earliest value in the column (informational only)
Latest	The latest value in the column (informational only)

Duplicate Column

Duplicate Column creates a new column in the query from the content of an existing column.

Duration

Duration takes an age and translates it to various durations. The result is placed in a new column. Here are the possible durations:

- Days
- Hours
- Minutes
- Seconds
- Total Years
- Total Days
- Total Hours
- Total Minutes
- Total Seconds

Duration will also multiply an age by a value or divide an age by a value. Alternatively, Duration will perform statistical analysis on an age. The statistical analysis is informational only. Available statistics include the following:

- Sum
- Minimum
- Maximum
- Median
- Average

Extract

Extract creates a new column with values based on information about or the partial content of a selected column. One of the following methods is used:

- **Length** New value is the length of the value in each row.
- **First Characters** New value is the first N characters of the value in each row.
- **Last Characters** New value is the last N characters of the value in each row.
- **Range** New value is N characters starting at character X.
- **Text Before Delimiter** New value is the characters before a specified delimiter.
- **Text After Delimiter** New value is the characters after a specified delimiter.
- **Text Between Delimiters** New value is the characters between the delimiter specified as the start delimiter and the delimiter specified as the end delimiter.

An example of the Extract Text Range dialog box is shown in Figure 10-12.

Format

Format applies formatting to text in a given column. Here are the valid formats:

- Lowercase
- Uppercase
- Capitalize Each Word
- Trim (Remove leading and trailing whitespace)

- Clean (Remove non-printable characters)
- Add Prefix
- Add Suffix

The resulting formatted text is placed in a new column.

Index Column

Index Column creates a new column in the query with a sequential number for each row based on the current sort order of the rows. The sequential numbering starts with 0 by default. You can specify to have the numbering start with 1. You can also specify a custom starting value and a custom increment using the Add Index Column dialog box shown in Figure 10-20.

Information

Information creates a new column reflecting information about the value in the selected column. Information has the following options:

- Is Even
- Is Odd
- Sign

When indicating the sign, 1 means positive, −1 means negative, and 0 means the value was 0.

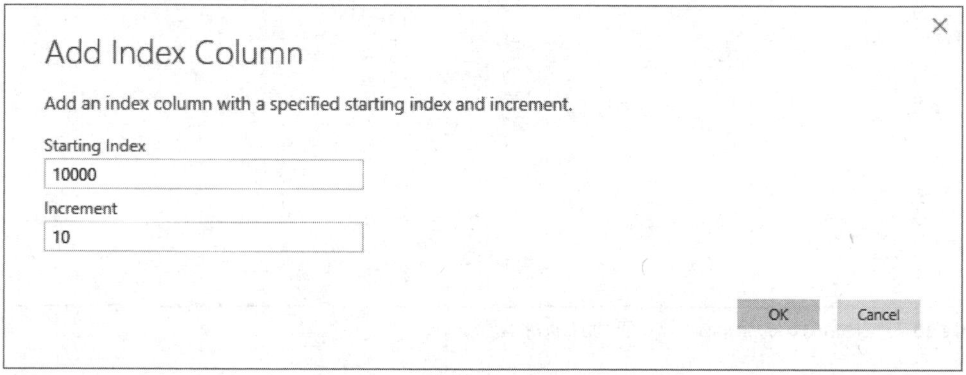

Figure 10-20 *The Add Index Column dialog box*

Invoke Custom Function

Invoke Custom Function allows you to use a custom function to calculate the values in a new column. Custom functions are created by right-clicking in the Queries area and selecting New Query | Blank Query from the context menu, as shown in Figure 10-21. The definition of the function is then entered, as shown in Figure 10-22, with parameters defined between the parentheses and the function calculation on the right side of the "=>" symbol.

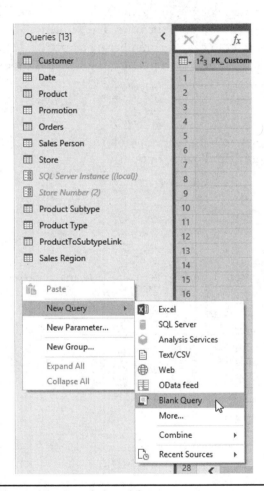

Figure 10-21 *Creating a blank query for a custom function definition*

Figure 10-22 *Defining a custom function*

Once the function is defined, it can be invoked using the Invoke Custom Function transformation. The Invoke Custom Function dialog box allows you to define the name of the new column and to select the custom function to use. This is shown in Figure 10-23.

Merge Columns

Merge Columns joins the content of two columns into a new column. The new column replaces the source columns in the query. A separator can be specified for insertion between the two values. The Merge Columns dialog box is used to define the new column, as shown earlier in Figure 10-14.

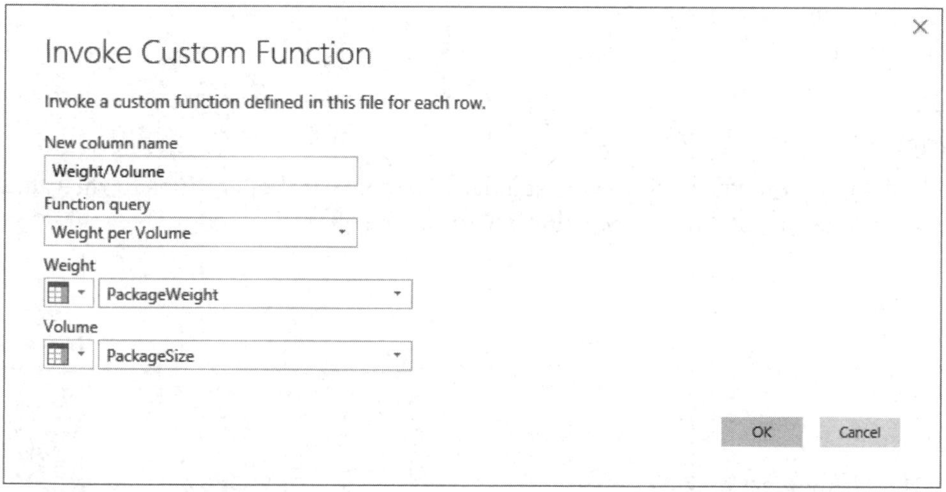

Invoke Custom Function

Invoke a custom function defined in this file for each row.

New column name

Weight/Volume

Function query

Weight per Volume

Weight

PackageWeight

Volume

PackageSize

OK   Cancel

Figure 10-23 *The Invoke Custom Function dialog box*

Parse

Parse interprets the selected column as either an XML or JSON structure. The contents are parsed and placed in an embedded table. Click the button to the right of the column header to expand the embedded record into columns.

Rounding

Rounding removes some or all of the decimal portion of a value. Round Up moves the value up to the closest integer. Round Down moves the value down to the closest integer. Round . . . performs rounding to the specified decimal place. The Round dialog box, shown earlier in Figure 10-16, is used to specify the number of decimal places to round to.

Scientific

Scientific applies one of the following scientific operations to the values in a numeric column, creating a new column with the result:

- Absolute Value
- Power
- Square Root
- Exponent
- Logarithm
- Factorial

Standard

Standard applies one of the following standard mathematical operations to the values in a numeric column, creating a new column with the result:

- Add
- Multiply
- Subtract
- Divide
- Divide (Integer)
- Modulo

- Percentage
- Percent Of

Statistics

Statistics performs one of the following statistical analyses on the selected column:

- Sum
- Minimum
- Maximum
- Median
- Average
- Standard Deviation
- Count Values
- Count Distinct Values

The statistical analysis is informational only. Once you have noted the statistic that was requested, you can delete this transformation from the Applied Steps list.

Trigonometry

Trigonometry applies one of the following trigonometric operations to the values in a numeric column, creating a new column with the result:

- Sine
- Cosine
- Tangent
- Arcsine
- Arccosine
- Arctangent

Time

When Time is applied to a column containing time-related values, it creates a new column containing a value calculated from the time value. When Time is applied to a column of type Text, it converts the text to a time value. Alternatively, a date and a time value can be combined into a single value.

The following values can be calculated from a time-related data type:

Time Only	Removes any date portion of the value
Local Time	Changes the values to local time
Parse	Parses a text column to extract a time value
Hour | Hour	The hour portion of the value as a number
Hour | Start of Hour	The first minute and second of the hour containing the value
Hour | End of Hour	The last minute and second of the hour containing the value
Minute	The minute portion of the value as a number
Second	The second portion of the value as a number
Subtract	The duration between two selected time columns
Combine Date and Time	Combines a selected date column and a selected time column into a single column
Earliest	The earliest value in the column (informational only)
Latest	The latest value in the column (informational only)

Model Building

Now that you know how to get data from a myriad of sources and transform that data into the format you need, it is time to look at the steps to define the data model itself. You learn to do that in Chapters 11 through 14.

Chapter 11

Creating a Tabular Model in Power BI

In This Chapter

- Relationships
- User-Friendly Models
- Formatting and Categories

In Chapter 9, we used the Power BI Query Editor to pull data into our data models. We were able to manipulate that data to get it just the way we needed it before it was loaded. That data serves as the raw material for our data models.

Now we need to do the work required to present the data in a manner useful to our business users. Our data models need relationships, hierarchies, and measures in order to allow users to get the most out of the data. We also need to apply some basic formatting to make our models business-user friendly.

Relationships

As our Population-GDP-CO2 by Country model in the "Population-GDP-CO2 by Country from Scratch.pbix" file currently sits, we can analyze the data in one table at a time to get insights into population growth or changes in CO_2 output. However, there are no relationships between our tables. Therefore, we cannot do things like look for a correlation between population growth and changes in CO_2 output. This is a severe limitation of our data model that needs to be addressed.

Creating Relationships

We added intermediate tables in Chapter 9 to facilitate relationships in the Population-GDP-CO2 by Country model. Now it is time to put those intermediate tables to work. We need to create those relationships.

Creating Relationships Using the Manage Relationships Dialog Box

1. Open the "Population-GDP-CO2 by Country from Scratch.pbix" file in Power BI Desktop.
2. In the Modeling tab of the ribbon, click Manage Relationships. The "Manage relationships" dialog box appears.
3. Click New, as shown in Figure 11-1. The "Create relationship" dialog box appears.

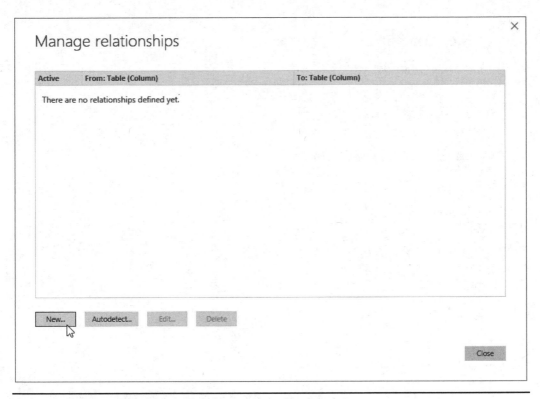

Figure 11-1   *Adding a new relationship in the Manage relationships dialog box*

4. Select the Population table from the upper dropdown list, as shown in Figure 11-2.
5. Select the "Country (or dependent territory)" column from the columns in the Population table, as shown in Figure 11-3.
6. Select the Country table from the middle dropdown list, as shown in Figure 11-4.
7. Select the PopulationTableCntry/Terr column from the columns in the Country table, as shown in Figure 11-5.

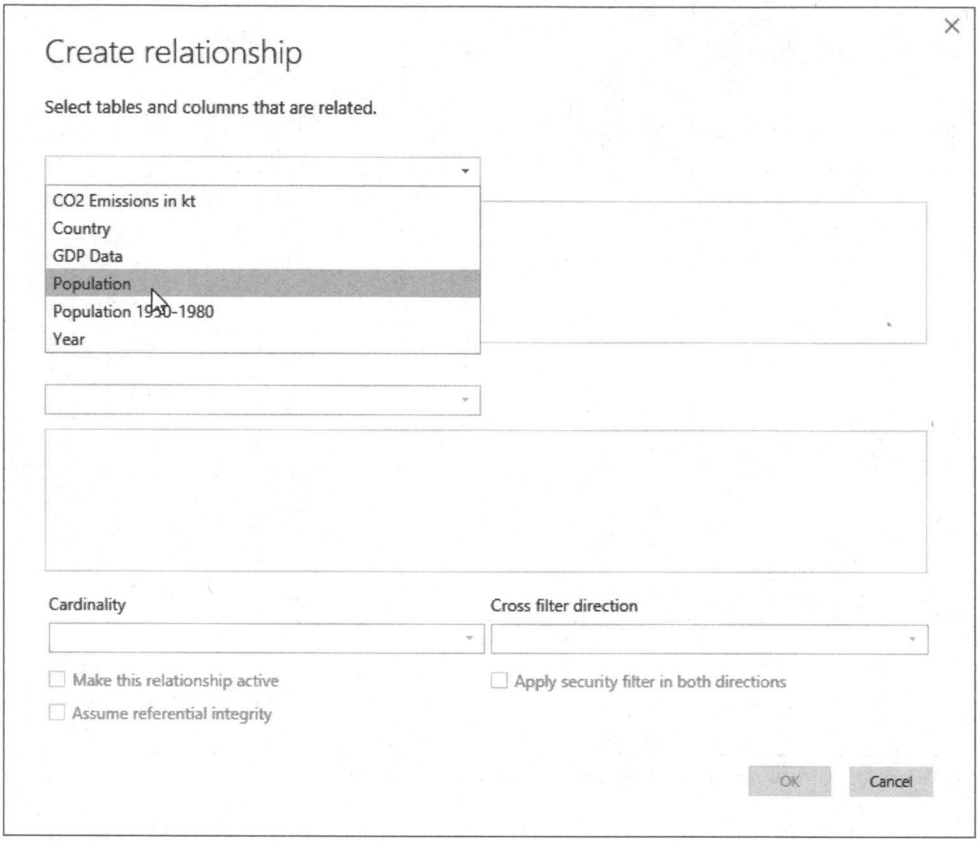

Figure 11-2   *Selecting the first table in the relationship*

8. Click OK to close the "Create relationship" dialog box.
9. Click New.
10. Select the GDP Data table from the upper dropdown list.
11. Select the Country Name column from the columns in the GDP Data table.
12. Select the Country table from the middle dropdown list.

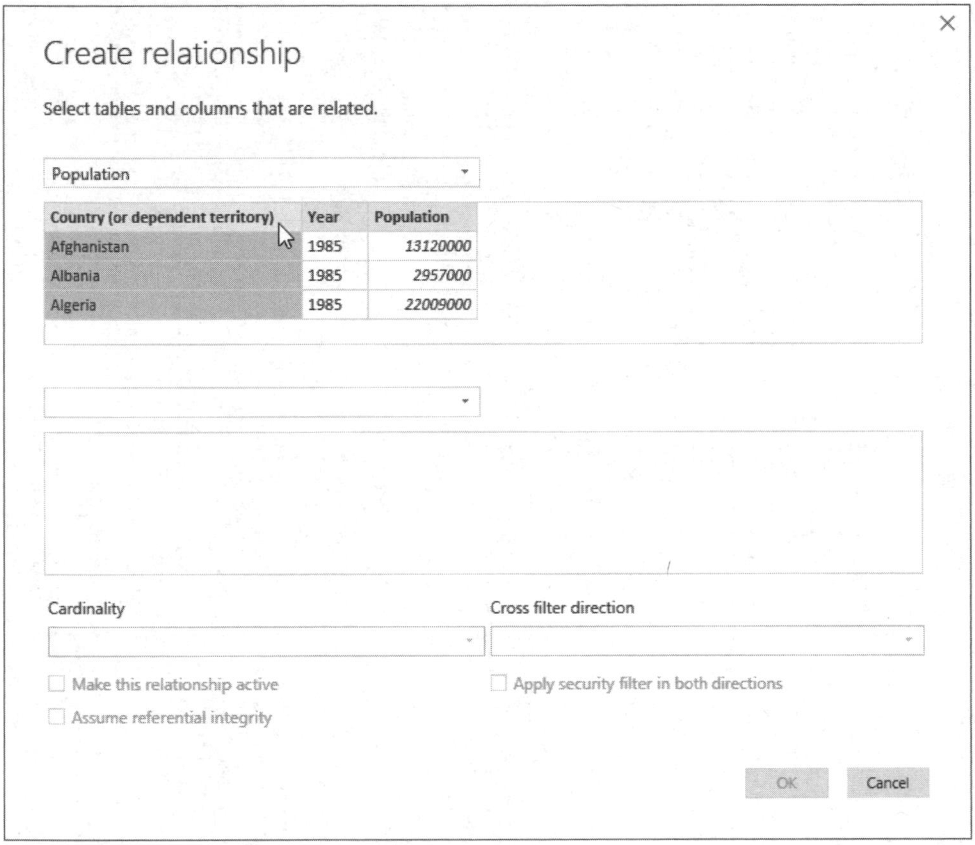

Figure 11-3 *Selecting the column in the first table in the relationship*

13. Scroll right and select the GDPCntry/Terr column from the columns in the
    Country table.
14. Click OK.
15. Click New.
16. Select the "CO2 Emissions in kt" table from the upper dropdown list.

328 Data Analysis with Microsoft Power BI

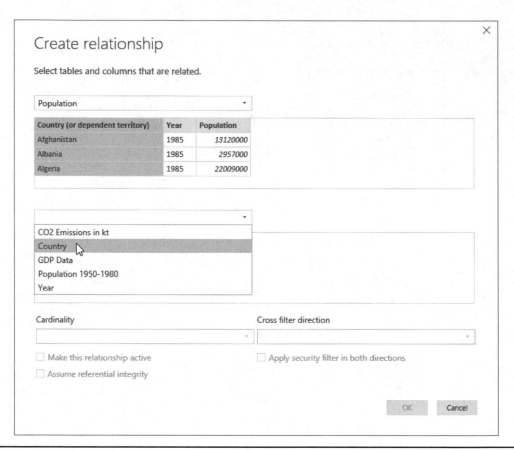

Figure 11-4 *Selecting the second table in the relationship*

17. Select the Country Name column from the columns in the "CO2 Emissions in kt" table.
18. Select the Country table from the middle dropdown list.
19. Scroll right and select the CO2TableCntry/Terr column from the columns in the Country table.
20. Click OK.
21. Click Close to close the "Manage relationships" dialog box.

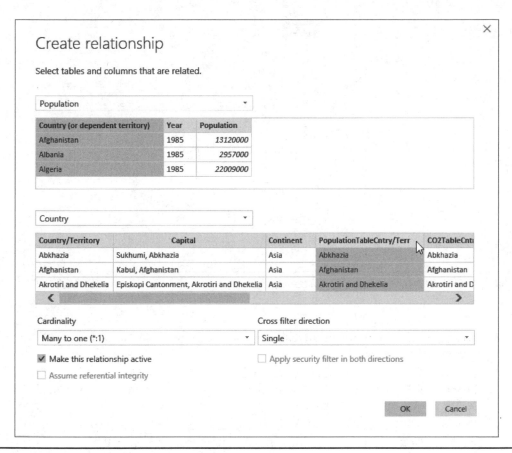

Figure 11-5   *Selecting the column in the second table in the relationship*

Creating Relationships in the Model View

1. On the left side of the Power BI Desktop window, select Model, as shown in Figure 11-6. The Model view of the data model appears.

2. Click the "Fit to screen" button at the bottom of the Power BI Desktop window so all tables are visible in the Model view. This is shown in Figure 11-7. You can also use the -/+ slider (next to the "Fit to screen" button) to zoom in or zoom out.

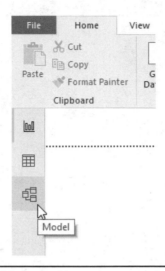

Figure 11-6 *Selecting the Model view of the data model*

3. Drag the tables into the arrangement shown in Figure 11-8 and click the "Fit to screen" button again.

4. In the "CO2 Emissions in kt" table, click Year. Drag and drop it on Year in the Year table. An active, one-to-many relationship is created from the Year table to "CO2 Emissions in kt" table.

5. In the GDP Data table, click Year. Drag and drop it on Year in the Year table. An active, one-to-many relationship is created from the Year table to the GDP Data table.

Figure 11-7 *The Model view Fit to screen button*

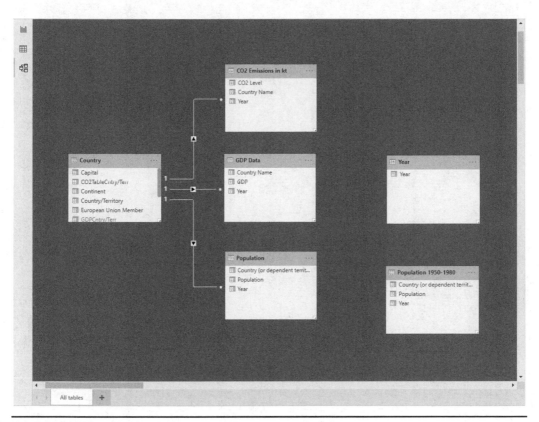

Figure 11-8 *The rearranged Model view*

6. In the Population table, click Year. Drag and drop it on Year in the Year table. An active, one-to-many relationship is created from the Year table to the Population table. The Model view should appear as shown in Figure 11-9.

7. Click Save.

Notice the small arrows on the relationship connections all go from the Country table to the other tables or from the Year table to the other tables. Therefore, when we select a country in the Country table, it will filter the other tables to display just the data for that country. When we select a year in the Year table, it will filter the other tables to display just the data from that year.

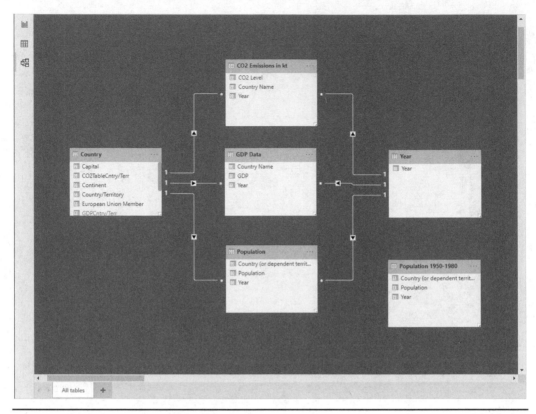

Figure 11-9 *The Model view with additional relationships*

User-Friendly Models

After our models are published, they can be used by other users to explore the data and create additional reports. (Of course, that is only true if those users are granted permission to use a given data model.) In order for other users to be as productive as possible, we want those users to be comfortable with our models. That means making our models user friendly.

A user-friendly model reflects the natural structure of the organization. Names should appear normal to the user, not some form of techie abbreviation. Tables in the model used solely as intermediate tables should be hidden from the user. Likewise, fields that are in the model just to facilitate relationships should be hidden from the user.

In this section, we will continue our formatting of the Population-GDP-CO2 by Country model. Once that is complete, we will work on the formatting of the Max Min Sales Information model. By the end of this chapter, we will have two models that present data in a user-friendly manner. You never know when a model might go from being your personal playground to a tool to be shared with others. Get in the habit of performing these formatting operations on all of your models to ensure they are always ready for public consumption.

Hiding Columns from the End User

In the previous section, we set up relationships so filtering on countries should be done using fields in the Country table and filtering on year should be done using fields in the Year table. We don't want to select countries and years in the tables containing the data. Therefore, let's hide the Year- and Country-related fields in the data tables. Likewise, when filtering, we don't want the special linking fields in the Country table to be selected (that is, PopulationTableCntry/Terr, GDPCntry/Terr, and CO2TableCntry/Terr).

In addition, the data from the Population 1950-1980 table was appended to the Population table. Therefore, we do not want to use the Population 1950-1980 table in our reporting. This is simply a staging table for use during the data load process. To simplify our model, we will hide that table, too.

Hiding the Internal-Use Columns and the Staging Table

1. Right-click the "Country (or dependent territory)" field in the Population table.
2. Select "Hide in report view" from the context menu. The field is grayed out.
3. Right-click the Year field in the Population table.
4. Select "Hide in report view" from the context menu.
5. Right-click the Country Name field in the "CO2 Emissions in kt" table.
6. Select "Hide in report view" from the context menu.
7. Right-click the Year field in the "CO2 Emissions in kt" table.
8. Select "Hide in report view" from the context menu.
9. We can also hide fields while viewing the model through the Data view. Click the Data button on the left side of the window, as shown in Figure 11-10. Power BI Desktop switches to Data view.
10. Select the GDP Data table in the Fields pane on the right.
11. Right-click the Country Name column heading and select "Hide in report view" from the context menu.

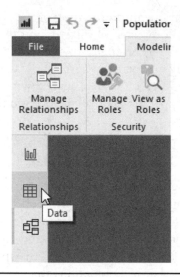

Figure 11-10 *Selecting the Data view*

12. Right-click the Year column heading and select "Hide in report view" from the context menu.

13. Select the Country table in the Fields pane.

14. Right-click the PopulationTableCntry/Terr column heading and select "Hide in report view" from the context menu.

15. Right-click the CO2TableCntry/Terr column heading and select "Hide in report view" from the context menu.

16. Right-click the GDPCntry/Terr column heading and select "Hide in report view" from the context menu.

17. Right-click the heading of the Population 1950-1980 table and select "Hide in report view" from the context menu. The table is grayed out.

18. Click Save.

Column Names and Descriptions

We have a few fields in the Country table of the Population-GDP-CO2 by Country model that have column names using "camel case." In camel case formatting, the spaces of a phrase are removed and the first letter in each word in the phrase is capitalized. This creates an effect like the humps of a camel in the middle of each phrase. EuropeanUnionMember and GroupOf20Member are two examples.

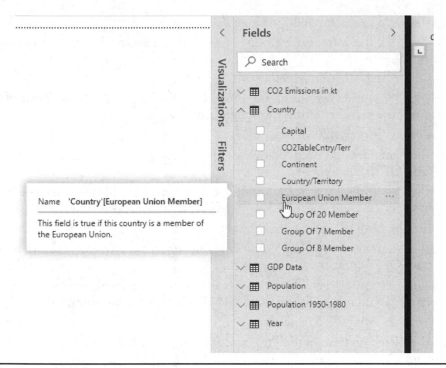

Figure 11-11 *Displaying the description of a field in a tooltip*

Camel case is often used when naming fields in database tables because embedded spaces in field names are either not allowed or make the fields more cumbersome to use. Our data model in Power BI does not have any issue with embedded spaces. Therefore, we will modify those column names to make them more familiar to nontechnical users.

At the same time, we will add descriptions to these columns. A description can be used to record information about where the data comes from or how it should be used. The content of the description is visible to the user if they hover over the field in the Fields pane, as shown in Figure 11-11. The description is specified on the Properties pane visible in the Model view.

Renaming Columns and Adding Descriptions

1. Click the Model button on the left side of the window.
2. Select the Country table.
3. In the Description textbox on the Properties pane, type **Use this table to slice the data by geographic information.**

4. In the Fields pane, expand the Country table.

5. Right-click the EuropeanUnionMember field and select Rename from the context menu.

6. Type **European Union Member** and press ENTER.

7. In the Description textbox on the Properties pane, type **This field is true if this country is a member of the European Union.**

8. Select the GroupOf20Member field.

9. In the Name textbox on the Properties pane, replace the current content with **Group Of 20 Member** and press ENTER.

10. In the Description textbox on the Properties pane, type **This field is true if this country is a member of the 20 largest IMF advanced economies.**

11. Select the GroupOf7Member field.

12. In the Name textbox on the Properties pane, replace the current content with **Group Of 7 Member** and press ENTER.

13. In the Description textbox on the Properties pane, type **This field is true if this country is a member of the 7 largest IMF advanced economies.**

14. Select the GroupOf8Member field.

15. In the Name textbox on the Properties pane, replace the current content with **Group Of 8 Member** and press ENTER.

16. In the Description textbox on the Properties pane, type **This field is true if this country is a member of the 8 largest IMF advanced economies.**

17. Click the Report button on the left side of the window. Notice the Population 1950-1980 table is no longer visible.

18. In the Fields pane, expand the Country table. Notice the internal-use fields are no longer visible.

19. In the Fields pane, hover over the Group Of 20 Member field and note the description in the tooltip.

20. Click Save.

21. Close Power BI Desktop.

Formatting and Categories

We switch now from the Population-GDP-CO2 by Country model to the Max Min Sales Information Incomplete Model. This model already has most of the required relationships defined. Most of what is needed in this model is to take care of formatting and naming. As previously noted, our Power BI data models should be as friendly and familiar as possible.

One Final Relationship

In Chapter 9, we manually created the Date table in the Max Min Sales Information Incomplete Model. We did not, however, relate this new table to any of the existing tables in the model. We will begin our work with this model in this chapter by creating that missing relationship.

Creating a Final Relationship in Max Min
Sales Information Incomplete Model

1. Locate the "Max Min Sales Information Incomplete Model.pbix" file in the file system location where you saved it.
2. Double-click the "Max Min Sales Information Incomplete Model.pbix" file. This will open the file in Power BI Desktop.
3. On the left side of the window, select Data. The Data view of the model appears.
4. On the Home tab of the ribbon, click Manage Relationships. The "Manage relationships" dialog box appears.
5. Click New.
6. Select Date from the upper dropdown list.
7. Select the Date column from the columns in the Date table.
8. Select Sales_Information from the middle dropdown list.
9. Select the FK_Date column from the columns in the Sales_Information table.
10. Click OK.
11. Click Close.
12. Click Save.

Data Categories

Power BI provides several data categories that can be assigned to columns in our tables. These categories tell Power BI how to use these columns during reporting. For example, we will assign the State or Province category to the State field. This tells Power BI it can use this field to assign values to a location on a map. The following data categories can be assigned to fields within a Power BI data model:

- Address
- Barcode
- City

- Continent
- Country/Region
- County
- Image URL
- Latitude
- Longitude
- Place
- Postal Code
- State or Province
- Web URL

We will also assign data categories to several fields in the Customer table. In addition, we will complete the final cleanup of several other tables in this model.

Cleaning Up the Customer Table

1. Select the Customer table in the Fields area, if it is not selected by default.
2. The PK_Customer field is used by a relationship in the model, but does not provide any value as we analyze the data. Right-click the PK_Customer heading in the grid and select "Hide in report view" from the context menu.
3. Right-click the Customer_Name heading and select Rename from the context menu.
4. Type **Customer** and press ENTER.
5. Click the Address heading.
6. On the Modeling tab of the ribbon, select Address from the Data Category dropdown list.
7. Click the City heading.
8. On the Modeling tab of the ribbon, select City from the Data Category dropdown list.
9. Click the State heading.
10. On the Modeling tab of the ribbon, select State or Province from the Data Category dropdown list.
11. Click the ZipCode heading.

12. On the Modeling tab of the ribbon, select Postal Code from the Data Category dropdown list.

13. Right-click the ZipCode heading and select Rename from the context menu.

14. Type **Zip Code** and press ENTER.

15. Right-click the Homeowner heading and select Rename from the context menu.

16. Type **Home Owner?** and press ENTER.

17. Right-click the MaritalStatus heading and select Rename from the context menu.

18. Type **Married?** and press ENTER.

19. Right-click the NumCarsOwned heading and select Rename from the context menu.

20. Type **Number of Cars Owned** and press ENTER.

21. On the Modeling tab of the ribbon, select Average from the Default Summarization dropdown list.

22. Right-click the NumChildrenAtHome heading and select Rename from the context menu.

23. Type **Number of Children at Home** and press ENTER.

24. On the Modeling tab of the ribbon, select Average from the Default Summarization dropdown list.

25. Right-click the SalesRegion heading and select Rename from the context menu.

26. Type **Sales Region** and press ENTER.

Cleaning Up the Date Table

In the Date table, there is a human-readable version of each field and a sortable version of each field. We will hide the sortable version of each field while renaming and setting the Sort By property for the human-readable version of each field.

1. Select the Date table in the Fields area.

2. Click the Date heading.

3. In the Format dropdown list on the Modeling tab of the ribbon, select Date Time | 3/14/2001 (M/d/yyyy).

4. Right-click the YearSort heading and select "Hide in report view" from the context menu.

5. Click the Year heading.

6. Click the Sort By Column button on the Modeling tab of the ribbon and select YearSort from the menu.

7. Right-click the QtrSort heading and select "Hide in report view" from the context menu.

8. Click the Quarter heading.

9. Click the Sort By Column button and select QtrSort from the menu.

10. Right-click the MnSort heading and select "Hide in report view" from the context menu.

11. Click the Month heading.

12. Click the Sort By Column button and select MnSort from the menu.

13. Right-click the MnOfYrSort heading and select "Hide in report view" from the context menu.

14. Click the Month of Year heading.

15. Click the Sort By Column button and select MnOfYrSort from the menu.

Cleaning Up the Product and Promotion Tables

1. Select the Product table in the Fields area.

2. The PK_Product field is used for creating relationships in the model, but does not provide any value as we analyze the data. Right-click the PK_Product heading in the grid and select "Hide in report view" from the context menu.

3. Right-click the Product_Name heading and select Rename from the context menu.

4. Type **Product** and press ENTER.

5. Click the RetailPrice heading and select Rename from the context menu.

6. Type **Retail Price** and press ENTER.

7. In the Format dropdown list on the Modeling tab of the ribbon, select Currency | $ English (United States).

8. In the Default Summarization dropdown list on the Modeling tab of the ribbon, select Average.

9. Click the Weight heading.

10. In the Default Summarization dropdown list on the Modeling tab of the ribbon, select Average.

11. Right-click the ProductSubtype heading and select Rename from the context menu.

12. Type **Product Subtype** and press ENTER.

13. Right-click the ProductType heading and select Rename from the context menu.

14. Type **Product Type** and press ENTER.

15. Right-click the ProductTypeColor heading and select Rename from the context menu.

16. Type **Product Type Color** and press ENTER.

17. Select the Promotion table in the Fields area.

18. The PK_Promotion field is used for creating relationships in the model, but does not provide any value as we analyze the data. Right-click the PK_Promotion heading in the grid and select "Hide in report view" from the context menu.

19. Right-click the Promotion_Name heading and select Rename from the context menu.

20. Type **Promotion** and press ENTER.

Cleaning Up the Sales_Information Table

We will rename the Sales_Information table itself to better reflect its content—orders. We will also hide all the foreign key fields used to link this table to the other tables in the model. Finally, we will delete the Sales_Tax and Shipping columns, which do not contain any data.

1. In the Fields area, right-click the Sales_Information table and select Rename from the context menu.

2. Type **Orders** and press ENTER.

3. Select the Orders table in the Fields area.

4. Right-click the FK_Date heading in the grid and select "Hide in report view" from the context menu.

5. Repeat Step 4 to hide the following fields:

    - FK_Customer

    - FK_Product

    - FK_Promotion

    - FK_Sales_Person

    - FK_Store

6. Right-click the Sales_in_Dollars heading and select Rename from the context menu.

7. Type **Sales in US Dollars** and press ENTER.

8. In the Format dropdown list on the Modeling tab of the ribbon, select Currency | $ English (United States).

9. Right-click the Sales_in_Units heading and select Rename from the context menu.

10. Type **Sales in Units** and press ENTER.
11. In the Format dropdown list on the Modeling tab of the ribbon, select Whole number.
12. In the Formatting area on the Modeling tab of the ribbon, click the "," (Thousands separator) button.
13. Right-click the Sales_Tax heading and select Delete from the context menu. The "Delete column" dialog box appears.
14. Click Delete.
15. Right-click the Shipping heading and select Delete from the context menu. The "Delete column" dialog box appears.
16. Click Delete.

Cleaning Up the Sales_Person and Store Tables

1. In the Fields area, right-click the Sales_Person table and select Rename from the context menu.
2. Type **Sales Person** and press ENTER.
3. Select the Sales Person table in the Fields area.
4. Right-click PK_Sales_Person and select "Hide in report view" from the context menu.
5. Right-click Sales_Person_Name and select Rename from the context menu.
6. Type **Sales Person** and press ENTER.
7. Right-click Sales_Person_SCD_Original_ID and select "Hide in report view" from the context menu.
8. Right-click Sales_Person_SCD_Status and select Rename from the context menu.
9. Type **Status** and press ENTER.
10. Right-click Sales_Person_SCD_Start_Date and select Rename from the context menu.
11. Type **Sales Person Start Date** and press ENTER.
12. In the Format dropdown list on the Modeling tab of the ribbon, select Date Time | 3/14/2001 (M/d/yyyy).
13. Right-click Sales_Person_SCD_End_Date and select Rename from the context menu.
14. Type **Sales Person End Date** and press ENTER.
15. In the Format dropdown list on the Modeling tab of the ribbon, select Date Time | 3/14/2001 (M/d/yyyy).

16. Right-click Sales_Person_Territory and select Rename from the context menu.
17. Type **Sales Territory** and press ENTER.
18. In the Default Summarization dropdown list in the Modeling tab of the ribbon, select "Don't summarize."
19. Select the Store table in the Fields area.
20. Right-click PK_Store and select "Hide in report view" from the context menu.
21. Right-click Store_Name and select Rename from the context menu.
22. Type **Store** and press ENTER.
23. Right-click Store_Type and select Rename from the context menu.
24. Type **Store Type** and press ENTER.
25. Click Save.

Hierarchies, Groups, and Bins

Data often has a natural organization or clusters. There may be hierarchies such as customers within cities and cities within states. There may be groupings of a particular category, such as all the British soldier miniatures or all the French soldier miniatures. There may be ranges of continuous quantities we want to consider together in a "bin." For example, we may want to consider all the products with weights over 70 ounces together for certain analysis.

We can define each of these types of data organization and clustering in our data model. This makes it easy to utilize these structures on our reports. It also ensures that all users of the data model have the same definition for these structures. We will add hierarchies, groups, and bins to our model.

Adding Hierarchies

1. In the Fields area, expand the entry for the Customer table.
2. Right-click the entry for the State field. You can also click the ellipsis (…) button to see the same context menu.
3. Select "New hierarchy" from the context menu. A new hierarchy called State Hierarchy is created. The State field is set as the highest level in the hierarchy.
4. Right-click the State Hierarchy entry and select Rename from the context menu.
5. Type **Geographic Hierarchy** and press ENTER. The hierarchy moves so it is in the correct sort order among the fields in the Customer table.
6. Click the City field. Drag and drop it on top of the Geographic Hierarchy entry. City is added as a lower level of the hierarchy.

7. Click the Customer field. Drag and drop it on top of the Geographic Hierarchy entry. Customer is added as a lower level of the hierarchy. The Fields area should appear, as shown in Figure 11-12.

8. Collapse the entry for the Customer table.

9. Expand the entry for the Date table.

10. Click the Quarter field. Drag and drop it on top of the Year field. A new hierarchy is created called Year Hierarchy with Year as the highest level and Quarter as the lowest level.

11. Right-click Year Hierarchy and select Rename from the context menu.

12. Type **Date Hierarchy** and press ENTER.

13. Click the Month field. Drag and drop it on top of the Date Hierarchy entry. Month is added as a lower level of the hierarchy.

14. Click the Date field. Drag and drop it on top of the Date Hierarchy entry. Date is added as a lower level of the hierarchy.

15. Collapse the Date Hierarchy entry. We are doing this to make it easier to correctly complete the following steps.

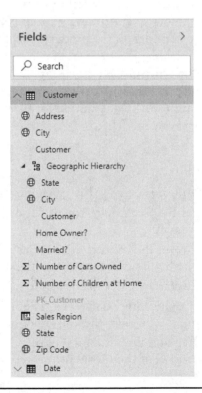

Figure 11-12 *The geographic hierarchy in the Customer table*

16. Right-click the Year field entry (the Year field entry not in the Date Hierarchy) and select "Hide in report view" from the context menu.

17. Repeat Step 16 for the Quarter, Month, and Date fields. Now, if we want to use Year, Quarter, Month, or Date in our report, we must access it through the Date Hierarchy.

18. Collapse the entry for the Date table.

19. Expand the entry for the Store table.

20. Select the Store field and drop it on top of the Store Type field. A new hierarchy called Store Type Hierarchy is created.

21. Right-click the Store field entry that is not part of the hierarchy and select "Hide in report view" from the context menu.

22. Right-click the Store Type field entry that is not part of the hierarchy and select "Hide in report view" from the context menu.

23. Click Save.

Creating Groups

1. In the Fields pane, expand the Product table.

2. Right-click the Product field and select "New group" from the context menu. The Groups dialog box appears.

3. Replace the content of the Name textbox with **Soldiers Grouped by Country**.

4. In the "Ungrouped values" list, select British Artillery.

5. In the "Ungrouped values" list, hold down SHIFT and click British Tank Commander. All four British military miniatures are now selected in the list.

6. Click Group. A new group is created in the "Groups and members" area.

7. Type **British Military** and press ENTER.

8. In the "Ungrouped values" list, scroll down until you can see all three French items.

9. Select French Artillery.

10. SHIFT-click French Infantry.

11. Click Group.

12. Type **French Military** and press ENTER. The Groups dialog box should appear, as shown in Figure 11-13.

13. Check the "Include Other group" check box. This will create a group called "Other" that will contain all the ungrouped items.

14. Click OK. The new group appears in the Fields pane, as shown in Figure 11-14.

15. Let's continue by creating a quick chart to show how our Soldiers Grouped by Country group works. Click the Report button on the left side of the window.

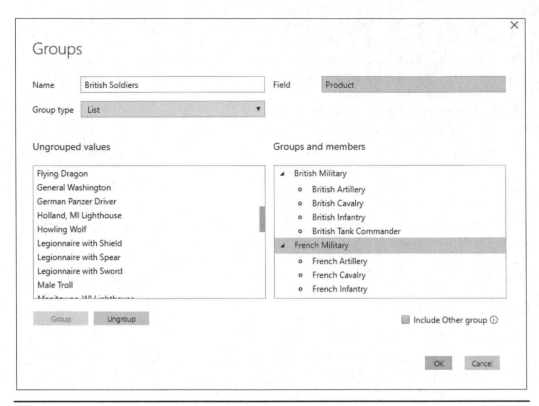

Figure 11-13 *The Groups dialog box with Country Groups*

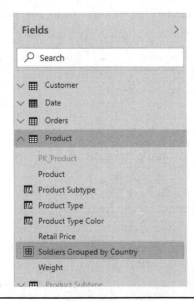

Figure 11-14 *The group entry in the Fields pane*

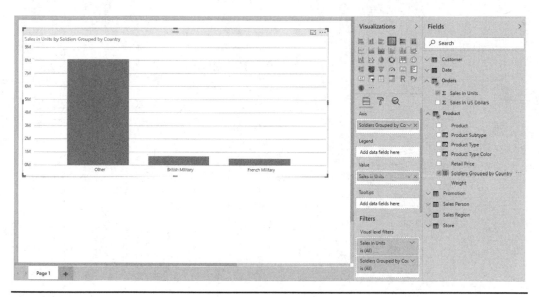

Figure 11-15 *A chart using a group*

16. In the Fields pane, expand the Orders table.

17. Check the box next to Sales in Units. This creates a column chart showing the total sales in units.

18. Check the box next to Soldiers Grouped by Country in the Product table. This will create entries on the chart's horizontal access for each of the groups in our grouping, as shown in Figure 11-15.

Creating Bins

1. In the Fields pane, right-click the Weight field in the Product table and select "New group" from the context menu. We see a different Groups dialog box this time because Weight has a numeric data type rather than a text data type. The Group type defaults to Bin. We can create bins based on the weight range covered by each bin ("Size of bins") or by the total number of bins that result. We will create our bins based on the size of each bin.

2. In the "Bin size" textbox, type **10**. The Groups dialog box should appear, as shown in Figure 11-16.

3. Click OK.

4. Again, let's create a quick chart to show how our Weight bins work. Click the plus sign in the yellow box at the bottom of the window to create a new tab.

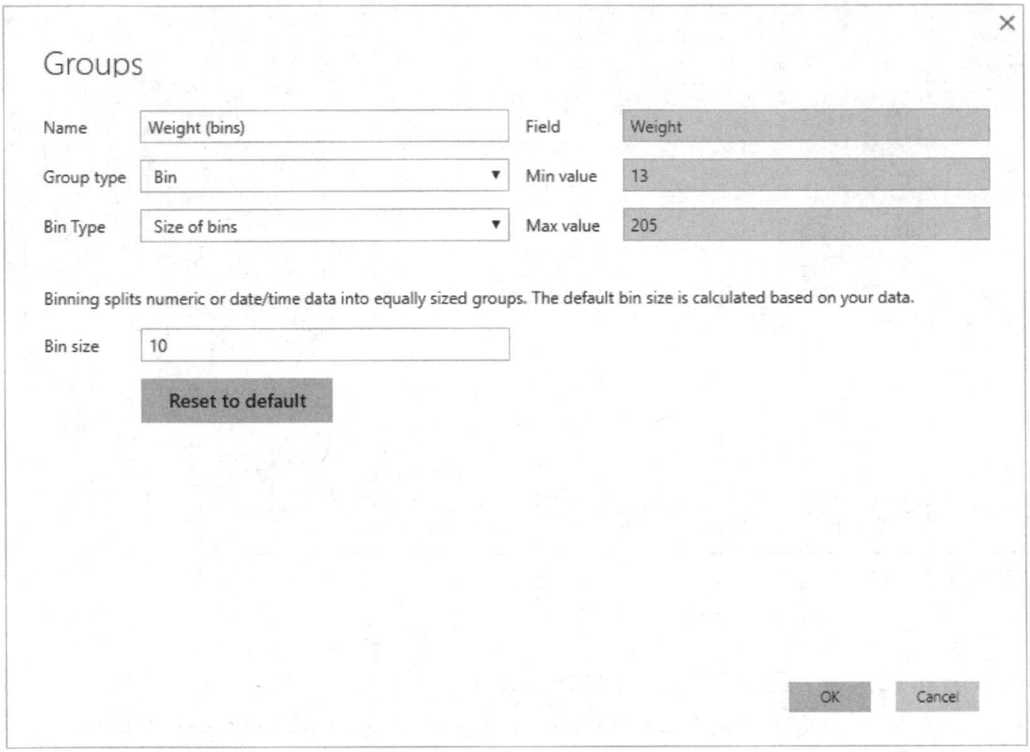

Figure 11-16   *The Groups dialog box for the Weight field*

5. In the Fields pane, check the box next to "Weight (bins)" in the Product table.
6. Click Table on the Visualizations pane to change this to a table visualization.
7. In the Fields pane, check the box next to Sales in Units in the Orders table. This creates a table showing the sales in units for each ten-ounce range or bin of product weight. This is shown in Figure 11-17.

   In our table, the "10.00" entry is for the bin containing products with weights between 10.00 ounces and 19.99 ounces. The "20.00" entry is for the bin containing products with weights between 20.00 ounces and 29.99 ounces, and so on. There are no products with a weight between 110.00 ounces and 119.99 ounces, so the "110.00" bin is not included in our table.
8. Click Save.
9. Close Power BI Desktop.

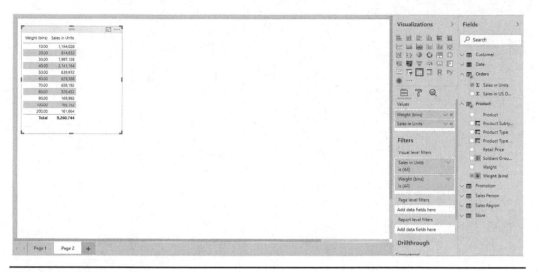

Figure 11-17 *A table using bins*

Measuring Up

We have come a long way toward creating user-friendly models. Relationships have been created, unnecessary items have been hidden, and the tables and fields have names that are familiar to our business users.

Now we need to capture business logic in our models. This is done through measures and calculated columns. That is our task in Chapter 12.

Chapter 12

Measures and Calculated Columns

In This Chapter

- Calculated Columns
- Measures
- DAX Variables

We made great progress building and refining our data models in Chapter 11. Tables are properly related. Tables and rows are nicely named and formatted. We also created hierarchies, groups, and bins. However, one major piece is missing. We have not captured the business logic in our model.

The business logic of an organization is the calculations used to determine its key performance indicators, such as those formulas and equations used to evaluate year-over-year performance, manufacturing efficiency, or customer retention. These calculations are what make the data models useful to users as decision-making tools.

In Power BI data models, business logic is defined using measures and calculated columns. Measures and calculated columns, in turn, are defined using the Data Analysis Expressions (DAX) language. DAX provides an extremely capable platform for creating business calculations within our models.

The DAX language relies heavily on functions that are strung together to create DAX expressions. This is very similar to the way expressions are created in Excel. If you are comfortable creating expressions in Excel, you should be comfortable creating expressions with DAX.

For an in-depth look at DAX and DAX functions, see Chapter 13. In this chapter, you will see how to utilize DAX functions to create calculated columns and measures in our data models. We will also discover the all-important context concepts that make DAX so powerful.

Calculated Columns

We begin with calculated columns. A calculated column has a value for each and every row in the data model. That value is defined by a single DAX expression that is evaluated for each row in the table. This expression is evaluated when the data is loaded into the table to determine the values for that column.

Creating a Calculated Column

We will begin by creating calculated columns in the Orders table of our Max Min Sales Information Incomplete model. Our goal is to create a column showing the total weight for each order line. We do this by taking the number of units sold and multiplying it by the weight of the product in that order line.

We have one issue we need to overcome before we can accomplish this calculation. The Sales in Units field is present in the Orders table and the product key is present in the Orders table, but the product weight is not. We will need to look up the weight of the product in the Product table using the product key.

Fortunately, DAX has a function for doing this type of lookup. The RELATED() function enables us to find the value of a column in the corresponding record of a related table. We will create a calculated column in the Orders table that contains the product weight from the related record in the Product table. Next, we will create a second calculated column in the Orders table using the product weight to calculate the order weight.

Adding a Calculated Column to the Orders Table

1. Open the Max Min Sales Information Incomplete Model.pbix file in Power BI Desktop.
2. Click Data on the left to go to the Data screen.
3. Select the Orders table in the Fields area on the right. You see the data in the Orders table.
4. On the Home tab of the ribbon, click New Column. A new column is created, and the formula bar appears ready for you to enter the formula for that column.
5. Delete the "Column =" text and type the following in the formula bar:

```
Product Wt = RELATED('Product'[Weight])
```

The text to the left of the equal sign becomes the name of the new column.

6. Press ENTER. After a few moments a new column called Product Wt will be added to the Orders table. The Weight will be brought into the new column from the Product table based on the existing relationship between the two tables.
7. Our goal was to have the total weight for the order line, not just the weight of an individual product. Let's add a second calculated column. On the Modeling tab of the ribbon, click New Column. (You can use the New Column item on either the Home tab or the Modeling tab of the ribbon to create the new column.)
8. Delete the "Column =" text and type the following in the formula bar:

```
Order Product Wt = 'Orders'[Sales in Units] *
                        'Orders'[Product Wt]
```

9. Press ENTER. After you have completed these steps, the formula bar and the Orders table appear as shown in Figure 12-1.
10. Click Save.

The Context for Calculated Columns

DAX expressions rely heavily on the context in which they are evaluated. It is essential to know the default context for each DAX expression you create. Expressions used in calculated columns have a different default context than expressions used in measures. In addition, the default context can be changed in various ways using various functions within the expressions.

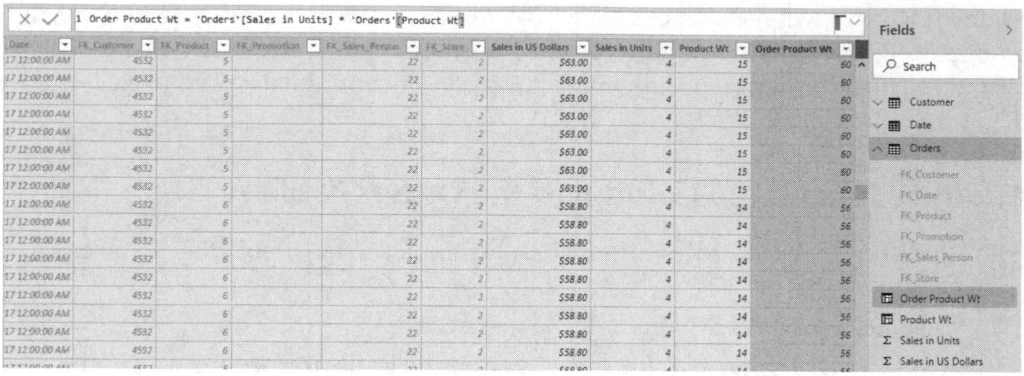

Figure 12-1 *The Order Product Wt calculated column*

The Default Context for Calculated Columns

For calculated columns, the default context of the calculation is the row itself. To calculate the product weight for an order, we used the following expression:

```
'Orders'[Sales in Units] * 'Orders'[Product Wt]
```

This expression is evaluated for each row in the table. As this is done, the values for the "Sales in Units" column and the Product Wt in that row are used to calculate a result for that row. You can see the result of the units times the product weight for each row in Figure 12-1.

Aggregate Functions in Calculated Columns

Some of the most-used functions within DAX expressions are aggregate functions. These functions perform an operation on multiple records to return a single result. That operation could be adding values together to return a sum, averaging values to return the mean, or perhaps evaluating the relative size of values to return the maximum. As you will see shortly, aggregate functions are required when defining measures, but they can also be used in DAX expressions for calculated columns.

When an aggregate function is used in a calculated column, it has its own default context. The default context for an aggregate function is the entire table (see Figure 12-2). When evaluating the expression for the row indicated by the large white arrow, the AVERAGE() function finds the average of the values in the Order Product Wt column from all of the rows in the table. The resulting average value is 112.

Orders

Overall Avg Order Wt = AVERAGE('Orders'[Order Product Wt])

Date of Order	Product Code	Order Product Wt	Overall Avg Order Wt
1/1/2017	5	60	112
1/1/2017	11	140	112
1/1/2017	14	288	112
1/2/2017	10	36	112
1/2/2017	16	96	112
1/3/2017	6	56	112
1/3/2017	19	108	112

Figure 12-2 *An aggregate function in a calculated column*

NOTE
If you add the calculated column shown in Figure 12-2 to the Orders table in your model, you will get a different result for the average value. Figure 12-1 and those that follow use a simplified version of the Orders table data for clarity and simplicity of illustration. Also in the name of clarity and simplicity, the text and illustrations refer to the Date Of Order and Product Code fields as if they are in the Orders table. When creating measures later in this chapter, we will actually use the fields in the related Date and Product tables.

This difference in default context can be useful. We can do things like compare an order's weight to the average order weight. This is done using the following expression, as shown in Figure 12-3:

```
% of Avg Order Wt=
'Orders'[Order Product Wt] / AVERAGE('Orders'[Order Product Wt])
```

The first reference to the Order Product Wt column is in the default context of the calculated column; therefore, when evaluating the value for the row indicated by the large white arrow, it will return the value for the Order Product Wt column in that row. The second reference to the Order Product Wt column is in the default context of the aggregate function, so the result of the aggregate function will be the average of all the values in the Order Product Wt column for all the rows. When we take the first and divide it by the second, and then format as a percentage, we get the percent of total.

Let's add this calculated column to our data model.

Orders

% of Avg Order Wt = 'Orders'[Order Product Wt]) / AVERAGE('Orders'[Order Product Wt])

60 / 122 = .5357

Date of Order	Product Code	Order Product Wt	% of Avg Order Wt
1/1/2017	5	60	0.5357
1/1/2017	11	140	1.2500
1/1/2017	14	288	2.5714
1/2/2017	10	36	0.3214
1/2/2017	16	96	0.8571
1/3/2017	6	56	0.5000
1/3/2017	19	108	0.9642

Figure 12-3 *Calculating percent of average*

Creating a Calculated Column Using an Aggregate Function

1. On the Modeling tab of the ribbon, click New Column.
2. Delete the "Column =" text and type the following in the formula bar:

```
% of Avg Order Wt=
       'Orders'[Order Product Wt] / AVERAGE('Orders'[Order Product Wt])
```

3. Press ENTER.
4. In the Formatting area of the Modeling tab of the ribbon, click "%". When you have completed these steps, the formula bar and the Orders table appear as shown in Figure 12-4.
5. Click Save.

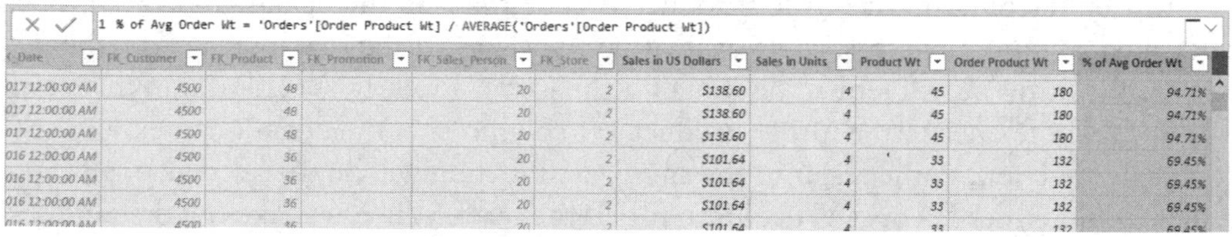

Date	FK_Customer	FK_Product	FK_Promotion	FK_Sales_Person	FK_Store	Sales in US Dollars	Sales in Units	Product Wt	Order Product Wt	% of Avg Order Wt
017 12:00:00 AM	4500	48		20	2	$138.60	4	45	180	94.71%
017 12:00:00 AM	4500	48		20	2	$138.60	4	45	180	94.71%
017 12:00:00 AM	4500	48		20	2	$138.60	4	45	180	94.71%
016 12:00:00 AM	4500	36		20	2	$101.64	4	33	132	69.45%
016 12:00:00 AM	4500	36		20	2	$101.64	4	33	132	69.45%
016 12:00:00 AM	4500	36		20	2	$101.64	4	33	132	69.45%
016 12:00:00 AM	4500	36		20	2	$101.64	4	33	132	69.45%

Figure 12-4 *The % of Avg Order Wt calculated column*

Measures

Whereas calculated columns provide one value for each row encountered, measures deal with multiple rows at the same time. As mentioned previously, measures use aggregate functions to sum (or count, or average, and so on) numbers in multiple records to get a single result. We need measures to unlock the power of the DAX language.

Default Summarization

The Power BI data model creates some default summarizations for us. Any column with a numeric value will be automatically set up to sum across multiple records. These default summarizations act as implicit measures in our model. They are indicated by a Greek letter sigma (Σ) in front of the entry in the Fields pane. "Sales in Units" and "Sales in US Dollars" are examples of default summarizations in the Orders table of the Max Min Sales Information data model, as shown in Figure 12-5.

We can choose to use a different aggregate for the default summarization for a given column by using the Default Summarization dropdown list on the Modeling tab of the ribbon. We have already used this dropdown several times to tell Power BI not to create

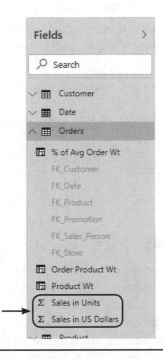

Figure 12-5 *Default summarizations*

a default summarization for numeric columns in our model. We did this for columns such as identification numbers and years that do not result in any meaningful value when aggregated.

Explicit Measures

The default summarizations work just fine for basic aggregations in our model. However, if we want to create more complex business logic, we need to create our own explicit measures. We may also want to replace default summarizations with our own explicit measures. This might be done for consistency or to change the name of the default summarization to something other than the column name.

We will begin creating measures by replacing the "Sales in US Dollars" default summarization with our own measure, giving it a slightly different name.

Creating a Measure

1. Select the Orders table.
2. On either the Home tab or the Modeling tab of the ribbon, click New Measure.
3. Delete the "Measure =" text and type the following in the formula bar:

   ```
   Sales in Dollars = SUM('Orders'[Sales in US Dollars])
   ```

4. Press ENTER. The measure will appear in the Fields pane. The measure will not appear in the data grid showing the rows and columns of the Orders table.
5. On the Modeling tab of the ribbon, click the "$" dropdown in the Formatting area.
6. Select "$ English (United States)" from the dropdown list. This will format the measure as U.S. dollars.
7. Right-click the "Sales in US Dollars" column in the data area and select "Hide in report view" from the context menu.
8. On the Modeling tab of the ribbon, use the Default Summarization dropdown list to select "Don't summarize."
9. Click Save.

Measures and Context

One of the features that makes measures so powerful is their ability to react to the context in which they are used. In other words, the result returned by a measure changes depending on the way the measure is currently being used in a visualization environment. Using DAX in our measures, we also have the ability to override what is going on in the visualization environment and enforce our own context on the measure calculation.

In this section of the chapter, we will see just how that works.

The Default Context for Measures

Measures are not created as a table column. Instead, they exist as a construct of the table itself. This difference provides a reminder of the measure's context.

The default context for a measure is the entire table. As noted previously, we must utilize aggregate functions when creating measures. We need to give the model a way to take values from multiple rows in the table and calculate a single result. In the "Sales in Dollars" measure, the SUM() aggregate function is used.

Let's validate the default context by creating a new visualization using our new "Sales in Dollars" measure.

1. Select Report on the left side of the Power BI Desktop window to switch to the Report view.
2. Click the plus sign in the yellow square at the bottom of the Power BI Desktop window to create a new report page.
3. In the Fields pane, check the box next to "Sales in Dollars" in the Orders table. A column chart is created on the report layout.
4. In the Visualizations pane, select Matrix to change the chart to a matrix.

In this default context, the "Sales in Dollars" measure shows the total of the "Sales in US Dollars" column for all rows in the Orders table. This is shown in Figure 12-6.

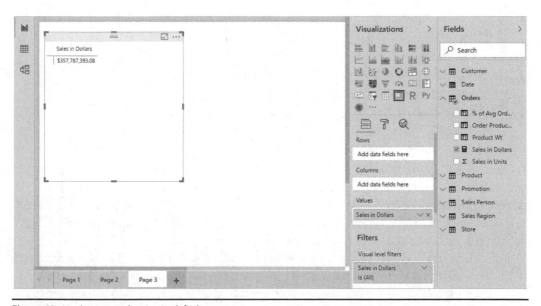

Figure 12-6 *A measure showing its default context*

Context Created by Filters and Slicers

We can make our report visualization more complex, and the measure will continue to respond to the context created. Let's give it a try.

1. In the Fields pane, expand the Product table.
2. Check the box next to Product Type. Product Type rows are created in the matrix visualization.
3. In the Fields pane, expand the Sales Person table.
4. Check the box next to Sales Person. Sales Person columns are created in the matrix visualization.
5. Select the Format tab in the Visualizations pane.
6. Expand the Subtotals area.
7. Set the "Row subtotals" slider switch to Off.
8. Set the "Column subtotals" slider switch to Off.
9. Expand the Title area.
10. Set the Title slider switch to On.
11. In the "Title text" text box, type **Sales in Dollars**.
12. Use the sizing handles to size the matrix so all the data is showing.
13. In the Fields pane, expand the Date table.
14. In the Date table, expand the Date Hierarchy.
15. Select the Year field in the hierarchy and drop it on the report layout to the right of the matrix.
16. In the Visualizations pane, select Slicer to change this to a slicer.
17. Use the sizing handles to size the slicer appropriately.
18. Select "Calendar 2018" in the slicer.
19. Select the matrix. The report should appear as shown in Figure 12-7.
20. Click Save.

Figure 12-7 shows how the "Sales in Dollars" measure reacts to the context of each cell in the matrix, along with the selected value in the slicer. It is the same DAX expression in the Sales in Dollars measure—SUM('Orders'[Sales in US Dollars])—that produces all of the values in all of the various calculated cells in the matrix. Each value is different because the context of each cell is different.

The cell in the upper-left corner of the matrix (called out in Figure 12-7) is restricted by the Year slicer on the report page, so it only includes sales made in calendar year 2018. That cell is in the Guiding Lights row of the matrix, so it only includes sales for the Guiding Lights product type. Finally, that cell is in the column for sales person Eddie, so it only includes sales made by Eddie.

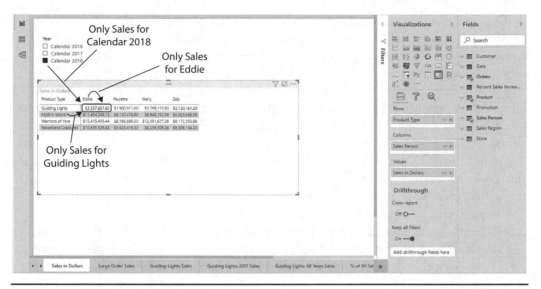

Figure 12-7   *A report showing measure context*

We can think of this as follows: Our report begins with the default context for our measure, All Orders. This is shown on the far left of Figure 12-8. Any slicers and filters that are in place in our report restrict the data to create a new "sub-table" containing the data that passes the restriction. In our example, this first sub-table contains only those orders placed in 2018.

Figure 12-8   *A conceptual model of measure context using sub-tables*

The rows then divide the data from our sub-table into additional smaller sub-tables, one for each row in the matrix. In this example, there would be four sub-tables. For clarity, only the first sub-table, containing 2018 Guiding Lights orders, and the last sub-table, containing 2018 Woodland Creatures orders, are shown in Figure 12-8.

The row-level sub-tables are then divided by the columns into further sets of sub-tables. In our example, this will create 16 sub-tables at this level. Again, only the first sub-table, containing 2018 Guiding Lights orders for Eddie, and the last sub-table, containing 2018 Woodland Creatures orders for Zeb, are shown in Figure 12-8.

Finally, the DAX expression is evaluated to aggregate the records in each of these 16 sub-tables to create 16 results. Those results are placed in the appropriate locations in the matrix cells. This produces the results shown in Figure 12-7.

I want to emphasize this is a conceptual view of what is happening to create the results seen in our Power BI report. I am not saying this is the way that the Vertipaq engine actually manipulates the data as it is processing a query. Instead, this conceptual view provides a convenient thought picture to use as we continue to explore context in this chapter.

Defining Context Within a Measure

In addition to reacting to the context in which it is used, a measure can also define its context. One of the ways this is done is by defining filter conditions within a measure. To do this, we need to leverage the functions available in DAX. One of the most-used functions, when it comes to defining measures, is the CALCULATE() function.

The CALCULATE() Function

The CALCULATE() function is a workhorse in the DAX world. You will find the CALCULATE() function appears in a large number of the measures we define. The CALCULATE() function's ability to create its own filter context is the reason for its popularity.

The CALCULATE() function has the following format:

```
CALCULATE(Expression, Filter1, Filter2, …)
```

The first parameter defines the DAX expression to be evaluated in the new context. The filter parameters define that new context. The expression parameter is required. The filter parameters are optional.

Let's put the CALCULATE() function to work and create a new measure with its own context.

1. Select the Orders table.
2. On the Modeling tab of the ribbon, click New Measure.

3. Delete the "Measure =" text and type the following:

```
Large Order Sales = CALCULATE([Sales in Dollars],
                              'Orders'[Sales in US Dollars]>150)
```

4. Press ENTER.
5. On the Modeling tab of the ribbon, click the "$" dropdown in the Formatting area.
6. Select "$ English (United States)" from the dropdown list. This will format the measure as U.S. dollars.

Maximum Miniatures defines large orders as any order over $150. The business goal of this measure is to find the total sales for orders where each individual order was over $150. Let's look at each of the two parameters of the CALCULATE() function in turn to see how this works.

The first parameter of the CALCULATE() function in the Large Order Sales measure is another measure—namely, the "Sales in Dollars" measure we just created. It is perfectly legal to reference one measure inside another measure. In this way, we can take advantage of any business logic coded in the measure without having to duplicate that business logic in other measures.

The second parameter of the CALCULATE() function in the Large Order Sales measure is a filter condition: 'Orders'[Sales in US Dollars] > 150. The first thing to note about this filter condition is we need to specify both the name of the table, in single quotes, and the name of the column, in square brackets, that are being referenced. This complete naming of columns is always required in measures.

The second thing to note is our filter applies to each individual row in the Orders table. We aren't filtering for the total sales to be greater than $150. We are filtering for each individual row to have a sales value greater than $150. The CALCULATE() function creates a situation where the filter condition(s) are evaluated row by row within the table. The context for the evaluation of "Sales in Dollars" measure becomes the set of rows in the Orders table where the "Sales in US Dollars" column value is greater than 150.

Let's put our new measure to the test.

1. Right-click the "Page 3" tab at the bottom of the Power BI Desktop window and select Rename Page from the context menu.
2. Type **Sales in Dollars** and press ENTER.
3. Right-click the newly named "Sales in Dollars" tab and select Duplicate Page from the context menu.
4. Right-click the "Duplicate of Sales in Dollars" tab and select Rename Page from the context menu.
5. Type **Large Order Sales** and press ENTER.

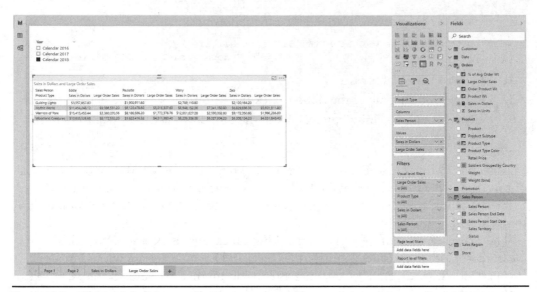

Figure 12-9   *The Large Order Sales report page*

6. Select the matrix.
7. In the Fields pane, check the box for the Large Order Sales measure in the Orders table. The Large Order Sales measure will be added in the Values area of the matrix.
8. In the Visualizations pane, select the Format tab.
9. Expand the Title area.
10. Add the following text to the end of the current title: **and Large Order Sales**. The report page should appear as shown in Figure 12-9.
11. Click Save.

Looking at the matrix on the Large Order Sales report page, we can see how much individual orders over $150 accounted for the sales of each product type made by each sales person in 2018. Right away we see there are no orders over $150 for any of the Guiding Lights products in 2018. We also see a large portion of the sales of Mythic World and Woodland Creatures products in 2018 come from orders over $150.

Figure 12-10 shows the sub-table conceptual updated to add the filter within the measure. As before, we can think of our data being filtered to include only 2018 sales. Sub-tables are created from the filtered data for each product type row, and then further sub-tables are created for each combination of product type and sales person column.

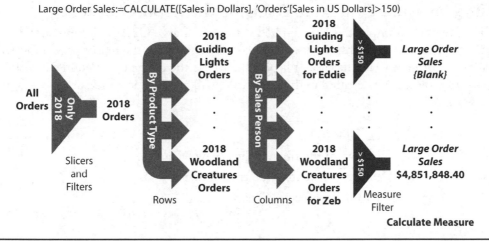

Figure 12-10 *The sub-table conceptual model with a measure filter*

Finally, the filter within the measure is applied to each sub-table, and the aggregation is evaluated on the records in each of the 16 filtered sub-tables, creating 16 results.

In some of the sub-tables, the final filter condition filters out all the rows in the sub-table. When the aggregate function is applied to an empty sub-table, the result is a blank value. This is different from an aggregate that returns a value of zero. If there are no records to aggregate, the result will always be blank.

Rows or columns that contain only blank values are not displayed in Power BI visualizations. In Figure 12-9, the row for the Guiding Lights product type is displayed because there are values for the Sales in Dollars measure. Let's see what happens when we remove that measure from the visualization.

1. Make sure the matrix is selected on the Large Order Sales report page.
2. In the Visualizations pane, select the Fields tab.
3. In the Visualizations pane, click the "X" for the "Sales in Dollars" measure in the Values area. This will remove the "Sales in Dollars" measure from the matrix.
4. In the Visualizations pane, select the Format tab.
5. Expand the Title area.
6. Delete "Sales in Dollars and" from the Title text.
7. Click Save.

As expected, there is no longer a Guiding Lights product type shown in the matrix.

Using Measure Context to Override the Report Context

In the previous example, the filter applied within the Large Order Sales measure did not involve any of the attributes used to create the context in the report page. However, that does not have to be the case. It is possible to use the context created in a measure to override the context created in the report. We will create a new measure to see how this works.

1. Select the Orders table.
2. On the Modeling tab of the ribbon, click New Measure.
3. Delete the "Measure =" text and type the following:

```
Guiding Lights Sales = CALCULATE([Sales in Dollars],
                            'Product'[Product Type]="Guiding Lights")
```

4. Press ENTER.
5. On the Modeling tab of the ribbon, click the "$" dropdown in the Formatting area.
6. Select "$ English (United States)" from the dropdown list. This will format the measure as U.S. dollars.

This measure gives us the sales of Guiding Lights product types. The first parameter of the CALCULATE() function is the same as before, the "Sales in Dollars" measure. The second parameter is a filter condition, 'Product'[Product Type] = "Guiding Lights".

This time, the filter condition uses a column from a table other than the Orders table. This works because this table, the Product table, is related to the Orders table. In the previous example, we saw that the CALCULATE() function evaluates the filter condition row by row in the table it is associated with. Here we see this behavior also extends to related tables. The CALCULATE() function evaluates filter conditions row by row in related tables.

Let's put this measure to the test.

1. Right-click the Large Order Sales tab and select Duplicate Page from the context menu.
2. Right-click the "Duplicate of Large Order Sales" tab and select Rename Page from the context menu.
3. Type **Guiding Lights Sales** and press ENTER.
4. Select the matrix.
5. In the Fields pane, check the box for the Guiding Lights Sales measure in the Orders table. The Guiding Lights Sales measure will be added in the Values area of the matrix.
6. In the Visualizations pane, click the "X" for the Large Order Sales measure in the Values area. This will remove the Large Order Sales measure from the matrix.

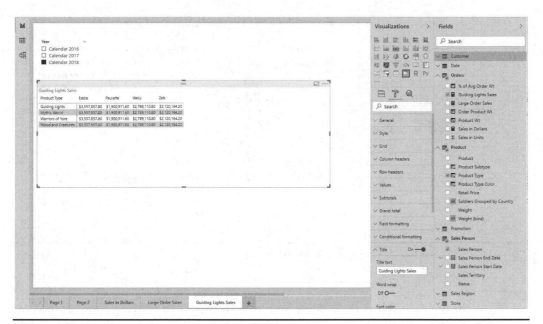

Figure 12-11 *The Guiding Lights Sales report page*

7. In the Visualizations pane, select the Format tab.
8. Expand the Title area.
9. Replace the current Title text with **Guiding Lights Sales**. The report page should appear as shown in Figure 12-11.
10. Click Save.

Looking at the results in the matrix, we see the values are the same in each column for all four of the product types. At first, it seems there must be an error here. Actually, the Guiding Lights Sales measure is working just as it should. The context created in the measure overrides the context created by the rows in the matrix. Figure 12-12 shows this context override at work in our sub-table conceptual model.

Our sub-tables are created as before. This time, however, the measure filter overrides the mechanism that created row sub-tables. The result of this override is the Mythic World records in the sub-tables for the Mythic World row are replaced with Guiding Lights records. Likewise, the Warriors of Yore records in the sub-tables for the Warriors of Yore row and the Woodland Creatures records in the sub-tables for the Woodland Creatures row are replaced with Guiding Lights records. The result is all four rows in the matrix contain aggregate results for Guiding Lights. This is why all of the rows in the matrix have the same values in each column.

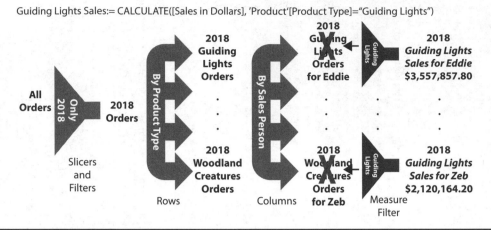

Guiding Lights Sales:= CALCULATE([Sales in Dollars], 'Product'[Product Type]="Guiding Lights")

Figure 12-12 *The sub-table conceptual model with context override*

This behavior is different from what we saw with the Large Order Sales measure in Figure 12-9 and Figure 12-10. The filter in the Large Order Sales does not involve a field that is already present in the report context. Therefore, the filter in the Large Order Sales simply filters out records from our sub-tables. The filter in the Guiding Lights measure uses a field that happens to be present in the report context as well. In this case, the filter in the measure overrides the report context. The rows for the four product types are still created in the matrix, but the measure result acts as if those groupings never actually filtered the sub-tables.

As before, keep in mind Figure 12-12 is a conceptual model. Don't get hung up trying to figure out how the query engine replaces one set of records with another. What is important is learning how measures react when the DAX expression for a measure contains a filter on a field that is also used to create a filter, a slicer, a row, or a column in the visualization context.

Using Multiple Filters

When the CALCULATE() function was introduced, we noted that it can have multiple filter expression parameters. Let's create a measure using two CALCULATE() function filter parameters.

1. Select the Orders table.
2. On the Modeling tab of the ribbon, click New Measure.

3. Delete the "Measure =" text and type the following:

```
Guiding Lights 2017 Sales = CALCULATE([Sales in Dollars],
                    'Product'[Product Type]="Guiding Lights",
                    'Date'[Year]="Calendar 2017")
```

NOTE

You can use CTRL-ENTER to put your DAX expression on multiple lines. Use any combination of spaces and tabs to align the DAX expression appropriately. The down arrow in the upper-right corner of the formula bar can be used to expand the formula bar to show multiple lines, when necessary.

4. Press ENTER.
5. On the Modeling tab of the ribbon, click the "$" dropdown in the Formatting area.
6. Select "$ English (United States)" from the dropdown list. This will format the measure as U.S. dollars.

This measure gives us the sales of Guiding Lights product types for calendar year 2017 based on our two filter conditions. Both the Product table and the Date table are related to the Orders table, so we can use both tables in our filter conditions.

Let's see what this measure looks like in a matrix.

1. Right-click the Guiding Lights Sales tab and select Duplicate Page from the context menu.
2. Right-click the "Duplicate of Guiding Lights Sales" tab and select Rename Page from the context menu.
3. Type **Guiding Lights 2017 Sales** and press ENTER.
4. Select the matrix.
5. In the Fields pane, check the box for the Guiding Lights 2017 Sales measure in the Orders table. The Guiding Lights 2017 Sales measure will be added in the Values area of the matrix.
6. In the Visualizations pane, click the "X" for the Guiding Lights Sales measure in the Values area. This will remove the Guiding Lights Sales measure from the matrix.
7. In the Visualizations pane, select the Format tab.
8. Expand the Title area.
9. Replace the current Title text with **Guiding Lights 2017 Sales**. The report page should appear as shown in Figure 12-13.
10. In the Year slicer, select Calendar 2016. Notice the values in the matrix do not change. This is due to the fact that the filter in the measure is overriding the slicer.

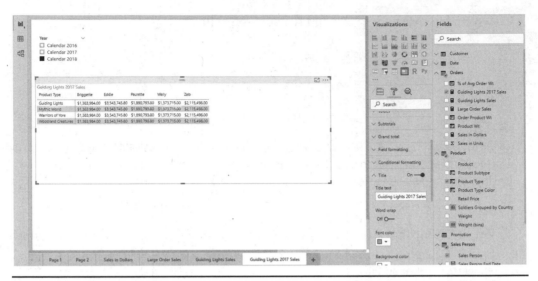

Figure 12-13 *The Guiding Lights 2017 Sales report page*

11. In the Year slicer, select Calendar 2018.
12. Click Save.

A new column for Briggette appeared in the matrix as soon as the Guiding Lights 2017 measure was added. This is due to that fact that Briggette had sales in calendar year 2017 but does not have any sales in 2018. Figure 12-14 shows the double context override in our sub-table conceptual model.

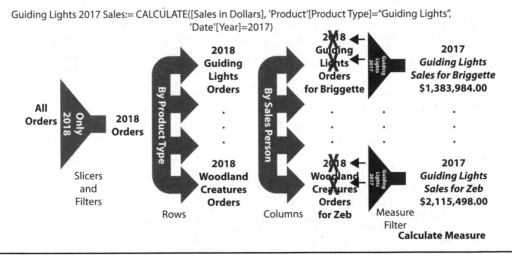

Figure 12-14 *The sub-table conceptual model with double context override*

This time, both the Year slicer and the Product Type rows in the matrix are overridden by the filters in the measure. No matter which year you select in the slicer, you will always see the aggregations for calendar year 2017. No matter which product type row you look at in the matrix, you will always see the aggregations for Guiding Lights.

NOTE
Obviously, this report would not be acceptable to a user in the real world. We wouldn't create a Power BI report where the slicer does not change the displayed values (at least not on purpose). The report pages in this chapter are simply to demonstrate the interaction of measures and context.

Filtering with a Table Expression

In our previous two examples, we overrode a portion of the report context by including the same field in a logical expression filter within the measure. Now, we will see it is possible to override report context using a DAX function. To understand how this works, we need to explore two other concepts first.

Up to this point, we have used a logic expression to define the filter parameters in the CALCULATE() function. This just makes sense. The logic expression must be true for a given row in order for it to be included in the final aggregation. However, this is not the only type of filtering we can do using the CALCULATE() function.

As an alternative to a logic expression, we can pass a table expression as one of the filter parameters of the CALCULATE() function. Only values present in this table can be included in the final aggregation. For those of you familiar with SQL queries, you can think of this as something akin to an INNER JOIN of this filtering table to the rest of the query. (This is not an exact analogy, but something close enough to give you a bit of a thought picture.)

Table Expressions and the ALL() Function

In DAX, table expressions are usually created using a DAX function that returns a table as its result. To this point, we have been working with DAX functions that return a single value in each context in which they are evaluated. The SUM() function or the AVERAGE() function works with lots of rows and returns a single number. The CALCULATE() function evaluates the DAX expression passed as its first parameter within the context it creates and returns a single value.

Many DAX functions return a table of values rather than a single value. In fact, DAX is highly optimized to create and process these table result sets very quickly. This is one of the features of DAX that makes it extremely powerful!

For our next measure, we will use the ALL() function. This function creates a context that ignores all filters on a particular field or on a particular table. The ALL() function has the following format:

```
ALL(TableNameOrTableFieldReference1, TableFieldReference2, …)
```

Each parameter identifies a particular table or a particular field within a table that should be included in the result set with all existing filters ignored. The ALL() function returns a table containing all of the values in the specified field(s) or specified table(s).

Using the ALL() Function

Now, we put these two new concepts together to create a measure. This measure will ignore filters on the year and provide sales information on Guiding Lights sales for all years in our data.

1. Select the Orders table.
2. On the Modeling tab of the ribbon, click New Measure.
3. Delete the "Measure =" text and type the following:

```
Guiding Lights All Years Sales = CALCULATE([Sales in Dollars],
                      'Product'[Product Type]="Guiding Lights",
                      ALL('Date'[Year]))
```

4. Press ENTER.
5. On the Modeling tab of the ribbon, click the "$" dropdown in the Formatting area.
6. Select "$ English (United States)" from the dropdown list. This will format the measure as U.S. dollars.

Let's put this measure to the test.

1. Right-click the Guiding Lights 2017 Sales tab and select Duplicate Page from the context menu.
2. Right-click the "Duplicate of Guiding Lights 2017 Sales" tab and select Rename Page from the context menu.
3. Type **Guiding Lights All Years Sales** and press ENTER.
4. Select the matrix.
5. In the Fields pane, check the box for the Guiding Lights All Years Sales measure in the Orders table. The Guiding Lights All Years Sales measure will be added in the Values area of the matrix.
6. In the Fields pane, uncheck the box for the Guiding Lights 2017 Sales measure in the Orders table. This is another way we can remove the Guiding Lights 2017 Sales measure from the matrix.

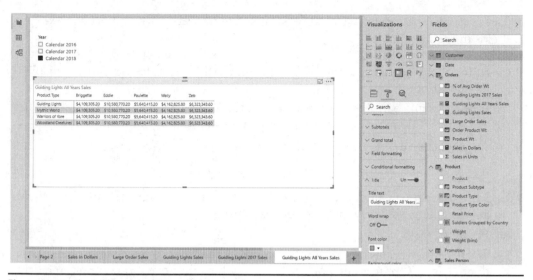

Figure 12-15 *The Guiding Lights All Years Sales report page*

7. In the Visualizations pane, select the Format tab.

8. Expand the Title area.

9. Replace the current Title text with **Guiding Lights All Years Sales**. The report page should appear as shown in Figure 12-15.

10. In the Year slicer, select Calendar 2016. Notice the values in the matrix do not change. This is due to the fact that the ALL('Date'[Year]) filter in the measure is overriding the slicer.

11. In the Year slicer, select Calendar 2018. Again, the values in the matrix do not change.

12. In the Fields pane, expand the Date table.

13. Select the Month of Year field and drop it on the report layout area near the Year slicer. A table of month of year values is created.

14. In the Visualizations pane, select Slicer.

15. In the Month of Year slicer, try selecting various months.

The values in our matrix change as different months are selected. This is due to the fact that we told the ALL() function to include all values of the Year field in the Date table. We did not instruct the ALL() function to override any report context slicing done on the Month of Year field in the Date table. The result is that we see the values for the selected month for all years.

Let's see what happens if we modify our measure to override the report context for all fields in the Date table.

1. In the Fields pane, click the Guiding Lights All Years Sales measure to display its definition.
2. In the formula bar, delete the reference to the Year field, including the "[" and "]" characters. The measure expression should now appear as follows:

```
Guiding Lights All Years Sales = CALCULATE([Sales in Dollars],
                            'Product'[Product Type]="Guiding Lights",
                            ALL('Date'))
```

3. Move the edit cursor to the very end of the measure expression. (If you don't do this, autocomplete will likely mess up your expression!)
4. Press ENTER.
5. Try selecting various months in the Month of Year slicer. The values in the matrix don't change. Our measure now overrides anything in the report context referencing the Date table.
6. Click Save.

Whenever you use the ALL() function to override report context, be sure to use the appropriate reference as the ALL() function parameter. If you want to override one field in a table but let the context created by other fields in the same table stand, then reference a single field in the ALL() function parameter. However, if you want to override all fields in a table, be sure to simply specify the table in the ALL() function parameter. Figure 12-16 shows the conceptual model of the ALL() function override.

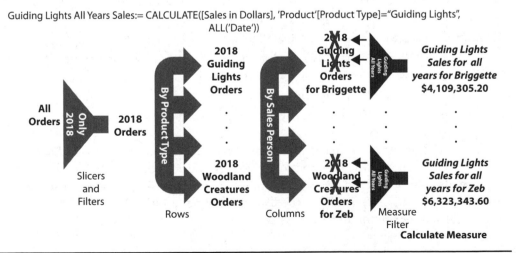

Figure 12-16   *Using the ALL() function for context override*

Using Multiple Contexts in a Measure

We have seen how to override the default report context by creating a new context within a measure. It is also possible to use both the default report context and an overridden context in the same measure to perform some interesting analytics. In this example, we will compare the sales of each sales person, as specified by the default report context, with the sales of all sales people in the same report context.

1. In the Fields pane, select the Orders table.
2. On the Modeling tab of the ribbon, click New Measure.
3. Delete the "Measure =" text and type the following in the formula bar:

```
% of All Sales People = SUM('Orders'[Sales in US Dollars])  /
            CALCULATE(SUM('Orders'[Sales in US Dollars]),
                                        ALL('Sales Person'))
```

4. Press ENTER.
5. On the Modeling tab of the ribbon, select Percentage from the Format dropdown list.
6. Right-click the "Sales in Dollars" tab. You may need to scroll left to find it.
7. Select Duplicate Page from the context menu.
8. Right-click the "Duplicate of Sales in Dollars" tab and select Rename Page from the context menu.
9. Type **% of All Sales People** and press ENTER.
10. Select the matrix.
11. In the Fields area, check the box for the "% of All Sales People" measure. The "% of All Sales People" measure is added to the matrix.
12. Size and rearrange appropriately. Your report page should appear as shown in Figure 12-17.
13. Click Save.

The report shows the sales for each sales person as well as what percent of the sales for all sales people that represents. Because Sales Person forms the columns in our matrix, the percentages across each row should add up to 100%. In other words, all of the column values in a single row make up the total sales for all sales people.

The measure we created uses an override to get the sales for all sales people. This is the only part of the report context it overrides. Therefore, the percentages being calculated are only for sales in calendar year 2018 when Calendar 2018 is selected in the Year slicer. The percentages represent percent of total sales of the Guiding Lights product type in the Guiding Lights row of the matrix. All of the report context not associated with Sales Person still affects the calculations in our matrix.

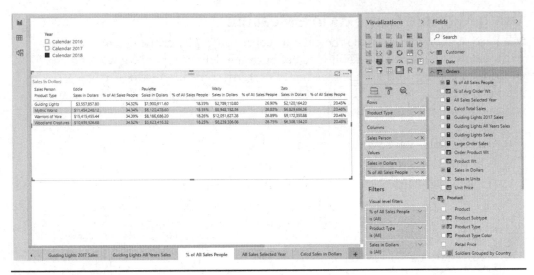

Figure 12-17 *The % of All Sales People report*

Using the ALLEXCEPT() Function

The ALL() function enables us to specify fields or tables and create a table result set ignoring all report context dealing with those fields or tables. The ALLEXCEPT() function works in the opposite manner. It only honors report context dealing with the fields and tables specified. Any other report context is overridden.

The ALLEXCEPT() function has the following format:

```
ALLEXCEPT(TableName, TableFieldReference1, TableFieldReference2, …)
```

The first parameter of this function, TableName, specifies the name of the table whose rows we are filtering. The second parameter, and subsequent parameters, specify a table or field whose filters are exceptions whose report context will apply to the aggregation context. Everything else from the report context will be overridden.

For this example, we will create a measure that shows all sales for the selected year. Any other filters that might be in place in the report are ignored. Only the year selected within the report affects the value of the measure.

1. Select the Orders table.
2. On the Modeling tab of the ribbon, click New Measure.
3. Delete the "Measure =" text and type the following:

```
All Sales Selected Year = CALCULATE([Sales in Dollars],
                          ALLEXCEPT('Orders', 'Date'[Year]))
```

4. Press ENTER.
5. On the Modeling tab of the ribbon, click the "$" dropdown in the Formatting area.
6. Select "$ English (United States)" from the dropdown list. This will format the measure as U.S. dollars.

Now, let's see how this measure works.

1. Right-click the Guiding Lights All Years Sales tab and select Duplicate Page from the context menu.
2. Right-click the "Duplicate of Guiding Lights All Years Sales" tab and select Rename Page from the context menu.
3. Type **All Sales Selected Year** and press ENTER.
4. Select the matrix.
5. In the Fields pane, check the box for the All Sales Selected Year measure in the Orders table.
6. In the Fields pane, uncheck the box for the Guiding Lights All Years Sales measure in the Orders table.
7. In the Visualizations pane, select the Format tab.
8. Expand the Title area.
9. Replace the current Title text with **All Sales Selected Year**. The report page should appear as shown in Figure 12-18. Notice additional sales people columns showed up. Also notice the values for all cells in the matrix are exactly the same.

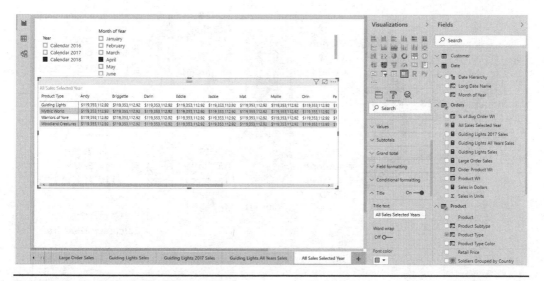

Figure 12-18 *The All Sales Selected Year report page*

10. In the Month of Year slicer, try selecting several different months. The value in the matrix does not change.

11. In the Year slicer, select Calendar 2016. The value in the matrix changes.

12. Click Save.

In the All Sales Selected Year measure, we used the ALLEXCEPT() function to override any report filters except those on 'Date'[Year]. When Calendar 2018 is selected in the slicer, every cell in the matrix displays the total sales for all product types made by all sales people in 2018. When Calendar 2016 is selected in the slicer, every cell in the matrix displays the total sales for all product types made by all sales people in 2016.

Selecting different months in the Month of Year slicer does not change our numbers. The ALLEXCEPT() function causes our measure to ignore all report context except for that based specifically on the Year field in the Date table. As with the ALL() function, when you use the ALLEXCEPT() function to override report context, be sure to use the appropriate reference as the function parameter. If you want to override all except one field in a table, then reference a single field in the ALLEXCEPT() function parameters. However, if you want to override all report context except that resulting from any fields in a given table, be sure to simply specify the table in the ALLEXCEPT() function parameter. Figure 12-19 shows the conceptual model of the ALLEXCEPT() function override.

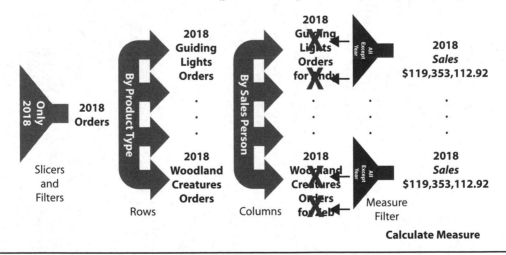

Figure 12-19 *Using the ALLEXCEPT() function for context override*

Time Analytics

Time analytics enable us to easily make comparisons of values across time. How do sales this month compare to the same month last year? What were the total sales to date as of this time last year?

DAX provides a number of functions we can use to perform time analytics. In many cases, these are table-valued functions. They return a table of rows we can use as a filter parameter to obtain the time-related values we are looking for.

For example, suppose our report context includes a slicer that selects a particular month or a particular quarter. We may want to create a measure that will show us the sales in the selected time period relative to the same time period last year. The best way to do this in DAX is with a function that returns a table containing the dates from the previous year relative to the dates in the report context. The table of date values created represents the context for the same period last year. As we have seen with ALL() and ALLEXCEPT(), DAX functions that return tables in this manner can be used as filter parameters within a CALCULATE() function. The SAMEPERIODLASTYEAR() function has the following format:

```
SAMEPERIODLASTYEAR(Dates)
```

Many of the DAX time analytics functions require a Dates parameter. This Dates parameter must be one of the following:

- A reference to a field containing date/time values
- A table-valued function that returns a table with a single column of dates
- A Boolean expression that defines a single-column table of date/time values.

In our data model, the Date field of the Date table ('Date'[Date]) provides the fields containing the date/time values.

A number of DAX time analytics functions work in a manner similar to the SAMEPERIODLASTYEAR() function. Each creates a table of date values for a new date context relative to the current dates present in the report context. The DATESMTD(), DATESQTD(), and DATESYTD() functions each create tables of dates to calculate the corresponding period-to-date values. The NEXTDAY(), NEXTMONTH(), NEXTQUARTER(), and NEXTYEAR() functions each create tables of dates to calculate the corresponding next period values. The PREVIOUSDAY(), PREVIOUSMONTH(), PREVIOUSQUARTER(), and PREVIOUSYEAR() functions each create tables of dates to calculate the corresponding previous period values.

The PARALLELPERIOD() function creates a table of dates that is a specified distance from the report context. The PARALLELPERIOD() function has the following format:

```
PARALLELPERIOD(Dates, NumPeriods, Period)
```

NumPeriods is the number of periods to move relative to the report context. A positive number of periods moves forward in time. A negative number of periods moves backward in time. MONTH, QUARTER, and YEAR are valid values for period. Chapter 13 provides a complete list and description of each of these table-valued time analytics functions.

There are a few other DAX time analytics functions that not only create the new date context, but also evaluate a DAX expression in that new context. The DAX functions act as a combination table-valued function and CALCULATE() function, all rolled into one. For example, the TOTALYTD() function will return the year-to-date value of a DAX expression. It has the following format:

```
TOTALYTD(Expression, Dates, [Filter],[YearEndDate])
```

Expression is automatically evaluated in a date context to return a year-to-date result. In addition to TotalYTD(), there are also TOTALQTD() and TOTALMTD() functions available in the DAX language.

Creating Measures Using Time Analytics

Let's try creating a few measures using DAX functions to create time analytics.

1. In the Fields pane, select the Orders table.
2. On the Modeling tab of the ribbon, click New Measure.
3. Delete the "Measure =" text and type the following in the formula bar and press ENTER:

```
Sales in US Dollars Last Year = CALCULATE(
                    SUM('Orders'[Sales in US Dollars]),
                            SAMEPERIODLASTYEAR('Date'[Date]))
```

4. Press ENTER.
5. On the Modeling tab of the ribbon, click the "$" dropdown in the Formatting area.
6. Select "$ English (United States)" from the dropdown list. This will format the measure as U.S. dollars.
7. On the Modeling tab of the ribbon, click New Measure.

8. Delete the "Measure =" text and type the following in the formula bar:

```
Sales YTD = TOTALYTD(SUM('Orders'[Sales in US Dollars]),
                                              'Date'[Date])
```

9. Press ENTER.
10. On the Modeling tab of the ribbon, click the "$" dropdown in the Formatting area.
11. Select "$ English (United States)" from the dropdown list. This will format the measure as U.S. dollars.
12. On the Modeling tab of the ribbon, click New Measure.
13. Delete the "Measure =" text and type the following in the formula bar:

```
Sales LY YTD = CALCULATE(SUM('Orders'[Sales in US Dollars]),
              PARALLELPERIOD(DATESYTD('Date'[Date]), -12, MONTH))
```

14. Press ENTER.
15. On the Modeling tab of the ribbon, click the "$" dropdown in the Formatting area.
16. Select "$ English (United States)" from the dropdown list. This will format the measure as U.S. dollars.

Creating the YOY Comparison Report

1. Click the yellow tab containing the plus sign to add a new report page.
2. Right-click the new page and select Rename Page from the context menu.
3. Type **YOY Comparison** and press ENTER.
4. In the Fields pane, check the box for the "Sales in Dollars" measure.
5. In the Fields pane, check the box for the "Sales in US Dollars Last Year" measure.
6. Expand the Date table, if necessary.
7. Check the box for the Date Hierarchy. We see a column chart with columns for the current year's sales and columns for last year's sales.
8. Click the down arrow in the upper-right corner of the column chart to turn on drilldown.
9. Click one of the bars for Calendar 2017. The chart drills into the four quarters of 2017.
10. Click one of the bars for Quarter 3, 2017. Your report appears as shown in Figure 12-20. The chart drills into the three months of that quarter. Notice how our "Sales in US Dollars Last Year" measure adapts to the level we are at in the drilldown, displaying year, quarter, or month values, as appropriate.
11. Click Save.

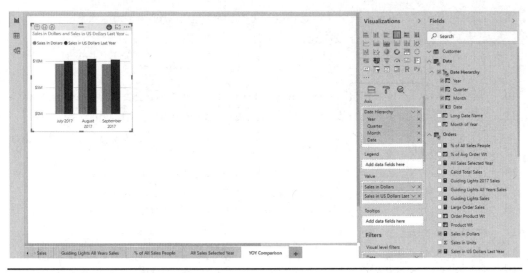

Figure 12-20 *The YOY Comparison report*

Creating the YTD KPI Report

1. Click the yellow tab containing the plus sign to add a new report page.
2. Right-click the new page and select Rename Page from the context menu.
3. Type **YTD KPI** and press ENTER.
4. In the Fields pane, expand the Date table.
5. Expand the Date Hierarchy.
6. Check the box for Month. A table containing the month, quarter, and year levels of the hierarchy is created.
7. In the Visualizations pane, click the "X" next to Quarter in the Values area. Quarter is removed from the table.
8. In the Visualizations pane, click the "X" next to Year in the Values area. Year is removed from the table.
9. In the Visualizations pane, select Slicer.
10. In the Month slicer, scroll down and select March 2018.
11. Click anywhere in the report page to unselect the slicer.
12. In the Fields pane, check the box for the Sales YTD measure. A column chart is created.

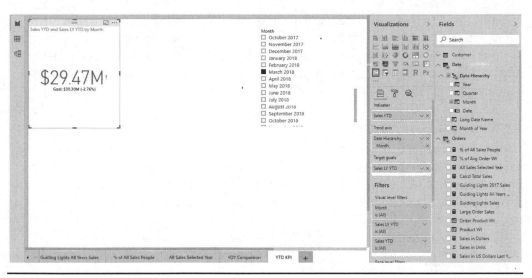

Figure 12-21 *The YTD KPI report*

13. In the Visualizations pane, select KPI. The column chart becomes a blank KPI. We need to provide a couple additional values before the KPI will display.

14. In the Fields pane, select Month under the Date Hierarchy and drop it on "Trend axis" | "Add data fields here."

15. In the Fields pane, select the Sales LY YTD measure and drop it on "Target goals" | "Add data fields here." The YTD KPI report is shown in Figure 12-21. We can see we had $29.47M to date as of March 2018. This is 2.76% behind the $30.30M in sales YTD for March 2017.

16. In the Month slicer, select April 2018. In April 2018, we were only 0.52% behind the previous year's sales year-to-date through April 2017.

17. In the Month slicer, select May 2018. In May 2018, we moved ahead of last year's YTD sales!

18. Click Save.

Row-by-Row Calculations

We have noted the CALCULATE() function evaluates the filter conditions one row at a time. The DAX expression in the first parameter of the CALCULATE() function, however, is evaluated once on the entire context that results. This works for most situations, but there are some where this will not produce the correct result.

Suppose, for a moment, we didn't have the "Sales in US Dollars" field in the Orders table. Suppose, instead, we needed to take the retail price and multiply it by the number of units sold and then add those results to get the total sales. This type of calculation must be done row by row. Fortunately, DAX includes a set of alternative aggregation functions that operate row by row.

Iterating Aggregators

Iterating aggregate functions have the same name as their regular aggregation counterparts, but with an "X" on the end. For example, SUMX() creates an aggregate by evaluating a DAX expression row by row and adding the results from each row. AVERAGEX() creates an aggregate by evaluating a DAX expression row by row and finding the mean of the result.

The SUMX() function has the following format:

```
SUMX(TableExpression,Expression)
```

AVERAGEX() and the other iterative aggregate functions have a similar format. Consult Chapter 13 for a complete list of the iterating aggregate functions.

Let's put one of these iterative aggregate functions to the test. As we were supposing earlier, we are going to pretend for a moment that we need to calculate total sales from "Sales in Units" and Retail Price. To do this, we will first need to create a calculated column using the RELATED() function to bring Retail Price into the Orders table. Here's how it's done:

1. Select the Orders table.
2. On the Modeling tab of the ribbon, click New Column.
3. Delete the "Column =" text and type the following:

   ```
   Unit Price = RELATED('Product'[Retail Price])
   ```

4. Press ENTER.
5. On the Modeling tab of the ribbon, click the "$" dropdown in the Formatting area.
6. Select "$ English (United States)" from the dropdown list. This will format the measure as U.S. dollars.
7. On the Modeling tab of the ribbon, click New Measure.
8. Delete the "Measure =" text and type the following:

   ```
   Calcd Total Sales = SUMX('Orders',
                   'Orders'[Sales in Units] * 'Orders'[Unit Price])
   ```

9. Press ENTER.
10. On the Modeling tab of the ribbon, click the "$" dropdown in the Formatting area.

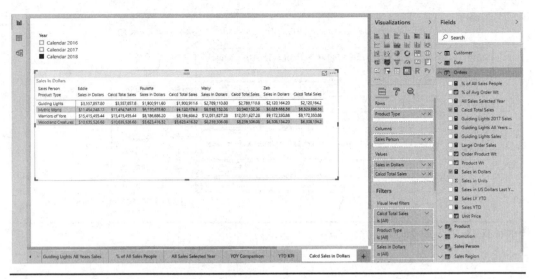

Figure 12-22 *The Calcd Sales in Dollars report*

11. Select "$ English (United States)" from the dropdown list. This will format the measure as U.S. dollars.

12. Right-click the "Sales in Dollars" tab. You may need to scroll left to see this tab.

13. Select Duplicate Page from the context menu.

14. Right-click the "Duplicate of Sales in Dollars" tab and select Rename Page from the context menu.

15. Type **Calcd Sales in Dollars** and press ENTER.

16. Select the matrix.

17. In the Fields pane, check the box for the Calcd Total Sales measure in the Orders table.

18. Rearrange and size appropriately. The report is shown in Figure 12-22.

19. Click Save.

If we did everything correctly, the values in the "Sales in Dollars" columns of the matrix should match the values in the Calcd Total Sales columns. Figure 12-23 shows how the SUMX() function operates. As was the case with the figures earlier in the chapter, Figure 12-23 shows a simplified version of the Orders table. Therefore, the value for Calcd Total Sales shown in the figure will not match any of the numbers in your Power BI report.

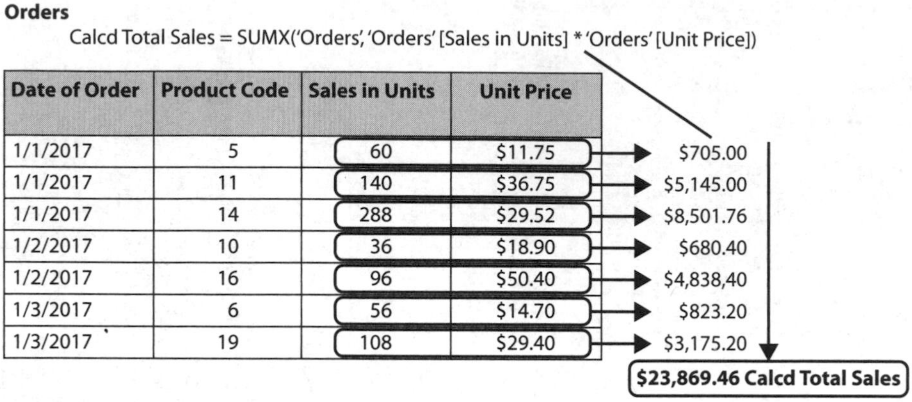

Orders

Calcd Total Sales = SUMX('Orders', 'Orders' [Sales in Units] * 'Orders' [Unit Price])

Date of Order	Product Code	Sales in Units	Unit Price	
1/1/2017	5	60	$11.75	$705.00
1/1/2017	11	140	$36.75	$5,145.00
1/1/2017	14	288	$29.52	$8,501.76
1/2/2017	10	36	$18.90	$680.40
1/2/2017	16	96	$50.40	$4,838,40
1/3/2017	6	56	$14.70	$823.20
1/3/2017	19	108	$29.40	$3,175.20

$23,869.46 Calcd Total Sales

Figure 12-23 *The SUMX() function in operation*

The FILTER() Function

There is one more very important table-valued function we want to take a look at here. This is the FILTER() function. The FILTER function applies a filter to a table to create a new table with the resulting subset of the initial table. The FILTER() function has the following format:

```
FILTER(TableExpression, Filter)
```

TableExpression is either a reference to a table in the data model or a table-valued function, and Filter is a Boolean expression that is evaluated for each row in the specified table. Rows where the Boolean expression evaluates to true are included in the resulting table.

Creating a Measure Using the FILTER() Function

The FILTER() function can be used anywhere a table expression can be used as a parameter. This could be as one of the filter parameters in a CALCULATE() function or as the first parameter in any of our iterating aggregation functions. Let's try an example with the latter of these two.

1. Select the Orders table.
2. On the Modeling tab of the ribbon, click New Measure.
3. Delete the "Measure =" text and type the following:

```
Total Sales for Medium Priced Items =
    SUMX(FILTER('Orders',
        'Orders'[Unit Price] >= 20.00 && 'Orders'[Unit Price] <= 30.00),
            'Orders'[Unit Price] * 'Orders'[Sales in Units])
```

NOTE
The && operator is a logical AND. In this measure, the Unit Price must be greater than or equal to 20.00 AND must be less than or equal to 30.00. More on && and other operators in Chapter 13.

4. Press ENTER.
5. On the Modeling tab of the ribbon, click the "$" dropdown in the Formatting area.
6. Select "$ English (United States)" from the dropdown list. This will format the measure as U.S. dollars.
7. Right-click the "Calcd Sales in Dollars" tab and select Duplicate Page from the context menu.
8. Right-click the "Duplicate of Calcd Sales in Dollars" tab and select Rename Page from the context menu.
9. Type **Medium Priced Sales** and press ENTER.
10. Select the matrix.
11. In the Visualizations pane, click the "X" next to "Calcd Total Sales" in the Values area.
12. In the Fields pane, check the box for the "Total Sales for Medium Priced Items" measure in the Orders table.
13. Rearrange and size appropriately. The report is shown in Figure 12-24.
14. Click Save.

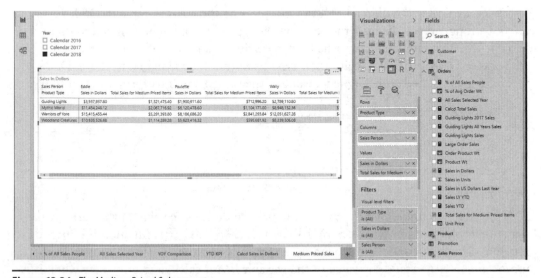

Figure 12-24 *The Medium Priced Sales report*

In the "Total Sales for Medium Priced Items" measure, the FILTER() function works on the records in the Orders table. Only rows where the Unit Price is greater than or equal to $20 and is less than or equal to $30 are included in the table output by the function. The DAX logic operator && is used to get the logical AND of the two Boolean expressions. The output of the FILTER() function is passed as the first parameter of the SUMX() function.

The first parameter of the SUMX() function is the table that the SUMX() function iterates through as it performs the calculation passed as its second parameter. Therefore, the result of the SUMX() returns the sum of only those records that passed through the filter condition. The result is the total sales of items priced between $20 and $30, inclusive.

DAX Variables

Variables were added to the DAX language to make complex DAX expressions easier to read and troubleshoot. They help us organize DAX expressions and break them down into smaller segments in order to better understand what is happening at each point in the evaluation. A DAX variable can hold any value returned by a DAX function. That includes the ability to hold a table created by a table-valued function. This flexibility makes DAX variables very powerful.

Declaring DAX Variables and Assigning a Value

Variables are declared within a DAX expression using the VAR statement. DAX variables are not strongly typed. Instead, they take on the type of the content assigned to them. The variable can hold either a scalar value (text, date/time, numeric, and so on) or a table.

Because DAX variables receive their type from the value assigned to them, DAX variables are declared and assigned a value at the same time. The format is as follows:

```
VAR <variable name> = <expression>
```

Here's an example:

```
VAR LastYearTotalSales = CALCULATE([Sales in Dollars],
                            SAMEPERIODLASTYEAR('Date'[Date]))
```

Note in the example that the expression used to define the value of the variable is dependent on the context. The SAMEPERIODLASTYEAR() function is going to return a different set of dates depending on what period the user is looking at. It is important to understand the value of the variable is not calculated only once when it is first defined in the model. It is part of a dynamic calculation that is being reevaluated each time the context of the expression changes.

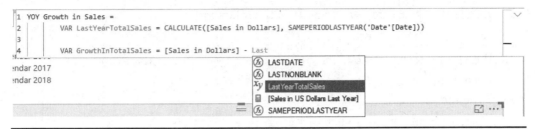

Figure 12-25 *A DAX variable in autocomplete*

Using a DAX Variable

Once our variable has been declared, we can use it in other locations in our DAX expression. For example, we can use the LastYearTotalSales variable in the initialization of another variable as follows:

```
VAR GrowthInTotalSales = [Sales in Dollars] - LastYearTotalSales
```

Power BI is even smart enough to recognize the variable and include it in the context-sensitive autocomplete, as shown in Figure 12-25.

Using Return in a Measure

Up to this point, our measures have consisted of a single DAX function. There may have been other functions nested within that function, but there was always a single outer DAX function. Whatever value was returned by this outermost function became the value of the measure.

When using DAX variables, our measure code looks more like a function written in C# or a stored procedure written in T-SQL. Similar to those two situations, we need a way to specify what is to be used as the final value for the C# function or the T-SQL stored procedure. As with those constructs, we use a return to specify our final result. The return includes an expression that is evaluated to determine the ultimate value for the measure.

In the example we have been building in this section, this is the statement that would return the final year-over-year growth calculation:

```
return DIVIDE(GrowthInTotalSales, LastYearTotalSales)
```

Creating a Measure Using DAX Variables

1. In the Fields pane, select the Orders table.
2. On the Modeling tab of the ribbon, click New Measure.

3. Delete the "Measure =" text and type the following:

```
Sales Qtr Over Qtr Growth =
```

4. Press ALT-ENTER to move the cursor to the second line of the formula bar.

5. Press TAB.

6. Type the following:

```
VAR SalesCurrQtr = CALCULATE([Sales in Dollars],
DATESBETWEEN('Date'[Date],
```

7. Press ALT-ENTER.

8. Press TAB twice.

9. Type the following:

```
        STARTOFQUARTER('Date'[Date]), ENDOFQUARTER('Date'[Date])))
```

10. Press ALT-ENTER twice.

11. Press TAB.

12. Type the following:

```
VAR SalesPrevQtr = CALCULATE([Sales in Dollars],
```

13. Press ALT-ENTER.

14. Press ESC to get rid of the autocomplete pop-up list.

15. Press TAB twice.

16. Type the following:

```
PARALLELPERIOD('Date'[Date],-1, QUARTER))
```

17. Press ALT-ENTER twice.

18. Press TAB.

19. Type:

```
VAR QtrOverQtrDiff = SalesCurrQtr - SalesPrevQtr
```

20. Press ALT-ENTER twice.

21. Press TAB.

22. Type the following:

```
RETURN DIVIDE(QtrOverQtrDiff, SalesPrevQtr)
```

The DAX code should appear as shown in Figure 12-26.

23. Press ENTER.

24. Click Save.

If you like, you can add a new report page and create a visualization using the Sales Qtr Over Qtr Growth measure.

```
 1  Sales Qtr Over Qtr Growth =
 2      VAR SalesCurrQtr = CALCULATE([Sales in Dollars], DATESBETWEEN('Date'[Date],
 3          STARTOFQUARTER('Date'[Date]), ENDOFQUARTER('Date'[Date])))
 4
 5      VAR SalesPrevQtr = CALCULATE([Sales in Dollars],
 6          PARALLELPERIOD('Date'[Date],-1, QUARTER))
 7
 8      VAR QtrOverQtrDiff = SalesCurrQtr - SalesPrevQtr
 9
10      RETURN DIVIDE(QtrOverQtrDiff, SalesPrevQtr)
```

Figure 12-26 *A measure using DAX variables*

Everything DAX

This chapter provided you with a good introduction to DAX expressions and the DAX functions that give them their power. The following chapter is a reference to all things DAX to give you a deeper understanding of the breadth of what is available.

Chapter 13

DAX Language Reference

In This Chapter

- DAX Operators
- DAX Functions

Entire books could be written, and have been written, about the DAX language. We worked with DAX expressions in Chapter 12. In this chapter, we take a closer look at the DAX language.

The power of the DAX language comes from functions. Almost all DAX expressions will include at least one DAX function. Therefore, the majority of this chapter will be about DAX functions. Before we get to that, let's make sure you understand the very basics—DAX operators.

DAX Operators

DAX operators can be divided into four categories: comparison operators, arithmetic operators, text operator, and logic operators.

Comparison Operators

Comparison operators are used to make a comparison between two values and return either true or false. The comparison operators are shown in Table 13-1.

Arithmetic Operators

Arithmetic operators are used to perform mathematical calculations and provide a numeric result (see Table 13-2).

Text Operator

Use the ampersand (&) to concatenate two text values, creating a single string as shown in Table 13-3.

Comparison Operator	Meaning	Example
=	Equal to	[Product] = "Soaring Eagle"
>	Greater than	[Revenue] > 10000
<	Less than	[Cost of Sales] < 5000
>=	Greater than or equal to	[Rating] >= 1
<=	Less than or equal to	[Expenses] <= 2000
<>	Not equal to	[Country] <> "United States"

Table 13-1   *DAX Comparison Operators*

Arithmetic Operator	Meaning	Example
+	Addition	[Cost of Sales] + [Expenses]
–	Subtraction or sign	[Revenue] – [Cost of Sales]
*	Multiplication	–1 * [Expenses]
/	Division	[Cost of Sales] / [Revenue]
^	Exponentiation	8 ^ 2

Table 13-2   *DAX Arithmetic Operators*

Text Operator	Meaning	Example
&	Concatenate	[Month Name] & " " & [Year]

Table 13-3   *DAX Text Operator*

Logical Operators

Logical operators are used to combine multiple conditional expressions into a single logical result. The logical operators are shown in Table 13-4.

Logical Operator	Meaning	Example
&&	Creates an AND condition between two logical expressions. Both expressions must evaluate to true in order for this to return true; otherwise, false is returned.	([Country] = "Germany") && ([Year] = 2015)
||	Creates an OR condition between two logical expressions. If either expression evaluates to true, then true is returned; both values have to return false in order for the result to be false.	([City] = "Chicago") || ([City] = "Dallas")
NOT	Reverses the logical meaning of an expression.	NOT ([City] = "Chicago")

Table 13-4   *DAX Logical Operators*

DAX Functions

Now that we have touched on DAX operators, we turn our attention to DAX functions. Functions are truly the heart and soul of the DAX language. A solid knowledge of the functions available and how they work is an important factor in success with Power BI.

Modifying Context

As demonstrated in Chapter 12, the most powerful concept in the DAX language is the ability to modify context within a measure. The most common way to do that is with the CALCULATE() function and its filter parameters. Due to the fact the CALCULATE() function is used so frequently, we put it first in our reference.

CALCULATE(Expression, Filter1, Filter2, ...)

The CALCULATE() function creates a framework for executing an expression in a context other than its default context. The first parameter is a valid DAX expression. The second and following parameters are DAX filters. The DAX expression is executed in the context resulting from the application of the filters. This resulting context is a table whose rows all satisfy the filter conditions. The filter parameters are optional.

The following example returns "Sales in Dollars" for orders that have a value of more than $150:

```
Large Order Sales = CALCULATE([Sales in Dollars],
                              'Orders'[Sales in US Dollars]>150)
```

Table-Valued Functions

In the section of the chapter following this one, we are going to look at the aggregate functions available in the DAX language. Before we do that, however, we need to look at another group of DAX functions—those that return a table. These table-valued functions are used as input to some types of aggregate functions, thus our need to consider the table-valued functions first.

A table-valued function takes a table as its input. It applies a filter to that table or in some other way manipulates the rows in that table and, in turn, produces a table as its output. That resulting table cannot be displayed directly. It can only be used as the input to another function that requires a table as one of its input parameters.

ALL(TableNameOrTableFieldReference1, TableFieldReference2, …)

The ALL() function creates an alternative result set or table for our aggregate function to use as its context when it is calculating a value. The function creates the alternative context by essentially overriding specific user-created filters that are in place at the time the measure expression is evaluated. A specific example will make this easier to understand.

In this example, we have created a measure called Sales All Years. This measure returns the sum of the sales in dollars across all dates in the dataset. To prevent any user-created filters from getting in the way of this calculation, we are going to add the ALL() function as a filter within the CALCULATE() function. Here is syntax for our measure:

```
Sales All Years = CALCULATE([Sales in Dollars], ALL('Date'[Year]))
```

The ALL() function requires at least one parameter. In our example, the parameter is the Year column in the Date table. Essentially, this expression says that when calculating this measure, ignore *all* filters that might be in place on 'Date'[Year]. Instead, use *all* of the rows available in the current context and any filters on this particular column are disregarded.

The ALL() function can have more than one parameter. Each parameter is a table reference or a reference to a specific field in a table. The ALL() function builds the new aggregation context table, ignoring filters on each and every field or table specified as a parameter.

ALLEXCEPT(TableName, TableFieldReference1, TableFieldReference2, …)

Whereas the ALL() function enables us to specify a field or table and instructs the aggregation to ignore all filters on that field or table, the ALLEXCEPT() function enables us to specify a field or table and instructs the aggregate to ignore all filters except for those on that field or table. The first parameter of this function, TableName, specifies the name of the table whose rows we are filtering. The second parameter, and subsequent parameters, specify a table or field whose filters are exceptions and will apply to the aggregation context.

The following example ignores all filters on the Orders table except those that apply to the Year field in the Date table:

```
All Sales Selected Year = CALCULATE([Sales in Dollars],
                ALLEXCEPT('Orders', 'Date'[Year]))
```

FILTER(TableExpression, Filter)

The FILTER() function applies a filter to a table to create a new table with the resulting subset of the initial table. The filter is a Boolean expression that is evaluated for each row in the specified table. Rows where the Boolean expression evaluates to true are included in the resulting table.

The following example creates a table of all the rows in the Orders table that have a Unit Price between $20 and $30 dollars, inclusive:

```
FILTER('Orders',
       'Orders'[Unit Price] >= 20.00 && 'Orders'[Unit Price] <= 30.00)
```

RELATEDTABLE(TableExpression)

The RELATEDTABLE() function is similar to the RELATED() function we saw in Chapter 12. It makes use of a one-to-many relationship between the table where the function is used and the table specified by the TableExpression parameter. The RELATED() function takes a foreign key and uses the relationship to find the record containing the matching primary key. The RELATEDTABLE() function takes a primary key and uses the relationship to find all the rows containing a matching foreign key. Whereas the RELATED() function works from the "many" side of the relationship to find the "one," the RELATEDTABLE() function works from the "one" side of the relationship to find the "many." Note that the TableExpression can be a table in the model or it can be the result set from another table-valued function.

The following example can be used in the Products table to create a table of all the rows in the Orders table related to each product:

```
RELATEDTABLE('Orders')
```

We can use the table that results from the RELATEDTABLE() function as a parameter to an aggregate function. This enables us to sum a field or count rows in a related table.

CALCULATETABLE(TableExpression, Filter1, Filter2)

The CALCULATETABLE() function is almost identical to the RELATEDTABLE() function. Even though the word "RELATED" is not present in the name of the function, the CALCULATETABLE() function utilizes any relationship that exists between the table where the function is used and the table specified by the TableExpression parameter. The only difference is the CALCULATETABLE() function allows you to add filters by specifying additional filter parameters. Note that the TableExpression can be a table in the model or it can be the result set from another table-valued function.

The following example can be used in the Products table to create a table of all the rows in the Orders table related to each product where the FK_Sales_Person is 1:

```
CALCULATETABLE('Orders', 'Orders'[FK_Sales_Person] = 1)
```

DATATABLE(FieldName1, DataType1,…, {{Value1, …}, {ValueN, …}})

The DATATABLE() function creates a table and populates that table with hardcoded values. The first pairs of parameters define the fields, specifying the name and data type of each field. Valid data types include INTEGER, DOUBLE, STRING, BOOLEAN, CURRENCY, and DATETIME. The curly brackets enclose the set of values to populate the table. The values for each row are enclosed in a second set of curly brackets.

The following example creates a table with two fields: Sales Region and Sales Quota. This table is populated with values for four sales regions.

```
=DATATABLE("Sales Region", STRING,
      "Sales Quota", CURRENCY,
      {    {"East", 10000000},
           {"North", 5000000},
           {"South", 8000000},
           {"West", 15000000}
      }
   )
```

TREATAS(TableExpression, Column1 [, Column2 [, Column3 [,…]]])

The TREATAS() function creates a table of values that will act as if they came from a different table or column. For example, if our context has a set of values from 'Customer'[Sales Region] and we want to use them in a calculation as if they were from 'Sales Region'[Sales Region], we can use the following:

```
CALCULATE([Sales in Dollars],
   TREATAS(VALUES('Customer'[Sales Region]), 'Sales Region'[Sales Region])
   )
```

Additional Filter and Table Functions

DAX includes a number of additional filter and table functions enabling us to create exactly the context needed for our analysis. More information on these functions is available through the Microsoft Developer Network (MSDN) online. These are shown in Table 13-5.

Syntax	Result
ADDCOLUMNS(Table, NewColumnName1, NewColumnExpression1 [, NewColumnName2, NewColumnExpression2] [,...])	Returns the content of Table with one or more calculated columns added. The column name(s) and defining expression(s) are passed as parameters.
ADDMISSINGITEMS(ShowAllColumn[, ShowAllColumn]..., Table, GroupingColumn [, GroupingColumn]...[, FilterTable]...)	Adds combinations of items from each ShowAllColumn that are not present in a result set table. For example, if the Date table contains years 2016 through 2018, but a result set table only contains rows with values for 2016 and 2017, ADDMISSINGITEMS() would add a row for 2018.
ALLNOBLANKROW(TableOrColumn)	Using the parent table of a relationship, this function returns all rows excluding the blank row or all distinct values in a column excluding the blank row. It disregards any context filter that might be in place.
ALLSELECTED(TableOrColumn)	Removes all context filters from columns and rows in the current query.
CROSSFILTER(Column1, Column2, Direction)	Specifies the cross-filtering direction to be used for an existing relationship in a calculation.
CROSSJOIN(Table1, Table2 [, Table3]...)	Returns the Cartesian product of all rows in the specified tables.
DETAILROWS(Measure)	If the specified measure has a DetailRows expression defined, this function returns the table data corresponding to that expression. Otherwise, this function returns the entire table to which the specified measure belongs.
DISTINCT(Column)	Returns a one-column table containing the distinct values from a specified column.
EARLIER(Column, EvaluationLevel))	Returns the value of the specified column in a previous context. This is used when multiple calculations or measures are nested one inside the other with each changing the context. EARLIER() can be used to retrieve the value of a column as it existed in an earlier (or outer, if you visualize nesting) context. EvaluationLevel specifies the number of context iterations to go back.
EARLIEST(Column)	This function is similar to the EARLIER() function, but it is evaluated in the earliest (or outermost context).
FILTERS(Column)	Returns a table of the values that are creating filters directly applied to the specified column. For example, if the current context filters the Year column to 2016 and 2017, FILTERS() would return a table containing two rows: one containing 2016 and one containing 2017.
GENERATE(Table1, Table2)	Returns a table with the Cartesian product between each row in Table1 and the table that results from evaluating Table2 in the context of the current row from Table1.

Table 13-5   *Additional Filter and Table Functions*

Syntax	Result
GENERATEALL(Table1, Table2)	Returns a table with the Cartesian product between each row in Table1 and the table that results from evaluating Table2 in the context of the current row from Table1. The row from Table1 is included in the returned table, even if no rows are produced for Table2 from that context.
GENERATESERIES(StartValue, EndValue [, IncrementValue])	Returns a table with a single column, called Value, containing the arithmetic series of values between StartValue and EndValue, inclusive. The values are incremented by IncrementValue, if it is specified; otherwise, the increment is 1.
HASONEFILTER(Column)	Returns true when there is only one filter directly affecting the values in the specified column in the current context; otherwise, it returns false.
HASONEVALUE(Column)	Returns true when the specified column contains only one distinct value; otherwise, it returns false.
ISCROSSFILTERED(Column)	Returns true when the specified column or another column in the same or a related table is being filtered; otherwise, it returns false. A column is said to be cross-filtered when a filter applied to another column in the same table or a related table limits the values in the column. For example, if Year is filtered to 2017, Month is cross-filtered to only the months in 2017.
ISFILTERED(Column)	Returns true when the specified column is being filtered directly; otherwise, it returns false.
KEEPFILTERS(Expression)	Modifies how filters are applied within a CALCULATE() or CALCULATETABLE() function. Normally, filters in a CALCULATE() or CALCULATETABLE() function replace any filters on the same columns. When KEEPFILTERS() is placed around the filter expression it returns the intersection of the existing filter context for that column and the new context created by the filter expression.
ROW (ColumnName1, ColumnExpression1 [[, ColumnName2, ColumnExpression2]...])	Returns a table with a single row from columns with the specified names and defined by the column expressions.
SAMPLE(SampleSize, Table, OrderByExpression1 [, Order1 [, OrderByExpression2 [, Order2]]...])	Returns a sample of SampleSize rows from Table. If "order by" expressions are specified, the same sample will be returned by repeated calls of this function. If no "order by" expressions are specified, the sample will be random and will vary from one call of this function to the next.

Table 13-5   *Additional Filter and Table Functions (Continued)*

Syntax	Result
SELECTCOLUMNS(Table, NewColumnName1, NewColumnExpression1 [, NewColumnName2, NewColumnExpression2] [,...])	This function works the same as the ADDCOLUMNS() function, except it starts with an empty table and adds rows rather than starting with Table.
SUBSTITUTEWITHINDEX(Table, IndexColumn, IndexColumnsTable, [OrderBy, [Order], ...)	Returns a table with all of the rows in Table and all of the columns in Table except for those in common with IndexColumnsTable. The common columns are replaced by a column with the name specified in the IndexColumn parameter. The content of this column is a zero-based index integer. Essentially, this function creates a normalized version of Table with a surrogate key that can be used for linking to IndexColumnsTable.
TOPN(N, Table, OrderByExpression1 [, Order1 [, OrderByExpression2 [, Order2]]...])	Returns the Top N rows from Table.
VALUES(TableOrColumn)	Returns a one-column table containing the distinct values from the specified table or column.

Table 13-5 *Additional Filter and Table Functions (Continued)*

Aggregate Functions

Now that you know a bit about table-valued functions, let's take a look at some of the basic aggregate functions available in the DAX language. The aggregate functions come in several varieties. Standard aggregate functions calculate their aggregation on a field found in the table where they are used.

Aggregate functions with an "X" appended to their name require a table as their first parameter. (This is where the FILTER(), RELATEDTABLE(), CALCULATETABLE(), and other table-valued functions can come into play.) These "X" functions calculate their aggregation in the context of the table passed as that first parameter and evaluate the expression row by row before aggregating. The standard and "X" aggregate functions are able to perform aggregations on fields with numeric and date types only.

Aggregate functions with an "A" appended to their name will work with additional types of data. They will work with Boolean values and with text values. When working with Boolean values, true is considered to be 1 and false is considered to be 0. A text value is always considered to be 0.

The final types of aggregate functions have an "AX" appended to their function name. These functions combine the characteristics of both the "X" and "A" aggregate functions. They require a table as their first parameter and calculate in the context of that table. They handle Boolean and text values as described earlier.

You should be aware of the fact that there is a performance difference between the various types of aggregate functions. Aggregate functions that use a field as their only parameter are able to use the data model very efficiently to obtain their results. Aggregate functions that allow an expression as one of their parameters (those ending in "X") must be evaluated row by row and can be slower when working with large tables.

AVERAGE(Field)

Calculates the mean of the values in the specified field. Works with numeric and date types only.
Example:

```
=AVERAGE([Sales in Dollars])
```

AVERAGEA(Field)

Calculates the mean of the values in the specified field. Handles Boolean and text data types as well as numeric and date data types.
Example:

```
=AVERAGEA([Group Of 8 Member])
```

AVERAGEX(Table, Expression)

Calculates the mean of the values yielded by the expression in the context of the specified table.
Example:

```
=AVERAGEX(RELATEDTABLE('Orders'), 'Orders'[Sales in Dollars])
```

CONCATENATEX(Table, Field, [Delimiter])

Concatenates string values from multiple rows in a table.
Example:

```
=CONCATENATEX('Products', [ProductName], ", ")
```

COUNT(Field)

Counts the number of rows in which the specified field contains a numeric or date value.
Example:

```
=COUNT([Sales in Dollars])
```

COUNTA(Field)

Counts the number of rows in which the specified field contains a value. Handles Boolean and text data types as well as numeric and date data types.
    Example:

```
=COUNTA([Is Group Of 8 Member])
```

COUNTAX(Table, Expression)

Counts the number of rows in which the expression yields a value in the context of the specified table.
    Example:

```
=COUNTAX(RELATEDTABLE('Orders'), 'Orders'[Sales in Dollars])
```

COUNTBLANK(Field)

Counts the number of rows in which the specified field is blank. If no rows have a blank value, a blank is returned by the function.
    Example:

```
=COUNTBLANK([Guiding Lights 2017 Sales])
```

COUNTROWS(Table)

Counts the number of rows in the specified table.
    Example:

```
=COUNTROWS(RELATEDTABLE('Orders'))
```

COUNTX(Table, Expression)

Counts the number of rows in which the expression yields a numeric or date value in the context of the specified table.
    Example:

```
=COUNTX(RELATEDTABLE('Orders'), 'Orders'[Sales in Dollars])
```

DISTINCTCOUNT(Field)

Counts the number of distinct values in the specified field.
    Example:

```
=DISTINCTCOUNT('Product'[Product Type])
```

DISTINCTCOUNTNOBLANK(Field)

Counts the number of distinct values in the specified field.
DISTINCTCOUNTNOBLANK() does not include the BLANK value in its count.
Example:

```
=DISTINCTCOUNTNOBLANK('Product'[Product Type])
```

GEOMEAN(Field)

Returns the geometric mean of the values in the specified field. Works with numeric
and date types only.
Example:

```
=GEOMEAN([Sales in Dollars])
```

GEOMEANX(Table, Expression)

Returns the geometric mean of the values yielded by the expression in the context of
the specified table.
Example:

```
=GEOMEANX(RELATEDTABLE('Orders'), 'Orders'[Sales in Dollars])
```

MAX(Field)

Returns the maximum of the values in the specified field. Works with numeric and date
types only.
Example:

```
=MAX([Sales in Dollars])
```

MAXA(Field)

Returns the maximum of the values in the specified field. Handles Boolean and text
data types as well as numeric and date data types.
Example:

```
=MAXA([Group Of 8 Member])
```

MAXX(Table, Expression)

Returns the maximum of the values yielded by the expression in the context of the
specified table.
Example:

```
=MAXX(RELATEDTABLE('Orders'), 'Orders'[Sales in Dollars])
```

MEDIAN(Field)

Returns the median of the values in the specified field. Works with numeric and date types only.

Example:

```
=MEDIAN([Sales in Dollars])
```

MEDIANX(Table, Expression)

Returns the median of the values yielded by the expression in the context of the specified table.

Example:

```
=MEDIANX(RELATEDTABLE('Orders'), 'Orders'[Sales in Dollars])
```

MIN(Field)

Returns the minimum of the values in the specified field. Works with numeric and date types only.

Example:

```
=MIN([Sales in Dollars])
```

MINA(Field)

Returns the minimum of the values in the specified field. Handles Boolean and text data types as well as numeric and date data types.

Example:

```
=MINA([Group Of 8 Member])
```

MINX(Table, Expression)

Returns the minimum of the values yielded by the expression in the context of the specified table.

Example:

```
=MINX(RELATEDTABLE('Orders'), 'Orders'[Sales in Dollars])
```

PRODUCT(Field)

Multiplies the values in the specified field by each other.

Example:

```
=PRODUCT([Multiples])
```

PRODUCTX(Table, Expression)

Multiplies the values yielded by the expression in the context of the specified table by each other.

Example:

```
=PRODUCTX(RELATEDTABLE('Multiples Table'), 'Multiples Table'[Multiples])
```

SUM(Field)

Calculates the total of the values in the specified field.

Example:

```
=SUM([Sales in Dollars])
```

SUMX(Table, Expression)

Calculates the total of the values yielded by the expression in the context of the specified table.

Example:

```
=SUMX(RELATEDTABLE('Orders'), 'Orders'[Sales in Dollars])
```

DAX Functions for Time Analytics

One of the reasons we create a model is to capture time analytics within the model. We do this in a Tabular model through the use of DAX functions. Here is a basic overview of a few of the time analytic functions available to us.

The DAX time analytics functions work with a standard Gregorian calendar year. They can also work with your organization's fiscal year, if that year is based on Gregorian calendar months. All you need to do is specify the year-end date for that fiscal calendar. If your organization uses a week-based fiscal calendar, such as those used in retail or manufacturing, you will need to use more complex DAX expressions to create your own custom time analytics.

CLOSINGBALANCEMONTH(Expression, Dates, Filter)
CLOSINGBALANCEQUARTER(Expression, Dates, Filter)
CLOSINGBALANCEYEAR(Expression, Dates, Filter, YearEndDate)

The CLOSINGBALANCE*period*() functions enable us to perform calculations with semi-additive measures. A semi-additive dimension may be summed across certain slicers but not across others. Inventory levels are the classic example. The sum of the inventory amounts for each product yields the total number of products in the warehouse. However, the sum of the first three months' inventory amounts does not give the inventory amount at the end of the first quarter. It is the inventory amount for the last month of the quarter, the "closing balance for the quarter," that is the inventory amount for the quarter.

The CLOSINGBALANCE*period*() functions provide a way to find these end-of-period amounts. Three different periods are supported. There are functions for end of month, end of quarter, and end of year.

The Expression parameter must return a numeric value. This is the quantity we want to find the closing balance for. In the example discussed earlier, this would be the number of products in the warehouse.

The Dates parameter must be one of the following:

- A reference to a field containing date/time values
- A table-valued function call that returns a table with a single column of dates
- A Boolean expression that defines a single-column table of date/time values

This parameter is used to determine which numeric quantity is the one for the end of the period. The Filter parameter is optional. It is a filter expression used to modify the context of the function.

Example:

```
=CLOSINGBALANCEMONTH(SUM('Inventory Info'[InventoryLevel]), 'Date'[Date])
```

DATEADD(Dates, NumberOfIntervals, Interval)

The DATEADD() function starts with a given date and adds a set number of time intervals—years, months, and so on—to it to produce a new date. The number of intervals may be either positive to move forward in time or negative to move backward in time. Valid values for Interval are as follows:

- Year
- Quarter
- Month
- Day

Note that Interval should not be enclosed in quotes.

Example:

```
=DATEADD('Date'[Date], 1, year)
```

DATESBETWEEN(Dates, StartDate, EndDate)

The DATESBETWEEN() function returns a table with a single column that contains all of the dates between the start date and the end date.

Example:

```
Accepted June to Mid July:=CALCULATE(SUM('Orders'[Sales In US Dollars]),
          DATESBETWEEN('Date'[Date],
          DATE(2017,6,1), DATE(2017,7,15))
```

DATESINPERIOD(Dates, StartDate, NumberOfIntervals, Interval)

The DATESINPERIOD() function works similar to the DATESBETWEEN() function in that it returns a table with a single column of dates. However, DATESINPERIOD() uses the number of time intervals relative to a starting date to calculate the date range. Valid values for Interval are as follows:

- Year
- Quarter
- Month
- Day

Note that Interval should not be enclosed in quotes.

Example:

```
Sales for Past 3 Weeks:=CALCULATE(SUM('Orders'[Sales in Dollars]),
          DATESINPERIOD('Date'[Date],
          DATE(2017,6,1), -21, day)
```

DATESMTD(Dates)
DATESQTD(Dates)
DATESYTD(Dates, [YearEndDate])

In the discussion of the CLOSINGBALANCE*period*() functions, one possibility for the second parameter was a table-valued function returning a single column of dates. The DATES*period*() functions do just that. Given a column containing dates, these functions return a table of dates up to and including the current date in the context. There are functions for month to date, quarter to date, and year to date.

The Dates parameter must be one of the following:

- A reference to a field containing date/time values
- A table-valued function call that returns a table with a single column of dates
- A Boolean expression that defines a single-column table of date/time values

For example, suppose the DATESMTD() function is called in a column containing a reference to January 15, 2018. January 15, 2018 becomes the context for the function call. The function would return a table with rows for January 1, 2018 through January 15, 2018.

Example:

```
=CALCULATE(SUM('Orders'[Sales in Dollars]),
 ALLEXCEPT('Orders', 'Product'[Product Type]),
 DATESYTD('Date'[Date]))
```

ENDOFMONTH(Dates)
ENDOFQUARTER(Dates)
ENDOFYEAR(Dates)

The ENDOF*period*() functions return a single-column, single-row table containing the last date in the month, quarter, or year in the given context. This allows you to easily find the last date in a period without doing a lot of fancy date calculations. Those of you who have had to do those date calculations know how nice these functions are to have in the arsenal.

Example:

```
=ENDOFMONTH('Date'[Date])
```

FIRSTDATE(Dates)

The FIRSTDATE() function returns a single-column, single-row table containing the first date in the current context.

Example:

```
=FIRSTDATE('Date'[Date])
```

FIRSTNONBLANK(Field, Expression)

The FIRSTNONBLANK() function returns the first value in Field where Expression is non-blank in the current context.

Example:

```
=FIRSTNONBLANK('Date'[Date], [Large Order Sales])
```

LASTDATE(Dates)

The LASTDATE() function returns a single-column, single-row table containing the last date in the current context.

Example:

```
=LASTDATE('Date'[Date])
```

LASTNONBLANK(Field, Expression)

The LASTNONBLANK() function returns the last value in Field where Expression is non-blank in the current context.

Example:

```
=LASTNONBLANK('Date'[Date], [Large Order Sales])
```

NEXTDAY(Dates)
NEXTMONTH(Dates)
NEXTQUARTER(Dates)
NEXTYEAR(Dates)

The NEXT*period*() functions return a table containing all of the dates within the next period in the current context.

Example:

```
=CALCULATE(SUM('Orders'[Sales in Dollars]), NEXTMONTH('Date'[Date]))
```

OPENINGBALANCEMONTH(Expression, Dates [, Filter])
OPENINGBALANCEQUARTER(Expression, Dates [, Filter])
OPENINGBALANCEYEAR(Expression, Dates [, Filter])

The OPENINGBALANCE*period*() functions evaluate the given expression on the first day of the specified period.

Example:

```
=OPENINGBALANCEQUARTER(SUMX('Orders',
  'Orders'[Sales in Dollars] - 'Orders'[Large Order Sales]),
  'Date'[Date])
```

PARALLELPERIOD(Dates, NumPeriods, Period)

The PARALLELPERIOD() function also returns a table of dates. It takes the dates passed as the first parameter and shifts those dates by the specified number of periods. The PARALLELPERIOD() function always returns all of the dates in the specified period. For example, if the Dates parameter contains dates from June 10, 2017 through June 20, 2017, the NumPeriods is –1, and the Period parameter is month, the PARALLELPERIOD() function will return a table of dates from June 1, 2016 to June 30, 2016.

The Dates parameter must be one of the following:

- A reference to a field containing date/time values
- A table-valued function call that returns a table with a single column of dates
- A Boolean expression that defines a single-column table of date/time values

A period can be any of the following:

- Month
- Quarter
- Year

The Period value is not put in quotes.

Example:

```
=CALCULATE(SUM('Orders'[Sales in Dollars]),
 ALLEXCEPT('Orders', 'Product'[Product Type]),
 PARALLELPERIOD('Date'[Date], -1, month))
```

PREVIOUSDAY(Dates)
PREVIOUSMONTH(Dates)
PREVIOUSQUARTER(Dates)
PREVIOUSYEAR(Dates)

The PREVIOUS*period*() functions return a table containing all of the dates within the previous period in the current context.

Example:

```
=CALCULATE(SUM('Orders'[Sales in Dollars]), PREVIOUSMONTH('Date'[Date])
```

SAMEPERIODLASTYEAR(Dates)

The SAMEPERIODLASTYEAR() function is similar to a call to the PARALLELPERIOD() function with the NumPeriods parameter set to –1 and the Periods parameter set to year. The difference is the SAMEPERIODLASTYEAR() function returns one and only one date in the output table for each date in the Dates parameter. It does not fill in the entire period as the PARALLELPERIOD() function does.

The Dates parameter must be one of the following:

- A reference to a field containing date/time values
- A table-valued function call that returns a table with a single column of dates
- A Boolean expression that defines a single-column table of date/time values

Example:

```
=CALCULATE(SUM('Orders'[Sales in Dollars]),
 ALLEXCEPT('Orders', 'Product'[Product Type]),
 SAMEPERIODLASTYEAR('Date'[Date]))
```

STARTOFMONTH(Dates)
STARTOFQUARTER(Dates)
STARTOFYEAR(Dates)

The STARTOF*period*() functions return a single-column, single-row table containing the first date in the month, quarter, or year in the given context. This allows you to easily find the first date in a period.

Example:

```
=STARTOFMONTH('Date'[Date])
```

TOTALMTD(Expression, Dates, Filter)
TOTALQTD(Expression, Dates, Filter)
TOTALYTD(Expression, Dates, Filter,[YearEndDate])

The TOTAL*period*() functions enable us to total a numeric quantity to get a period-to-date value. There are functions for month to date, quarter to date, and year to date. The Expression parameter must return a numeric value.

The Dates parameter must be one of the following:

- A reference to a field containing date/time values
- A table-valued function call that returns a table with a single column of dates
- A Boolean expression that defines a single-column table of date/time values

The Filter parameter is optional. It is a filter expression used to modify the context of the function.

Example:

```
=TOTALYTD(SUM('Orders'[Sales in Dollars]), 'Date'[Date])
```

Parent/Child Relationships

A parent/child relationship is a special type of one-to-many relationship. It is built on a table that contains a self-referential relationship. An employee table that contains a supervisor field is a good example. Figure 13-1 shows a table with a Supervisor field. The Supervisor field contains the employee number of the person to whom the employee reports. This field is a foreign key field that points to the primary key in the same table.

A parent/child dimension creates its own hierarchy. Each step from child to parent creates another level in that hierarchy. What is unique about this is there are an undetermined number of levels to the hierarchy. The number of hierarchy levels depends on the number of links in the parent/child chain you are following.

In the Employee dimension shown in Figure 13-1, we can start at Eva, the developer, and follow the chain of supervisors up to Maya, the CEO. There are six levels to the hierarchy along this path. If, however, we start at Juan, the system administrator, and follow the chain of supervisors up to Maya, there are four levels to the hierarchy. (Not saying that system administrators are more important than developers. That's just the way this company happens to be structured!)

When a table containing the records shown in Figure 13-1 is imported into a Power BI data model, we use DAX functions to turn the parent/child relationship into a hierarchy.

Path(PrimaryKeyField, ParentForeignKeyField)

The PATH() function uses the primary key field and the parent foreign key field to traverse up the parent/child relationship. As it does, it builds a list of each of the primary key values it encounters along the way. The primary key values are delimited by the "|" character.

In the structure shown in Figure 13-1, we could use the following PATH() function:

```
=PATH([EmpNum], [Supervisor])
```

Employees

EmpNum	Name	Position	Supervisor
129	Sandra	Team Leader	239
235	Eva	Developer	129
239	Peter	Development Manager	303
293	Maya	CEO	
303	Frank	IT Director	470
470	Tia	CFO	293
487	Juan	System Administrator	303

Figure 13-1 *An employee table with a self-referential field*

In the record for Eva, this function returns the following path:

```
293|470|303|239|129|235
```

This path results because Eva is employee number 235 and Eva's supervisor is employee number 129, Sandra. Sandra's supervisor is employee number 239, Peter. Peter's supervisor is employee number 303, Frank. Frank's supervisor is employee number 470, Tia. Tia's supervisor is employee number 293, Maya. Maya is the CEO, so her supervisor field is empty.

PATHITEM(PathField, PathLevel)

The PATHITEM() function extracts one of the primary key values from the delimited list created by the PATH() function. To use the PATHITEM() function, a calculated column must first be created using the PATH() function. The "path field" can then be referenced as the first parameter (PathField) of the PATHITEM() function.

The value extracted from the list is determined by the second parameter (PathLevel) of the PATHITEM() function. A PathLevel value of 1 extracts the leftmost primary key value in the path. A PathLevel value of 2 extracts the primary key value that is second from the left, and so on.

If we use the PATH() function to create a calculated column called SupervisorPath for our structure in Figure 13-1, we can then use the following PATHITEM() function:

```
=PATHITEM ([SupervisorPath], 3)
```

In the record for Eva, this function returns the following foreign key value:

```
303
```

This is the third item from the left in the list created by the PATH() function.

PATHITEMREVERSE(PathField, PathLevel)

The PATHITEMREVERSE() function works the same as the PATHITEM() function, except it starts from the rightmost item in the path. Again, using our example from Figure 13-1, the PATHITEMREVERSE() function

```
=PATHITEMREVERSE([SupervisorPath], 3)
```

would return the following foreign key value in the Eva record:

```
239
```

This is the third item from the right in the list created by the PATH() function.

PATHCONTAINS(PathField, Item)

The PATHCONTAINS() function determines if a given item is contained somewhere along the specified path. It returns true if the item was found along this path and false if it was not. Continuing with our example from Figure 13-1, we can use this function to determine if employee number 129 is in the supervisory path:

```
=PATHCONTAINS([SupervisorPath], 129)
```

This function will return true for the path in the Eva record and false for the path in the Peter record.

PATHLENGTH(PathField)

The PATHLENGTH() function returns a count of the number of items in a given path. The expression

```
=PATHLENGTH([SupervisorPath])
```

returns

```
6
```

in the record for Eva.

LOOKUPVALUE(ReturnValueField, PrimaryKeyField, PrimaryKeyValue)

In most cases, finding the primary key value at a certain level in the parent/child relationship is not enough. In our example here, we probably want to know the name of the supervisor or their position. We do this with the LOOKUPVALUE() function. This function returns the value in the ReturnValueField for the row where the PrimaryKeyField matches the PrimaryKeyValue.

Again, using the example from Figure 13-1, we use the following expression to get the name of the person at the third level in the relationship:

```
=LOOKUPVALUE ([Name], [EmpNum], PATHITEM ([SupervisorPath], 3))
```

In the record for Eva, this function returns

```
Frank
```

because Frank is the name corresponding to the employee number found at the third level of the path.

Additional DAX Functions

Along with the workhorse functions we've covered so far, DAX has a number of other functions that aid us in producing exactly the values we and our users need. We take a quick look at those functions here.

Date and Time Functions

The date functions in DAX allow us to manipulate date/time data types, as shown in Table 13-6.

Syntax	Result
CALENDAR(StartDate, EndDate)	Returns a table with a date field containing one row for each date between StartDate and EndDate.
CALENDARAUTO([FiscalYearEndMonth])	Returns a table with a date field containing one row for each date between the earliest date and the latest date found in the data model. The table includes the complete fiscal years containing the earliest date and the latest date. Optionally, the ending month of the fiscal year can be specified as an integer (1–12).
DATE(Year, Month, Day)	Returns a date/time data type value with the specified year, month, and day.
DATEDIFF(StartDate, EndDate, Interval)	Returns the number of intervals between two dates where Interval can be one of the following: • Year • Quarter • Month • Week • Day • Hour • Minute • Second
DATEVALUE(DateText)	Converts a textual representation of a date into a date/time data type value.
DAY(DateTime)	Returns the day of the month of the specified date.
EDATE(StartDate, NumberOfMonths)	Returns the date that is the specified number of months before or after the given date.
EOMONTH(StartDate, NumberOfMonths)	Returns the date that is the last day of the month which is NumberOfMonths before or after the specified date.

Table 13-6 *DAX Date and Time Functions (Continued)*

Syntax	Result
HOUR(DateTime)	Returns the hour portion of the specified date/time.
MINUTE(DateTime)	Returns the minute portion of the specified date/time.
MONTH(DateTime)	Returns the month portion of the specified date/time.
NOW()	Returns a date/time data type value containing the current date and current time.
SECOND(DateTime)	Returns the seconds portion of the specified date/time.
TIME(Hour, Minute, Second)	Returns a date/time data type value with the specified hour, minute, and second.
TIMEVALUE(TimeText)	Converts a textual representation of a time into a date/time data type value.
TODAY()	Returns the current date as a date/time data type. The time portion is always midnight.
UTCNOW()	Returns the current UTC date/time.
UTCTODAY()	Returns the current UTC date.
WEEKDAY(DateTime, ReturnType)	Returns the day of the week number of the specified date/time. ReturnType may be one of the following: ● **1**—The week begins on Sunday, with Sunday as day 1 and Saturday as day 7. ● **2**—The week begins on Monday, with Monday as day 1 and Sunday as day 7. ● **3**—The week begins on Monday, with Monday as day 0 and Sunday as day 6.
WEEKNUM(DateTime, ReturnType)	Returns the week number in the current year for the specified date/time. ReturnType may be one of the following: ● **1**—Weeks begin on Sunday. ● **2**—Weeks begin on Monday.
YEAR(DateTime)	Returns the year portion of the specified date/time.
YEARFRAC(StartDate, EndDate [, Basis])	Returns the number of whole days between the two dates. Basis may be one of the following: ● **0**—US (NASD) 30/360 ● **1**—Actual/Actual ● **2**—Actual/360 ● **3**—Actual/365 ● **4**—European 30/360

Table 13-6 *DAX Date and Time Functions (Continued)*

Informational Functions

The informational functions in DAX tell us something about a column, an expression, or the environment in which we are working, as shown in Table 13-7.

Syntax	Result
CONTAINS(Table, Column, Value [, Column, Value]...)	Returns true if the specified values exist or are contained in those specified columns.
CONTAINSROW(Table, Expression1, [Expression2, ...])	Returns true if the specified row of values exists or is contained in the table; otherwise returns false.
CUSTOMDATA()	Returns the content of the CustomData property in the connection string.
ERROR(ErrorMessage)	Raises an error with ErrorMessage as the error message.
ISBLANK(Value)	Returns true if the specified value is blank; otherwise returns false.
ISEMPTY(Table)	Returns true if the specified table is blank; otherwise returns false.
ISERROR(Value)	Returns true if the specified value is in error; otherwise returns false.
ISEVEN(Number)	Returns true if the specified number is even; otherwise returns false.
ISINSCOPE(Field)	Returns true if the specified field is the current level in a hierarchy; otherwise returns false.
ISLOGICAL(Value)	Returns true if the specified value is a logical data type; otherwise returns false.
ISNONTEXT(Value)	Returns true if the specified value is not textual; otherwise returns false.
ISNUMBER(Value)	Returns true if the specified value is numeric; otherwise returns false.
ISODD(Number)	Returns true if the specified number is odd; otherwise returns false.
ISONORAFTER(ScalarExpression1, ScalarExpression2 [, SortOrder [, ScalarExpression3, ScalarExpression4 [, SortOrder]], ...)	Compares each pair of scalar values based on the sort order specified or ascending if no sort order is specified. If each pair of values is in the designated sort order, the function returns true; otherwise, it returns false.
ISSELECTEDMEASURE(Measure1, Measure2, ...)	Returns true if the measure currently in context is one of the parameters specified; otherwise returns false.
ISSUBTOTAL(Column)	Returns true if the current row contains a subtotal for the specified column; otherwise returns false.
ISTEXT(Value)	Returns true if the specified value is textual; otherwise false.
SELECTEDMEASURE()	Returns a reference to the measure that is currently in context.

Table 13-7 *DAX Informational Functions (Continued)*

Syntax	Result
SELECTEDVALUE(Field, [AlternateResult])	Returns the value in the specified field when the current context has filtered this field to a single value; otherwise, AlternateResult is returned.
USEROBJECTID()	Returns the user's Object ID from Azure Active Directory.
USERNAME()	Returns the domain name and user name for the credentials used to connect to Analysis Services.
USERPRINCIPALNAME()	Returns the user principal name.

Table 13-7   *DAX Informational Functions (Continued)*

Logical Functions

The logical functions in DAX allow us to perform true/false decision making in our expressions, as shown in Table 13-8.

Syntax	Result
AND(LogicalExpression, LogicalExpression)	Returns true if both logical expressions are true; otherwise returns false. This is equivalent to the && operator.
CONTAINSSTRING(TextToSearch, TextToFind)	Returns true if TextToFind exists within TextToSearch; otherwise returns false. CONTAINSSTRING() is not case-sensitive.
CONTAINSSTRINGEXACT(TextToSearch, TextToFind)	Returns true if TextToFind exists within TextToSearch; otherwise returns false. CONTAINSSTRINGEXACT() is case-sensitive.
FALSE()	Returns false.
IF(LogicalExpression, Expression1, Expression2)	Returns the content of expression 1 if the logical expression is true; otherwise returns the content of expression 2.
IFERROR(Expression1, Expression2)	If expression 1 is in error, returns the content of expression 2; otherwise returns the content of expression 1.
NOT(LogicalExpression)	Returns the opposite of the logical expression. This is equivalent to the NOT and ! operators.
OR(LogicalExpression, LogicalExpression)	Returns true if either logical expression is true; otherwise returns false. This is equivalent to the || operator.
SWITCH(Expression, Value1, Result1 [, Value2, Result2]...[, ElseResult])	If the expression evaluates to value 1, result 1 is returned. If the expression evaluates to value 2, result 2 is returned. If the expression does not match any of the specified values, the else result is returned.
TRUE()	Returns true.

Table 13-8   *DAX Logical Functions*

Text Functions

The text functions in DAX allow us to manipulate textual data, as shown in Table 13-9.

Syntax	Result
BLANK()	Returns a blank textual value.
COMBINEVALUES(Delimiter, String1, String2 [, String3]…)	Returns the concatenation of the specified strings separated by the delimiter.
CONCATENATE(String1, String2)	Returns the concatenation of the two strings.
EXACT(String1, String2)	Returns true if the two strings are exactly the same; otherwise returns false.
FIND(Search, Target [, [StartPosition] [, NotFound]])	Returns the starting position of the search text within the target text, optionally beginning at the starting position. If the search text is not found, the NotFound value is returned, if it has been specified. FIND() is case-sensitive. FIND() does not support wildcards. To include wildcards, use SEARCH().
FIXED(Number, Decimals, NoCommas)	Rounds a number to the specified number of decimals and returns the result as a textual value.
FORMAT(Value, FormatString)	Formats the specified value according to the format string and returns the result as a textual value.
LEFT(String, NumCharacters)	Returns the specified number of characters from the left of the string.
LEN(String)	Returns the length of the string.
LOWER(String)	Converts the string to all lowercase text.
MID(String, StartPosition, NumCharacters)	Returns the specified number of characters from the string starting at the specified location.
REPLACE(OldString, StartPosition, NumCharacters, NewString)	Replaces the specified number of characters in the old string at the starting position with the content of the new string.
REPT(String, Repetitions)	Creates a new string by concatenating the specified string with itself the given number of repetitions.
RIGHT(String, NumCharacters)	Returns the specified number of characters from the right of the string.
SEARCH(Search, Target [, [StartPosition] [, NotFound]])	Returns the starting position of the search text within the target text, optionally beginning at the starting position. If the search text is not found, the NotFound value is returned, if it has been specified. SEARCH() is case-insensitive and accent-sensitive. The SEARCH() function allows ? to be used as a wildcard placeholder for a single character and * to be used as a wildcard placeholder for multiple characters.

Table 13-9   *DAX Text Functions (Continued)*

Syntax	Result
SELECTEDMEASUREFORMATSTRING()	Returns a string containing the format string of the measure that is currently in context.
SELECTEDMEASURENAME()	Returns a string containing the name of the measure that is currently in context.
SUBSTITUTE(Target, OldString, NewString, InstanceNum)	Replaces the specified instance of the old string with the new string within the target text.
TRIM(String)	Removes all spaces from the string except for single spaces between words.
UNICHAR(Number)	Returns the Unicode character referenced by Number.
UNICODE(String)	Returns the numeric Unicode value of the first character in the string.
UPPER(String)	Converts the string to all uppercase text.
VALUE(String)	Converts the string to a numeric value.

Table 13-9   *DAX Text Functions (Continued)*

Grouping and Set Functions

The grouping and set functions in DAX allow us to create and manipulate tables as sets of rows, as shown in Table 13-10.

Syntax	Result
ALLCROSSFILTERED(Table)	Clears all filters on the specified table.
EXCEPT(Table1, Table2)	Returns the rows of Table1 that do not appear in Table2.
GROUPBY(Table, [GroupByColumn1] [, GroupByColumn2]... [, Name, Expression]...)	Groups the rows of the specified table on the given values, creating new aggregated rows as specified. This function does not do an implicit CALCULATE on each aggregation expression.
IGNORE(Measure)	Used with the SUMMARIZECOLUMNS() function to indicate measures to be ignored when determining nonblank rows.
INTERSECT(Table1, Table2)	Returns the rows present in both Table1 and Table2, retaining duplicates.

Table 13-10   *DAX Grouping and Set Functions*

Syntax	Result
NATURALINNERJOIN(LeftTable, RightTable)	Performs an inner join of the two tables based on columns with the same name in both tables.
NATURALLEFTOUTERJOIN(LeftTable, RightTable)	Performs a left outer join of the two tables based on columns with the same name in both tables.
NONVISUAL(Expression)	Used with the SUMMARIZECOLUMNS() function to designate a filter as nonvisual.
SUMMARIZE(Table, [GroupByColumn1] [, GroupByColumn2]... [, Name, Expression]...)	Groups the rows of the specified table on the given values, creating new aggregated rows as specified. This function does an implicit CALCULATE on each aggregation expression.
SUMMARIZECOLUMNS(GroupByColumn1 [GroupByColumn2]...,[FilterTable]...,[Name, Expression]...)	Groups the rows on the given values within the specified filter context, creating new aggregate rows as specified.
UNION(Table1, Table2 [, Table3]...)	Creates a union of the specified tables.

Table 13-10 *DAX Grouping and Set Functions (Continued)*

Lookup/Relationship Functions

The lookup functions in DAX allow us to find a value or values in a table, as shown in Table 13-11.

Syntax	Result
LOOKUPVALUE(ReturnValueField, PrimaryKeyField1, PrimaryKeyValue1, [PrimaryKeyField2, [PrimaryKeyValue2], ..., [AlternativeResult])	Returns the value in the ReturnValueField for the row where the PrimaryKeyField(s) match the PrimaryKeyValue(s). If there is no matching row found, AlternativeResult is returned.
RELATED(ReturnValueField)	Returns the value in ReturnValueField in the related row.
USERELATIONSHIP(Field1, Field2)	Specifies the relationship to use in a specific calculation. A relationship must be defined between Field1 and Field2.

Table 13-11 *DAX Grouping and Set Functions*

Math and Trigonometric Functions

The math and trigonometric functions in DAX allow us to do complex mathematical calculations, as shown in Table 13-12.

Syntax	Result
ABS(Number)	Returns the absolute value of a number.
ACOS(Number)	Returns the arccosine of a number in radians.
ACOSH(Number)	Returns the inverse hyperbolic cosine of a number.
ACOT(Number)	Returns the arccotangent of a number in radians.
ACOTH(Number)	Returns the inverse hyperbolic cotangent of a number.
ASIN(Number)	Returns the arcsine of a number in radians.
ASINH(Number)	Returns the inverse hyperbolic sine of a number.
ATAN(Number)	Returns the arctangent of a number in radians.
ATANH(Number)	Returns the inverse hyperbolic tangent of a number.
CEILING(Number, Significance)	Rounds the number up to the nearest integer or the nearest multiple of the significance.
COMBIN(NumberOfItems, NumberInEachCombination)	Returns the number of combinations for a given number of items.
COMBINA(NumberOfItems, NumberInEachCombination)	Returns the number of combinations for a given number of items with repetitions.
COS(Number)	Returns the cosine of a given number in radians.
COSH(Number)	Returns the hyperbolic cosine of a given number.
COT(Number)	Returns the cotangent of a number in radians.
COTH(Number)	Returns the hyperbolic cotangent of a number.
CURRENCY(Number)	Returns the given number as a currency data type.
DEGREES(Angle)	Returns the angle in radians converted to degrees.
DIVIDE(Numerator, Denominator [, AlternateResult])	Returns the numerator divided by the denominator or an optional alternate result if there is a divide-by-zero error.
EVEN(Number)	Returns the number rounded up to the nearest even integer.
EXP(Number)	Returns e raised to the power of the given number.
FACT(Number)	Returns the factorial of a number.
FLOOR(Number, Significance)	Rounds the number down to the nearest multiple of the significance.
GCD(Integer, Integer, . . .)	Returns the greatest common divisor of the integers specified.

Table 13-12 *DAX Math and Trigonometric Functions*

Syntax	Result
INT(Number)	Returns the number rounded down to the nearest integer.
ISO.CEILING(Number, Significance)	An ISO-compatible version of the CEILING function.
LCM(Integer, Integer, ...)	Returns the least common multiple of the integers specified.
LN(Number)	Returns the natural logarithm of a number.
LOG(Number, base)	Returns the logarithm of a number using the specified base.
LOG10(Number)	Returns the base-10 logarithm of a number.
MOD(Numerator, Denominator)	Returns the remainder after integer division is performed on the numerator and denominator.
MROUND(Number, Multiple)	Returns the number rounded to the desired multiple.
ODD(Number)	Returns the number rounded up to the nearest odd number.
PI()	Returns the value of pi to 15 digits.
POWER(Number, Power)	Returns a number raised to the specified power.
QUOTIENT(Numerator, Denominator)	Returns the integer portion after integer division is performed on the numerator and denominator.
RADIANS(Angle)	Returns the angle converted from degrees to radians.
RAND()	Returns a random number greater than or equal to 0 and less than 1.
RANDBETWEEN(LowerLimit, UpperLimit)	Returns a random number between the lower limit and the upper limit.
ROUND(Number, NumberOfDigits)	Returns the number rounded to the specified number of digits to the right of the decimal point.
ROUNDDOWN(Number, NumberOfDigits)	Returns the number rounded down to the specified number of digits to the right of the decimal point.
ROUNDUP(Number, NumberOfDigits)	Returns the number rounded up to the specified number of digits to the right of the decimal point.
SIGN(Number)	Returns 1 if the number is positive, 0 if the number is zero, or −1 if the number is negative.
SIN(Number)	Returns the sine of a given number in radians.
SINH(Number)	Returns the hyperbolic sine of a given number.
SQRT(Number)	Returns the square root of a given number.
TAN(Number)	Returns the tangent of a given number in radians.
TANH(Number)	Returns the hyperbolic tangent of a given number.
TRUNC(Number)	Returns the integer portion of a number.

Table 13-12 *DAX Math and Trigonometric Functions (Continued)*

Statistical Functions

The statistical functions enable us to add statistical analysis to our DAX expressions, as shown in Table 13-13.

Syntax	Meaning
BETA.DIST(X, Alpha, Beta, Cumulative, [A], [B])	Returns the beta distribution.
BETA.INV(Probability, Alpha, Beta, [A], [B])	Returns the inverse of the BETA.DIST() function.
CHISQ.DIST(X, DegreesOfFreedom, Cumulative)	Returns the chi-squared distribution.
CHISQ.DIST.RT(X, DegreesOfFreedom)	Returns the inverse of the right-tailed probability of the chi-squared distribution.
CHISQ.INV(Probability, DegreesOfFreedom)	Returns the inverse of the left-tailed probability of the chi-squared distribution.
CHISQ.INV.RT(Probability, DegreesOfFreedom)	Returns the inverse of the right-tailed probability of the chi-squared distribution.
CONFIDENCE.NORM(Alpha, StandardDeviation, SampleSize)	Returns the Confidence.Norm.
CONFIDENCE.T(Alpha, StandardDeviation, SampleSize)	Returns the confidence interval for a population mean, using a Student's t-distribution.
EXPON.DIST(X, Lambda, Cumulative)	Returns the exponential distribution.
NORM.DIST(X, Mean, StdDeviation, Cumulative)	Returns the normal distribution for the specified mean and standard deviation.
NORM.INV(Probability, Mean, StdDeviation)	Returns the inverse of the normal cumulative distribution for the specified mean and standard deviation.
NORM.S.DIST(Z, Cumulative)	Returns the standard normal distribution with a mean of zero and a standard deviation of one.
NORM.S.INV(Probability)	Returns the inverse of the standard normal cumulative distribution. The distribution has a mean of zero and a standard deviation of one.
PERCENTILE.EXC(Column, K)	Returns the K-th percentile of values in a range, where K is in the range 0..1, exclusive.
PERCENTILE.INC(Column, K)	Returns the K-th percentile of values in a range, where K is in the range 0..1, inclusive.
PERCENTILEX.EXC(Table, Expression, K)	Returns the percentile number of an expression evaluated for each row in a table, where K is in the range 0..1, exclusive.

Table 13-13 *DAX Statistical Functions*

Syntax	Meaning
PERCENTILEX.INC(Table, Expression, K)	Returns the percentile number of an expression evaluated for each row in a table, where K is in the range 0..1, inclusive.
PERMUT(Number, NumberChosen)	Returns the number of permutations possible for a group of Number objects, where NumberChosen are chosen.
POISSON.DIST(X, Mean, Cumulative)	Returns the Poisson distribution.
RANK.EQ(Value, Column [, Order])	Returns the ranking of a number in a list of numbers.
RANKX(Table, Expression [, Value [, Order [, Ties]]])	Returns the ranking of a number in a list of numbers for each row.
STDEV.P(Column)	Returns the standard deviation of the entire population.
STDEV.S(Column)	Returns the standard deviation of a sample population.
STDEVX.P(Table, Expression)	Returns the standard deviation of the entire population for the specified table.
STDEVX.S(Table, Expression)	Returns the standard deviation of a sample population for the specified table.
SQRTPI(Number)	Returns the square root of (number * pi).
T.DIST(X, DegreesOfFreedom, Cumulative)	Returns the left-tailed Student's t-distribution.
T.DIST.2T(X, DegreesOfFreedom)	Returns the two-tailed Student's t-distribution.
T.DIST.RT(X, DegreesOfFreedom)	Returns the right-tailed Student's t-distribution.
T.INV(Probability, DegreesOfFreedom)	Returns the left-tailed inverse of the Student's t-distribution.
T.INV.2T(Probability, DegreesOfFreedom)	Returns the two-tailed inverse of the Student's t-distribution.
VAR.P(Column)	Returns the variance of the entire population.
VAR.S(Column)	Returns the variance of a sample population.
VARX.P(Table, Expression)	Returns the variance of the entire population for the specified table.
VARX.S(Table, Expression)	Returns the variance of a sample population for the specified table.
XIRR(Table, Values, Dates [, Guess])	Returns the internal rate of return for a schedule of cash flows that is not necessarily periodic.
XNPV(Table, Values, Dates, Rate)	Returns the present value for a schedule of cash flows that is not necessarily periodic.

Table 13-13   *DAX Statistical Functions (Continued)*

Additional Modeling

Chapter 14 wraps up our work with tabular models. We explore a number of additional features to round out your modeling knowledge. From there, we move on to sharing your tabular models with others.

Chapter 14

Additional Power BI Desktop Features

In This Chapter

- Additional Power BI Data Model Features
- Performance Analyzer
- Import and Export

We have spent a number of chapters working in Power BI Desktop, learning the ins and outs of building data models, creating visualizations, and using those visualizations to explore your data. In Chapters 15 and 16, we move from Power BI Desktop to the environments used for sharing Power BI content. Before we do that, there are a few remaining capabilities within Power BI Desktop we should examine.

In the first part of this chapter, we explore some additional features within the Power BI data model. From there, we move on to a feature that combines an aspect of the Power BI data model with a special structure in the data model—namely, what-if parameters. Next, we look at security roles. We finish the chapter examining several features of Power BI Desktop—performance analyzer, import, and export.

Additional Power BI Data Model Features

There are a few remaining features that help us provide a better user experience and secure our data models. Synonyms and linguistic schemas help us enable more natural interaction with the Q&A feature. Using display folders, we can better organize the items in the data model for our users. Roles allow us to secure portions of the data.

Synonyms

In Chapter 4, we used the Q&A tool to query our data model using natural language. Q&A worked well for our example in that chapter. However, if you use this feature for any length of time, you will discover it can be finicky about the way you enter your natural language query. In order to make the Q&A feature more robust and easier to use, Power BI provides a mechanism to define synonyms for the tables and fields in your data model.

The synonym information is entered and maintained using the Properties pane on the Model page of Power BI Desktop. When you select a table, a column, or a measure, you will see a Synonyms entry area in the Properties pane, as shown in Figure 14-1. You can type a comma-separated list of other names your users are likely to use when referring to this object. Tweaking the list of synonyms for the various items in the data model to give your users the expected natural language results will require some experimentation.

Working with Q&A Synonyms

Let's give synonyms a try. We will use the Q&A tool to create a new visualization on a new report page without the synonym in place. Then, we will add the synonym and try the same text in Q&A a second time.

1. Open the Max Min Sales Information Incomplete Model.pbix file in Power BI Desktop.
2. Click Report on the left to go to the Report screen.

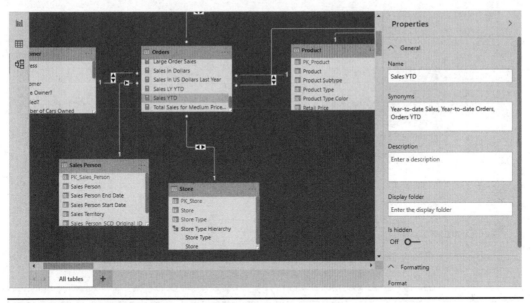

Figure 14-1 *The Synonyms entry area on the Properties pane*

3. Click the plus sign in the yellow square at the bottom of the Power BI Desktop window to create a new report page.

4. Right-click the tab for the new report page and select Rename Page from the context menu.

5. Type **Q&A Synonym Test** for the name of the new tab and press ENTER.

6. On the Home tab of the ribbon, click Ask A Question. The Q&A entry area will appear.

7. In the Q&A entry area, type **Year-to-date sales for guiding lights**.

8. Size and position the chart appropriately. The chart produced shows sales for several years. It does not show year-to-date sales.

9. Click Model on the left to go to the Model screen.

10. Select Sales YTD in the Orders table.

11. Expand the Properties window on the right, if necessary.

12. Replace the content of the Synonyms entry area with **Year-to-date Sales, Year-to-date Orders, Orders YTD**. The Model screen will appear similar to Figure 14-1.

13. Click Report on the left to go to the Report screen.

14. On the Home tab of the ribbon, click Ask A Question. The Q&A entry area will appear.

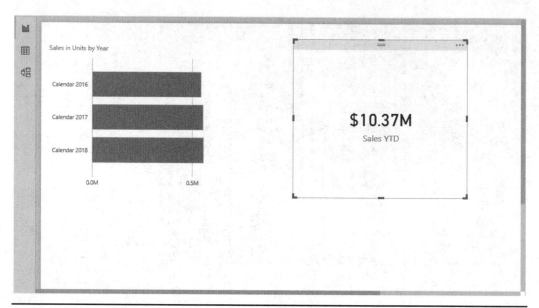

Figure 14-2   *The incorrect Q&A visualization and the correct Q&A visualization using synonyms*

15. In the Q&A entry area, type **Year-to-date sales for guiding lights**. The card produced now shows the year-to-date sales measure, as desired. This is shown in Figure 14-2.
16. Click Save.

Linguistic Schemas

In addition to adding synonyms to the data model, you can further enhance the user's Q&A experience by editing the model's linguistic schema. The linguistic schema is generated by the Q&A engine. It defines how tables, columns, and measures in the model relate to natural language concepts.

To better understand what a linguistic schema does for us, let's explore an example. Suppose we use Q&A to ask the question "Which products are heaviest?" The Q&A engine needs to determine that we want a list of records from the Products table. Next, it needs to know that the Weight field is what determines whether something is heavy. Finally, it needs to understand that the heaviest things are those where the weight is greatest. Figure 14-3 shows that the linguistic schema generated for our data model by the Q&A engine allows this question to be answered properly. Q&A parses our natural language question and creates a list of products sorted by weight in descending order.

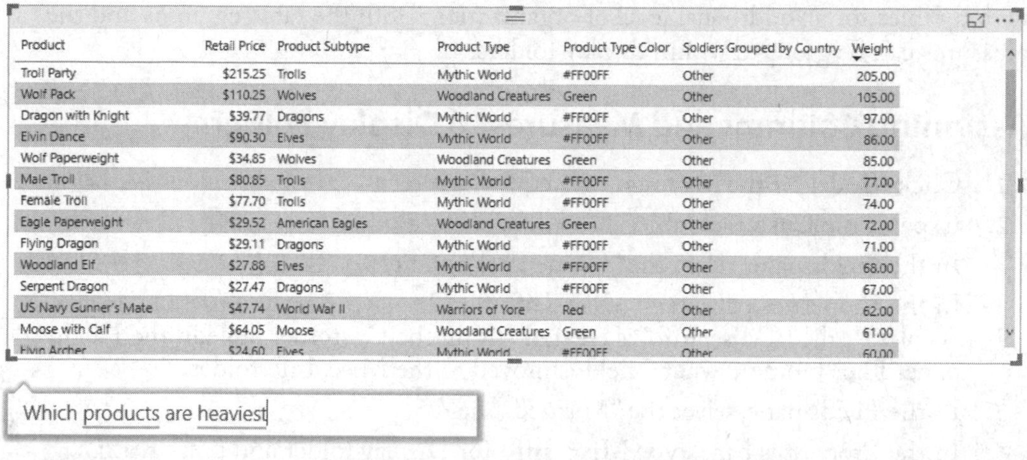

Product	Retail Price	Product Subtype	Product Type	Product Type Color	Soldiers Grouped by Country	Weight
Troll Party	$215.25	Trolls	Mythic World	#FF00FF	Other	205.00
Wolf Pack	$110.25	Wolves	Woodland Creatures	Green	Other	105.00
Dragon with Knight	$39.77	Dragons	Mythic World	#FF00FF	Other	97.00
Elvin Dance	$90.30	Elves	Mythic World	#FF00FF	Other	86.00
Wolf Paperweight	$34.85	Wolves	Woodland Creatures	Green	Other	85.00
Male Troll	$80.85	Trolls	Mythic World	#FF00FF	Other	77.00
Female Troll	$77.70	Trolls	Mythic World	#FF00FF	Other	74.00
Eagle Paperweight	$29.52	American Eagles	Woodland Creatures	Green	Other	72.00
Flying Dragon	$29.11	Dragons	Mythic World	#FF00FF	Other	71.00
Woodland Elf	$27.86	Elves	Mythic World	#FF00FF	Other	68.00
Serpent Dragon	$27.47	Dragons	Mythic World	#FF00FF	Other	67.00
US Navy Gunner's Mate	$47.74	World War II	Warriors of Yore	Red	Other	62.00
Moose with Calf	$64.05	Moose	Woodland Creatures	Green	Other	61.00
Elvin Archer	$24.60	Elves	Mythic World	#FF00FF	Other	60.00

Which products are heaviest

Figure 14-3 *Q&A linguistic schema example*

In some environments, where Q&A is going to be used extensively, the linguistic schema created by the Q&A engine might not be adequate. In those situations, it is necessary to edit the linguistic schema to add more information about the model's relationships to natural language constructs such as nouns, verbs, adjectives, and prepositions. This is done by exporting the linguistic schema from the model into a file using the YAML markup format. This is done from the Modeling tab of the ribbon using Linguistic Schema | Export linguistic schema.

The YAML file can then be edited using a text editor that understands the YAML format. Microsoft suggests downloading and using Microsoft Studio Code. The ins and outs of enhancing a data model's linguistic schema is beyond the scope of this book. Additional information can be found by following the Linguistic Schema | How to edit linguistic schema link. An updated linguistic schema YAML file can be imported into the model using Linguistic Schema | Import linguistic schema.

Display Folder

As we continue to add content to our data models, they can become rather complex. This is especially true as we continue to add specialized measures to the model to get us the exact analysis we are looking for. The more we can do to organize items within the data model, the easier they will be to use and the more we can be sure we are using the correct item for the correct purpose.

The tables provide one level of organization within our data models. Measures and columns exist within a given table. We can take things further by using display folders within tables for an additional level of organization. Both the table columns and the measures can be grouped within display folders.

Assigning Columns and Measures to Display Folders

1. Click Model on the left to go to the Model screen.
2. Expand the Customer table.
3. In the Fields pane, select the "Home Owner?" field.
4. In the Properties pane, type **Misc. Info** for Display folder and press ENTER. A folder called "Misc. Info" is created within the Customer table in the Fields pane. The "Home Owner?" field is moved to the Misc. Info folder.
5. In the Fields pane, select the "Married?" field.
6. In the Properties pane, type **Misc. Info** for Display folder and press ENTER.
7. In the Fields pane, select the "Number of Cars Owned" field.
8. In the Properties pane, type **Misc. Info** for Display folder and press ENTER.
9. In the Fields pane, select the "Number of Children at Home" field.
10. In the Properties pane, type **Misc. Info** for Display folder and press ENTER.
11. Collapse the Misc. Info folder.
12. Expand the Orders table.
13. Select the Guiding Lights 2017 Sales measure.
14. In the Properties pane, type **Guiding Lights Measures** for Display folder and press ENTER.
15. Select the Guiding Lights All Years Sales measure.
16. In the Properties pane, type **Guiding Lights Measures** for Display folder and press ENTER.
17. Select the Guiding Lights Sales measure.
18. In the Properties pane, type **Guiding Lights Measures** for Display folder and press ENTER.
19. Collapse the Guiding Lights Measures folder.
20. Click Save.

What-If Parameters

There are times as we analyze our data that we want to play the game of "what if." What if we decreased our overhead cost by one cent per item? Or two cents per item? What if we increased sales by five percent? Or seven percent?

Seeing what our data looks like in the what-if scenarios can be very helpful for decision making. Fortunately, Power BI includes a feature enabling us to implement reports using what-if scenarios. This feature is known as What-If Parameters.

The What-If Parameter is always a range of either a numeric quantity or a percentage we want to try out in calculations with existing measures in our model. As in the previous examples, we may want to see what profit margin would result if we increased or decreased our overhead cost by this amount or that amount. We may want to see what future sales would be if they increased by this percent or that percent in the future.

We implement these what-if scenarios by defining a range of values the report user can select from, using either a whole number or a decimal number. This range of values is added to our data model as a calculated table. If we choose, we can also automatically add a slicer to the current report page for selecting the current what-if value. We can also create that slicer from the what-if value later on, if desired.

A measure is also defined in the calculated what-if table. This measure provides access to the what-if value currently selected in the slicer. We can now include this currently selected value in our own measures to create the what-if scenarios.

Let's give this a try. We will create a What-If Parameter to calculate future sales if they increase a certain percentage from the most recent year's sales.

Creating a What-If Parameter

1. Click Report on the left to go to the Report screen.
2. Add a new report page.
3. Right-click the new tab and select Rename Page.
4. Type **What If Parameter Test** and press ENTER.
5. On the Modeling tab of the ribbon, click New Parameter. The "What-if parameter" dialog box appears.
6. Replace the content of the Name text box with **Percent Sales Increase** to change the name of the What-If Parameter.
7. From the Data type dropdown, select "Decimal number."
8. Replace the content of the Minimum text box with **0.5**.
9. Replace the content of the Maximum text box with **4.0**.
10. Replace the content of the Increment text box with **0.5**.
11. Replace the content of the Default text box with **2.0**. The "What-if parameter" dialog box should appear as shown in Figure 14-4.
12. Click OK. The Percent Sales Increase calculated table is created in the model and a Percent Sales Increase slicer is added to the report page.

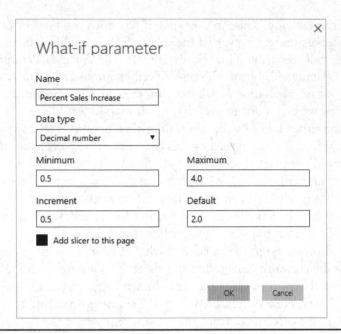

Figure 14-4 *The "What-if parameter" dialog box*

13. Size the Percent Sales Increase slicer appropriately.

14. In the Fields pane, expand the Percent Sales Increase table. You can see the GENERATESERIES() DAX function is used to create the calculated table, as shown in Figure 14-5. When the Percent Sales Increase table is expanded, you can also see the column and the measure created in this table.

Figure 14-5 *The Percent Sales Increase calculated table*

Using a What-If Parameter

1. In the Fields pane, select the Orders table.
2. On the Modeling tab of the ribbon, select New Measure.
3. In the formula bar, replace "Measure =" with the following:

```
Predicted Sales = [Sales in Dollars]
               + ([Sales in Dollars] * [Percent Sales Increase Value])
```

4. Press ENTER. We now have a measure using the value selected for our What-If Parameter.
5. Click the background of the report page so the slicer is no longer selected.
6. In the Fields pane, check the box for the "Sales in Dollars" measure in the Orders table. A column chart is created.
7. In the Fields pane, check the box for the Predicted Sales measure in the Orders table. This measure is added as a second column in the chart.
8. In the Fields pane, expand the Product table and check the box for the Product Type field. Our chart now has a pair of columns for each product type.
9. Size the column chart appropriately. The report page should appear as shown in Figure 14-6.
10. Use the Percent Sales Increase slicer to try different increase values.
11. Click Save.

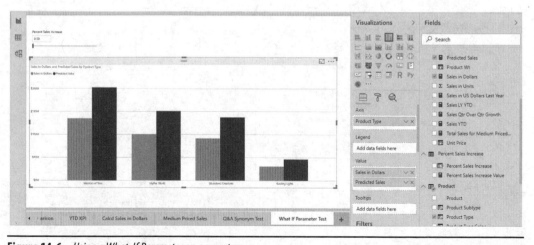

Figure 14-6 *Using a What-If Parameter on a report page*

Roles

Roles enable us to control data security within a Power BI data model. Without roles, the Power BI security story is all or nothing. Either we let someone see everything in the data model or we have to lock them out of the entire data model altogether.

With roles, we can allow access to certain aspects of our data model while limiting access to other areas. This is done by defining DAX expressions that determine what a given security role can see and what it cannot. We can set these limits on one table within the data model or create a restriction on each table in the data model.

When you click the Manage Roles button on the Modeling tab of the ribbon, you see the "Manage roles" dialog box. Roles are added and removed using the Create and Delete buttons on the left. Once a role is created, you can rename it and set up its filters.

To add a filter to a role, click the ellipsis (…) button next to the table you want to filter. From the pop-up menu you can choose Add filter. You will then select the field in the table you want to use to create the filtering expression or choose to filter all rows in this table. Figure 14-7 shows the Sales Territory 8 role with a filter to display only rows from the Sales Person table where Sales Territory is set to 8.

We can test a role using the "View as Roles" button on the Modeling tab of the ribbon. Clicking this button displays the "View as roles" dialog box. We can select our new Sales

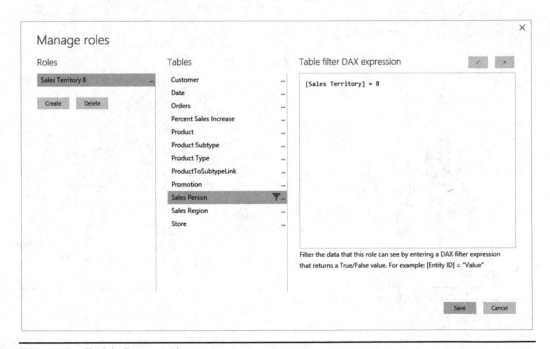

Figure 14-7   *The Sales Territory 8 role*

Figure 14-8   *The "View as roles" dialog box*

Territory 8 role, as shown in Figure 14-8. Once we click OK, we are interacting with the data as if we are a member of that role. For instance, if we view the "% of All Sales People" report page while functioning as a member of the Sales Territory 8 report, we will only see data for Briggette and Wally, as shown in Figure 14-9. These are the only two salespeople who have sold in Sales Territory 8. To stop viewing the data as a member of the selected role, click the "Stop viewing" button located just above the report page.

The roles come into play when we publish our Power BI content and allow others to have access. After content is published, we can assign users to a role when we give them rights to see the published content. Those users will then be limited by the restrictions placed on that role.

Roles and DAX Context Override Functions

The "% of All Sales People" report page includes the "% of All Sales People" measure. You might recall we used the ALL() function in that measure to ignore all filters on the Sales Person table in the existing context and get the sales in dollars for all sales people. We then used that total for all sales people to calculate a percent of total.

Can the ALL() function and other functions override the filter created by a role? The answer is no. The filters created by a role are not considered part of the report context.

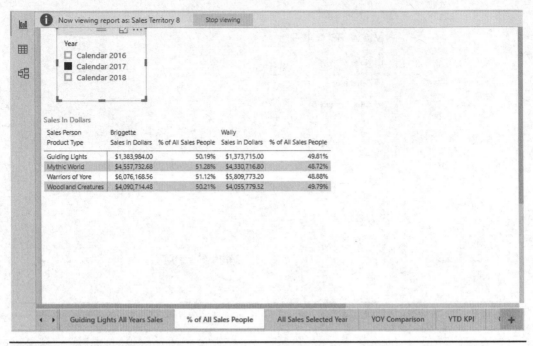

Figure 14-9 *Viewing the "% of All Sales People" report through the Sales Territory 8 role*

They are applied before any of the DAX functions in our measures or calculated columns are evaluated. Further, the filters in the role cannot be overridden by the DAX functions in the measures or calculated columns.

Creating a Role

1. On the Modeling tab of the ribbon, click Manage Roles. The "Manage roles" dialog box appears.
2. Click Create. A new role is created.
3. Replace "New role" with **Sales Territory 8** and press ENTER.
4. In the Table area, click the ellipsis (…) button next to Sales Person.
5. Hover over Add Filter in the pop-up menu and select the [Sales Territory] column. The expression "[Sales Territory] = 0" is created in the Table filter DAX expression area.
6. Replace the "0" with **8**. The "Manage roles" dialog box should appear, as shown earlier in Figure 14-7.
7. Click Save.

Testing a Role

1. Select the "% of All Sales People" tab to view the "% of All Sales People" report page.
2. In the Year slicer, select Calendar 2017. Note there are columns for five sales people.
3. In the Modeling tab of the ribbon, select "View as Roles." The "View as roles" dialog box appears.
4. Check the box for Sales Territory 8. The "View as roles" dialog box should appear, as shown earlier in Figure 14-8.
5. Click OK. You are now viewing the report content in the security context of a member of the Sales Territory 8 role. The "% of All Sales People" report page now includes only two sales people, as shown Figure 14-9. Further, the "% of Sales People" measure totals to 100% across each row for these two sales people.
6. Click the "Stop viewing" button at the top of the report page.
7. Click Save.
8. Close Power BI Desktop. (We are switching to a different Power BI report file for the final exercises in this chapter.)

Performance Analyzer

The Performance Analyzer enables us to get information about the rendering of report pages. We can see how much time was spent on each aspect of the rendering process for each visualization on the report page. We can also see the underlying query being run to extract data from the data source. Using this information, we can find the specific bottlenecks in report pages that take a long time to render and make changes to be more efficient.

Capturing Performance Information

Performance information is captured on the "Performance analyzer" pane. This pane is accessed using the Performance Analyzer check box on the View tab of the ribbon. Click "Start recording" to begin capturing performance data.

We can capture performance data on the current report page by clicking "Refresh visuals." We can also change selected values in a slicer or filter to determine how their settings affect performance. Once we are done analyzing one page, we can navigate to another report page to gather additional performance data.

The performance data will contain an entry for each visualization on the report page. Use the plus sign to see the detail of the rendering information for a given visual. The "Performance analyzer" pane is shown in Figure 14-10.

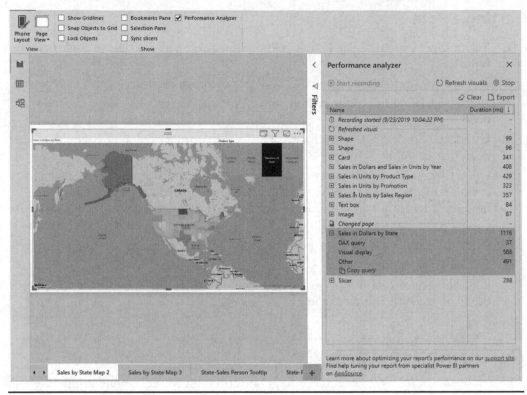

Figure 14-10 *The "Performance analyzer" pane*

The detailed performance information is grouped into three categories—"DAX query," "Visual display," and Other:

- **DAX query** The DAX query segment is the time required for the query to be sent to the data model and the resulting data returned. If this portion of the render time is too long, you should make sure the measures being used are coded efficiently.

- **Visual display** The Visual display segment is the time required for the visual to be drawn on the report page. This includes time to retrieve any required images or for any geocoding to be done. If this portion of the render time is too long, you should try to return fewer rows to be rendered.

- **Other** The Other segment is the time required for preparing the queries, the time spent waiting for other visuals to complete, and the time spent performing other background processing. There's usually not a lot to be optimized here.

We can click Clear to remove all performance information from the "Performance analyzer" pane and gather new information. We can click Export to save the "Performance analyzer" pane content as a JSON file for later analysis. We can click Stop to terminate the gathering of performance data.

Using Performance Analyzer

1. Open the Max Min Sales Information.pbix file in Power BI Desktop.
2. Select the Sales Person Detail tab.
3. On the View page of the ribbon, check Performance Analyzer. The "Performance analyzer" pane is visible.
4. On the "Performance analyzer" pane, click "Start recording."
5. On the "Performance analyzer" pane, click "Refresh visuals." Performance information for the rendering of this report page is displayed in the "Performance analyzer" pane.
6. Select the "Sales by State Map 2" tab.
7. In the "Performance analyzer" pane, click the plus sign next to Sales in Dollars by State to expand this entry. The "Performance analyzer" pane should appear as shown in Figure 14-10.
8. Click Stop.

Viewing the DAX Query

Once the performance entry for a given visualization is expanded, we can click "Copy query" to obtain the query generated for this visualization. The query is copied to the clipboard. The query can be pasted into a query window for execution and analysis. This could be DAX studio or a DAX query window in SQL Server Management Studio connected to a SQL Server Analysis Services tabular model.

Copying an Underlying DAX Query

1. In the "Performance analyzer" pane under "Sales in Dollars by State," click "Copy query." The underlying DAX query is copied to the clipboard.
2. If you have DAX Studio or SQL Server Management Studio connected to a tabular model, open a DAX query window. If you do not have either of these tools available, open your favorite text editor.
3. Paste the query into the editor opened in Step 2.
4. After viewing the query, close the editor without saving.
5. In the View tab of the Power BI Desktop ribbon, uncheck the box for Performance Analyzer.
6. Click Save.

Import and Export

Power BI is designed to be a self-service data environment. Even though that may be the case, there are still times we want to share some of what we have created or load content created elsewhere. This can be done by importing Excel workbook contents and through the use of Power BI templates.

Excel Workbook Content

If you have content created using the Power Query, Power Pivot, or Power View add-ons in Microsoft Excel, you can import that into Power BI Desktop. Select File | Import | "Power Query, Power Pivot, Power View" to bring these items into Power BI Desktop. Once these items are imported, you can work with them within Power BI Desktop.

Power BI Templates

A Power BI template is a specially created version of your Power BI content stored in a file with a .pbit extension. The template contains all of the content created within a Power BI Desktop file. However, it is in a file format not designed to be opened directly but rather intended to be imported by others as a starting point or to assist with their projects.

To create a Power BI template, build out your data model and reports in Power BI Desktop to the point where you would like to provide them to others. Next, select File | Export | Power BI Template. Then name your template and choose the location where you would like to save the new .pbit file.

When someone would like to utilize your template file, they select File | Import | Power BI Template. They will receive all of your content to build upon.

Spreading the Word

You have learned how to create Power BI content, both data models and visualizations, in Power BI Desktop. The final two chapters in this book discuss the sharing of that content with others. This is done through PowerBI.com in the cloud and Power BI Report Server on premises.

Let's share some content and spread the word!

Part V

Sharing Content

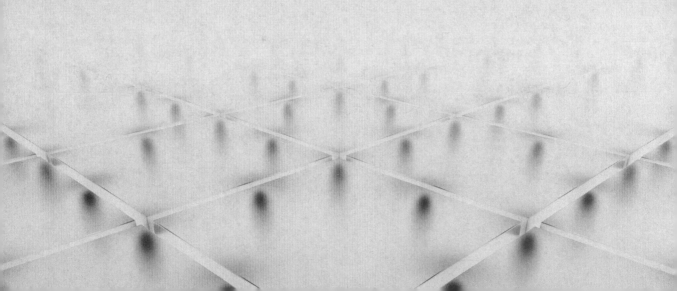

Chapter 15

Sharing Content on the Power BI Service (PowerBI.com)

In This Chapter

- The Power BI Service and Data Refresh
- The Power BI Service and Sharing
- The Power BI Service and Row-Level Security

We have spent a number of chapters learning how to create great content in Power BI. The purpose of this content is to allow users to explore the data, discover insights, and make data-driven decisions. In order for any of that to happen, we need to find a way to share this content with the users.

We can use two platforms to share content with users. The first is the Power BI Service (PowerBI.com). The other is the Power BI Report Server. The Power BI Service is part of Microsoft's Azure platform and, therefore, as we saw in Chapter 5, resides in the cloud. Power BI Report Server is designed to be an on-premises installation.

The remaining chapters of this book are dedicated to these two Power BI report-sharing environments. In this chapter, we explore the mechanisms for sharing content within the Power BI Service. In Chapter 16, we explore the operation of the on-premises Power BI Report Server.

The Power BI Service and Data Refresh

In Chapter 5, we explored the operation of PowerBI.com. You learned how to navigate and work with the various content created and published by Power BI Desktop. You created a dashboard from the published report content.

We won't rehash the use of PowerBI.com here. If you need a refresher, please reread Chapter 5. Instead, most of this chapter will focus on sharing content. You will learn how to create content packs and apps in order to deliver Power BI content to others. Before we get to that, we need to cover one other very important process. How do we make updated data coming from our on-premises sources available to data models deployed in the cloud?

The On-premises Data Gateway

Eventually, you will want to load new data into the data models loaded on PowerBI.com. This is not a problem if the data was taken from a public source somewhere in the cloud. It is also pretty straightforward if the data source resides on Microsoft Azure.

Things get a bit more complicated if the data source is on one of your organization's private servers. This is where the On-premises Data Gateway comes in. The On-premises Data Gateway provides a secure conduit from your on-premises data sources to data consumers in Azure like Power BI data models. Once in place, the On-premises Data Gateway provides a safe path for your Power BI data models to refresh their data either on a scheduled basis or on demand. The On-premises Data Gateway will also support Live Connect access to on-premises SQL Server Analysis Services instances as well as Direct Query access to SQL Server relational instances and to SQL Server Analysis Services.

The On-premises Data Gateway operates on an organization's server infrastructure and is usually maintained by the IT department. It is set up to be shared by a number of applications at that organization needing to move data to the Microsoft cloud. A personal version, the On-premises Data Gateway (personal mode), is also available.

The personal version operates from a workstation rather than a server. As the name implies, it is intended for personal, not organization-wide, use. The On-premises Data Gateway (personal mode) only supports data refresh for Power BI models using Import mode. It does not support Direct Query or Live Connect.

The On-premises Data Gateway Architecture

The On-premises Data Gateway operates by making a secure, outbound HTTP connection to the Microsoft Azure environment. The gateway operates using the same communication path a browser does when making a secure connection to a website. Because this connection uses the standard secure HTTP protocol, the On-premises Data Gateway does not require any special ports or security holes to be opened in your organization's firewall.

Figure 15-1 shows the operation of the On-premises Data Gateway. The gateway can be used to support Power BI operating in Import, Direct Query, or Live Connect mode. In fact, a single installation of the On-premises Data Gateway can handle data requests for all three modes of operation.

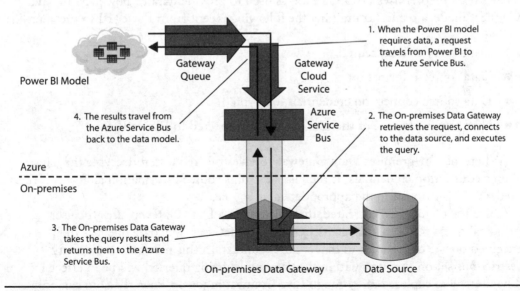

Figure 15-1 *The On-premises Data Gateway architecture*

Import Mode Data Model Refresh and Direct Query

When the On-premises Data Gateway is used to refresh a model in Import mode or is used to provide data to a model in Direct Query mode, a request containing the following is sent from the Power BI model to the gateway:

- Data query to be executed
- Data source information
- Data source connection credentials (encrypted)

When the On-premises Data Gateway receives this request, it decrypts the data source connection credentials. It then uses the data source information along with the credentials to connect to the appropriate data source. A single installation of the On-premises Data Gateway may connect to multiple on-premises data sources based on the data source information in the request. The gateway installation just has to have a path through the on-premises infrastructure to connect to each specified data source.

Once the connection is created, the On-premises Data Gateway executes the data query on that data source. The result set from that query execution is returned to Azure. Azure, in turn, gets the result set back to the Power BI model.

Live Connect

When the On-premises Data Gateway is used to provide data to Power BI in Live Connect mode, a request containing the following is sent from Power BI to the gateway:

- Data query to be executed
- Data source information
- Data source connection credentials (encrypted)
- User principal name of the user currently connected to PowerBI.com

When the On-premises Data Gateway receives this request, it decrypts the data source connection credentials. It then uses the data source information along with the credentials to connect to the appropriate data source.

Once the connection is created, the On-premises Data Gateway uses the user principal name to create the security context of that user. The data query is then executed on the data source in that security context. In this manner, any security restrictions set on that user within the data model being queried will be in effect. The users who explore data through Live Connect mode on PowerBI.com can only retrieve data they have rights to see. As before, the result set from that query execution is returned to Azure, and Azure gets the result set back to Power BI.

NOTE
The following descriptions are intended to serve as a guide should you need to install and configure an On-premises Data Gateway. They are not meant to be a step-by-step exercise. If you do wish to try this process with the "Max Min Sales Information.pbix" file, you will need to restore several SQL Server databases on a default instance of SQL Server 2017 (or later) on the same computer where the On-premises Data Gateway is installed. The database backup files for this process can be found in the "Databases to Use with Data Gateway Example" folder in the supporting materials for this book.

Installing the On-premises Data Gateway

The On-premises Data Gateway software is available as a free download from Microsoft. To download, sign in to PowerBI.com, click the Download button (down arrow icon) in the Power BI toolbar, and then select Data Gateway. This is shown in Figure 15-2 and will open the On-premises Data Gateway browser page in a new tab.

Click the Download Gateway button to download a copy of the installation executable. Execute this file to begin the gateway installation process. Follow the prompts during the installation process. As part of the install process, you can select whether this is a regular installation or a personal mode installation, as shown in Figure 15-3.

The personal mode On-premises Data Gateway can be installed on your personal computer—hence the name. Just keep in mind this gateway will only be active when your computer is running. Also keep in mind this program generates some overhead as it looks for data requests.

The regular version of the gateway does not need to be installed on the same server where the data source is running. However, this can be a good idea if that server has the available capacity. This will reduce the network overhead of data-request data moving between the data source and the gateway software.

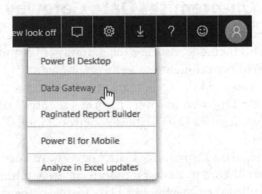

Figure 15-2   *The Download Data Gateway menu option*

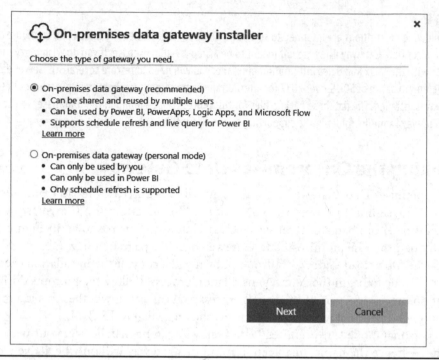

Figure 15-3 *Choosing the On-premises Data Gateway type*

If you installed the regular On-premises Data Gateway, the install program will display the screen shown in Figure 15-4 when complete. This screen shows the Azure programs, including Power BI, that are ready to use the gateway.

Managing the On-premises Data Gateway

Once you have installed the On-premises Data Gateway, you can manage the gateway from PowerBI.com. This includes ensuring the gateway is up and running and configuring your PowerBI.com content to use the gateway for its data needs. The On-premises Data Gateway and the On-premises Data Gateway (personal mode) are managed a bit differently. This section covers the On-premises Data Gateway processes. The "Managing the On-premises Data Gateway (personal mode)" section covers the personal mode processes.

If you installed the regular On-premises Data Gateway, you can use the Manage Gateway pages of PowerBI.com to view and modify gateway settings. These pages will not function if you installed the On-premises Data Gateway (personal mode) version, as noted in the "Managing the On-premises Data Gateway (personal mode)" section of

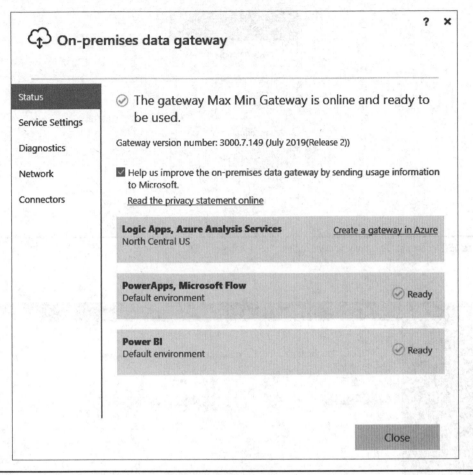

Figure 15-4   *The completed On-premises Data Gateway installation*

this chapter. To view the Manage Gateway pages, click the Settings button (cog icon) in the Power BI toolbar and then select "Manage gateways." This is shown in Figure 15-5.

Selecting "Manage gateways" displays the Gateway Cluster Settings tab of the Gateways page, as shown in Figure 15-6. Even if you only have a single gateway installed, the tab will be titled "Gateway Cluster Settings." In addition to setting data identifying this gateway, you can set the following options:

- **Allow user's cloud data sources to refresh through this gateway cluster**   When this option is enabled, data from on-premises sources can be combined with data from cloud sources in the same query.

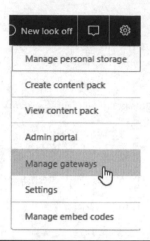

Figure 15-5 *The Manage gateways menu option*

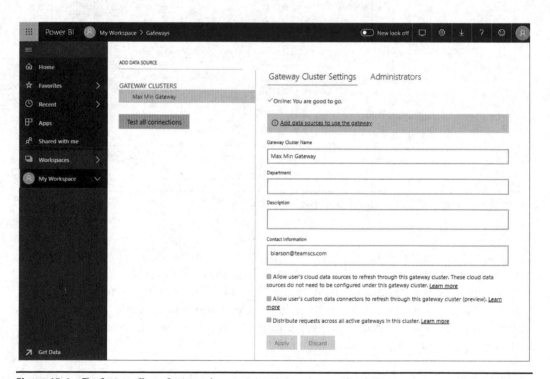

Figure 15-6 *The Gateway Cluster Settings tab*

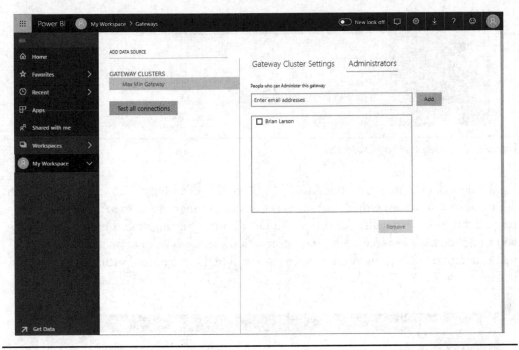

Figure 15-7   *The Gateway Administrators page*

- **Allow user's custom data connectors to refresh through this gateway cluster**   If you have developed custom data connectors using the Data Connector SDK (software development kit), you must enable this option to allow those connectors to use the gateway.

- **Distribute requests across all active gateways in this cluster**   When this option is enabled and there are multiple gateways configured in this cluster, enabling this option will allow for load balancing across all active gateways.

Clicking Administrators at the top of the page takes you to the Administrators tab of the Gateways page, as shown in Figure 15-7. This tab enables you to define who has rights to administer each gateway. The person who installed the gateway is automatically added as an administrator of the gateway.

Adding a Data Source to an On-premises Data Gateway

In order for the On-premises Data Gateway to be used by your published Power BI content, you must define data sources for the gateway. Again, this does not apply to an On-premises Data Gateway (personal mode) installation. See the "Managing the On-premises Data Gateway (personal mode)" section of this chapter for the personal mode process.

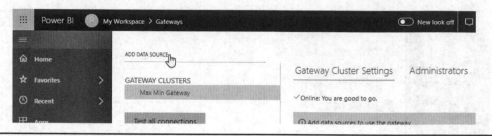

Figure 15-8   *Adding a gateway data source*

To add a data source, click the ADD DATA SOURCE link, as shown in Figure 15-8. This can be done from either the Gateway Cluster Settings tab or the Administrators tab. Clicking this link will take you to the Data Source Settings tab. This tab enables you to define a data source, including information such as type of connection, server name, database name, and Windows credentials. The Data Source Settings tab is shown in Figure 15-9.

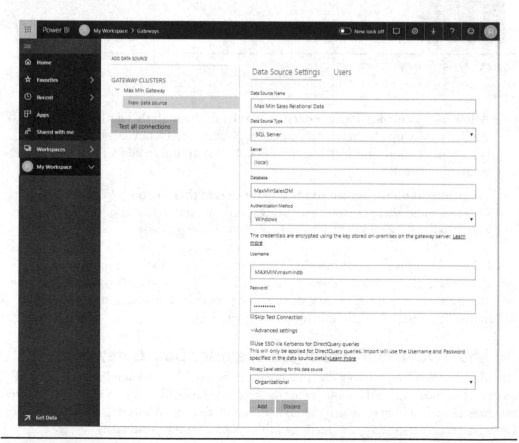

Figure 15-9   *The Data Source Settings tab*

NOTE
The server name and database name used in a gateway data source definition must exactly match the server name and database name in the Power BI dataset in order for that dataset to use the gateway to access on-premises data.

Once the data source is defined, the Users tab is used to specify those people who can use this gateway data source. Users in this list may publish Power BI content and then configure that content to access on-premises data through this data source. The Users tab is shown in Figure 15-10.

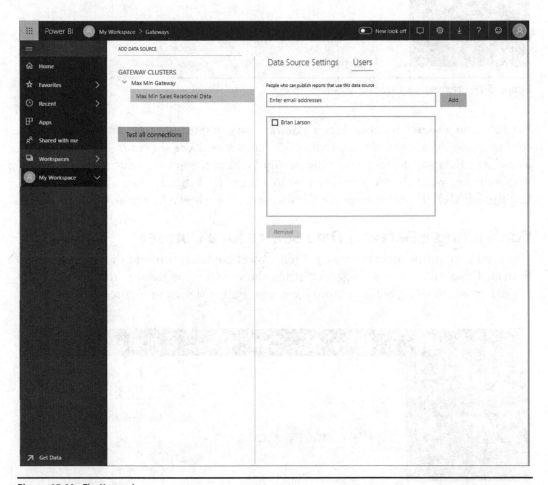

Figure 15-10 *The Users tab*

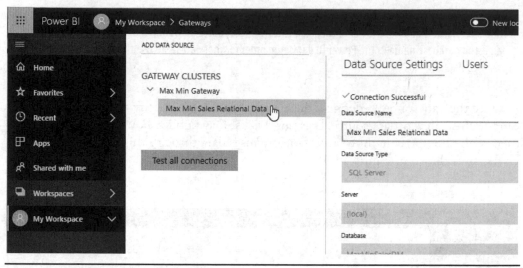

Figure 15-11 *Returning to a data source definition*

Once a data source is defined for a gateway, you can return to that data source's configuration information by expanding the gateway entry, as shown in Figure 15-11. To delete a data source, hover over the far-right end of the gray box surrounding the data source name and click the "Open menu" button (…) that appears to the right. Use the REMOVE option to delete the data source, as shown in Figure 15-12.

Configuring a Gateway Data Source for a Dataset

The final step in this process is to configure Power BI datasets to use the gateway data sources. To accomplish this, click the Settings button (the cog icon) in the Power BI toolbar and then select Settings from the menu. This is shown in Figure 15-13.

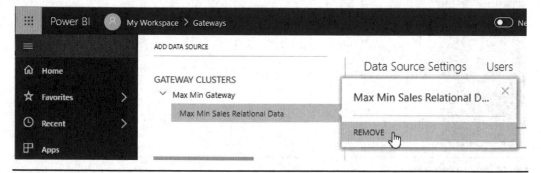

Figure 15-12 *Removing a data source*

Figure 15-13   *The Settings menu option*

This will take you to the General tab of the Settings page. Click Datasets to navigate to the Datasets tab. Once on the Datasets tab, you can click a dataset to view the property settings for that dataset. Finally, expand the "Gateway connection" item, as shown in Figure 15-14.

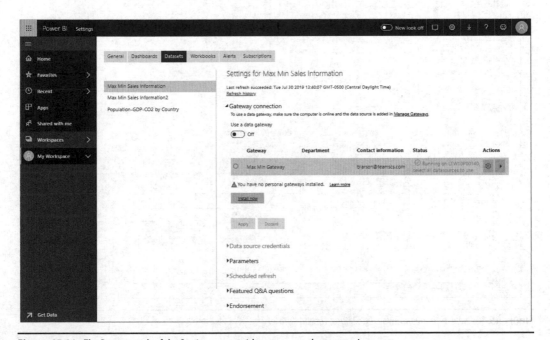

Figure 15-14   *The Datasets tab of the Settings page with no gateway data source in use*

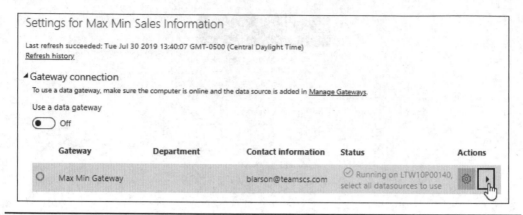

Figure 15-15   *Expanding a gateway to configure for a dataset*

To configure a gateway data source for a dataset, click the arrow at the far end of the gateway entry, as shown in Figure 15-15. Use the "Maps to" dropdown list to select the appropriate gateway data source for each data source in the Power BI dataset, as shown in Figure 15-16. (Selecting the gateway data sources will automatically turn on the

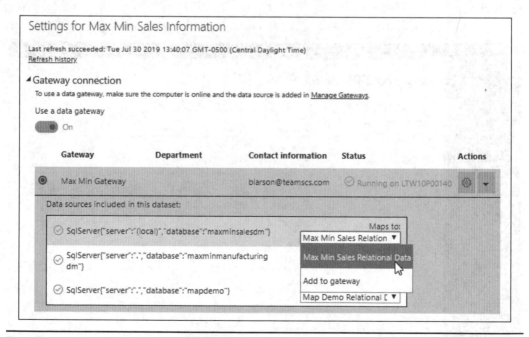

Figure 15-16   *Selecting the gateway data source for the dataset*

"Use a data gateway" slider.) Once all of the dataset data sources are configured with gateway data sources, click Apply.

Managing the On-premises Data Gateway (personal mode)

Once you have installed the On-premises Data Gateway (personal mode), you can configure Power BI datasets to use the gateway in PowerBI.com. To accomplish this, click the Settings button (the cog icon) in the Power BI toolbar and then select Settings. This is shown earlier in Figure 15-13. This will take you to the General tab of the Settings page. Click Datasets to navigate to the Datasets tab.

NOTE
The personal mode gateway does not require us to configure gateway data sources.

Once on the Datasets tab, you can click a dataset to view the property settings for that dataset. Finally, expand the "Gateway connection" item as shown in Figure 15-17. Figure 15-17 shows a dataset that can use the available personal gateway. Simply select the radio button next to Personal Gateway and click Apply. (Clicking the Personal Gateway radio button will automatically turn on the "Use a data gateway" slider.) If required, edit the data source credentials to provide a valid user name and password.

Setting a Dataset for Scheduled Refresh

Once you have an import dataset configured to use the On-premises Data Gateway, you may set up that dataset to perform a scheduled data refresh. This is done on the Datasets tab of the Settings page. You can reach the Datasets tab of the Settings page through the Settings menu, as we did in the previous section, or you can click the "Schedule refresh" button on the entry for that dataset in the Datasets area of the workspace, as shown in Figure 15-18.

Once on the Dataset tab, expand the "Scheduled refresh" item. Change the "Keep your data up to date" slider to On. Enter the required information on the refresh schedule you would like to use for this dataset and provide an email to be contacted if there is an issue during data refresh. Once completed, the schedule refresh configuration should appear similar to Figure 15-19. Click Apply to begin using this scheduled refresh.

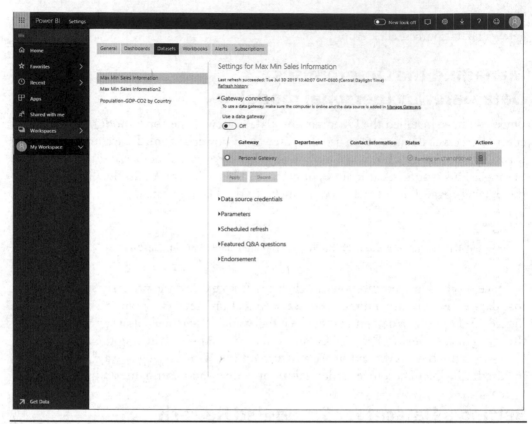

Figure 15-17 *A dataset eligible to use the personal gateway*

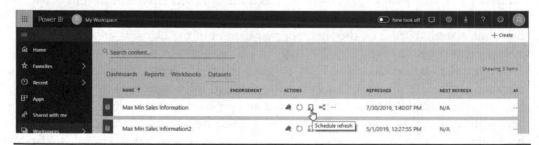

Figure 15-18 *The "Schedule refresh" button for a dataset*

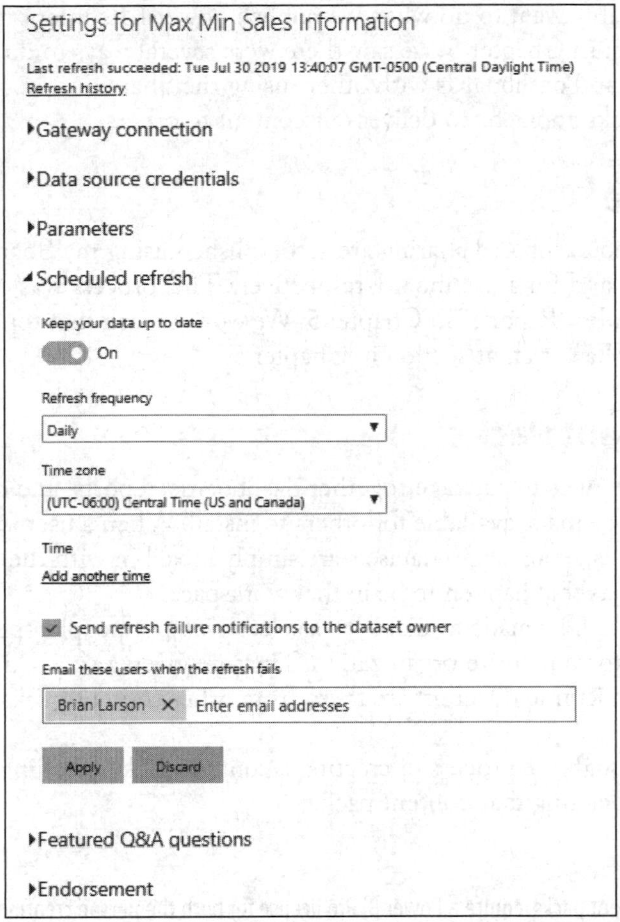

Settings for Max Min Sales Information

Last refresh succeeded: Tue Jul 30 2019 13:40:07 GMT-0500 (Central Daylight Time)
Refresh history

▶Gateway connection

▶Data source credentials

▶Parameters

◢Scheduled refresh

Keep your data up to date

⬤ On

Refresh frequency

Daily ▼

Time zone

(UTC-06:00) Central Time (US and Canada) ▼

Time
Add another time

☑ Send refresh failure notifications to the dataset owner

Email these users when the refresh fails

Brian Larson ✕	Enter email addresses

[Apply] [Discard]

▶Featured Q&A questions

▶Endorsement

Figure 15-19 *Configuring a scheduled refresh*

The Power BI Service and Sharing

Publishing content to PowerBI.com puts a copy of our Power BI reports in an environment where we can easily access our own content through a browser-based interface. However, our Power BI content works pretty well for us in Power BI Desktop. Just having the Power BI content available through a browser may not be a good enough reason to publish content.

What we probably want to do when we publish Power BI content is to make it available to others. In Chapter 5, we saw there were several ways to do that. First, we can share reports and dashboards with others using the Share button. We can also create content packs and apps to deliver our content to others.

Using Share

Report sharing and dashboard sharing are accomplished using the Share button in the entry for a report and for a dashboard, respectively. This process was covered in the "Share" section under "Reports" in Chapter 5. We won't rehash that topic here. For more information, refer back to that section in Chapter 5.

Using Content Packs

Content packs allow us to package together dashboards, reports, and datasets. The package can then be made available for others to install. When a user installs a content pack, its dashboards, reports, and datasets are simply mixed in with the other dashboards, reports, and datasets that happen to be in that workspace.

Content packs can be made available to a select group of people, specified by email address, or to your entire organization. They are given a title, a description, and, optionally, an icon to differentiate them from other content packs that might be available to a user.

We'll walk through the process of creating a content pack, installing that content pack, and finally deleting that content pack.

NOTE
Organizational content packs require a Power BI Pro license for both the person creating the content pack and the person installing the content pack.

Creating a Content Pack

1. As part of this exercise, we will use the "Analytics Icon.jpg" image file. Locate this file in the supporting materials download and copy it to a location in your file system.
2. Open a browser and navigate to PowerBI.com.
3. Click "Sign in" at the top of the page.
4. Complete the sign-in process.

Figure 15-20 *The "Create content pack" menu option*

5. Select My Workspace on the left side of the web page. My Workspace opens with the Dashboards tab active.

6. Click the "Data Analysis with Microsoft Power BI" dashboard. This dashboard opens in the browser.

7. Click the Settings button (the cog icon) in the Power BI toolbar and select "Create content pack" from the menu. This is shown in Figure 15-20.

8. Select the "My entire organization" option.

9. For Title, enter **Data Analysis with Power BI Test Content Pack**.

10. For Description, enter **This is a test content pack**.

11. In the phrase "Upload an image or company logo," click the word "Upload." This opens a file selection dialog box.

12. Navigate to the folder where you copied the "Analytics Icon.jpg" image file.

13. Select the "Analytics Icon.jpg" image file and click Open.

14. In the "Select items to publish" area, click the check box for the "Data Analysis with Microsoft Power BI" dashboard. (The dashboard name may be shortened with an ellipsis at the end.) The reports that this dashboard depends on are automatically selected. The datasets that those reports depend on are also automatically selected. The content pack creation page should appear, as shown in Figure 15-21.

15. Click Publish. The content pack is created.

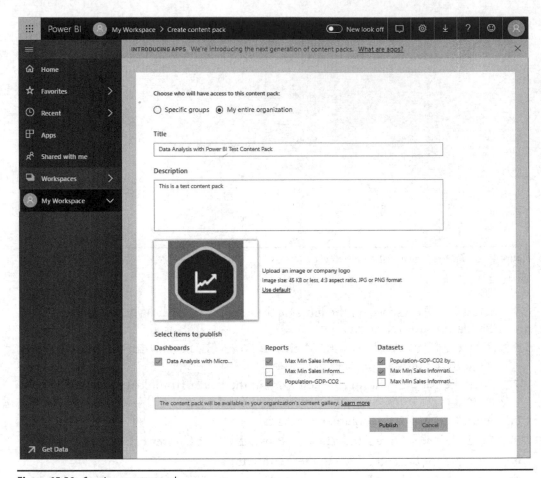

Figure 15-21 *Creating a content pack*

Installing a Content Pack

For a moment, we will play the role of another user who wants to get the dashboard and reports in our content pack. Our fictional user will find the content pack we just created and install its content.

1. Click Get Data in the lower-left corner of the Power BI page in your browser. The Get Data page appears.

2. Click the Organizational Content Packs link, as shown in Figure 15-22.

3. Click the "Get it now" button for the "Data Analysis with Power BI Test Content Pack," as shown in Figure 15-23.

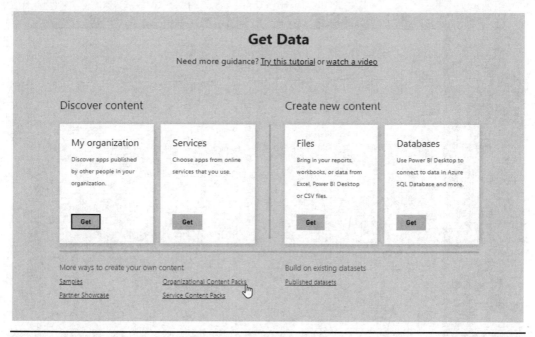

Figure 15-22 *The Organizational Content Packs link on the Get Data page*

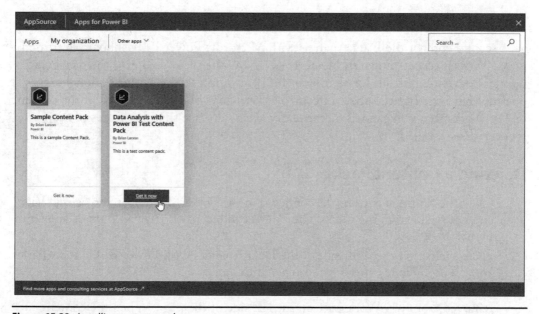

Figure 15-23 *Installing a content pack*

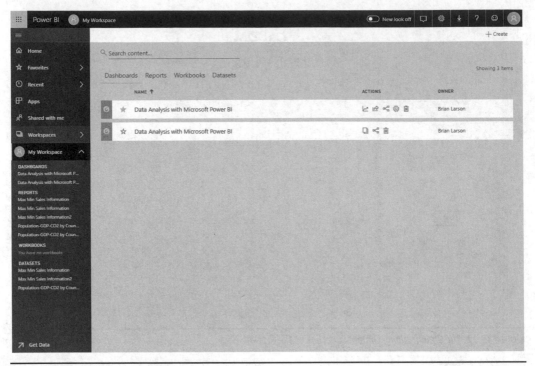

Figure 15-24 *The results of the content pack installation*

A second copy of the Data Analysis with Microsoft Power BI dashboard is created in My Workspace, as shown in Figure 15-24. Note the second copy of the dashboard does not have the buttons for sharing or for controlling settings. Our fictional user does not have the right to share or control the settings of our dashboard. If the content of My Workspace is expanded on the left, you can also see that duplicates of the reports were installed.

Deleting a Content Pack

1. Click the Settings button (the cog icon) in the Power BI toolbar and select "View content pack" from the menu. The "View content pack" page appears, as shown in Figure 15-25.

2. Click Delete on the right side of the Data Analysis with Power BI Content Pack entry. The "Delete content pack" dialog box appears.

3. Click Delete. Note the duplicate items created from the content pack have been removed from My Workspace on the left side of the page. When the content pack is deleted, its installed items are also deleted.

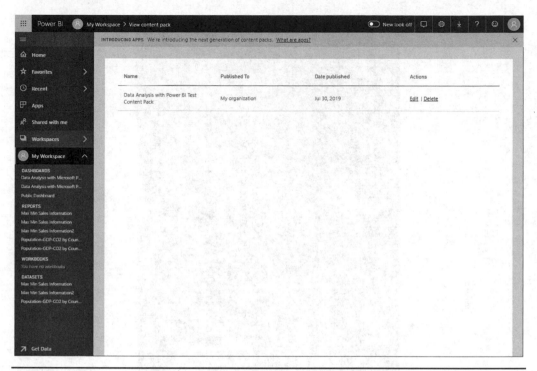

Figure 15-25   *The "View content pack" page*

Using Apps

Currently, apps are preferred over content packs for sharing content. Like content packs, apps package together dashboards, reports, and datasets for sharing with others. Unlike content packs, installed apps end up in their own area within PowerBI.com. Each app has its own name and icon. The dashboards, reports, and datasets from each app remain separate, and the app content is accessed through the app icon.

We'll try creating an app, installing that app, and finally deleting that app.

Creating an App

1. Click Workspaces on the left side of the PowerBI.com page.
2. Click "Create a workspace" at the bottom of the workspaces listing, as shown in Figure 15-26. The "Create a workspace" dialog box appears.
3. For Workspace name, enter **Data Analysis with Power BI Test App**.

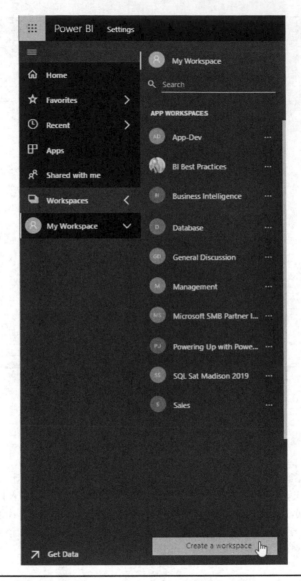

Figure 15-26 *"Create a workspace" button*

4. For Description, enter **This is for a test app.** The completed dialog box should appear as shown in Figure 15-27.

5. Click Save. The new workspace appears in the workspaces listing.

6. Open the "Max Min Sales Information.pbix" file in Power BI Desktop. We will deploy content from here into our new workspace.

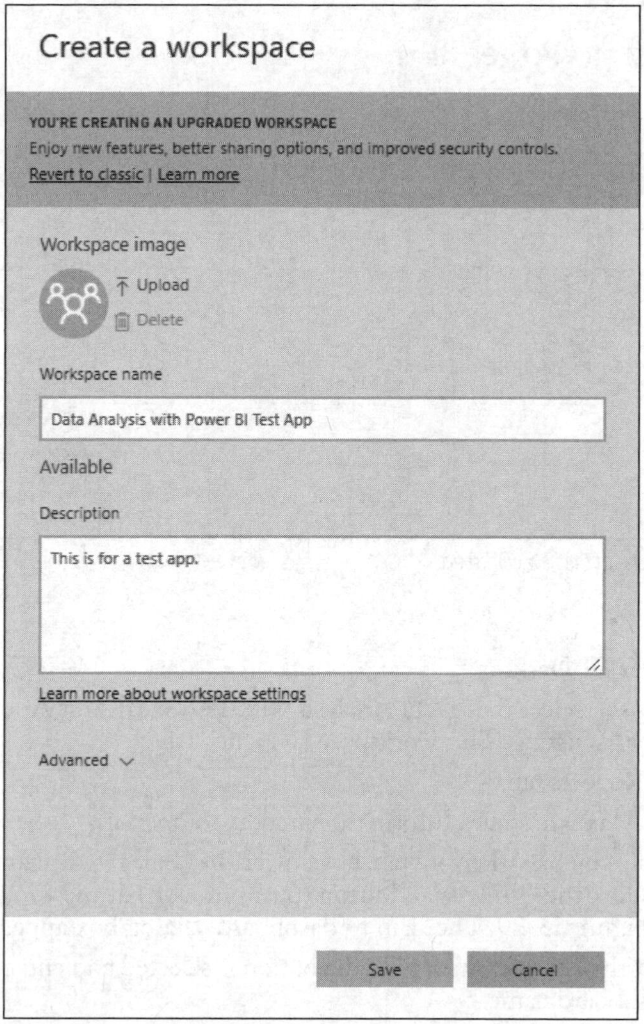

Figure 15-27 *Creating a new workspace*

7. On the Home tab of the ribbon, click Publish. The Publish to Power BI dialog box appears.
8. Select the "Data Analysis with Power BI Test App" workspace, as shown in Figure 15-28.
9. Click Select. The content is deployed to the "Data Analysis with Power BI Test App" workspace on PowerBI.com.
10. When the Success! dialog box appears, click "Got it."

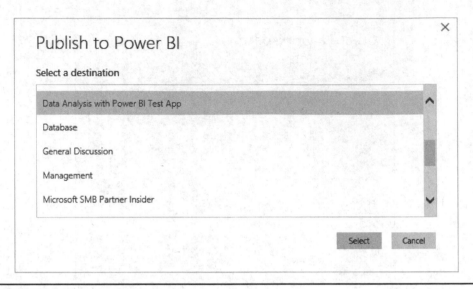

Figure 15-28 *Publishing to the new workspace*

11. Close Power BI Desktop.
12. In the browser, select the "Data Analysis with Power BI Test App" workspace in the workspaces listing. This workspace is opened.
13. Select the Reports tab.
14. Click the "Max Min Sales Information" report to open it.
15. On the "Sales by Sales Person" tab, hover over the "Sales in Dollars by Sales Person" chart and click the "Pin visual" button (pushpin icon) at the top of the chart, as shown in Figure 15-29. The "Pin to dashboard" dialog box appears.
16. Ensure that the "New dashboard" radio button is selected and enter **App Dashboard** for the Dashboard name.
17. Click Pin.
18. Select the "Sales Units by Promotion" tab.
19. Hover over the "Sales in Units by Promotion" treemap and click the Pin visual button.
20. Ensure App Dashboard is selected and click Pin. Close any popup messages that may appear.
21. Return to the Data Analysis with Power BI Test App workspace using the breadcrumbs at the top of the page, as shown in Figure 15-30.
22. On the Dashboards tab, ensure the INCLUDED IN APP toggle is set for App Dashboard, as shown in Figure 15-31. The report that this dashboard comes from will also be included in the app.

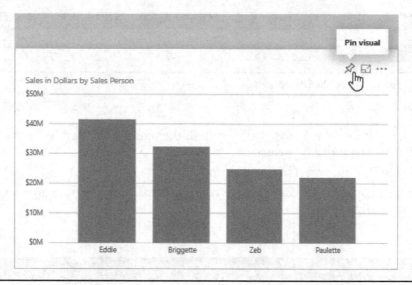

Figure 15-29 *Pinning a chart to a dashboard*

Figure 15-30 *Returning to the workspace page*

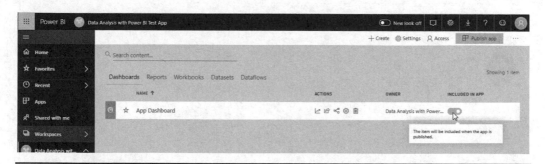

Figure 15-31 *Including content in the app*

Figure 15-32 *Starting the app-publishing process*

23. Click the Publish app button at the top of the screen, as shown in Figure 15-32. The App Setup page appears.
24. For Description, type **This is a test app.**
25. Select an app theme color using the color picker. The Setup page appears, as shown in Figure 15-33.

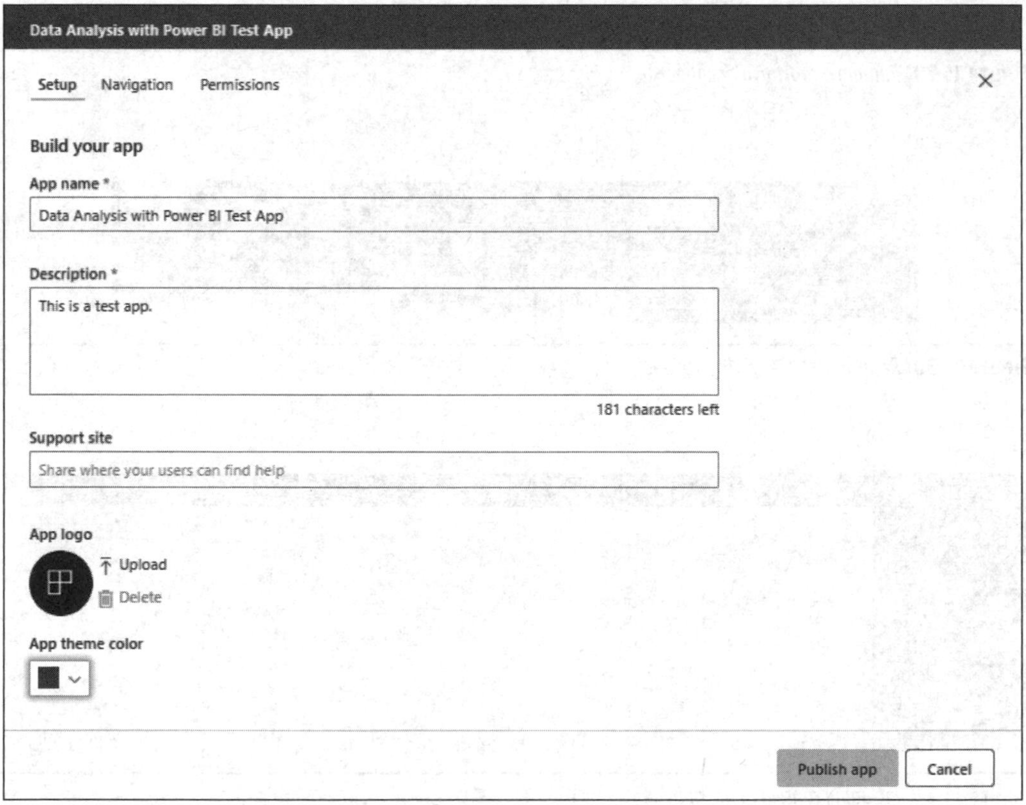

Data Analysis with Power BI Test App

Setup   Navigation   Permissions   ✕

Build your app

App name *

    Data Analysis with Power BI Test App

Description *

    This is a test app.

                                                    181 characters left

Support site

    Share where your users can find help

App logo

    ⊞ ⤒ Upload
        🗑 Delete

App theme color

    ⬛ ⌄

                                        Publish app   Cancel

Figure 15-33 *The Setup page*

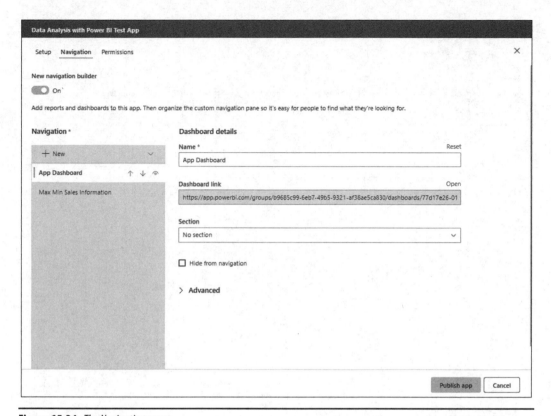

Figure 15-34 *The Navigation page*

26. Select Navigation at the top of the page. Using the Navigation area on the left, you can select which content will be the landing location for the app. Leave the App Dashboard at the top of the list. The Navigation page appears, as shown in Figure 15-34.

27. Select Permissions at the top of the page.

28. Select "Entire organization" to allow the entire organization access to this app. The Permissions page appears as shown in Figure 15-35.

29. Click the "Publish app" button. A confirmation dialog box appears.

30. Click Publish.

31. When the "Successfully published" dialog box appears, click Close.

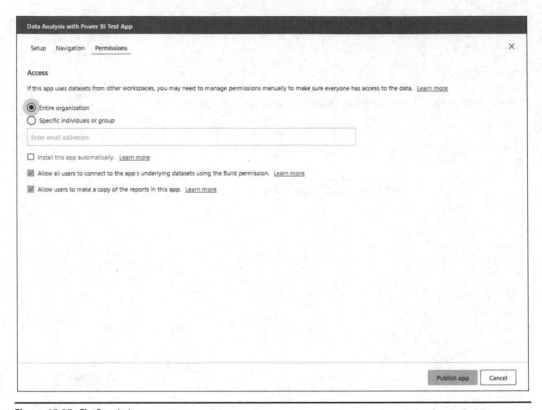

Figure 15-35 *The Permissions page*

Installing an App

As we did with the content pack, we will play the role of another user who wants to get the dashboard and reports in our app. Our fictional user will find the app we just created and install its content.

1. Click Get Data in the lower-left corner of the page.
2. Click the "My organization" box under "Discover content," as shown in Figure 15-36.
3. Click the "Get it now" button for "Data Analysis with Power BI Test App," as shown in Figure 15-37.
4. Click the entry for "Data Analysis with Power BI Test App" in the Apps area, as shown in Figure 15-38. You are taken to the dashboard deployed with the app.

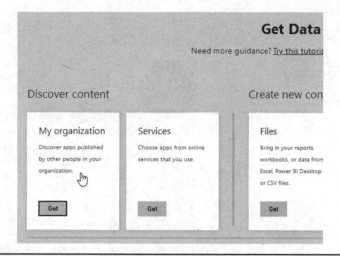

Figure 15-36 *Discover content from My organization*

5. The app content is kept separate from the workspaces. Use the menu on the left to navigate through the app content, as shown in Figure 15-39.

6. Click "Go back" on the left side of the screen to leave the app.

7. On the left side of the screen, click Apps. Note the "Data Analysis with Power BI Test App" is now available on the Apps page.

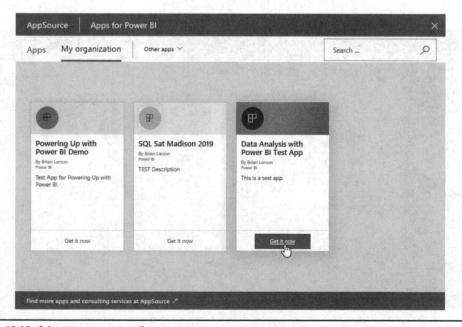

Figure 15-37 *Selecting an app to install*

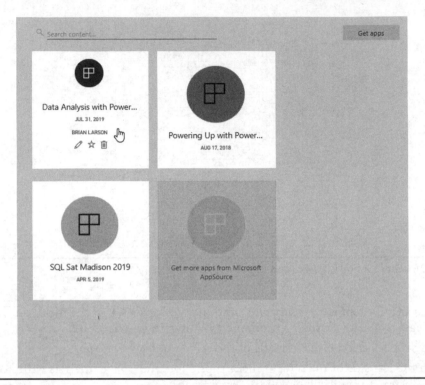

Figure 15-38 *Opening an app*

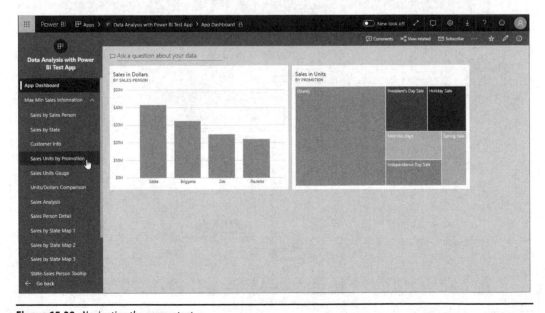

Figure 15-39 *Navigating the app content*

Deleting an App

1. On the left side of the page, click Workspaces and then click the More (…) button to the right of the "Data Analysis with Power BI Test App" workspace item.
2. Click "Workspace settings," as shown in Figure 15-40. The Workspace Settings dialog box appears.
3. Click "Delete workspace," as shown in Figure 15-41. The "Delete workspace?" confirmation dialog box appears.
4. Click Delete. The workspace and the corresponding app are deleted. Eventually, the app will disappear from our installed apps as well.

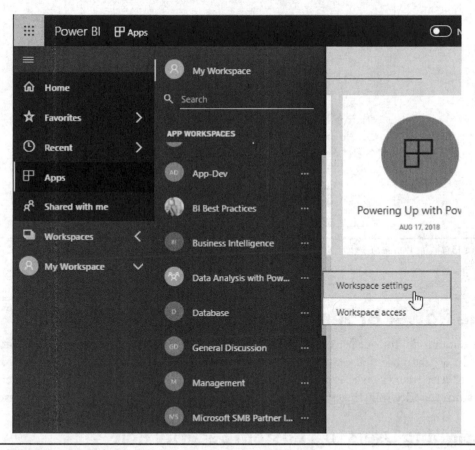

Figure 15-40 *Accessing workspace settings*

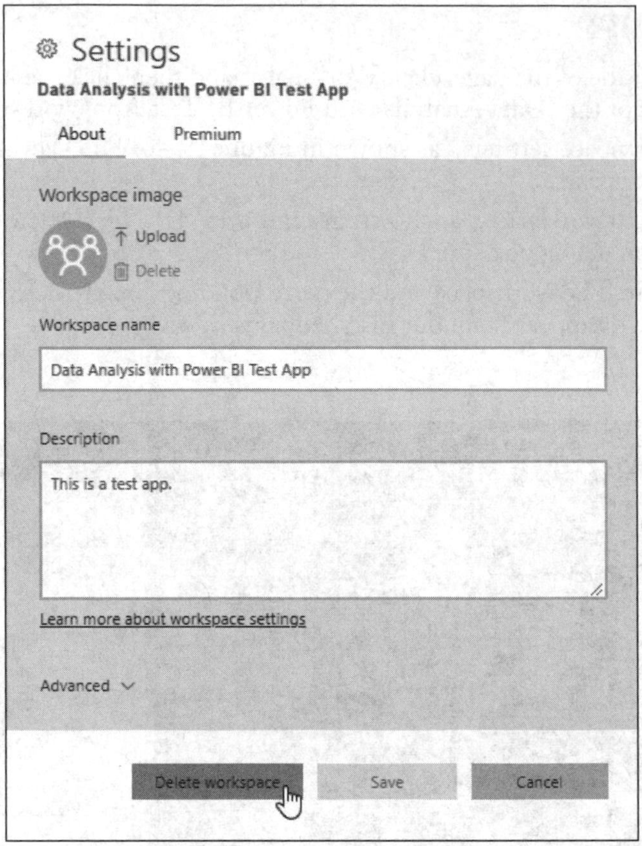

Figure 15-41 *The Workspace Settings dialog box*

The Power BI Service and Row-Level Security

The data model for our Max Min Sales Information report includes a custom security role. In order to use this security role in the Power BI Service, we must assign users to this security role. If a user is given access to a report (or its dataset) and is not assigned to a custom security role, they will not have proper security for that report (or that dataset).

Assigning Users to a Custom Security Role

Users are assigned to a custom security role at the dataset level. Once assigned, that user is restricted by that security role. That is true whether they are using a report dependent on that dataset or exploring the data in the dataset directly.

Let's look at how we manage the members of a security role.

Managing Users in a Custom Security Role

1. On the left side of the page, select "My workspace."
2. Select the Datasets tab.
3. In the entry for the Max Min Sales Information dataset, click the ellipsis (…) button.
4. Select Security from the menu, as shown in Figure 15-42. The Row-Level Security page appears.
5. The "Sales Territory 8" role is selected. Enter the email address of a valid Power BI user and press ENTER.
6. Click Add. This user is added as a member of the Sales Region 8 role, as shown in Figure 15-43.
7. Click Save.
8. To remove this user from the role membership, click the "X" to the right of the user name.
9. Click Save.

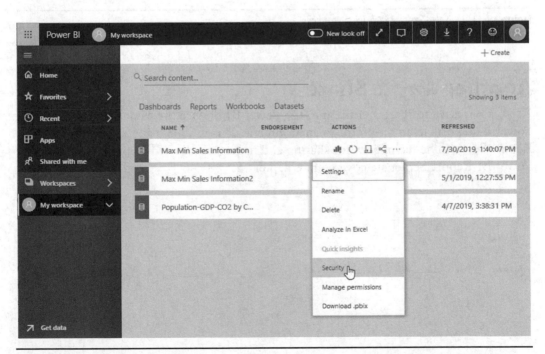

Figure 15-42 *The Security menu option*

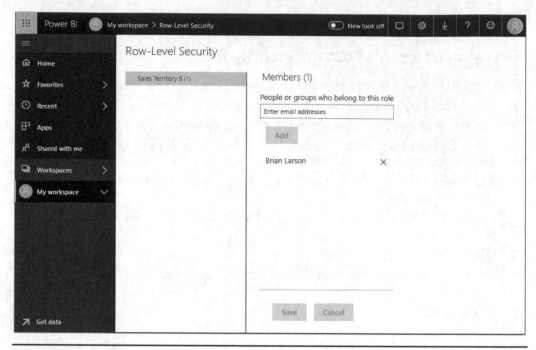

Figure 15-43 *The Sales Territory 8 role with a member*

Another Way to Share

As an alternative to sharing content in the Power BI Service, we can also share our Power BI reports in an on-premises environment. This is done using the Power BI Report Server. The techniques for sharing and managing Power BI content using the Power BI Report Server are covered in Chapter 16.

Chapter 16

Saving to the Power BI Report Server

In This Chapter

- Power BI Service and Power BI Report Server Comparison
- Installing Power BI Report Server
- The Report Catalog

- Security
- Branding the Power BI Report Server
- Powered Up and Ready to Go

Chapter 15 was all about sharing Power BI content using the Power BI Service (PowerBI.com). The Power BI Service contains a number of features to enhance the Power BI user experience. We can combine visualizations from multiple reports to create dashboards. We can easily access data stored on Microsoft Azure platforms. We can even leverage the On-premises Data Gateway to securely access on-premises data.

There is one thing, however, we can't get away from when using the Power BI Service, and that is the fact that it exists on cloud-based infrastructure. There are some organizations that are not ready, for one reason or another, to build their reporting platform in the cloud. Others don't mind having part of their reporting infrastructure in the cloud, but need to complement the cloud capabilities with an on-premises infrastructure. For those organizations, there is the Power BI Report Server.

Power BI Service and Power BI Report Server Comparison

As noted in Chapter 3, the Power BI Report Server is a customized version of SQL Server Report Server. This is the server for delivering SQL Server Reporting Services (SSRS) reports throughout an enterprise. The Power BI Report Server retains all the features of SQL Server Reporting Services and adds to it the ability to process data in Power BI tabular models and render Power BI reports.

The Power BI Report Server is licensed through Power BI Premium or through a SQL Server Enterprise Edition license as part of a Microsoft Enterprise Agreement/ Software Assurance (EA/SA). Be sure to check on licensing before pursuing a Power BI Report Server installation. In some cases, it can be a very expensive alternative to the Power BI Service.

Versions

Microsoft upgrades the Power BI Report Server frequently—about every three to five months. That is an aggressive upgrade cadence for an on-premises server application. Still, it's almost a snail's pace when compared to the monthly updates to the Power BI Service. Therefore, the Power BI Report Server is often several months behind the Power BI Service when it comes to feature updates. You may have to wait a bit for the latest features supported by the Power BI Service to reach a new version of the Power BI Report Server.

Power BI Desktop Optimizations

As noted in Chapter 3, there are two optimizations of Power BI Desktop—one optimized for Power BI Service and the other optimized for the Power BI Report Server. Because the Power BI Report Server is often several months behind the Power BI Service in

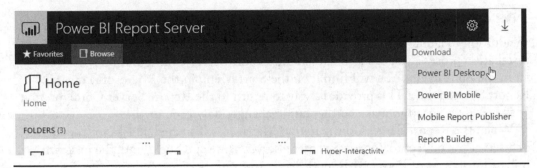

Figure 16-1   *Link for downloading the Power BI Desktop Report Server optimizations*

feature support, that means the Power BI Desktop optimized for the Power BI Report Server is behind the Power BI Desktop optimized for the Power BI Service. As of the writing of this chapter, the Power BI Service and associated Power BI Desktop were on the July 2019 release. The Power BI Report Server and its associated Power BI Desktop were on the May 2019 release.

Not surprisingly, the best way to obtain the appropriate version of Power BI Desktop optimized for the Power BI Service is through the Power BI Service. Likewise, the best way to obtain the appropriate version of Power BI Desktop optimized for Power BI Report Server is through the link on your local Power BI Report Server. This is shown in Figure 16-1.

Installing Power BI Report Server

Installing an instance of Power BI Report Server is a two-step process. The Power BI Report Server is installed by running an executable downloaded from PowerBI.com. Once the installation is done, the Report Server Configuration Manager is used to complete the final setup of the new Power BI Report Server instance.

The Power BI Report Server Installation Executable

The Power BI Report Server install program can be found using the Products menu at the top of the PowerBI.com landing page (prior to signing in). Selecting "Power BI Report Server" from the Products menus takes you to the Power BI Report Server information page. I find it works best to click the "Advanced download options" link and then download the PowerBIReportServer.exe installation executable from there.

Download and run (open) the executable file. Follow the steps to complete the installation. When the installation is done, you can use the button on the last screen of the installation program to launch the Report Server Configuration Manager.

The Report Server Configuration Manager

In addition to launching the Report Server Configuration Manager at the end of the installation process, you can also launch the Report Server Configuration Manager from the Start Menu. You will find it on the Start Menu in the Microsoft Power BI Report Server folder. This provides a way to return to the Report Server Configuration Manager if you need to make configuration changes down the road.

When the Report Server Configuration Manager is launched, it asks for the name of a server to connect to. Once you enter a server name and click Find, the program finds all instances of Power BI Report Server (or SQL Server Reporting Services) running on that server and displays them in the Report Server Instance dropdown box. You need to select an instance and click Connect to enter the utility program with the configuration information for that Report Server instance loaded. (These will be filled in by default during your initial installation/configuration process.)

The Report Server Configuration Manager contains a number of pages, each geared toward configuring a different aspect of the Report Server.

Report Server Status Page

The Report Server Status page displays status information about the Report Server instance you selected. This page provides buttons to start or stop this Report Server instance.

Service Account Page

The Service Account page enables you to view and change the credentials used to run the Report Server service.

Web Service URL Page

The Web Service URL page enables you to create or change the URL used by the Report Server web service. Power BI Desktop uses the Report Server web service to communicate with the Report Server when deploying reports. Use this page to configure the ports to be used when communicating with the Report Server web service and to specify whether a secure connection is required.

Report Server Database Page

The Report Server Database page enables you to select the set of databases that will serve as the Report Catalog. The Report Catalog stores all the configuration information and the reports saved to this Report Server. You can select the database server name, the name of the database on that server, and the credentials used to connect to that server. A SQL Server instance is required to host the Report Catalog.

Web Portal URL Page

The Web Portal URL page enables you to view and change the name of the virtual directory used by the web portal. The web portal serves as the main user interface for interacting with the Report Server.

E-mail Settings Page

The E-mail Settings page enables you to identify an SMTP server that can be used by the Report Server. The SMTP server is used for delivering report subscriptions via e-mail. At the time of this writing, subscriptions could be used with SQL Server Reporting Services reports on the Report Server but were not available for Power BI reports.

Execution Account Page

The Execution Account page enables you to specify a set of login credentials to be used by the Report Server when it needs to access a file or other resource.

Encryption Keys Page

The Report Server uses an encryption key to encrypt and store sensitive information, such as credentials. You can use the Backup button to create a backup copy of the encryption key. This guards against corruption of the encryption key, which would cause all of the sensitive information stored on the Report Server to becoming unreadable.

Subscription Settings Page

The Subscription Settings page is used to specify credentials to be used by subscriptions to allow it to gain rights to create a file in a file share. At the time of this writing, subscriptions could be used with SQL Server Reporting Services reports on the Report Server but were not available for Power BI reports.

Scale-out Deployment Page

The Scale-out Deployment page is used to add servers to a scale-out installation of the Power BI Report Server. A scale-out deployment allows us to spread the rendering load across multiple servers. Each server added to the scale-out list uses the same encryption key. In this way, encrypted data stored in the common Report Catalog can be decrypted by any Report Server in the scale-out installation.

Power BI Integration Page

SQL Server Reporting Services reports can be pinned to a Power BI dashboard hosted on PowerBI.com. In order for PowerBI.com to display these reports for a user, it must know how to find a Report Server that can render the reports. The Power BI Integration page is used to register this Report Server with PowerBI.com. To register, simply enter your PowerBI.com credentials.

NOTE This feature has nothing to do with rendering Power BI reports. It is used solely to support the ability of PowerBI.com to host SQL Server Reporting Services reports.

Menu Bar

The Connect button, at the top of the page's menu area, lets you connect to a different server and then select a Report Server instance on that server.

The Report Catalog

Before we deploy reports to the Power BI Report Server, we need to have an understanding of the way the Report Server organizes reports. In the Power BI Service, our content was organized in workspaces and apps. On the Power BI Report Server, content is stored in the Report Catalog and organized in folders.

Folders

In the Report Catalog, reports are arranged into a system of folders similar to the Windows or Mac file system. Folders can contain reports, supporting files, and even other folders. The easiest way to create, view, and maintain these folders is through the web portal.

Although the Report Catalog folders look and act like Windows file system folders, they are not actual file system folders. You cannot find them anywhere in the file system on the computer running the Report Server. Report Catalog folders are screen representations of records in the Report Catalog database.

Each folder is assigned a name. Folder names can include just about any character, including spaces. However, folder names cannot include any of the following characters:

```
; ? : @ & = + $ , \ * < > | " /
```

Also, a folder name cannot consist exclusively of dots or spaces.

In addition to a name, folders can be assigned a description. The description can contain a long explanation of the contents of the folder. It also can help users determine what types of reports are in a folder without having to open that folder and look at the contents. Both the folder name and the description can be searched by a user to help them find a report.

The Web Portal

The web portal provides a straightforward method for creating and navigating folders in the Report Catalog. When you initially install the Power BI Report Server, the Home folder is created by default. This is the only folder that exists at first.

The default Uniform Resource Locator (URL) for accessing the web portal site on the computer running the Power BI Report Server is

```
http://ComputerName/reports
```

where *ComputerName* is the name of the computer on which the Power BI Report Server was installed. If you are using a secure connection to access the web portal, replace **http:** with **https:**. If you are on the same computer where the Power BI Report Server is running, you can use the following URL:

```
http://localhost/reports
```

No matter how you get there, when you initially access the web portal, it appears similar to Figure 16-2.

Notice the URL shown in Figure 16-2 is a bit different from the URLs given previously. This is because the web portal web application redirects you to browse mode. The browse mode is used to display folder contents.

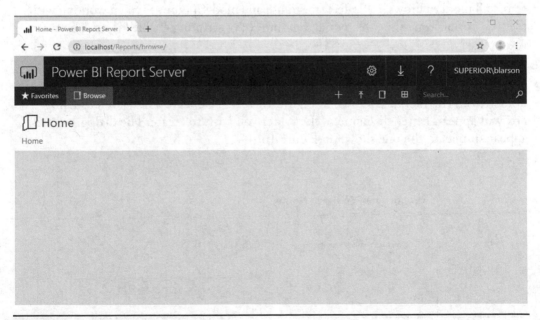

Figure 16-2   *The web portal with no folders defined*

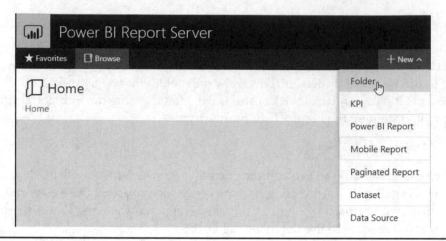

Figure 16-3   *The Folder menu option*

NOTE
Figure 16-2 shows the web portal as it appears for a user with content manager privileges. If you do not see the same items in the toolbar, you do not have content manager privileges.

The web portal follows the HTML5 standard. This should get you great compatibility across all modern browsers. So feel free to use any modern browser when working with the web portal. To use the web portal, you must have scripting enabled in your browser.

Adding a New Folder Using the Web Portal

To create a new folder, click the New button in the web portal toolbar and select Folder from the menu, as shown in Figure 16-3. The "Create a new folder" dialog box will appear. Enter the name of the folder you wish to create. The dialog box will appear similar to the one shown in Figure 16-4.

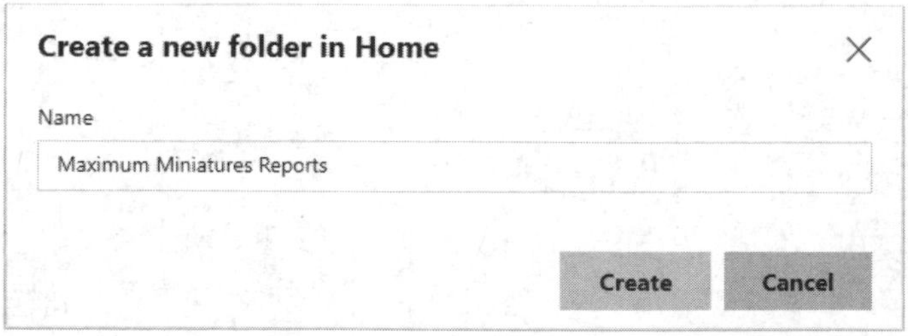

Figure 16-4   *The "Create a new folder" dialog box*

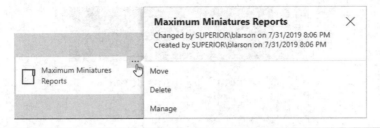

Figure 16-5   *The Folder menu*

Folder Properties

We noted earlier that each folder can also have a description. To add a description to a folder, click the ellipsis (…) button for the folder, as shown in Figure 16-5. Select Manage from the popup box. This will display the Properties page for the folder. You can enter the folder description.

There is also a check box titled "Hide this item." When this box is checked, the folder is not visible when the folder contents are displayed in tile view. This hidden option plays a role with the SQL Server Reporting Services content that the web portal user interface was originally designed to work with. It does not really come into play when working with Power BI content.

The folder Properties page is shown in Figure 16-6.

Manage Maximum Miniatures Reports

Home > Maximum Miniatures Reports > Manage > Properties

| Properties | Move   Delete |
| Security | |

Changed by SUPERIOR\blarson on 7/31/2019 8:06 PM
Created by SUPERIOR\blarson on 7/31/2019 8:06 PM

Properties

Name

Maximum Miniatures Reports

Description

This folder will create Power BI Reports showing information about Maximum Miniatures.

☐ Hide this item

Apply   Cancel

Figure 16-6   *The folder Properties page*

Figure 16-7 *Navigating to the Home folder using the breadcrumbs*

Navigating Folders

To view the contents of the new folder, click the folder name. The name of the current folder appears in bold text near the top of the page. Below the name of the current folder is the path from the Home folder to the current folder. This is the breadcrumb path you can use to return to any folder you clicked through to get to the current location. To return to any folder in the current path, click that folder name in the breadcrumb path. You can return to the Home folder by clicking Home at the beginning of the breadcrumb path, as shown in Figure 16-7. You can also return to the Home folder by clicking the main heading or logo in the upper-left corner of the page. By default, the main heading is "Power BI Report Server." Later in this chapter, you will see how to customize this heading to put your own brand on the web portal.

Saving a Report to the Power BI Report Server

Once we have created an appropriate folder structure to hold our Power BI reports, we can save our reports to the Power BI Report Server. This is done using the version of Power BI Desktop optimized for the Power BI Report Server. We simply save the report file somewhere in the Power BI Report Server folder structure.

With a Power BI .pbix file open in the Power BI Desktop version optimized for the Power BI Report Server, select File | Save as | Power BI Report Server, as shown in Figure 16-8. The Power BI Report Server Selection dialog box appears. This is shown in Figure 16-9.

The Power BI Report Server Selection dialog box shows the URLs for any Power BI Report Servers we have saved reports to in the past. The bottom portion of this dialog box has a text entry area where we can enter the URL for a new server. When the desired server is selected, we can click OK to continue.

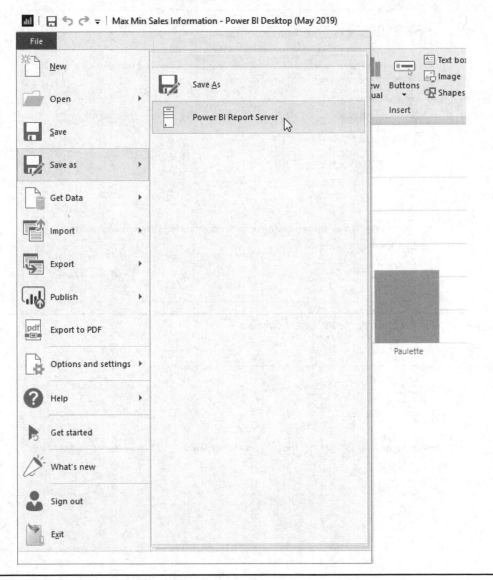

Figure 16-8 *Saving a Power BI report to the Power BI Report Server*

The "Save report" dialog appears next, as shown in Figure 16-10. The Save report dialog box starts out in the Home folder of the selected server. It shows the folders and the Power BI reports in the folder being displayed. We can double-click a folder name to navigate into that folder. We can click the up arrow next to the folder path to navigate back up a level if we went into the wrong folder. Once in the correct folder, we click OK to save the report.

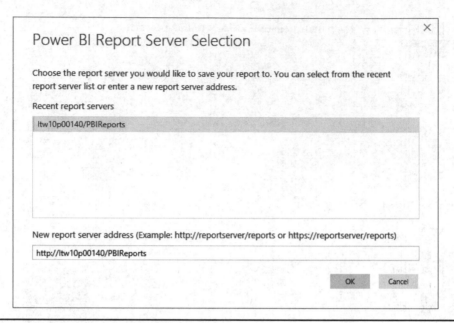

Figure 16-9 *The Power BI Report Server Selection dialog box*

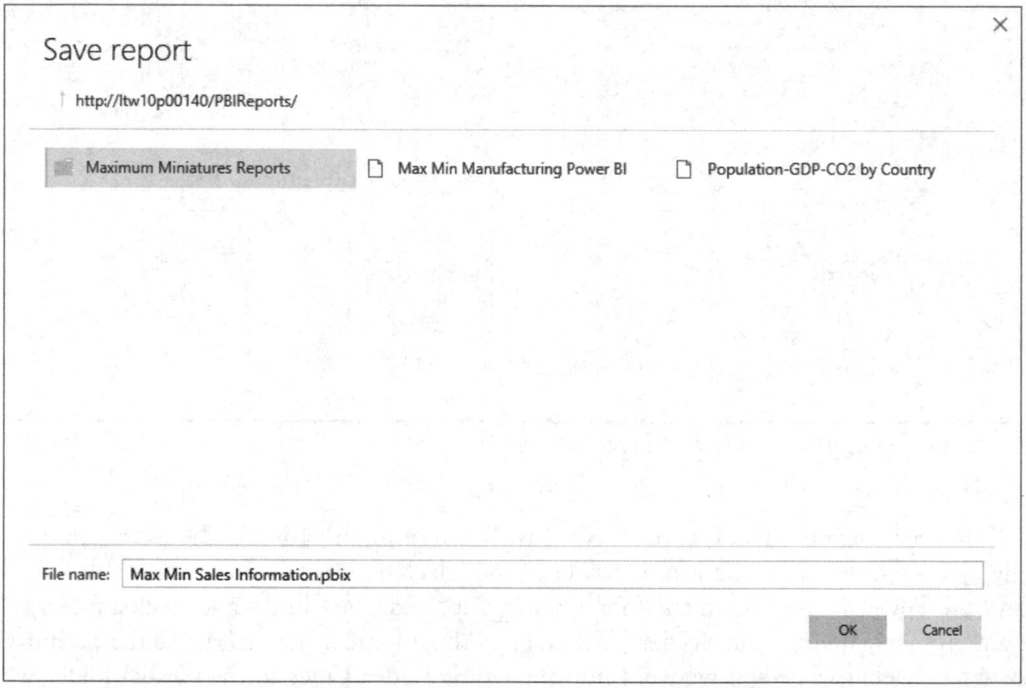

Figure 16-10 *The "Save report" dialog box*

Because this is a "save as" operation, the folder on the Power BI Report Server becomes the last saved location for this report. If we make changes to the report and click File | Save or click the Save button at the top of the window, the changes are saved to the Power BI Report Server, not to the original location in the file system.

NOTE
The Open menu in the version of Power BI Desktop optimized for Power BI Report Server supports opening a Power BI report from the Report Server.

The Power BI Report Server caches its pages for efficiency. That means your newly saved reports may not show up in the folder on the Power BI Report Server. You may need to use the browser's refresh button to get the Power BI Report Server to update the content of the folder being displayed in order to see a newly saved report.

Once the report is visible in the folder, you click the report and interact with it just as you would in the Power BI Service. This is shown in Figure 16-11.

NOTE
For Power BI reports that include roles, you may need to configure row-level security on the Power BI Report Server before the content of the report will display. See the "Row-Level Security" section of this chapter for more information.

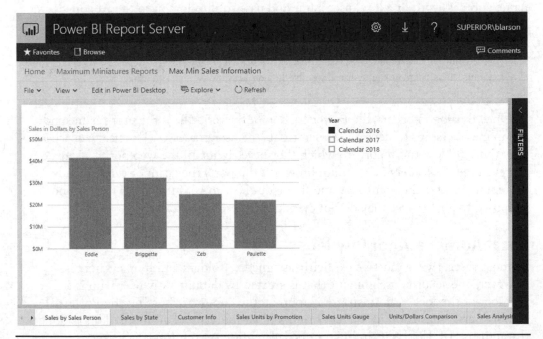

Figure 16-11 *Viewing a report on the Power BI Report Server*

Security

Security may be set at two levels on a Power BI Report Server. First, security is set on folders and reports to determine who can explore the folders and execute the reports as well as who can manage these items. Second, row-level security can be configured to use security roles created within a Power BI data model.

Folder and Report Security

In the Power BI Report Server, security was designed with both flexibility and ease of management in mind. Flexibility is provided by the fact that individual access rights can be assigned to each folder and to each report within a folder. You can specify exactly who has rights to each item and exactly what those rights are. Ease of management is provided by security inheritance, security roles, and integration with Windows security. We begin our discussion with the last entry in this list.

Integration with Windows Security

The Power BI Report Server does not maintain its own list of users and passwords. Instead, in its default configuration, it depends entirely on integration with Windows security. When a user accesses the Power BI Report Server, that user must authenticate with the Report Server. In other words, the user must have either a valid domain user name and password or a local user name and password to log on to the Report Server.

NOTE
If it is impossible for each report user to have their own credentials on the Power BI Report Server, it is possible to configure the server to use forms-based security through a custom security extension.

Once this logon occurs, the Power BI Report Server utilizes the user's name and group memberships to determine what rights the user possesses. The user can access only those folders and reports to which they have rights. In the web portal, users do not even see the folders they cannot browse and reports they cannot run. There is no temptation for the user to try and figure out how to get into places they are not supposed to go, because they do not even know these places exist.

Local Administrator Privileges

In most cases, rights must be explicitly assigned to folders and items. There is, however, one security assignment that is created by default. Any user who is a member of the local administrators group on the computer hosting the Power BI Report Server has content manager rights to all folders and all items. This is done through the BUILTIN\Administrators designation on the Report Server.

Figure 16-12 *The Folder Properties button*

Viewing the Security Rights for a Folder

To view the rights for a given folder, we look at the properties of that folder. Earlier, you learned we could do this by clicking the ellipsis (…) button for that folder and selecting Manage from the popup menu. We can view the properties of the folder whose contents we are currently viewing by clicking the Folder Properties button, as shown in Figure 16-12.

Either method takes us to the Folder Properties. Click the Security tab on the left side of the page to see the security settings. This is shown in Figure 16-13.

Security Roles

The rights to perform tasks are grouped together to create *roles*. Power BI Report Server includes a number of predefined roles to help you with security management.

Power BI Report Server	⚙ ↓ ? SUPERIOR\blarson

★ Favorites   ▢ Browse

▢ Manage Maximum Miniatures Reports

Home > Maximum Miniatures Reports > Manage > Security

Properties	✎ Customize security	
Security	**Group or user** ∧	**Roles**
	BUILTIN\Administrators	Content Manager
	SUPERIOR\blarson	Content Manager

Figure 16-13 *The Security tab of the Properties page*

The Browser Role   The Browser role is the basic role assigned to users who are going to view reports but who are not going to create folders or upload new reports. The Browser role has rights to perform the following tasks:

- View folders
- View reports

The Publisher Role   The Publisher role is assigned to users who are going to create folders and upload reports. The Publisher role does not have rights to change security settings. The Publisher role has rights to perform the following tasks:

- Manage folders
- Manage reports

The My Reports Role   The My Reports role is designed to be used only with a special folder called the My Reports folder. Within this folder, the My Reports role gives the user rights to do everything except change security settings. The My Reports role has rights to perform the following tasks:

- Manage folders
- Manage reports
- View folders
- View reports

The Content Manager Role   The Content Manager role is assigned to users who are managing the folders and reports. The Content Manager role has rights to perform all tasks, excluding system-wide tasks.

The Report Builder Role   The Report Builder role is a holdover from SQL Server Reporting Services.

The System User Role   The system-wide security tasks have two predefined roles. The System User role has rights to perform the following system-wide tasks:

- Execute reports
- View report server properties

The System Administrator Role   The System Administrator role provides the user with rights to complete any of the tasks necessary to manage the Power BI Report Server. This role has rights to perform the following system-wide tasks:

- Execute reports
- Manage report server properties
- Manage report server security
- Manage roles

Creating Security Role Assignments

As stated previously, role assignments are created when a Windows user or a Windows group is assigned a role for a folder or a report. Role assignments are created on the Security tab of the Properties page for the folder or report. These role assignments control what the user can see within a folder and what tasks the user can perform on the folder or report.

If the Security tab of the Properties page includes the "Customize security" button, as shown earlier in Figure 16-13, then the security settings for that folder or report are being inherited from its parent folder. Clicking the "Customize security" button will break that inheritance and enable you to make security role assignments for this item. When you click the "Customize security" button, you will see the confirmation dialog box shown in Figure 16-14. Click OK to confirm.

When a folder or report is not inheriting security settings from its parent folder, the Security tab of the Properties page appears as shown in Figure 16-15. We can click the "Add group or user" button to create a new security assignment. When we do, we see the New Role Assignment page.

On the New Role Assignment page, the group or user must be a valid domain user or group, or a valid local user or group. When using a domain user or group, this must be in the format *DomainName\UserName* or *DomainName\GroupName*. If you are using a local user or group, you can simply type the user name or group name. Once the user or group

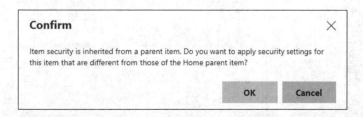

Figure 16-14 *The Confirm dialog box for breaking security inheritance*

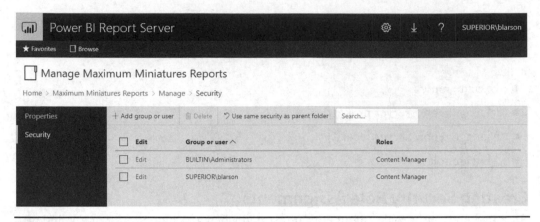

Figure 16-15 *The Security tab when security settings are not inherited*

is specified, you can select the role to assign to this user or group. The completed New Role Assignment page should appear similar to Figure 16-16.

Site-Level Security Role Assignments

Site-level security role assignments are created on the "Site settings" page. Click the Settings button (the cog icon) and select "Site settings" from the menu, as shown in Figure 16-17. The "Site settings" page appears. Click Security on the left to view the

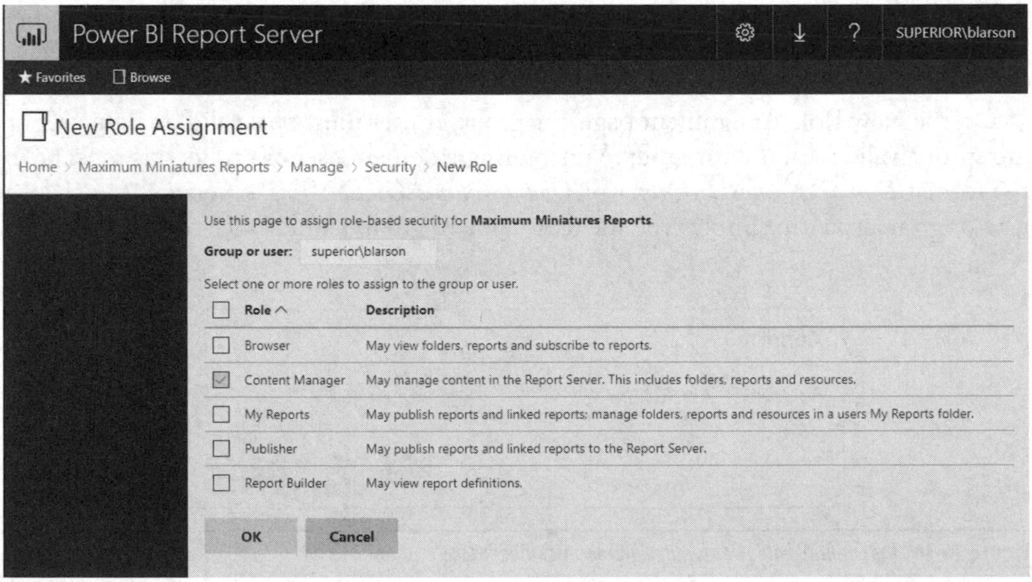

Figure 16-16 *The New Role Assignment page*

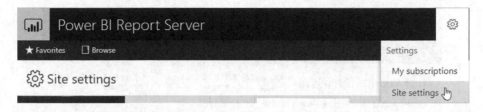

Figure 16-17 *The "Site settings" menu option*

Security tab of the "Site settings" page, as shown in Figure 16-18. The "Add group or user" button is used to create new security role assignments in the same manner as at the folder or report level.

Role Assignments Using Windows Groups

As mentioned previously, role assignments can be made to domain users or to domain groups. If you create your role assignments using Windows users, you need to create a new set of role assignments every time a new user needs to access the Power BI Report Server. This can be extremely tedious if you have a complex set of role assignments for various folders, reports, and resources.

In most cases, creating role assignments using domain groups is better. Then, as new users come along, you simply need to add them to the domain group that has the appropriate rights in Power BI Report Server. This is much easier!

Row-Level Security

We saw in Chapter 15 that we had to assign users to our custom row-level security role in the Power BI Service environment. The same is true for the Power BI Report Server.

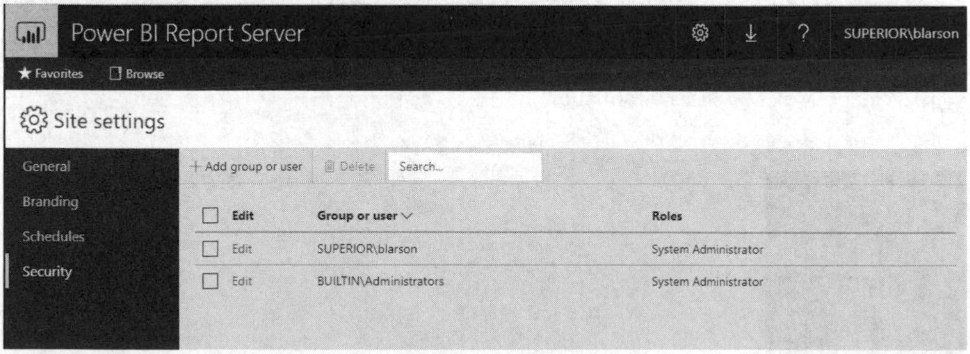

Figure 16-18 *The Security tab of the "Site settings" page*

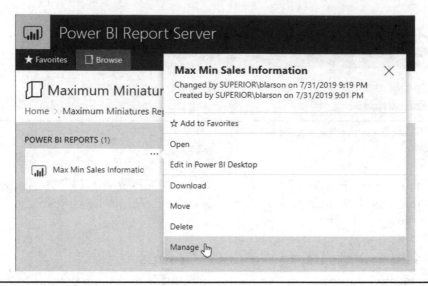

Figure 16-19 *The report menu*

We must assign users to the custom security role in order for that role to limit their data access.

On the Power BI Report Server, the role assignments are done at the report level. To add row-level security to a report, click the ellipsis (…) button for the report, as shown in Figure 16-19, and select Manage from the popup box. This will display the Properties page for the report.

On the left side of the page, select "Row-level security" to display the row-level security page. Click Add Member to add a member to a security role, as shown in Figure 16-20. The Add Member page appears.

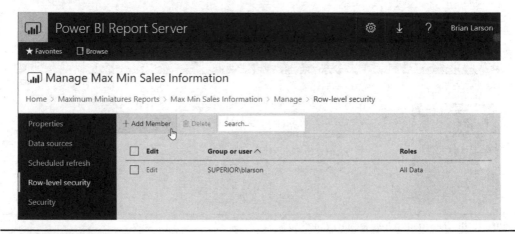

Figure 16-20 *The "Row-level security" page*

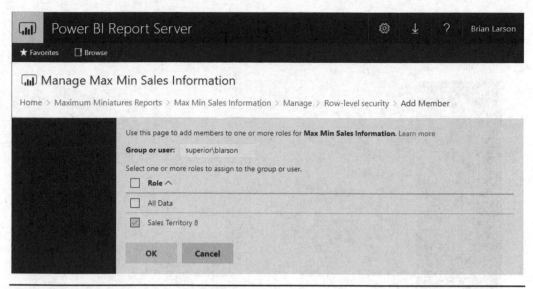

Figure 16-21 *Adding a user to a row-level security role*

In the "Group or user" area, enter the name of a valid domain user or group, or a valid local user or group. Check the box for the row-level security role or roles to assign to this user or group. This is shown in Figure 16-21. Click OK when complete.

Branding the Power BI Report Server

Branding enables us to customize the Power BI Report Server to better match our organization. There is one very quick and easy change we can make to provide a small customization and a larger change we can make for more comprehensive branding. We will take a look at both.

Modifying the Site Name

The small customization involves changing the name of the Power BI Report Server site. This is done on the General tab of the "Site settings" page. Use the "Site settings" menu option to navigate to the "Site settings" page, as shown previously in Figure 16-17. The General tab of the "Site settings" page is shown in Figure 16-22.

A custom site name is shown in Figure 16-22. Once we click Apply, the custom site name is shown in the upper-left corner of every Power BI Report Server page. This is shown in Figure 16-23.

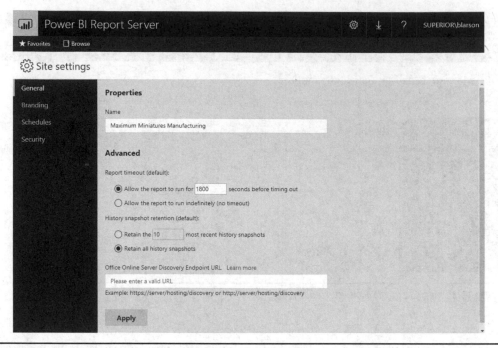

Figure 16-22 *The General tab of the "Site settings" page*

Creating a Brand Package

The Branding tab of the "Site settings" page enables us to load a brand package to customize the site. The brand package consists of three items packaged in a ZIP file:

- **Metadata.xml**   A table of contents for the package
- **Colors.json**   Custom color definitions for the site
- **Logo file**   An image file to use in place of the site name (optional)

Figure 16-23 *The Power BI Report Server with a custom site name*

Metadata.xml

The Metadata.xml file serves as the table of contents for the brand package. It provides references to the other two files in the package. Here is the format of the Metadata.xml file:

```
<?xml version="1.0" encoding="utf-8"?>
<SystemResourcePackage
   xmlns="http://schemas.microsoft.com/sqlserver/reporting/2016/01/
                                      systemresourcepackagemetadata"
   type="UniversalBrand" version="2.0.2" name="Data Analytics Brand Package">
 <Contents>
    <Item key="colors" path="colors.json" />
    <Item key="logo" path="Branding Logo.jpg" />
 </Contents>
</SystemResourcePackage>
```

(In the actual Metadata.xml file, `systemresourcepackagemetadata` should be on the same line as the rest of the xmlns property value.)

The name property in the Metadata XML structure can be set to whatever you like in order to identify your brand package. The path property associated with the logo file must be the name of the logo file loaded into the brand package. If no logo is included in the brand package, the entire Item element for the logo should be omitted from the Metadata.xml file.

Colors.json

The Colors.json file consists of sets of name/value pairs used to generate the cascading style sheet (CSS) that ultimately controls the look of the web portal. The Colors.json file will look similar to the following:

```
{
    "name":"Default brand",
    "version":"1.0",
    "interface":{
        "primary":"#bb2124",
        "primaryAlt":"#d31115",
        "primaryAlt2":"#671215",
        "primaryAlt3":"#bb2124",
        "primaryAlt4":"#00abee",
        "primaryContrast":"#fff",
        "secondary":"#FFFFFF",
        "secondaryAlt":"#229Fd8",
```